United States Edition

Workbook for **Lectors, Gospel Readers,** and **Proclaimers** of the **Word**®

Elaine Park, SSL, STD

Konrad Schaeffer, OSB, SSD

Douglas Leal

LTP
LITURGY
TRAINING
PUBLICATIONS

CONTENTS

New American Bible readings are taken from *Lectionary for Mass for Use in the Dioceses of the United States of America*, second typical edition © 1998, 1997, 1970 by the Confraternity of Christian Doctrine, Washington, DC, and are reproduced herein by license of the copyright owner. All rights reserved. No part of *Lectionary for Mass* may be reproduced in any form without permission in writing from the Confraternity of Christian Doctrine, Washington, DC.

Excerpts from the English translation of the Psalm Responses, Titles of the Readings from *Lectionary for Mass* © 1969, 1981, 1997, International Commission on English in the Liturgy Corporation (ICEL). All rights reserved. Texts contained in this work derived whole or in part from liturgical texts copyrighted by the International Commission on English in the Liturgy (ICEL) have been published here with the confirmation of the Committee on Divine Worship, United States Conference of Catholic Bishops. No other texts in this work have been formally reviewed or approved by the United States Conference of Catholic Bishops.

WORKBOOK FOR LECTORS, GOSPEL READERS, AND PROCLAIMERS OF THE WORD® 2019, United States Edition © 2018 Archdiocese of Chicago. All rights reserved.

Liturgy Training Publications, 3949 South Racine Avenue, Chicago, IL 60609, 800-933-1800, fax 800-933-7094, orders@ltp.org, www.LTP.org.

Cover art: Barbara Simcoe

This book was edited by Lorie Simmons and Victoria M. Tufano. Christian Rocha was the production editor, Anna Manhart was the designer, and Luis Leal was the production artist.

(continues on next page)

Easter Time

Ordinary Time

Printed in the United States
of America

ISBN: 978-1-61671-403-1
WL19

In accordance with c. 827,
permission to publish was granted
on March 28, 2018, by Very
Reverend Ronald A. Hicks, Vicar
General of the Archdiocese of
Chicago. Permission to publish is
an official declaration of ecclesiasti-
cal authority that the material is
free from doctrinal and moral error.
No legal responsibility is assumed
by the grant of this permission.

(see endnotes on page x)

The Authors

Two Scripture scholars have written
the commentaries. (Their initials
appear after the ones they have
written.)

Elaine Park has a licentiate in
Sacred Scripture (SSD) from the
Pontifical Biblical Institute and a
sacred theology doctorate from the
Gregorian University, both in Rome.
She has been a professor of biblical
studies and academic dean at
Mt. Angel Seminary in St. Benedict,
Oregon. Currently she is a pastoral
associate at Christ the King parish
in Milwaukie, Oregon, and
frequently gives talks and retreats
on biblical topics.

Fr. Konrad Schaefer, OSB, a monk of
Mount Angel Abbey, Oregon, holds
a doctorate in Sacred Scripture from
the École Biblique in Jerusalem. He
teaches at the Pontifical University
of Mexico and resides at Our Lady
of the Angels Priory in Cuernavaca,
Mexico.

Douglas Leal has written all of the
margin notes. He holds an MA in
pastoral ministry from Boston
College. He has written, directed,
and acted in numerous theater
productions, conducts lector training
workshops nationwide, and is the
author of *Stop Reading and Start
Proclaiming!*, available from
www.LTP.org.

MINISTRY OF THE WORD BASICS

The Word of God in the Liturgy

The Word of God proclaimed in the liturgy is a living Word with power to nourish and transform both those who proclaim it and those who hear it. In the words of the Second Vatican Council's *Constitution on Divine Revelation* (*Dei Verbum*), "The Church has always venerated the divine Scriptures just as she venerates the body of the Lord, since, especially in the sacred liturgy, she unceasingly receives and offers to the faithful the bread of life from the table both of God's word and of Christ's body" (DV, 21).

Throughout its history, the Church has affirmed over and over the close tie between the Word proclaimed in the liturgy and the Word made flesh received in the Eucharist, recognizing both as Christ present to give himself as food. Pope Francis, in his apostolic exhortation *Evangelii Gaudium*, writes that the hearts of the faithful who gather on the Lord's Day are nourished both by his Word and by the bread of eternal life (EG, 15). He emphasizes as well that being fed at both tables gives strength for the whole journey: "God's word, listened to and celebrated, above all in the Eucharist, nourishes and inwardly strengthens Christians, enabling them to offer an authentic witness to the Gospel in daily life. . . . The preaching of the word, living and effective, prepares for the reception of the sacrament, and in the sacrament that word attains its maximum efficacy" (EG, 174).

The image of food to refer to God's Word has a strong foundation in the Hebrew Scriptures. Moses tells the people prior to their entering the land, "it is not by bread alone that people live, but by all that comes forth from the mouth of the LORD" (Deuteronomy 8:3). The prophet Jeremiah, commanded to proclaim God's Word, cried out, "When I found your words, I devoured them; your words were my joy, the happiness of my heart" (Jeremiah 15:16). And God later instructed Ezekiel to open his mouth and eat the scroll. Ezekiel recounts the episode: "Feed your stomach and fill your belly with this scroll I am giving you. I ate it, and it was as sweet as honey in my mouth" (Ezekiel 3:1–3). Each of these passages, and many more, highlight God's gift of satisfying our deepest hungers with a Word that is life giving.

How does this Word of God actually feed us with joy, happiness, sweetness, and an abundance of life? Think of what goes into a lavishly prepared feast that gives delight and nourishment to guests. In the same way, the Word of God proclaimed in the liturgy also requires careful selection and preparation. Those proclaiming the Word are like good chefs who have done everything needed to present a nourishing meal. The Lectionary provides the selection of the food set at the table of the Word. Its

In the beginning was the WORD, and the WORD was with God, and the WORD was God.

design offers a rich variety, much like a well-chosen menu. The variety of fare means that the readings provide, as fully as possible, an overview of the biblical story and its great themes, even when they might not be people's favorite menu items. Although it isn't the role of the reader to make the selection, it is important for those who proclaim to see where particular texts fit into the broad sweep of the biblical story (our salvation history), how it harmonizes with the season or feast we are celebrating, and how it can offer insights for their particular community at this particular moment. Some questions we might ask are: Why was this text selected? How does it relate to the other readings of the day? How does it provide the variety of nourishment essential for a mature faith? Was the passage selected because of the season or feast, or as part of a continuous reading of a book, letter, or Gospel? How do we hear it echoed in the images and words of the prayers, music, liturgical environment, and ritual actions of this specific liturgy?

In addition to being nourishing food, the Word in the liturgy is also a very personal communication from God to his people: "When the Sacred Scriptures are read in the Church, God himself speaks to his people, and Christ, present in his word, proclaims the Gospel," (*General Instruction of the Roman Missal*, 29). Proclaimers of the Word, then, lend their voices for this personal communication, preparing themselves with sincere humility, through prayer, study, and practice to faithfully convey to the people what God intends.

Understanding the Word We Proclaim

Preparation for reading at the table of the Word can be just as multifaceted as preparing for a family feast. Consider the story of Philip and the Ethiopian eunuch, in which Philip asked the eunuch who was reading from Isaiah, "Do you understand what you are reading?" (Acts 8:30), a question that we should ask ourselves in preparing for liturgical proclamation. If we who proclaim do not understand our reading, how can we help the assembly understand it? In his apostolic exhortation *Verbum Domini*, Pope Benedict XVI commented: "Word and Eucharist are so deeply bound together that we cannot understand one without the other: the word of God sacramentally takes flesh in the event of the Eucharist. The Eucharist opens us to an understanding of Scripture, just as Scripture for its part illumines and explains the mystery of the Eucharist" (VD, 55).

Understanding Word and Sacrament comes partly through research that draws on the wisdom of others, and also through prayer that relies on the inspiration of the Holy Spirit. The wisdom of others may be both from written sources and from discussion and prayer flowing from the readings, perhaps with people from the parish. The biblical texts themselves, as well as prayers used in the liturgy of the day, are rich sources that can prepare one's mind and heart. Such careful reading, research, and prayer comprise the preparation we do in the days prior to our proclamation. Some additional quiet reflection immediately before the celebration of the liturgy is the final preparation.

Good preparation for proclamation aims at unleashing the power of the Word for the whole assembly. As at a festive meal, a hospitable attitude welcomes all who are gathered and also welcomes the Word that will be proclaimed. We taste, we chew, we savor, we digest and absorb the Word so that it becomes a part of us, going forth with the energy of the Holy Spirit. It is most particularly in the liturgy that God's Word becomes bread plentiful enough to feed five thousand and more, becoming an abundant source of nourishment. This is beautifully expressed by St. Ambrose: "This bread which Jesus breaks is, according to the mystery, the Word of God and a teaching about Christ. When this bread is distributed, it multiplies. . . . Jesus gives his words as bread" (*Treatise on Luke's Gospel*, 6:86).

Elaine Park

Proclaiming Effectively: The Art of the Storyteller

Jesus was an excellent storyteller. The evidence of his skill is right there in the Gospels. Everyone was "astonished" at his "gracious words" which had authority and impact (Matthew 7:28; Mark 11:18; Luke 4:22, 32). You don't attract more than five thousand people to a hillside on a hot day if you don't know how to tell a good story! His skills allowed the Word that he preached to touch the hearts and minds of those gathered. Isn't that what we hope to do with our proclamation?

Listen closely to the good storytellers you know. See how the stories they tell appear on their face, are colored by their voice, seem to flow from their whole being. These people are full of energy as they tell their stories; they work to connect with the family or community that listens; they have a desire, a need, to communicate well. We have the same desire to com-

This is my commandment: love one another as I love you.

municate that Word of God well, so these same skills will be crucial to our proclamation of the Word. This book is designed to help you develop those skills.

The commentaries on each reading are written by Scripture scholars who share their insights. The margin notes give you advice on proclaiming the readings, helping you incorporate essential skills into your ministry of the Word. Those notes are intended to coach you as you prepare for your proclamation.

Think of them as comments from a guide or mentor, standing alongside you as you practice, throwing out helpful ideas, hints, strategies, questions, cautions, and encouragements.

Preparing the Text

The ministry of a proclaimer is rooted in the text, so begin there. Read the Scripture commentary that accompanies each reading to help you understand what you're proclaiming. No matter how skilled a proclaimer you are, you can't proclaim what you can't understand! It's also helpful to read the passages from your Bible that come before and after the text, so you have a better idea of its context. For the same reason, it's important to read the other readings of the day, including the Responsorial Psalm. As you gain experience you'll also become interested in how your reading relates to the readings of the weeks prior, and following, and to the season as a whole.

Form or Purpose

The margin notes identify the *form* or *purpose* of each reading, which tells us a lot about how best to proclaim it. Different forms require different emphases, and different ways of proclaiming. Those who study Scripture classify texts into many different forms, but for the purposes of proclaiming, we will use three: *narrative, didactic,* and *exhortatory.*

A **narrative** text reads like a story, and may include characters, dialogue, a setting, and action. The point of view may be that of the narrator or any character in the story. Scripture is full of narratives—stories about creation, our ancestors in faith, the history of Israel, the life of Jesus, or the ministries of the first Apostles.

When proclaiming a narrative, strive to help your assembly know what's happening in the story. Keep characters distinct. Be clear about shifts in setting. Allow the community to *see* the story unfold as you proclaim. Some stories may be very familiar to your community through years of repetition. Your goal is to bring back a sense of wonder and anticipation to these stories, so they maintain their power to amaze. Avoid *telegraphing*—that is, resist allowing the end of the story to color how you proclaim the entire reading.

A **didactic** text makes a point or teaches something. The author may lay out an argument or make a case to support the point. The letters of Paul contain mostly didactic text, as do some of the history books, prophets, and wisdom books. The texts describing Jesus' teachings in the Gospel accounts are usually didactic. It's important to understand the author's point and the flow of any supporting argument or logic. Your goal is to help your community follow the argument and understand what's being taught.

Exhortatory texts make an urgent appeal to listeners. They may encourage, warn, or challenge, and often include a call to action. In these texts the emotions are heightened and the stakes are high. Sometimes, the exhortation is directed to God, pleading for mercy or justice or praising God's goodness and love. The speaker is sometimes the author; other times God directly addresses the people. They are most often found in the prophets and the epistles, or letters, but there is also exhortatory text in the Gospels, especially John. In an exhortatory text, it's essential to convey the urgency and passion behind the words.

Although most readings are primarily one of these three styles, some may combine styles. The notes will identify places where the style of the reading changes.

Literary Devices

As you study your text, identify any literary devices. The notes will point out some of these. They can reveal much about the meaning of the passage, so pay attention and make a choice about how they will affect your proclamation. The most common devices are *parallelism, thought rhyme, paradox,* and *repetition.*

Parallelism refers to phrases or sentences that have a similar structure or express a similar idea, as in these examples:

> for he has clothed me with a robe of salvation,
> and wrapped me in a mantle of justice.
> (Isaiah 61:10)

> I will bless those who bless you
> and curse those who curse you. (Genesis 12:3)

> Remain in me, as I remain in you. (John 15:4)

The rhythm of our proclamation—the words we choose to stress—will help the community hear the parallelism in these lines. If we disregard the parallel structure in our proclamation, we will obscure the meaning. Parallelism is one of the most frequently used literary devices in both testaments.

Thought rhyme is a form of parallelism used in Hebrew poetry. Hebrew poets showed their skill not in the cleverness of their rhymes but in their ability to be deeply descriptive of a thing or idea. Consider this passage from Sirach (15:18–20):

> Immense is the wisdom of the Lord;
>   he is mighty in power, and all-seeing.
> The eyes of God are on those who fear him;
>   he understands man's every deed.
> No one does he command to act unjustly,
>   To none does he give license to sin.

Notice that both lines of each couplet say the same thing, but each line says it in a different way. Thought rhyme occurs throughout wisdom literature and the prophets. When proclaiming, use care to keep the two lines together and use emphasis to show the parallelism.

Paradox uses parallelism to express an idea that seems to contradict itself. Jesus often employs paradox to show that the reign of God will turn our expectations upside down:

> Thus, the last will be first, and the first will be last. (Matthew 20:16)

> For every one who exalts himself will be humbled,
> but the one who humbles himself will be exalted. (Luke 14:11)

Again, use the rhythm of your proclamation to make the parallelism evident, with some extra emphasis on the contradictory phrase.

Repetition of the same word or phrase over the course of a reading emphasizes a point. Sometimes a word is doubled ("Amen, amen"). More often, a word, phrase, or idea is repeated a few times throughout a reading. When you proclaim, make each instance distinct, and build your intensity with each repetition.

Tools: Voice and Body

Studying the text is only the beginning of our work as proclaimers. Our ministry has a significant *physical* aspect—it requires the use of our bodies as well as our minds. Simply reading the words clearly from the ambo so they can be heard and understood is not enough for effective proclamation; we must also pay attention to what we are communicating with our tone, pace, volume, eyes, face, even our posture. In fact, those who study communication tell us that we read meaning more from nonverbal cues than from spoken words.

If I were to approach you with a concerned look and say, slowly, in a low tone and with sadness in my voice, "I have some news for you," you'd likely be very worried about this news. But if I were to run up to you excitedly, with eyes shining, energy in my voice, and quickly say, "I have some news for you," you'd probably be eager to hear the news. Notice that the words were exactly the same in both situations, yet the meaning was completely different. The difference was conveyed entirely through nonverbal cues. Nonverbal expression is critical to our ministry; without the right cues the community will never understand what we proclaim. The notes will help you work on this.

Pace refers to the speed of your proclamation—how fast you speak. The most common problem for proclaimers new to the ministry is going too fast to be understood. More important than finding the right pace, however, is making sure to *vary* your pace, since pace gives clues to the *meaning* of a reading. We express joy or anxiety at a faster pace and sorrow or sadness at a slower pace.

Volume pertains both to being heard (loudness or softness) and to *vocal energy* (the direction and strength of your intention to speak). The notes will suggest places where you might raise or lower your volume, but you should still have good vocal energy even when your volume is low. It's also important to

Magnify the LORD with me; let us exalt his name together.

articulate well so you can be clearly understood; the notes will warn you about any tricky phrases that might require extra attention to articulate correctly.

Inflection refers to the pitch or tone of our voice (high or low). It conveys attitude and feeling. The high end of our range of inflection might be used to express intensity and excitement, while the low end could express sadness or contrition. Find places to vary your inflection throughout your proclamation.

The notes will point out words or phrases in danger of being "swallowed"—that is, words which could be mumbled, and thus lost to the assembly. Make sure you articulate these so they are clearly heard.

Pauses are critical cues that allow your listeners to follow the sense of a text, especially one laying out an argument. Pause in order to break up separate thoughts, set apart significant statements, or indicate major shifts of thought. Never pause in the middle of a single thought. Your primary guide for pauses is punctuation. In general, pause and take a full breath at periods, question marks, exclamation points, and sometimes at semicolons and colons. Don't come to a full stop at commas; rather, break your speech briefly (and take a short, catch-up breath if needed).

There should always be a pause at the end of the reading, before you proclaim the closing dialogue ("The Word of the Lord" or "The Gospel of the Lord"). The notes will indicate when a reading might require a longer pause than usual.

Choice Words. Some words in the readings in this book are printed in bold. These are *choice words.* They're the key words that an effective proclaimer will use to convey the meaning, emotion, and intent of the reading. *They are not necessarily meant to be stressed.* Rather, they are flagged to encourage you to make some *choice* about them. They're significant words, so take some time in your preparation to consider how you will proclaim them.

Eye contact with the community is necessary for effective proclamation. You wouldn't trust someone who didn't make eye contact with you while they were speaking; you'd either dismiss or quickly lose interest in what they were saying. Making eye contact with the assembly connects us with them and connects them to the reading more deeply than using our voice alone. This helps the assembly stay with the story and keeps them engaged.

Except in a few instances, the notes don't indicate where you should be making eye contact in your proclamation because you are encouraged to do so *throughout* the text. Experienced proclaimers look down and scan the next part of the text quickly, then look up and proclaim it. They may make eye contact for as much as seventy-five percent of a reading, particularly on the more significant lines. Of course, this takes practice and experience to do well! If you're new to this skill, set modest goals at first, then increase steadily. Your skill with eye contact will grow over time as your confidence as a proclaimer increases.

Whenever you look up, include everyone in the assembly with your glance, looking most often at (or just above) the people farthest away from you. Link your vocal energy to eye contact; that is, direct your voice to where you look. This will help keep your vocal energy up so you can be both seen *and* heard by the whole assembly.

The notes will indicate difficult or awkward phrases which you might want to proclaim looking directly at the text. Apart from these, however, aim to make eye contact with the assembly as much as you comfortably can.

Posture and Facial Expression. Stand at the ambo in a relaxed posture, with your hands on the Lectionary or the ambo. Don't hunch over, hiding your face from the assembly. Share yourself freely.

Your face will communicate much to the assembly about the reading. It will especially tell them that you're proclaiming "Good News"—the meaning of the word "Gospel." When we share Good News from the ambo we should also share our joy—with a *smile* on our face (and in our eyes and voice). Our smile tells the assembly that we proclaim news of joy, love, mercy, forgiveness, and compassion. Without this cue, they may miss it, so allow yourself to smile when it's appropriate to the reading.

Intention

Our *need* to communicate *something in particular* gives our communication urgency and drive. One of the pitfalls of proclamation is that we don't always have a clear reason to communicate, other than "now it's time for the Liturgy of the Word." The result is a reading that's flat and unfocused. For our proclamation to be effective, we have to rediscover our reason to communicate, our *intention.*

The Scripture commentary will help you understand the original purpose for the text—a good starting point for discerning an intention. What does the reading ask your assembly to *do* or to *be* after hearing your proclamation? After all, we are to "be doers of the word and not hearers only" (James 1:22). Choosing an intention like, "This reading gives the origin of Passover" or "This reading tells about the Annunciation" is a weaker choice than "This reading shows that God will set you free" or "This reading urges you to trust God as Mary did." It's an even stronger choice to shorten the intention into a brief command: "Be free!" or "Trust God!"

Focus on an intention every time you proclaim. (The notes will offer suggestions for some of the readings.) An intention helps pull together all the necessary elements of good proclamation because when we have a *need* to communicate, we work hard to use all our skills to make sure our communication is clear. Of course, you are an *instrument* of the Holy Spirit. Your intention helps you focus your proclamation, but the effect of your proclamation on your listeners is always the work of the Holy Spirit, who gives to "each person individually everything that in the proclamation of the word of God is spoken for the good of the whole gathering of the faithful" (Introduction to the Lectionary, 9).

Expressive Proclamation

Although the Liturgy of the Word is not intended to be theatrical, proclamation cannot be effective unless it is expressive. Readers have little time and few words with which to convey the meaning of a Lectionary passage, and the judicious expression of emotion aids that process greatly. We read emotions very quickly. In the example given earlier, you would have determined a great deal of meaning in my approaching you with excitement or with sadness, before I even said, "I have some news for you." Emotion is a powerful nonverbal communicator, and thus a central element in proclamation.

As we prepare our proclamation we need to make choices about expression. Some choices are

The LORD's word is true; all his works are trustworthy.

already evident in the text. If it says Paul is rejoicing, or Jeremiah is grumbling, or God is acting with compassion, then the emotion we need to express is clear. In other cases, we must make our own choice. The notes offer some suggestions. In a narrative, find an emotion or point of view for each character, keeping in mind that these might change during the reading. In an exhortatory text, all the emotions are heightened, so make bold choices and practice conveying them with your voice, eyes, and face. A didactic text might seem emotion*less*, but assuredly there is emotion present. A teaching is usually given out of *love* for the community being taught.

Admittedly, proclaiming expressively can be a challenge. Many people aren't comfortable showing emotions in public. But the Scriptures we proclaim are not sterile, cold stories; they're dynamic and full of passion. If we fail to include emotion in our proclamation, we're leaving out meaning, thus making it even more difficult for our assembly to understand and connect with the Word. Of course, we shouldn't

proclaim with exaggerated emotion so that we draw attention to ourselves and away from the text. Rather we are called to faithfully proclaim the emotion as it is present in the text.

Pray the Text

You may have a favorite method of praying with Scripture; if so, use it with your text. If not, you can read and meditate on your text during prayer. If you proclaim a narrative text, you could imagine yourself in the story as one of the characters or as an onlooker. If you proclaim a didactic or exhortatory text, you could imagine yourself as the original writer of the text, or as one of the first hearers. If your text speaks directly to God, you can use it *as* your prayer. In your prayer you may discern an intention for your text, or certain emotions may arise that you'll want to use in your proclamation. Take note of these or any other insights.

Recognize That the Stakes Are High

Would you work harder to tell someone that they had a loose thread on their shirt or that their hair was on fire? Likely the latter! When the *stakes are high,* all your communication skills are heightened without your even thinking about them. That's why it's important to recognize how significant your ministry is to the community. The Word that you have the privilege of proclaiming is a Word that desperately needs to be heard by your community, and if you don't proclaim it well, an opportunity is lost. Remind yourself of this awesome responsibility each time you proclaim, and you'll be inspired to work hard to help the Word of God come alive for the community.

Douglas Leal

An Option to Consider

The third edition of *The Roman Missal* encourages ministers of the Word to chant the introduction and conclusion to the readings ("A reading from . . . "; "The word of the Lord"). For those parishes wishing to use these chants, they are demonstrated in audio files that may be accessed either through the QR codes given here (with a smartphone) or through the URL indicated beneath the code. This URL is case sensitive, so be careful to distinguish between the letter l (lowercase L) and the numeral 1.

The first QR code contains the tones for the First Reading in both a male and a female voice.

http://bit.ly/l2mjeG

The second QR code contains the tones for the Second Reading in both a male and a female voice.

http://bit.ly/krwEYy

The third QR code contains the simple tone for the Gospel.

http://bit.ly/iZZvSg

The fourth QR code contains the solemn tone for the Gospel.

http://bit.ly/lwf6Hh

Recommended Works

Find a list of recommended reading and assistance in considering and implementing chanted introductions and conclusions to the readings in downloadable PDF files at http://www.ltp.org/products/details/WL19.

Pronunciation Key

bait = bayt	thin = thin
cat = kat	vision = VIZH*n
sang = sang	ship = ship
father = FAH-<u>th</u>er	sir = ser
care = kayr	gloat = gloht
paw = paw	cot = kot
jar = jahr	noise = noyz
easy = EE-zee	poison = POY-z*n
her = her	plow = plow
let = let	although = ahl-<u>TH</u>OH
queen = kween	church = cherch
delude = deh-L<u>OO</u>D	fun = fuhn
when = hwen	fur = fer
ice = ī<u>s</u>	flute = fl<u>oo</u>t
if = if	foot = foot
finesse = fih-NES	

Shorter Readings

In the Scripture readings reproduced in this book, shorter readings are indicated by brackets and also by a citation given at the end of the reading.

Endnotes

(continued from page ii)

Quotations from *Verbum Domini* by Pope Benedict XVI and from *Evangelii gaudium* by Pope Francis, © Libreria Editrice Vaticana.

Excerpts from the English translation of the Introduction from *Lectionary for Mass* © 1969, 1981, 1997, International Commission on English in the Liturgy Corporation (ICEL); excerpts from the English translation of *The Roman Missal* © 2010, ICEL. All rights reserved.

FIRST SUNDAY OF ADVENT

Jeremiah = jayr-uh-Mī-uh

From the start, let your tone suggest the hope that permeates this prophecy.

God's promise, made and remade throughout Israel's history, was an enduring source of identity and hope. Use the word "promise" to awaken that hope.

This is an intentional repetition meant to achieve emphasis; such constructions require greater emphasis on the second phrase

Stress God's initiative in bringing about a new age and new reality.

As you speak "Israel" (IZ-ree-uhl) and "Judah" (JOO-duh), persuade your listeners that the promise includes them.

Speak the final line with a sense of awed gratitude: the goodness of God brands us; we bear his name and become icons of his justice.

For meditation and context:

LECTIONARY #3

READING I   Jeremiah 33:14–16

A reading from the Book of the Prophet Jeremiah

The days are **coming**, says the Lord,
   when I will fulfill the **promise**
   I made to the house of **Israel** and **Judah**.
In **those days**, in **that time**,
   I will **raise up** for **David** a **just shoot**;
   he shall do what is **right** and **just** in the land.
In **those days Judah** shall be **safe**
   and **Jerusalem** shall dwell **secure**;
   this is what they shall **call** her:
"**The Lord our justice.**"

RESPONSORIAL PSALM   Psalm 25:4–5, 8–9, 10, 14 (1b)

R. To you, O Lord, I lift my soul.

Your ways, O Lord, make known to me;
   teach me your paths,
guide me in your truth and teach me,
   for you are God my savior,
   and for you I wait all the day.

Good and upright is the Lord;
   thus he shows sinners the way.
He guides the humble to justice,
   and teaches the humble his way.

All the paths of the Lord are kindness and
      constancy
   toward those who keep his covenant and
      his decrees.
The friendship of the Lord is with those
      who fear him,
   and his covenant, for their instruction.

READING I   The first reading presents a text framed in a prophecy of the material and spiritual renewal of the Jerusalem population, devastated by the long siege by Babylon. Thus, the reader feels the tension between the routine of our daily life and the hope for a resolution of all stress in God's plan for humanity. Ever faithful, God does not renege on the promise to grant David a descendant, the Messiah, who "shall do what is right and just in the land" and forever occupy his throne.

READING II   The second reading begins with a prayer, "May the Lord make you increase and abound in love for one another and for all." Paul desires a mature, fraternal love, open to everyone in the community; that would be the finest preparation and guarantee to meet the Lord when he comes. To live in expectation of his coming does not imply a flight from everyday reality. Paul invites us to conduct ourselves in a way pleasing to God. If the full stature of the believer is Christ, the basic attitude of each one is

Thessalonians = thes-uh-LOH-nee-uhnz

After the salutation, pause briefly and assume a prayerful tone.

Note that the Lord will return "with all his holy ones." Perhaps some of us will be in that number.
The word "finally" provides an opportunity to command attention with increased intensity.

Remember, Paul's message is simple: You learned from me how to behave. You're doing very well. Now, try even harder.

Communicate both ideas in the last sentence: (a) You know how to behave. (b) You learned it from the Lord Jesus.

TO KEEP IN MIND
Always pause at the end of the reading, before you proclaim the closing dialogue ("The Word of the Lord" or "The Gospel of the Lord").

READING II   1 Thessalonians 3:12—4:2

A reading from the first Letter of Saint Paul to the Thessalonians

Brothers and sisters:
 May the Lord make you **increase** and **abound** in **love**
    for one **another and** for **all**,
    just as **we** have for **you,**
    so as to **strengthen** your **hearts**,
    to be **blameless** in **holiness** before our **God** and **Father**
    at the coming of our **Lord Jesus** with **all** his **holy** ones. Amen.

Finally, brothers and sisters,
    we earnestly **ask** and **exhort** you in the **Lord Jesus** that,
    as you received from **us**
    how you should conduct yourselves to please **God**
    —and as you **are** conducting yourselves—
    you do so **even more.**
For you **know** what **instructions** we **gave** you
        through the **Lord Jesus**.

---

practicing what we have attained by our Baptism in Christ. These words are directed to people prepared by the promise God made to his people, the promise Jeremiah recalls in the first reading: "I will raise up for David a just shoot."

GOSPEL Today's Gospel reading is part of a discourse about the end of time and the Last Judgment. Jesus announces his return to our world and how we are scheduled to meet him. He borrows images of the prophets: the signs in the sun, moon, and stars; the roar of the sea; the anguish that anticipates his arrival. To illustrate the suddenness of his coming, he employs the image of a trap. The upheaval that will accompany Jesus' coming might frighten us if we are not prepared. Even as a new world is born amid the birth pains, so the world as we know it is destined to disappear, agonizing in its death. Let us be prepared and not get drunk on the things of the passing world. The birth of the new world will arrive with the anguish that accompanies all life as it comes to its end and with the labor that escorts every new life into the world. What Jesus announces is not new; the prophets had already spoken of this final crisis. Some elements are novel, however, and they touch us closely: the new world that Jesus announces is about to be born. Why do we

The storm rages throughout the first paragraph. The tone is solemn and threatening and the pace is measured.

You're not trying to frighten, but don't dilute the powerful imagery that's meant to remind us Christ is a cosmic and awesome Lord.

We have no present-day equivalent for such an event. Speak of it with great solemnity.

For a moment, the storm subsides and the tone softens as you offer words of hope and redemption.

These words comprise a true warning, and they are offered to save us, even if at first they must frighten us.

The sudden and unexpected advent of these events must be stressed.

These words come right from Jesus as prescient advice meant to steel us for the storm that will surely come.

TO KEEP IN MIND
Always pause at the end of the reading, before you proclaim the closing dialogue ("The Word of the Lord" or "The Gospel of the Lord").

GOSPEL   Luke 21:25–28, 34–36

A reading from the holy Gospel according to Luke

Jesus said to his disciples:
"There will be **signs** in the **sun**, the **moon**, and the **stars**,
and on **earth nations** will be in **dismay**,
perplexed by the **roaring** of the sea and the waves.
People will **die** of **fright**
in **anticipation** of what is **coming** upon the **world,**
for the **powers** of the **heavens** will be **shaken**.
And then they will see the **Son of Man**
coming in a **cloud** with **power** and **great glory.**
But when these signs **begin** to happen,
stand erect and **raise** your heads
because your **redemption** is at **hand**.

"**Beware** that your **hearts** do not become **drowsy**
from **carousing** and **drunkenness**
and the **anxieties** of daily life,
and that day catch you by **surprise** like a **trap**.
For that day will assault **everyone**
who lives on the face of the earth.
Be **vigilant** at **all** times
and **pray** that you have the **strength**
to **escape** the tribulations that are **imminent**
and to **stand** before the **Son of Man**."

---

fear our next encounter with the one who will console us with the words, "Do not be afraid. It's me"?

Another novelty is that Jesus encourages us to live in patient expectation when he says, "stand erect and raise your heads because your redemption is at hand." This detail, the word *redemption,* from the Latin *redemptio,* could also be translated as *ransom,* the buying of freedom from slavery or captivity. What do we hope for at Christmas,

but freedom from the chains of an obstinate character, the liberation of our life from attitudes and unhealthy activities that enslave us in the present?

Labor pains before giving birth and the anguish accompanying death are two moments when the familiar world adjusts to a new phase of life. What Jesus announces will happen in heaven, on earth, and in the bedrock of the heart. We may be apprehensive in the face of the announcement of

God's coming "in a cloud with power and great glory," but the one whom we expect came first as a child, one like us, a child who offers freedom from the obstacles of an old world, and rewards us with the peace and joy of a new world, designed by our loving God. K.S.

THE IMMACULATE CONCEPTION OF THE BLESSED VIRGIN MARY

LECTIONARY #689

READING I   Genesis 3:9–15, 20

A reading from the Book of Genesis

After the **man**, **Adam**, had **eaten** of the **tree**,
    the Lord God **called** to the man and **asked** him,
        "**Where are you?**"
He answered, "I **heard** you in the garden;
    but I was **afraid**, because I was **naked**,
    so I **hid** myself."
Then he asked, "**Who told you** that you were naked?
You have **eaten**, then,
    from the **tree** of which I had **forbidden** you to eat!"
The man replied, "The **woman** whom you put here with me—
    she gave **me** fruit from the tree, and so **I ate it**."
The Lord God then asked the woman,
    "**Why** did you **do such** a **thing?**"
The woman answered, "The **serpent tricked me** into it,
    so I **ate** it."

Then the Lord **God** said to the **serpent**:
    "**Because you have done this**, **you** shall be **banned**
        from **all** the **animals**
        and from **all** the **wild creatures;**
    on your **belly** shall you **crawl,**
        and **dirt** shall you **eat**
        all the days of your **life**.

From the start, signal that Adam's eating of the apple was a dire offense.
Adam and Eve are not children hiding from a parent, but adults who have chosen rebellion.

God is not the victim here; though he inquires, he is fully aware and in full control.

Sin results immediately in alienation and mistrust. Adam is fearful, so he blames the woman.

The woman brazenly rejects responsibility and blames the serpent.

God's rebuke of the serpent is hard hitting and unequivocal. Your tone should reflect the harsher judgment God levies on the serpent.

This curse heaps humiliation on the serpent.

READING I   Adam and Eve, tempted by the serpent, mistrusted God's love and disobeyed the prohibition to eat the fruit of the tree of knowledge of good and evil. The tragic consequence of this forbidden breakfast was the revealing of their nakedness, a nudity not so much physical but with moral and spiritual implications. Rather than becoming like God, they tasted the fruit of their own insecurity, the fear of their own limits, as they met their friendly God in the role of judge. It is true that God intervenes as judge, sustaining the moral order inscribed on the created world; but God continues to show the friendly side of the divine essence in anticipation of the definitive triumph over evil, expressed in the sentence pronounced on the serpent: Their offspring "will strike at your head, while you strike at his heel." Even amid the darkness of a false start, the faces of Christ and his Mother are traced. Mary's "enmity" with Satan was total. At no moment of her existence did she debase herself with idolatry, as happens in our interior lives by virtue of the patrimony of that first sin that marked us from birth.

READING II   God's project "before the foundation of the world," realized in Jesus' coming, is our participation in the filial condition of Christ: "In love he destined us for adoption to himself through Christ Jesus." The goal is for us to be "holy and without blemish in his sight" so that we "might exist for the praise of his

4

I will put **enmity** between **you** and the **woman,**
    and between **your offspring** and **hers;**
he will **strike** at **your** head,
    while **you strike** at **his** heel."

The man called his wife **Eve,**
    because she became the **mother** of **all** the **living.**

The Church sees Mary as the "woman" and Christ as her offspring who will "strike" at the serpent's "head."
Pause before announcing that Eve became the mother of all humanity (as Mary is the mother of all who live in Christ).

RESPONSORIAL PSALM   Psalm 98:1, 2–3ab, 3cd–4 (1)

R. Sing to the Lord a new song, for he has done marvelous deeds.

Sing to the Lord a new song,
    for he has done wondrous deeds;
His right hand has won victory for him,
    his holy arm.

The Lord has made his salvation known:
    in the sight of the nations he has revealed
      his justice.
He has remembered his kindness and his
    faithfulness
      toward the house of Israel.

All the ends of the earth have seen
    the salvation by our God.
Sing joyfully to the Lord, all you lands;
    break into song; sing praise.

For meditation and context:

READING II   Ephesians 1:3–6, 11–12

A reading from the Letter of Saint Paul to the Ephesians

Brothers and sisters:
Blessed be the **God** and **Father** of our **Lord Jesus Christ,**
    who has **blessed** us in **Christ**
    with **every spiritual blessing** in the heavens,
    as he **chose** us **in him, before** the **foundation** of the **world,**
    to be **holy** and **without blemish** before him.
In **love** he **destined us** for **adoption** to himself
    through Jesus **Christ,**
    in accord with the **favor** of his **will,**
    for the **praise** of the **glory** of his **grace**
    that he **granted us** in the **beloved.** ≫

Ephesians = ee-FEE zhuhnz

With energetic rhythm, the opening sentence calls us to praise. Don't rush or you'll blur the several ideas expressed here. Start praying and don't stop praying until the end.

Blessed = BLES-uhd
blessed = blesd

We existed in the mind of God from all eternity! Share that profound insight with gravity.
"In love" = "because of love." Our status as children ("adoption") was always God's plan for humanity.

beloved = bee-LUHV-uhd
Joy should resound in these lines.

---

glory, we who first hoped in Christ." We should be attentive to the consequences that derive from the revelation of the mystery of the Immaculate Conception. It provides an impulse to let God's love take shape in us and forego the obstacle of sin. In our world where selfishness and corruption are all too evident, we are called to do our part to fashion a world where grace and Christian love are present, and invite every human being to imitate that quality of life.

GOSPEL   Today's feast recalls three women, three mothers, each with her own special appeal. The first is the mother of Mary, grandmother of our Savior, whom tradition knows as Anne, an elderly woman considered sterile. The birth of the Virgin Mary is due to God's intervention. The Hebrew name *Hannah*, "Anne" in English, means "mercy." The Immaculate Conception is due to God's wondrous operation in history and in the womb of the mother of the Immaculate Mary, the sec-

ond woman we celebrate today, whose will was none other than God's will. History is marked by humans who seek their own will, who cling to their own determination instead of relying on God. Today we celebrate the one whose will was not stained by the selfishness that destroys the harmony of the divine will.

The third woman is Eve, mother of all humanity. God created her, together with her partner, and arranged a marvelous garden as their home and work place. Our first

In Christ, God chose us to inherit the glory of the Kingdom.

Despite appearances, all things work toward the accomplishment of God's will.

Sustain eye contact with the assembly and slow your delivery on the final line. Then pause before, "The word . . . "

In him we were **also chosen,**
>destined in accord with the purpose of the One
>who accomplishes **all things** according to the **intention**
>>of his **will**,
>so that we might exist for the **praise** of **his glory**,
>we who **first hoped** in Christ.

GOSPEL   Luke 1:26–38

A reading from the holy Gospel according to Luke

Though familiar, these lines carry significant information packed into one sentence. Lift out each detail.

The angel **Gabriel** was sent from **God**
>to a town of **Galilee** called **Nazareth**,
>to a **virgin** betrothed to a man named **Joseph**,
>of the house of **David**,
>and the virgin's **name** was **Mary**.

Speak Mary's name with reverence and affection.
The angel's voice should be reassuring and gentle, not jarring.
This narration should convey Mary's confusion.

And coming to her, he said,
>"**Hail**, **full of grace**! The **Lord** is **with you**."
But she was greatly **troubled** at what was said
>and **pondered** what sort of **greeting** this might be.
Then the angel **said** to her,
>"Do **not** be **afraid**, Mary,
>for **you** have found **favor** with **God**.

Aware that his words are unsettling, the angel soothes and informs at the same time.

Behold, you will **conceive in your womb** and **bear a son**,
>and you shall **name** him **Jesus**.
He will be **great** and will be called **Son of the Most High**,
>and the **Lord God** will give him the throne of **David** his **father**,
>and he will **rule** over the house of **Jacob forever**,
>and of his **Kingdom** there will **be no end**."

The angel is fully aware of the great dignity and destiny of Mary's child.

But **Mary** said to the angel,
>"**How can this be**,
>since I have **no relations** with a **man**?"

Mary believes God will do this, but can't iMagine how.

---

parents began their story in perfect harmony with God and creation. But once at home, they dug a pit, a grave, wherein they fell. The hole they dug is called self-will, the channel to death. Since then, this pit of selfishness has held its own attraction for all her daughters and sons. Self-will has as collaborators our resentments, prejudices, excuses, and passions. Every human has fallen into that pit, driven by her or his own will, leading to death.

And so the story unfolded until a young woman, today's celebrated Mary Immaculate, took God's side. The grave and death had no attraction for that strong young woman, full of grace, who had the courage to deny the insinuations of self, as she united her life completely to God's plan of salvation. With grace and by her generous, selfless response to the angel, "May it be done to me according to your word," this woman short-circuited the program of death as the destiny of Eve's every daugh-

ter and son. Today, with the celebration of this great-granddaughter of Eve, Anne's only child, we are inspired to follow her marvelous example. God's will, not my own, brings about the salvation of the human race and will restore the beauty of creation. Today's collect puts it well: "O God, who by the Immaculate Conception of the Blessed Virgin prepared a worthy dwelling for your Son, grant, we pray, that as you preserved her from every stain by virtue of the death of your Son, which you foresaw, so

This is the climax of the passage and its most tender lines.

Don't change tone here: "And behold" extends the miraculous hand of God's love from Mary to her elder cousin.

Pause after "Mary said to the angel." Mary announces her decision with simplicity and strength.

And the angel said to her in **reply**,
  "The **Holy Spirit** will come **upon you**,
    and the **power** of the **Most High** will **overshadow you**.
Therefore the **child** to be **born**
    will be called **holy**, the **Son of God**.
And **behold**, **Elizabeth**, your relative,
    has **also conceived** a **son** in her **old age**,
    and this is the **sixth month** for her who was called **barren**;
    for **nothing** will be **impossible** for **God**."
Mary said, "**Behold, I am the handmaid of the Lord.**
May it be done to **me** according to **your** word."
Then the angel departed from her.

THE 4 STEPS OF *LECTIO DIVINA* OR PRAYERFUL READING

1. *Lectio:* Read a Scripture passage aloud slowly. Notice what phrase captures your attention and be attentive to its meaning. Silent pause.

2. *Meditatio:* Read the passage aloud slowly again, reflecting on the passage, allowing God to speak to you through it. Silent pause.

3. *Oratio:* Read it aloud slowly a third time, allowing it to be your prayer or response to God's gift of insight to you. Silent pause.

4. *Contemplatio:* Read it aloud slowly a fourth time, now resting in God's word.

---

through her intercession, we, too, may be cleansed and admitted to your presence."

The angel's greeting to Mary, "The Lord is with you," invigorates the present-day Christian with the knowledge that we are not alone in our task to live out our faith. With this formula that has been spoken to the prophets and heroes of the past, God guarantees continuing divine presence in the commission of our task. This greeting re-creates the consciousness that it is the work of God, who will bring our collabora-tion to fruition. As we celebrate the Immaculate Conception, we recognize the wonders God has worked in Mary for our salvation. She is our reason to rejoice. We pray that, like her, we may be filled with the benevolence of God and enlisted in the purpose of receiving the Messiah, convinced that God continues to fulfill the promise of salvation for all people. K.S.

SECOND SUNDAY
OF ADVENT

LECTIONARY #6

READING I   Baruch 5:1–9

Baruch = buh-ROOK

A reading from the Book of the Prophet Baruch

You begin with imperatives that express Israel's wondrous reversal of fortune!

Visualize these tangible items; they are sacred, like a wedding dress or a child's baptismal gown.

Speak with energy and conviction of what God will do.

IMagine speaking the name of your city when you call "Jerusalem" to rise up.

Being "remembered" is the difference between life and death.
Contrast the sorrow of being led away with the joy of returning home.
This is not a news report; you are joyfully sharing poetic images meant to rouse the iMagination.

Let the final sentence summarize the joyous good news that fills the entire reading.

Jerusalem, **take off** your robe of **mourning** and **misery**;
   put on the **splendor** of **glory** from **God forever**:
Wrapped in the cloak of **justice** from God,
   bear on your head the **mitre**
   that **displays** the **glory** of the **eternal name**.
For God will show **all** the **earth** your **splendor**:
   you will be **named** by **God forever**
   the **peace** of **justice**, the **glory** of God's **worship**.

Up, Jerusalem! stand upon the **heights**;
   look to the **east** and **see** your **children**
gathered from the **east** and the **west**
   at the **word** of the **Holy One**,
   rejoicing that **they** are **remembered by God**.
Led away on **foot** by their **enemies** they **left** you:
   but **God** will bring them **back** to you
   borne **aloft** in **glory** as on **royal thrones**.
For God has **commanded**
   that **every lofty mountain** be made **low**,
and that the **age-old depths** and **gorges**
   be **filled** to **level ground**,
   that **Israel** may advance **secure** in the **glory** of **God**.
The **forests** and every **fragrant** kind of tree
   have **overshadowed Israel** at God's **command**;

READING I Baruch consoles Jerusalem with the news that her children will return, that the dream of restoration is coming true. Jerusalem, emblem of God's people, is invited to take off her "robe of mourning and misery" and adorn herself with "the splendor of glory from God forever." Jerusalem acquires a new identity, endorsed by a new name that sums up the values she represents: "the peace of justice, the glory of God's worship." Her inhabitants will construct "peace," that is, living according to God's design; she will radiate "glory," the imprint of the divine mercy and justice. In language reminiscent of Isaiah, God commands "that every lofty mountain be made low"—a reference to the excesses of pride, arrogance, and materialism—while he commands "that the age-old depths and gorges be filled to level ground"—referring to the shortage of justice and obedience to God. Baruch's oracle projects how the wasteland of the human heart comes to life.

READING II Paul opens his letter with thanksgiving, and the dominant note is friendship between the apostle and his community. True friendship extends into eternity. One path hastens the arrival of that day: charity, the most effective instrument for infusing meaning in life. Paul prays "that your love increase ever more and more, both in knowledge and every kind of perception." The vocabulary of "understanding," or knowledge, enhances the love to which the apostle refers. With

for **God** is **leading Israel** in **joy**
    by the **light** of his **glory**,
    with his **mercy** and **justice** for company.

For meditation and context:

RESPONSORIAL PSALM Psalm 126:1–2, 2–3, 4–5, 6 (3)

R. The Lord has done great things for us; we are filled with joy.

When the LORD brought back the captives
    of Zion,
  we were like men dreaming.
Then our mouth was filled with laughter,
  and our tongue with rejoicing.

Then they said among the nations,
  "The LORD has done great things
    for them."
The LORD has done great things for us;
  we are glad indeed.

Restore our fortunes, O LORD,
  like the torrents in the southern desert.
Those who sow in tears
  shall reap rejoicing.

Although they go forth weeping,
  carrying the seed to be sown,
they shall come back rejoicing,
  carrying their sheaves.

READING II Philippians 1:4–6, 8–11

A reading from the Letter of Saint Paul to the Philippians

Brothers and sisters:
I pray always with **joy** in my **every prayer** for **all** of you,
    because of your **partnership** for the **gospel**
    from the **first day** until **now**.
I am **confident** of this,
    that the one who **began** a **good work** in you
    will **continue** to **complete** it
    until the day of **Christ Jesus**.
God is my **witness**,
    how I **long** for **all** of you with the **affection** of **Christ Jesus**.
And **this** is my **prayer**:
    that your **love** may **increase** ever **more** and **more**
    in **knowledge** and **every kind** of **perception**,
    to **discern** what is of **value**,
    so that you may be **pure** and **blameless** for the day of **Christ**, **»**

Philippians = fih-LIP-ee-uhnz

Remember, this is Paul's "letter of joy."
Be sure it sounds like it by establishing eye contact and speaking directly to your assembly.
Here is the reason Paul is so joyful: they are remaining faithful to the gospel.
The word "confident" sets the tone.
Be as confident as Paul as you speak to your community.

Paul is speaking not like a teacher but as a loving friend or parent.
Don't report the "prayer"; pray it.

Pray for yourself as well as for your assembly.
Paul's prayer contains several "intentions." Don't rush them together.

such an attitude, on the day of Christ Jesus, you may be "filled with the fruit of righteousness that comes through Jesus Christ for the glory and praise of God." God's coming in our flesh puts believers in tension and impels us to give our best. Paul reassures the Philippians that God will bring to fruition the work in them and in us.

GOSPEL The evangelist speaks ironically when he lists the names of the superstars of Jesus' day—Caesar Tiberius, Pontius Pilate, Herod and his brother Philip, Lisanias, the religious hierarchs Annas and Caiaphas—and then reports that the Word of God arrived in a secluded place to an unexpected person, John, son of Zechariah. The commercial center, the theaters of government and show business, have their appeal, but God's Word arrived in the desert. The evan-

gelist sketches a tension between two poles: wealth and power contrasted with seclusion. In both places God's Word risks not being heard—in the noise of politics and commerce for its lack of attention, but also in the austere desert, for its lack of audience. But the Word came to the desert. Humans experience the tension between the attraction of the spectacle and yearning for rest. But it is in the desert, severe in its landscape, where a new voice can be heard.

filled with the fruit of **righteousness**
that **comes** through **Jesus Christ**
for the **glory** and **praise** of **God**.

GOSPEL   Luke 3:1–6

A reading from the holy Gospel according to Luke

In the fifteenth year of the reign **of Tiberius Caesar,**
    when **Pontius Pilate** was **governor of Judea,**
    and **Herod** was **tetrarch** of **Galilee,**
    and his brother **Philip tetrarch** of the region
        of **Ituraea** and **Trachonitis,**
    and **Lysanias** was **tetrarch** of **Abilene,**
    during the high **priesthood** of **Annas** and **Caiaphas,**
    the **word** of **God** came to **John** the son of **Zechariah**
        in the **desert.**
John went throughout the **whole** region of the **Jordan,**
    proclaiming a **baptism** of **repentance** for the **forgiveness**
        of **sins,**
    as it is **written** in the book of the words of the prophet **Isaiah:**
    *A **voice** of one **crying out** in the **desert**:*
    *"**Prepare** the **way** of the **Lord,***
        *make **straight** his **paths.***
    *Every **valley** shall be **filled***
        *and **every mountain** and **hill** shall be made **low.***
    *The **winding roads** shall be **made straight,***
        *and the **rough ways made smooth,***
    *and **all flesh** shall see the **salvation** of **God.**"*

Side notes (left column):

Use ritardando (gradually slowing your rate) as you end the sentence.

These characters' names are from different arenas of first-century life; don't rush them, and change tone slightly from civil to religious authorities.

Tiberius = tĭ-BEER-ee-uhs; Caesar = SEE-zer
Judea = joo-DEE-uh
Ituraea = ih-too-REE-ah
Trachonitis = trak-uh-NĪ-tis
Lysanias = lĭ-SAY-nee-uhs
Annas = AN-uhs
Caiaphas = KĪ-uh-fuhs
Zechariah = zek-uh-RĪ-uh

Pause briefly before announcing the beginning of John's ministry.

Don't gloss over John's important ministry. You might speak the line in his proclamatory tone.

Isaiah's poetry is familiar; slow it down to make it fresh and help your listeners hear it as new.

Let conviction ring in your voice.

Rejoice in this final declaration that God's mercy is for all.

The encounter with God does not happen apart from our daily lives. Health, happiness, and integrity are not achieved by turning away from who we are; they are found in the fertile soil where God's Word takes root. It is in our concrete history, in the tapestry of joyful and sad events, in the fragmented projects of everyday life, where God is revealed. The call to conversion is not heard first in society, not even in the chapel, but in an individual's own life, in the freedom and calm that every person carries within. Our nearest inhospitable desert is ourselves! There the Baptist's message is received, there we prepare the way, iron out the roughness, fill in the potholes and level off the bumpy places of our character; there we smooth out the exaggerations and presumption, so our own eyes can see the Salvation of God. What did the prophet say? "Prepare the way of the Lord, make straight his paths." Here, in everyday life, under the appearance of seemingly insignificant happenings, in the interior life and consciousness, God desires to be born in each one of us. When the Church invites us to conversion, as our response to the Baptist's cry, she does not refer to a routine house cleaning. It is a question of our becoming the temple of God's beauty, generosity, and truth. Here is our vocation, our response to the love affair for which we have been created from the genesis of the world. K.S.

THIRD SUNDAY OF ADVENT

LECTIONARY #9

READING I   Zephaniah 3:14–18a

A reading from the Book of the Prophet Zephaniah

> **Shout** for **joy**, O daughter Zion!
>   Sing **joyfully, O** Israel!
> Be **glad** and **exult** with **all** your **heart**,
>   O **daughter Jerusalem**!
> The LORD has **removed** the **judgment against** you,
>   he has **turned away** your **enemies**;
> the **King of Israel**, the LORD, is in your **midst**,
>   you have no further **misfortune** to fear.
> On **that day**, it shall be said to **Jerusalem**:
>   **Fear not**, O Zion, **be not discouraged**!
> The LORD, your **God**, is in your **midst**,
>   a **mighty savior**;
> he will **rejoice** over you with **gladness**,
>   and **renew** you in his **love**,
> he will **sing joyfully** because of **you**,
>   as one **sings** at **festivals**.

Zephaniah = zef-uh-NĪ-uh

"Shout for joy . . . sing joyfully" is a form of repetition that characterizes biblical poetry. To convey the emphasis it intends, you must increase energy in your voice from the first expression to the second.

Keep in mind the trials the nation has endured as you speak these comforting words.

Renew your energy here as if noticing a face that remains unconvinced. "Fear not" is a consistent and important biblical theme.

The tone becomes more personal and intimate, and perhaps softer.

TO KEEP IN MIND
Smile when you share good news in a reading. Nonverbal cues like a smile help your assembly better understand your reading.

READING I The prophet addresses the people affectionately with the term "daughter Zion"; and, in spite of her infidelities, announces salvation: "The Lord, your God, is in your midst, a mighty savior; he will rejoice over you . . . and renew you in his love." At a time when Israel felt the threat of formidable enemies and did not expect the solution to their difficulties, God promises salvation that will gladden the people. What wonderful news! God's judgment brings with it the promise of salvation! In the face of danger and struggles, God is on our side, ever ready to save us because he loves us. Zephaniah announces the end of the exile and the return from Babylon with a vibrant oracle, a joyful hymn to Jerusalem. The reasons for joy are twofold. First, God revoked the sentence of condemnation and has dispersed the enemies; second, the Lord promises never to abandon his people; he guarantees salvation.

For meditation and context:

RESPONSORIAL PSALM   Isaiah 12:2–3, 4, 5–6 (6)

R. Cry out with joy and gladness: for among you is the great and Holy One of Israel.

God indeed is my savior;
  I am confident and unafraid.
My strength and my courage is the LORD,
  and he has been my savior.
With joy you will draw water
  at the fountain of salvation.

Give thanks to the LORD, acclaim his name;
  among the nations make known
    his deeds,
  proclaim how exalted is his name.

Sing praise to the LORD for his glorious
    achievement;
  let this be known throughout all
    the earth.
Shout with exultation, O city of Zion,
  for great in your midst
    is the Holy One of Israel!

READING II   Philippians 4:4–7

Philippians = fil-LIP-ee-uhnz

A reading from the Letter of Saint Paul to the Philippians

Offer Paul's command joyfully. Then repeat it with even greater energy.

Each short sentence conveys a new and distinct thought. Don't run them together.

Stress the "thanksgiving" that should characterize our prayers of petition.

Communicate all three ideas here: (a) God's peace, (b) that's like no other, (c) will protect us.

Brothers and sisters:
Rejoice in the **Lord always**.
I shall say it **again: rejoice**!
Your **kindness** should be known to **all**.
The **Lord** is **near**.
Have **no anxiety** at **all**, but in **everything**,
  by **prayer** and **petition**, with **thanksgiving**,
  make your **requests known** to **God**.
Then the **peace** of God that surpasses **all understanding**
  will **guard your hearts** and **minds** in **Christ Jesus**.

READING II   Paul encourages the Philippians even as he challenges them: "Rejoice in the Lord always. . . . Your kindness should be known to all. The Lord is near." When we are kind and perform our service with a view to the good of all, we can live free from the anxiety that spoils peace and harmony. God's nearness is the source of joy that frees the believing community from dread of judgment. The encouragement "Have no anxiety at all" moves the Church to be at peace even amidst persecution, with the guarantee that "The peace of God that surpasses all understanding will guard your hearts and minds in Christ Jesus." These consoling words do not eliminate the rude drama of life, but they dismiss panic and despair. Paul's counsel, like those of the Baptist, announces the nearness of salvation, which we celebrate in every Eucharist.

The prophet's theme of joy is accentuated in Philippians. To the various reasons for joy throughout the letter, Paul has added "The Lord is near." The eschatological dimension of faith makes the heart of the Christian vibrate with joy. Knowing that the Lord is near relieves all sorrow, to the effect that, for the believer, Christ's coming is not "after" the suffering ends, but within the suffering. The challenge is to correct our vision and adjust our sensitivity so that we may see and sense Christ close when we are in pain, whether physical or spiritual.

GOSPEL   Announcing the urgency of conversion, John the Baptist advised his audience to show forth the fruits of a change of attitude and life. When the people asked, "What should we do?" John answered, "Whoever has two cloaks should share with the person who

GOSPEL   Luke 3:10–18

A reading from the holy Gospel according to Luke

The **crowds** asked John the **Baptist**,
  "**What** should we **do**?"
He said to them in **reply**,
  "Whoever has **two** cloaks
  should **share** with the person who has **none**.
And whoever has **food** should do **likewise**."
Even tax collectors came to be baptized and **they** said to him,
  "**Teacher**, **what** should **we do**?"
He answered them,
  "**Stop** collecting **more** than what is **prescribed**."
Soldiers also asked him,
  "And **what** is it that **we** should **do**?"
He told them,
  "**Do not** practice **extortion**,
  do not falsely accuse anyone,
  and be **satisfied** with your **wages**."

Now the **people** were filled with **expectation**,
  and **all** were asking in their **hearts**
  whether **John might** be the **Christ**.
John answered them **all**, saying,
  "**I** am **baptizing** you with **water**,
  but one **mightier than I** is **coming**.
I am **not worthy** to **loosen** the **thongs** of his **sandals**.
He will **baptize** you with the **Holy Spirit** and **fire**.
His **winnowing fan** is in his **hand** to **clear** his **threshing** floor
  and to **gather** the **wheat** into his **barn**,
  but the **chaff** he will **burn** with **unquenchable fire**."
Exhorting them in **many other ways**,
  he preached **good news** to the people.

Be sure to stress that John is the baptizer, so your listeners don't assume it is Jesus.

Given what we know of John, his manner is likely not refined and his tone might sound abrupt.

The questions are asked with sincerity and urgency.
Though brief, John's replies provide a complete response to each questioner. Speak them with authority and an attitude of "This is all you need to do."

"And be satisfied . . . " might be delivered as a kind of afterthought.

Pause before starting this section that begins a new "beat" in the text.

John's tone should convey a desire to suffer no illusions about his identity. He's saying: "You're wondering who I am. Well, I'll tell you!"

Don't rush his reference to the "Holy Spirit and fire."

Pause briefly before this final summary statement. Let your tone suggest that John himself was "good news."

---

has none. And whoever has food should do likewise." Some government functionaries asked John, "Teacher, what should we do?" to which he replied: "Stop collecting more than what is prescribed." To soldiers who asked him, "And what is it that we should do?" he replied, "Do not practice extortion, do not falsely accuse anyone, and be satisfied with your wages." With such counsel, John teaches that conversion does not require anything extraordinary. In responding to people, to functionaries and soldiers,

the Baptist emphasizes the fidelity to one's responsibilities, integrity in one's state of life. It is as if he were saying "Do what you are committed to do; be sensible, honest, and normal in your dealings with other people, or, in a word, be human. Do not exaggerate, do not use your position to bully, defraud or impress anyone."

Recognizing that the Messiah was at the door, John pressed for a more compassionate, less selfish conduct. His advice astonishes us by its simplicity. Conversion

will be manifested in dealing with one's neighbor, being generous, kind, and compassionate. Conversion is about sharing one's property with the needy, being honest and fair in business, and moderate in the exercise of power. Our conversion consists in putting these counsels into practice; our attitudes, translated into behavior, prove the Messiah is near. K.S.

FOURTH SUNDAY OF ADVENT

LECTIONARY #12

READING I   Micah 5:1–4a

A reading from the Book of the Prophet Micah

> **Thus says** the LORD:
> **You**, **Bethlehem-Ephrathah**
>   **too small** to be among the **clans** of **Judah**,
> from **you** shall come **forth** for **me**
>   one who is to be **ruler** in **Israel**;
> whose **origin** is from of **old**,
>   from **ancient times**.
> **Therefore** the Lord will give them **up**, until the time
>   when **she** who is to give **birth** has **borne**,
> and the **rest** of his **kindred** shall **return**
>   to the **children** of **Israel**.
> He shall **stand firm** and **shepherd** his **flock**
>   by the **strength** of the LORD,
>   in the **majestic name** of the LORD, his **God**;
> and they shall **remain**, for **now his greatness**
>   shall reach to the **ends** of the **earth**;
>   **he** shall be **peace**.

Micah = MĪ-kuh

After the introductory line, shift to the voice of God.

Bethlehem-Ephrathah = BETH-luh-hem-EPH-ruh-thuh

These words, spoken as if to an insecure young person, are meant to encourage and embolden.

"Old . . . ancient times" evokes the regal dignity of King David.

This is good news: those scattered will return home.

He will be both strong and gentle, shepherding not with his own strength but God's.

The final line should be set off with a pause before and after. Speak each word with great conviction and joy.

READING I Micah announces the coming of a messianic king in Bethlehem, David's hometown, but insignificant among the villages of Judah. Rather than a geographical precision about where the Messiah is to be born, this is a theological oracle announcing his humble style: his triumph is not with the sword nor with a spectacle of power, but "He shall be peace." But first, a time of purification is necessary, during which Israel will be subjected to foreign powers. This preparation will end with the birth of the king who will rule his people—or "pasture" the flock—with firmness, and he will act in God's name.

READING II The author of the Letter to the Hebrews addresses the theme of salvation by comparing the ultimate efficacy of Christ's sacrifice with the inefficacy of the sacrifices of the first covenant. He presents a Christological interpretation of Psalm 40 to indicate the perfect submission to the will of the Father who presided over Christ's life and work. The sacrifices and expiatory victims prescribed by the first covenant do not earn salvation. Christ's coming into the world replaced the former offerings with the sacrifice of fulfilling God's will, with the perfect offering, once and for all, of his own body, which sanctifies us. The author puts in Christ's mouth the strong declaration of his mission: "I come to do your will, O God." In becoming flesh, Jesus showed how to live according to God's will. The author motivates the believer to do God's will, which is what Jesus Christ came to instill in his people.

For meditation and context:

RESPONSORIAL PSALM   Psalm 80:2–3, 15–16, 18–19 (4)

R. Lord, make us turn to you; let us see your face and we shall be saved.

O shepherd of Israel, hearken,
    from your throne upon the cherubim,
        shine forth.
Rouse your power,
    and come to save us.

Once again, O LORD of hosts,
    look down from heaven, and see;
take care of this vine,
    and protect what your right hand
        has planted,
    the son of man whom you yourself
        made strong.

May your help be with the man of your
    right hand,
    with the son of man whom you yourself
        made strong.
Then we will no more withdraw from you;
    give us new life, and we will call upon
        your name.

READING II   Hebrews 10:5–10

Communicate thoughts, not just words.

A reading from the Letter to the Hebrews

Brothers and sisters:
When **Christ** came into the **world**, he said:
    "**Sacrifice** and **offering** you did **not** desire,
        but a **body** you **prepared** for me;
    in **holocausts** and **sin** offerings you took **no delight**.
    Then I said, 'As is **written** of me in the **scroll**,
    behold, I come to do **your will**, O **God**.'"

"You" refers to God.

Suggest the greater value of obedience over sacrifice.

First he says, "**Sacrifices** and **offerings**,
    holocausts and **sin offerings**,
        you neither **desired** nor **delighted** in."
These are offered according to the **law**.
Then he says, "**Behold**, I come to do **your will**."
He takes away the **first** to establish the **second**.
By this "**will**," **we** have been **consecrated**
    through the offering of the **body** of **Jesus Christ once** for **all**.

The author is reviewing here.

"According to the Law," in the author's view, means they are of less value.

The author's emotion is most evident here in what is a clear declaration of faith.

GOSPEL

The drama of the Gospel presents four actors: the Old Testament, personified in Elizabeth; the New Testament, represented by the young Virgin; divine Grace incarnate, present in the Virgin's pregnancy, and John the Baptist, in Elizabeth's womb. Of the four, John takes the initiative; he moves behind the scene, leaps or dances in his mother's womb as he celebrates God's presence in Mary's womb. This cast of four suits us because, to some degree, we find ourselves there. The old self is Elizabeth, barren but now open to new frontiers. The fruit of her pregnancy is a child who moves under the vision and the impulse that is felt in the encounter with the Mother of Grace. We call this impulse conversion. Everyone receives life, painted in chiaroscuro—with darkness and light, possibilities and barriers —and many people get stuck in the same program, entangled in stale feelings, barraged by habitual disappointments, chained by habits or attitudes. The Old Testament teaches that we cannot free ourselves; God takes the initiative to save us. But once upon a time our humanity, without putting conditions to God's grace, responded in the person of the Blessed Virgin. Humanity, personified in John, previously trapped in a dark, enslaved history, begins to walk, run, and jump in the presence of God's grace, incarnate in the Virgin's womb. God's untiring love for us is a story of hope, because who does not long to move ahead and get free from the habitual rut? Who does not want to enjoy the freedom of grace? It is a story of faith and courage that inspires us to be conscious of and live the Christmas holidays and liturgies that celebrate God's birth in history and in our lives.

Mary has just experienced a stunning revelation from the angel Gabriel. Elizabeth's pregnancy provides assurance for Mary of Gabriel's promise.

Judah = JOO-duh

Zechariah = zek-uh-RĪ-uh

Creating a sense of "haste" doesn't require fast reading. Let your energy suggest her hurriedness.

Take delight in recounting this warm detail.

Blessed = BLES-uhd

Don't give Elizabeth's remark the sound of rote recitation as in the Hail Mary. It is a spontaneous and heart-felt exclamation! Elizabeth is not looking for explanations, but marveling at her good fortune!

Repeat this detail with Elizabeth's apparent joy.

Elizabeth's best insight is last: Mary is blessed because she believed God's word so much that it took root within her.

> ### TO KEEP IN MIND
> In a narrative, find an emotion or point of view for each character, keeping in mind that these might change during the reading.

GOSPEL   Luke 1:39–45

A reading from the holy Gospel according to Luke

Mary set out
    and **traveled** to the **hill** country in **haste**
    to a town of **Judah**,
    where she entered the house of **Zechariah**
    and greeted **Elizabeth**.
When **Elizabeth heard** Mary's greeting,
    the infant **leaped** in her womb,
    and Elizabeth, **filled** with the **Holy Spirit**,
    cried out in a **loud voice** and said,
    "**Blessed** are you among **women**,
    and **blessed** is the **fruit** of **your womb**.
And **how** does this **happen** to me,
    that the **mother** of my **Lord** should **come** to **me**?
For at the moment the sound of your greeting reached my **ears**,
    the **infant** in my **womb leaped** for **joy**.
Blessed are **you** who **believed**
    that what was spoken to you by the **Lord**
    would be **fulfilled**."

Dance transforms the natural movement of walking, transporting it to another level. The Israelites danced in the procession of the Ark to Jerusalem, and David danced fervently before the Ark of the Covenant (2 Samuel 6:14). St. Luke tells us how the forerunner of the Messiah, John the Baptist, danced in the womb of elderly Elizabeth before the Ark of the New Covenant, Mary, the Virgin Mother of the Son of God. Their dance communicates freedom and joy.

Days before the celebration of the birth of the one who would be God's new covenant with us, we meet John in the bosom of the Old Testament, in the presence of the New; his leap in the womb celebrates the change of our life and a break from our habitual rhythm. In the presence of the Messiah, our walk becomes more elegant, because with him our humanity is clothed with virtue, stripped of attitudes and conversations that are not of God, which do not dance to the new rhythm of the Messiah. Our dance is not practical; we may not leap forward with giant steps, but our world becomes more beautiful, peaceful, human, immersed in the grace of a lovely God who visits us, as we respond with the dance of our conversion. K.S.

THE NATIVITY OF THE LORD (CHRISTMAS): VIGIL

LECTIONARY #13

READING I   Isaiah 62:1–5

Note the pattern of couplets: the second line repeats what was stated in the first. Let your energy increase from the first line to the second.
These lines call for energetic proclamation and unmuted zeal.

Throughout, your tone must announce the Good News in these lines as surely as the words themselves.

God's people are held tenderly in God's own hand like a crown of precious jewels

God comes to reverse our fortunes. The times when we were "forsaken" and "desolate" are forever gone!

The imagery of lover and beloved conveys the profound intimacy between God and people.

Let your eye contact tell us "you" refers to all in the assembly.

A reading from the Book of the Prophet Isaiah

For **Zion's** sake I will not be **silent**,
    for **Jerusalem's** sake I will not be **quiet**,
until her **vindication** shines forth like the **dawn**
    and her **victory** like a burning **torch**.

Nations shall **behold** your vindication,
    and all the **kings** your **glory**;
you shall be called by a **new** name
    pronounced by the mouth of the **Lord**.
You shall be a glorious **crown** in the hand of the Lord,
    a **royal diadem** held by your God.
No **more** shall people call you "**Forsaken**,"
    or your land "**Desolate**,"
but you shall be called "My **Delight**,"
    and your **land** "**Espoused**."
For the Lord **delights** in you
    and makes your land his **spouse**.
As a young **man** marries a **virgin**,
    your **Builder** shall marry **you**;
and as a **bridegroom rejoices** in his **bride**
    so shall your **God** rejoice in **you**.

READING I Isaiah's enthusiastic vision refers to Jerusalem, the holy hill of Zion, which the prophet contemplates already reconstructed. Jerusalem is the object of God's tender love. After the fall of Babylon, following the providential edict of the Persian king Cyrus, the "remnant of Israel" has returned home and rebuilt the Lord's temple. The city has once again become the driving force behind the religious identity of the nation and the focal point of salvation.

The prophet describes this renewed covenant between God and Jerusalem with nuptial images: "You shall be a splendid crown in the hands of the Lord, a royal crown in the palm of your God," for the city will be the seat of justice, the place that praises God, and a beacon of peace and freedom for the people who recognize his glory in God's renewed presence among his people. The Lord will give Jerusalem a new name; it will no longer be spoken of as "Abandoned" and "Devastated," but will be called "My favorite" and "Espoused." This grand vision, in the context of the Christmas feast, refers to the new covenant and the perennial salvation that God, through the birth of Jesus, establishes with humanity in a matrimony of true and lasting

For meditation and context:

RESPONSORIAL PSALM   Psalm 89:4–5, 16–17, 27, 29 (2a)

R. For ever I will sing the goodness of the Lord.

I have made a covenant with my chosen one,
    I have sworn to David my servant:
forever will I confirm your posterity
    and establish your throne for
        all generations.

Blessed the people who know the
        joyful shout;
    in the light of your countenance, O LORD,
        they walk.
At your name they rejoice all the day,
    and through your justice they are exalted.

He shall say of me, "You are my father,
    my God, the rock, my savior."
Forever I will maintain my kindness
        toward him,
    and my covenant with him stands firm.

READING II   Acts of the Apostles 13:16–17, 22–25

A reading from the Acts of the Apostles

When **Paul** reached **Antioch** in **Pisidia** and entered the **synagogue**,
    he **stood** up, motioned with his **hand**, and said,
        "Fellow **Israelites** and you **others** who are God-fearing, **listen**.
The God of this people **Israel** chose our **ancestors**
    and **exalted** the people during their sojourn in the land
        of **Egypt**.
With uplifted **arm** he led them **out** of it.
Then he removed **Saul** and raised up **David** as **king**;
    of him he **testified**,
    'I have found **David**, son of **Jesse**, a man after my own **heart**;
    he will carry out my every **wish**.'

Paul is speaking in a setting similar to yours—the weekly gathering place for worship.

Paul is quite deliberate in securing people's attention before speaking. Do the same!

To gain their attention, Paul must speak with authority. He reviews their salvation history in order to arrive at Jesus, who culminates that history!

David is always a point of reference in Israelite history. But in Jesus, they have one even greater than David!

---

love. The prophet encourages his audience, only lately returned from exile, assuring them that God will indeed restore David's city, Jerusalem. The people who live here will be God's delight and bride. The Lord's promises are forever valid. Even after the destruction and desolation of the exile, God has not forgotten the promise.

READING II Paul's preaching in the synagogue of Antioch of Pisidia is rich in scene changes: first, the enthusiastic welcome of the Word, when the apostle reviews the principal stages of salvation history from the patriarchs, through slavery and liberation from Egypt, the desert experience, the occupation of the Promised Land, Saul, King David, and finally to John's "Baptism of conversion";

from there the history reaches to Jesus, the Savior. The Messiah's forerunner was the first to welcome his coming: "Look for the one who comes after me. I am not worthy to unfasten the sandals on his feet."

What follows is the rejection of the Word and the persecution of the announcer, but such rejection was providential for the conversion of the pagan world and those who were not scandalized

From David came the "savior." This makes Jesus far greater than his ancestor.

Now he cites John, another hero superseded by Jesus. John insists they be clear about his identity.

Speak "one is coming after me . . . " with simple sincerity, as if John could see Jesus coming from a distance.

From this man's **descendants** God, according to his **promise**,
  has brought to Israel a **savior**, **Jesus**.
John **heralded** his coming by proclaiming a **baptism** of **repentance**
  to all the people of **Israel**;
  and as John was **completing** his course, he would say,
  'What do you suppose that I **am**? I am not **he**.
Behold, one is coming **after** me;
  I am not **worthy** to unfasten the **sandals** of his **feet**.'"

GOSPEL   Matthew 1:1–25

A reading from the holy Gospel according to Matthew

The book of the **genealogy** of Jesus **Christ**,
  the son of **David**, the son of **Abraham**.

Abraham became the father of **Isaac**,
  Isaac the father of **Jacob**,
  Jacob the father of **Judah** and his brothers.
Judah became the father of **Perez** and **Zerah**,
  whose **mother** was **Tamar**.
Perez became the father of **Hezron**,
  Hezron the father of **Ram**,
  Ram the father of **Amminadab**.
Amminadab became the father of **Nahshon**,
  Nahshon the father of **Salmon**,
  Salmon the father of **Boaz**,
  whose **mother** was **Rahab**.
Boaz became the father of **Obed**,
  whose **mother** was **Ruth**.
Obed became the father of **Jesse**,
  Jesse the father of **David** the **king**. »

Rehearse pronunciation of the names. Litanies like this make an impact through repetition, so don't rush this sacred listing. To sustain interest, renew your energy every few lines.

Abraham = AY-bruh-ham

Isaac = Ī-zik

Judah = JOO-duh

Perez = PAYR-ez

Zerah = ZEE-rah

Tamar = TAY-mahr: see Genesis 38.

Hezron = HEZ-ruhn

Ram = ram

Amminadab = uh-MIN-uh-dab

Nashon = NAH-shun

Salmon = SAL-muhn

Boaz = BOH-az

Rahab = RAY-hab: see Joshua 2:1–7

Obed = OH-bed

Ruth was the great-grandmother of King David.

Jesse = JES-ee

by the crucifixion. Then, finally, a multitude of women and men open to the gift of the Holy Spirit and conversion followed.

At all times in the history of the Church the announcement of the Good News is met with persecution. The child born in Bethlehem, wrapped in celestial glory, is the One who brings along with the gift of himself the royal emblems of passion. The disciple of Jesus is called to give

proof of fidelity and love—in peace, but above all in suffering—because the world habitually rejects the announcement and is uneasy in the face of the denunciation of an incoherent and selfish life.

GOSPEL   The genealogy of the family of the Son of God is presented like a column in a telephone directory, except the names are not in alphabetic

order. Or it might be the line-up for three football teams. The names reveal attributes and characteristics, as if they were nicknames of famous persons. Let us put the names in English: Abraham (Father of a great nation); Isaac (Jester); Jacob (Wrestler or Tripper); Perez (Breach), whose mother was Tamar (Palm Tree); Aram (Conceited); Aminadab (Prodigal or Highness); Nahshon (Snakey); Salmon (Sparky), whose mother

Uriah = yoo-RĪ-uh. His "wife" is Bathsheba: 2 Samuel 11:1–27.

Rehoboam = ree-huh-BOH-uhm

Abijah = uh-BĪ-juh

Asaph = AY-saf

Jehoshaphat = jeh-HOH-shuh-fat

Joram = JOHR-uhm

Uzziah = yuh-ZĪ-uh: Struck with leprosy for usurping role of priests: 2 Chronicles 26:16–20.

Jotham = JOH-thuhm

Ahaz = AY-haz

Hezekiah = hez-eh-KĪH-uh: One of the few "good" kings; a reformer.

Manasseh = muh-NAS-uh: The nation's worst king.

Josiah = joh-SĪ-uh: One of Judah's best kings; a reformer. Ascended the throne at age eight.

The exile was the nation's greatest trial.

Jechoniah = jek-oh-NĪ-uh

Shealtiel = shee-AL-tee-uhl

Zerubbabel = zuh-ROOB-uh-b*l

Abiud = uh-BĪ-uhd

Eliakim = ee-LĪ-uh-kim

Azor = AY-sohr

Zadok = ZAD-uhk

Achim = AH-kim

Eliud = ee-LĪ-uhd

Eleazar = el-ee-AY-zer

Matthan = MATH-uhn

"Fourteen" is a deliberate redundancy. Stress each recurrence.

David became the father of **Solomon**,
   whose **mother** had been the wife of **Uriah**.
Solomon became the father of **Rehoboam**,
   Rehoboam the father of **Abijah**,
   Abijah the father of **Asaph**.
Asaph became the father of **Jehoshaphat**,
   Jehoshaphat the father of **Joram**,
   Joram the father of **Uzziah**.
Uzziah became the father of **Jotham**,
   Jotham the father of **Ahaz**,
   Ahaz the father of **Hezekiah**.
Hezekiah became the father of **Manasseh**,
   Manasseh the father of **Amos**,
   Amos the father of **Josiah**.
Josiah became the father of **Jechoniah** and his brothers
   at the time of the Babylonian **exile**.

After the Babylonian exile,
   Jechoniah became the father of **Shealtiel**,
   Shealtiel the father of **Zerubbabel**,
   Zerubbabel the father of **Abiud**.
Abiud became the father of **Eliakim**,
   Eliakim the father of **Azor**,
   Azor the father of **Zadok**.
Zadok became the father of **Achim**,
   Achim the father of **Eliud**,
   Eliud the father of **Eleazar**.
Eleazar became the father of **Matthan**,
   Matthan the father of **Jacob**,
   Jacob the father of **Joseph**, the husband of **Mary**.
Of her was born **Jesus** who is called the **Christ**.

Thus the total number of **generations**
   from **Abraham** to **David**
   is **fourteen** generations;
   from **David** to the Babylonian **exile**,

was Rahab (Broad); Boaz (Tough Guy), whose wife is Ruth (Girlfriend); Obed (slave), the grandfather of David (Beloved), who was the father of Solomon (Peaceful), whose mother was the wife of Uriah.

IMagine Jesus reflecting on his family tree. He knows his foster father and perhaps his grandparents, the end of a long list of names. Of those farther up the family tree, he knows a few chance tidbits, stories told in the Bible. Four of the five women mentioned place his pedigree in jeopardy: Tamar, a Canaanite, conceived her son by her father-in-law, Judah; Rahab was the madam of a brothel in Jericho; Ruth, another foreigner, a Moabite; Bathsheba, the Hittite's wife, whose first son, by the illustrious King David, was conceived in adultery. Does it strike us as unlikely that Jesus, the Savior of the world, would be the fruit of this family tree? Yet at times we also find it most unlikely that Jesus might be found in the heart of this or that person with whom we do not agree.

We, too, may review the skeletons in our closet, the sins that shame us. But we have been born anew in Jesus our Lord, our next of kin. So we now have the duty and privilege to give birth to Jesus our brother in the world. We bring Jesus into the world

fourteen generations;
from the Babylonian exile to the **Christ**,
fourteen generations.

Matthew purposefully stresses details of Jesus' conception and the role of Joseph.

[Now this is how the **birth** of Jesus Christ came about.
When his mother **Mary** was betrothed to **Joseph**,
but before they **lived** together,
she was found with **child** through the Holy **Spirit**.

"Before they lived together" addresses the delicacy of the situation.

"Righteous man" should be stressed. Take a brief pause before the word "quietly."

Joseph her **husband**, since he was a **righteous** man,
yet unwilling to expose her to **shame**,
decided to divorce her **quietly**.
Such was his **intention** when, **behold**,
the **angel** of the Lord appeared to him in a **dream** and said,
"**Joseph**, son of **David**,
do not be **afraid** to take Mary your **wife** into your **home**.

The angel's role asserts Jesus' divine origin and his messianic destiny.

For it is through the Holy **Spirit**
that this child has been **conceived** in her.
She will bear a **son** and you are to name him **Jesus**,
because he will **save** his people from their **sins**."
All this took place to **fulfill**
what the Lord had said through the **prophet**:
*Behold, the **virgin** shall **conceive** and bear a **son**,
and they shall name him **Emmanuel**,*
which means **"God is with us."**

The word "Emmanuel" climaxes the reading. The name's translation should be vocally set apart.
Joseph is confident his dream has divine origin.

When Joseph **awoke**,
he **did** as the angel of the Lord had **commanded** him
and took his **wife** into his **home**.

Again, this detail regarding marital "relations" bears emphasis.

Sustain eye contact with the assembly after speaking "Jesus" and when announcing "The Gospel of the Lord."

He had no **relations** with her until she bore a **son**,
and he **named** him **Jesus**.]

[Shorter: Matthew 1:18–25 (see brackets)]

by recognizing him where he may be found. We ask in the collect for this vigil Eucharist, "Grant that, just as we joyfully welcome your Only Begotten Son as our Redeemer, we may also merit to face him confidently when he comes again as our Judge." K.S.

THE NATIVITY OF THE LORD (CHRISTMAS): NIGHT

LECTIONARY #14

READING I   Isaiah 9:1–6

Isaiah = i-ZAY-uh

Images of darkness and pain contrast with those of light and rejoicing. Greater energy goes to the positive images.

We all are among those who lived in "darkness." But we also are among those who have seen "light."
Your tone marvels at the goodness of God who has brought an abundance of joy.

Three negative images ("yoke," "pole," "rod") are offset by the single word "smashed." Take a slight pause between "smashed" and "as on the day . . . "

Even the refuse of war will be consumed and forgotten!

This is the reason that light is shining and oppression has ended: "a child"!

The four titles must each stand alone, as if spoken by four different voices. Don't rush.

Speak these closing lines with a sense of deep joy.

A reading from the Book of the Prophet Isaiah

The people who walked in **darkness**
 have seen a great **light**;
upon those who dwelt in the land of **gloom**
 a light has **shone**.
You have brought them abundant **joy**
 and great **rejoicing**,
as they rejoice before you as at the **harvest**,
 as people make **merry** when dividing **spoils**.
For the **yoke** that **burdened** them,
 the **pole** on their **shoulder**,
and the **rod** of their **taskmaster**
 you have **smashed**, as on the day of **Midian**.
For every **boot** that tramped in **battle**,
 every **cloak** rolled in **blood**,
 will be **burned** as fuel for **flames**.
For a **child** is born to us, a **son** is given us;
 upon his shoulder **dominion** rests.
They name him **Wonder-Counselor**, **God-Hero**,
 Father-Forever, **Prince** of **Peace**.
His dominion is **vast**
 and forever **peaceful**,
from **David's** throne, and over his **kingdom**,
 which he **confirms** and **sustains**

READING I Darkness and light are opposites. Light reveals color, volume, and distance; in the light we feel safe; we are awake, alive, and active when it is light. Darkness often inspires insecurity and fear; when we fall asleep we enter the shadows, an image of death. The antagonism of light and dark reminds us of the conflicts of good and evil, life and death, knowledge and ignorance. But the light celebrated tonight is resplendent, joyful; darkness is evicted from our lives. The cause of our joy is the birth of Emmanuel, a name to which the prophet adds descrip-

tive names of the greatness and mission of the Messiah: "Wonder-Counselor, God-Hero, Father-Forever, Prince of Peace," four titles that reveal the glory and salvation hidden in the newborn, titles that express the hope that his reign will be prosperous, peaceful, and just. To his people he is a representative of God; to God, a representative of the people.

In this messianic poem everything is light and joy, expressed in the images of harvest and victory. Three reasons for a joyful response? First, freedom from oppression: the yoke, the rod, and the scepter, symbols

of control and domination, are destroyed. Second, peace, a fire that consumes battle-worn footwear and bloodied military uniforms. And finally, "a child is born to us, a son is given us"—Emmanuel, enthroned as the sovereign.

READING II Paul, after advising his disciple Titus to stay faithful to his pastoral work, summarizes Christ's salvific work, accomplished by his offering of himself. The apostle encourages Titus (and us) to live in accord with God's marvelous gift: "reject godless ways and worldly

by **judgment** and **justice**,
both **now** and **forever**.
The **zeal** of the LORD of hosts will **do** this!

This is a promise. Speak it with great conviction.

For meditation and context:

RESPONSORIAL PSALM Psalm 96:1–2, 2–3, 11–12, 13 (Luke 2:11)

R. Today is born our Savior, Christ the Lord.

Sing to the LORD a new song;
    sing to the LORD, all you lands.
Sing to the LORD; bless his name.

Announce his salvation, day after day.
    Tell his glory among the nations;
        among all peoples, his wondrous deeds.

Let the heavens be glad and the
        earth rejoice;
    let the sea and what fills it resound;
    let the plains be joyful and all that is
        in them!
Then shall all the trees of the forest exult.

They shall exult before the LORD,
        for he comes;
    for he comes to rule the earth.
He shall rule the world with justice
    and the peoples with his constancy.

READING II Titus 2:11–14

A reading from the Letter of Saint Paul to Titus

Beloved:
The grace of **God** has appeared, **saving** all
    and training us to **reject** godless ways and **worldly** desires
    and to live **temperately**, **justly**, and **devoutly** in this age,
    as we await the blessed **hope**,
    the **appearance** of the glory of our great **God**
    and **savior** Jesus **Christ**,
    who **gave** himself for us to **deliver** us from all **lawlessness**
    and to **cleanse** for himself a people as his **own**,
    eager to do what is **good**.

Beloved = bee-LUHV-uhd
The first line is a birth announcement! Take time to announce that "The grace of God / has appeared / bringing salvation . . . ." When filled with gratitude and joy, turning away from such darkness is less difficult.

blessed = BLESS-uhd
God's grace has once appeared; now we await a second "appearance." Even on the night of Jesus' birth we contemplate how he gave himself that we might be cleansed.
The word "eager" is your guide to the tone of this reading. Doing good is our response to God's mercy.

Trust the simplicity of the story. You need no embellishment; just tell it simply and honestly.
The events recounted here touch "the whole world."

GOSPEL Luke 2:1–14

A reading from the holy Gospel according to Luke

In those days a **decree** went out from Caesar **Augustus**
    that the whole **world** should be **enrolled**. **»**

desires, and . . . live temperately, justly, and devoutly in this age," and this inspires in us the hope of the Parousia, "the appearance of the glory of our great God and savior Jesus Christ." Jesus is the foundation and model of the Christian life. God's free and merciful love, manifested in the birth of his Son, helps us overcome perverse inclinations and live in accord with his teaching and example. Let us live in justice and faithfulness as citizens in the reign of our sovereign God who announces salvation through the witness of our lives.

GOSPEL A Child was born in our world and in our consciousness, and he offers us something we cannot reject: God is born in our world, so we may be born in God. God opened the roof and descended into our dreary home; now we may ascend to God. A wondrous light has shone among us; now we may avoid the darkness where we tend to stray. But God does not hurry us and does not apply force. God's only argument is love. If a person wants to approach God, she or he does so in the same way that God approached us, as a small child, stripped of majesty. In

this way Christmas is inseparable from the cross of Christ, the triumph of invincible love achieved in weakness. In the infant of Bethlehem lying in a manger, as in the Crucified of Golgotha, surrender and unprotected love overpower the wisdom of the ages. Tonight we celebrate the logic of love born in our flesh, so that we may be born in eternity.

With God's birth in our flesh, human nature underwent an unprecedented surgery. The human race, mortally wounded from the serpent's venomous lies whispered in the Garden of Eden, recovers only

Quirinius = kwih-RIN-ee-uhs

This requirement brings Joseph, through whom Jesus receives his royal lineage, to the city of his ancestor, David.

Engagement and pregnancy were not incompatible.

Each phrase tells an important detail, so share one phrase/thought at a time.

Don't overstate this detail, but let it linger momentarily.

Your pace can quicken and your energy climb on these lines describing the sudden and shocking appearance of angels.

"Do not be afraid" is one of the most common exhortations in the New Testament.

Slow your delivery for these significant details.

Fast or slow, louder or softer, these lines must echo joy.

This was the **first** enrollment,
    when **Quirinius** was governor of **Syria**.
So all went to be **enrolled**, **each** to his own **town**.
And **Joseph** too went up from **Galilee** from the town
        of **Nazareth**
    to **Judea**, to the city of **David** that is called **Bethlehem**,
    because he was of the **house** and **family** of David,
    to be enrolled with **Mary**, his **betrothed**, who was with **child**.
While they were there,
    the time came for her to **have** her child,
    and she gave **birth** to her firstborn **son**.
She wrapped him in **swaddling** clothes and laid him in a **manger**,
    because there was no **room** for them in the **inn**.

Now there were **shepherds** in that region living in the **fields**
    and keeping the **night** watch over their flock.
The **angel** of the Lord **appeared** to them
    and the **glory** of the Lord **shone** around them,
    and they were struck with great **fear**.
The angel **said** to them,
    "Do not be **afraid**;
    for **behold**, I proclaim to you good **news** of great **joy**
    that will be for **all** the people.
For **today** in the city of **David**
    a **savior** has been born for you who is **Christ** and **Lord**.
And this will be a **sign** for you:
    you will find an **infant** wrapped in **swaddling** clothes
    and lying in a **manger**."
And **suddenly** there was a **multitude** of the heavenly host with
        the angel,
    praising God and saying:
    "**Glory** to God in the **highest**
        and on **earth peace** to those on whom his **favor** rests."

with the implantation of God into it. Since that divine intervention, when the heart of Jesus pulses, our hearts throb; when his eyes look, we see with the same eyes; when we listen, Jesus hears.

But our nature is capable of rejecting supernatural kindness and mercy; the patient may resist the life-giving gift of God in favor of a former existence. On one hand, it is recorded that women and men continue with the same illness of sin and delusion. But it would be a heresy for a Catholic Christian believer to hold that, with the coming of God in our flesh, nothing

has changed in our life and history. Since God became flesh, the human being has a future beyond death: now mercy relieves sin, now suffering and martyrdom make sense, now history reaches to eternity. With the birth of God in time, the human is born for eternity.

In the birth of God as a human child, we have received a new heart, new eyes, a new feeling, a new way of thought and action. If our celebration of the nativity of God in our flesh is no more than skin deep, if it does not go beyond the sensation, if it does not resound in the pulse of our inte-

rior life, if it was not enough to change our attitude and action, we would be the saddest people in the world. Because God has come as a child, the divine surgeon has transplanted his own heart in the hollow of our chest. He has touched our afflicted flesh, applied the medicine of his eternal love, so we are able to love beyond ourselves, because in this feast, at the threshold of eternity, there is no room for sadness or fear. We are one with God, who is united with us in the Incarnation of his Son, our Brother. K.S.

THE NATIVITY OF THE LORD (CHRISTMAS): DAWN

LECTIONARY #15

READING I   Isaiah 62:11–12

Isaiah = Ī-ZAY-uh

Short readings require slower pacing.

The operative word here is "proclaims." Let your tone become expansive and regal for you proclaim news for the whole world to hear.

On this special night, this line must be savored. Establish eye contact with the assembly.

The Savior's coming changes everyone's fortunes. Speak these new names as if to someone you love whose face you hold in your hands.

A reading from the Book of the Prophet Isaiah

See, the LORD proclaims
  to the **ends** of the **earth**:
say to daughter **Zion**,
  your **savior** comes!
Here is his **reward** with him,
  his **recompense** before him.
They shall be called the **holy** people,
  the **redeemed** of the LORD,
and you shall be called "**Frequented**,"
  a city that is **not forsaken**.

For meditation and context:

RESPONSORIAL PSALM   Psalm 97:1, 6, 11–12

R. A light will shine on us this day: the Lord is born for us.

The LORD is king; let the earth rejoice;
  let the many isles be glad.
The heavens proclaim his justice,
  and all peoples see his glory.

Light dawns for the just;
  and gladness, for the upright of heart.
Be glad in the LORD, you just,
  and give thanks to his holy name.

READING II   Titus 3:4–7

Beloved = bee-LUHV-uhd

"Not" and "but" are the keys to the major contrast of the opening lines: Christ appeared "not" because of what we did, "but" because of God's mercy.

A reading from the Letter of Saint Paul to Titus

Beloved:
When the **kindness** and generous **love**
  of God our savior appeared, »

READING I A prophet in the sixth or fifth century before Christ hoped for the restoration of God's city and the glory of God's people. He announced encouraging words to the people assembled in Jerusalem, who were awaiting the homecoming of the remnant of Israel who lived in exile in Babylon. The oracle is composed of two sections. The first part is addressed to Jerusalem, "daughter Zion," a phrase that refers to the whole nation; it announces the imminent release of the exiles by the people's Savior. The second part contains the glorious new titles of the people who lived far away, "holy people" and "rescued from the Lord"; and Jerusalem, as a young wife, will be called "Desired" and "Not forsaken." God takes the initiative, seeks his people, rescues them, and binds them to himself with renewed and faithful love. In the Christmas liturgy this oracle is a prophecy of the marvelous encounter God realizes through his only-begotten Son, born in Bethlehem. Now we approach the cradle of the Child, true Savior and liberator of humanity. Through him, with him, and in him, we now are called the "holy people" of God, the people "rescued from the Lord": to us he has manifested his tenderness.

READING II The apostle Paul, addressing his disciple Titus, confirms that we are saved not by our good works, but because the Spirit of God has poured favors upon us. By the initiative of divine love, God has made us friends, adopting us as children through the sacrament of Baptism. At Christmas God gives us the divine Son; in Baptism God breathes in us the divine Spirit, and thus we are heirs of eternal life, that is, we have experienced

"Bath of rebirth" is a reference to Baptism. Increase energy when you cite the work of the Holy Spirit.
Speak with both conviction and gratitude.

Here you have more than one idea to share: (a) we are justified by grace; (b) we become heirs in hope.

not because of any righteous **deeds** we had done
  but because of his **mercy**,
he **saved** us through the **bath** of **rebirth**
  and **renewal** by the Holy **Spirit**,
whom he richly **poured** out on us
  through Jesus **Christ** our **savior**,
so that we might be **justified** by his grace
  and become **heirs** in hope of eternal **life**.

GOSPEL   Luke 2:15–20

A reading from the holy Gospel according to Luke

The story reverberates with the sound of angel wings and the excitement of the shepherds. Sustain that joyful energy throughout.
The shepherds are full of belief and hurry to see the promise.
Though they go "in haste," don't race this important line.

When the **angels** went **away** from them to **heaven**,
  the **shepherds** said to one another,
  "Let us **go**, then, to **Bethlehem**
  to **see** this thing that has taken place,
  which the Lord has made **known** to us."
So they went in **haste** and found **Mary** and **Joseph**,
  and the **infant** lying in the **manger**.
When they **saw** this,
  they made known the **message**
  that had been **told** them about this child.
All who heard it were **amazed**
  by what had been **told** them by the shepherds.

Convey a sense of awe as they share the angels' message.

Take time with this classic line that speaks of Mary's own sense of wonder.

And Mary **kept** all these things,
  reflecting on them in her **heart**.
Then the shepherds **returned**,
  glorifying and **praising** God
  for all they had **heard** and **seen**,
  just as it had been **told** to them.

"Heard" refers to their expectation, "seen" to its fulfillment.

the personal knowledge of God. The multiple gifts open our hearts to be grateful for such generosity.

GOSPEL   The shepherds, instructed by the angel, find Mary and Joseph, and, lying in the manger, the infant. The shepherds, one of the lowest classes of people, are akin to transient migrants who live on the periphery of society. They move from place to place according to a seasonal pattern of grazing opportunities, and often wander far from the city and towns. Was it that bunch of itinerants who attended the premiere of salvation in Bethlehem? What about the less stable parts of our own lives? Might the unsteady, insecure part of humanity in us be more sensitive and open, less resistant, ready to receive a change in life, the good news of salvation that comes from outside the well-established, well-protected self? From the shepherds' visit to the manger is born proclamation and praise.

The first two readings, along with the psalm, are fine examples of how memory is key for the liturgy. The prophets glimpsed the dawn of salvation. The shepherds discovered God's light in the infant Christ, and we hope for the brightness of day, the fullness of our Baptism. The center of our hope is the birth of Christ in our lives, and the fulfillment won in his life, death, and Resurrection. In today's celebration the past and future of God's salvation is encapsulated as we sing of the Lord's birth, the light that shines on us today. K.S.

THE NATIVITY OF THE LORD (CHRISTMAS): DAY

LECTIONARY #16

READING I Isaiah 52:7–10

A reading from the Book of the Prophet Isaiah

How **beautiful** upon the **mountains**
 are the **feet** of him who brings glad **tidings**,
announcing **peace**, bearing good **news**,
 announcing **salvation**, and saying to **Zion**,
 "Your **God** is **King**!"

Hark! Your sentinels raise a **cry**,
 together they shout for **joy**,
for they see **directly**, before their **eyes**,
 the LORD **restoring** Zion.
Break out together in **song**,
 O **ruins** of Jerusalem!
For the LORD **comforts** his people,
 he **redeems** Jerusalem.
The LORD has **bared** his holy arm
 in the sight of all the **nations**;
all the ends of the **earth** will behold
 the **salvation** of our **God**.

Isaiah = ī-ZAY-uh

The first part of the text marvels at the beauty of one who brings news of peace. Recall the instinct to embrace or kiss someone who brings great news, and let that color your proclamation.
Pause briefly before announcing "Your God is King." Then pause again.

Sustain energy and joyous excitement, but don't speed through these elegant lines.

"Break out" is a command. Even the "ruins" will sing!

The final sentence both celebrates what God has done and promises God's mercy will extend to all the earth.

READING I A messenger arrives in Jerusalem. He has been spotted racing toward the city, and his voice arrives before he does. The poet proclaims the beauty of his worn and torn feet because they bring the wonderful news of God's triumph. A new horizon opens for God's people, living in the ruins of the holy city, now invited to celebrate God's saving action, evident to all nations: "Break out together in song, O ruins of Jerusalem! For the Lord comforts his people, he redeems Jerusalem. . . . All the ends of the earth will behold the salvation of our God."

READING II This introduction to Hebrews affirms that God has spoken "in partial and various ways" to save humanity. The one God, who is Creator and Redeemer, has a single purpose. As God's creative Word, the Son has been the foundation of the world and remains at the center of our future. Now the Son is present in all his glory in the culminating moment of salvation, when he brought revelation to fullness. The Son is the Father's one and definitive Word, the "heir of all things"; "he took his seat at the right hand of the Majesty on high."

For meditation and context:

RESPONSORIAL PSALM   Psalm 98:1, 2–3, 3–4, 5–6 (3c)

R. All the ends of the earth have seen the saving power of God.

Sing to the LORD a new song,
　for he has done wondrous deeds;
his right hand has won victory for him,
　his holy arm.

The LORD has made his salvation known:
　in the sight of the nations he has revealed
　　his justice.
He has remembered his kindness and his
　faithfulness
　toward the house of Israel.

All the ends of the earth have seen
　the salvation by our God.
Sing joyfully to the LORD, all you lands;
　break into song; sing praise.

Sing praise to the LORD with the harp,
　with the harp and melodious song.
With trumpets and the sound of the horn
　sing joyfully before the King, the LORD.

READING II   Hebrews 1:1–6

A reading from the Letter to the Hebrews

Brothers and sisters:
In times **past**, God spoke in **partial** and **various** ways
　to our **ancestors** through the **prophets**;
　in these **last** days, he has spoken to us through the **Son**,
　whom he made **heir** of all things
　and **through** whom he created the **universe**,
　who is the **refulgence** of his **glory**,
　　the very **imprint** of his **being**,
　and who **sustains** all things by his mighty **word**.
　When he had accomplished purification from **sins**,
　he took his **seat** at the **right** hand of the **Majesty** on high,
　as far **superior** to the **angels**
　as the **name** he has inherited is more **excellent** than theirs.

For to **which** of the angels did God ever say:
　You are my **son***; this day I have* **begotten** *you*?
Or again:
　I will be a **father** *to him, and he shall be a* **son** *to me*?
And again, when he leads the **firstborn** into the world, he says:
　Let all the **angels** *of God* **worship** *him*.

You are contrasting God's past and "partial" dialogue with Israel with the full and climactic communication of God in Jesus.

The author focuses on the divine and preexistent nature of Christ. Don't let the theology obscure the joy!

These lines come from an early liturgical hymn making them a prayer of praise.

With authority, you declare that Christ is superior to every rank of angels.

Christ is unique for he is not a creature but a "son." Speak the two affirmations not as a lawyer making a point but as a parent speaking of a beloved child.

IMagine the heavenly court and the angelic host being ordered to worship the "firstborn"!

GOSPEL

"In the beginning was the Word" that comes from God and returns to God. How many words spoken in the name of God cannot find their way back; they lose track on the way! But this Word was so full of life that it "lived," "made his dwelling," "settled down"—the Greek text reads "encamped"—among us. The verb deserves attention. The evangelist does not report that the Word hovered, inspired, perched, or breathed; the expression describes setting up camp, a specific action that requires decision, time, and effort; it also involves facing unforeseen circumstances. It is necessary to leave home, to break with one's routine. Before setting up camp, it is necessary to feel out the ground, that it is not too hard or too soft, that it is clear of stones or objects or creatures that might interrupt or hinder one's rest. For camping, it is necessary to coordinate with other people, and, once in the campground, in short order we discover the best and worst of our fellow campers. The experience of camping honors the discretion of those who speak less and do not impose on others, but rather renounce certain preferences for the good of everybody. Camping projects the ideal attitude of the Christian, who does not occupy a stable place in the present world: setting up the tent as firmly as possible, picking up and starting over after a brief time, trusting God to guide them where they are destined to go. The Word that became flesh camped among us.

God is Word, but God is also silence. The Word became an infant, incapable of speech; he took our flesh, and we have seen his glory. We are faced with the profoundest divine mystery: the Word of God and God's silence. However, that silence is

GOSPEL   John 1:1–18

A reading from the holy Gospel according to John

> Three distinct ideas that must be shared one at a time and each with great reverence.

[In the **beginning** was the **Word**,
  and the **Word** was with **God**,
  and the Word **was** God.
He was in the **beginning** with God.
All things came to be **through** him,
  and without him **nothing** came to be.
What came to be through him was **life**,
  and this life was the **light** of the human race;
  the light **shines** in the **darkness**,
  and the darkness has not **overcome** it.]

> This creed is the foundation for the narrative that follows. Speak each article of faith as both instruction and celebration.

> From the beginning, John is fascinated with the contrast between light and darkness.

A man named **John** was sent from **God**.
He came for **testimony**, to testify to the **light**,
  so that all might **believe** through him.
He was not the light,
  but came to **testify** to the light.

> The setting shifts from the cosmic realm to an earthly context. Your tone should signal the shift.

> Note the repetitions that name John as witness to Christ.

[The **true** light, which enlightens **everyone**,
  was coming into the world.
He was **in** the world,
  and the world came to **be** through him,
  but the world did not **know** him.
He came to what was his **own**,
  but his own people did not **accept** him. »

> There is a sense of regret in relating the blindness that kept "his own" from recognizing him.

---

the Word God pronounced, because the divine Word is not speech or logical argument, but Word. It does not interrupt or shatter the silence, but rather impregnates and enhances it. Suddenly life springs from the silence, pregnant with the Word that is born among us even as it penetrates God's inaccessible mystery.

There is another silence that is not of God. There is a deaf and leaden silence, made of nothing, in which there is neither word nor eloquence, because it speaks to itself, enters not into friendship. Where there is no respondent, the words are ster-

ile; there is no love because there is no relationship or personal encounter. If there is a god to be found there, it would be a fictitious or dead one. But we love the one and true God, who made us in the divine likeness and who bestows on us our true humanity. We want God to move among us, to embrace and speak to us. His presence is real, his Word is wrapped in the eloquence of silence.

Within the all-encompassing silence, when the night had come halfway, the Almighty Word came down from the heavenly throne and penetrated our

silence (see Wisdom 18:14–15). Here is the encounter between two silences: that of absurdity and meaningful silence. God's silence enters human silence, without fanfare, without speeches. Like the grain of sand that lodges in the oyster and irritates until a pearl is formed; like the yeast introduced in the dough and infects the whole loaf. The silence of God is the fertile seed that the good earth cannot resist; it germinates, sprouts, and grows to produce fruit in abundance.

If we enter the family home in Nazareth, what treasures might we find?

Adopt a more upbeat tone here to contrast with the previous lines.

Let your intensity grow as you move through the "not," "nor," and "but" phrases.

These sacred words conjure images of the birth of Bethlehem's child.

The voice of John penetrates without shattering the mood of awe in the previous lines.

John's voice returns, commenting on the gift of Christ on which we all have feasted.

Lift out John's contrast of "law" / "Moses" with "grace" / "Jesus Christ."

The intimacy between Father and Son is once again highlighted.

But to those who **did** accept him
  he gave power to become **children** of **God**,
  to those who **believe** in his name,
  who were born not by **natural** generation
  nor by human **choice** nor by a **man's** decision
  but of **God**.
    And the **Word** became **flesh**
      and made his **dwelling** among us,
      and we saw his **glory**,
      the glory as of the Father's only **Son**,
      full of **grace** and **truth**.]
John **testified** to him and cried out, saying,
  "This was he of whom I said,
  'The one who is coming **after** me ranks **ahead** of me
  because he existed **before** me.'"
From his **fullness** we have all received,
  grace in place of **grace**,
  because while the **law** was given through **Moses**,
  grace and **truth** came through Jesus **Christ**.
No one has ever **seen** God.
The only **Son**, **God**, who is at the Father's **side**,
  has **revealed** him.

[Shorter: John 1:1–5, 9–14 (see brackets)]

TO KEEP IN MIND
Repetition of the same word or phrase over the course of a reading emphasizes a point. Make each instance distinct, and build your intensity with each repetition.

Probably we would find in that home the silence that is the admirable and indispensable habit of the Spirit of God, so necessary for us who are stunned by so much noise and tumult, so many voices of our hectic life. And there, once having found silence, we can pray: "Silence of Nazareth, open the treasure of our interior lives, teach us to listen to your inspiration and divine instruction. Open the ears of our head and heart to the words of our families, and to the good example of our parents. Instruct us as to the value of obedience, humility, and respect for people, mutual forgiveness, and patience. Reserve a seat for yourself in our interior lives, a space and time, to enter into friendship with you. And above all, dear Silence, open a generous space for love, the perfection of the virtues." K.S.

THE HOLY FAMILY OF JESUS, MARY, AND JOSEPH

LECTIONARY #17

READING I   1 Samuel 1:20–22, 24–28

A reading from the first Book of Samuel

In those days **Hannah conceived,** and at the end of her **term**
  bore a **son**
whom she called **Samuel,** since she had **asked** the Lord
  for him.
The next time her husband **Elkanah** was going up
  with the rest of his **household**
to offer the customary **sacrifice** to the **Lord** and to **fulfill**
  his **vows,**
  Hannah did **not** go, **explaining** to her husband,
  "Once the child is **weaned,**
  I will **take** him to **appear** before the Lord
  and to **remain** there **forever;**
  I will **offer** him as a **perpetual nazirite.**"

Once Samuel was **weaned,** Hannah **brought him up** with her,
  along with a three-year-old **bull,**
  an **ephah** of flour, and a skin of **wine,**
  and **presented** him at the **temple** of the Lord in **Shiloh.**
After the boy's **father** had **sacrificed** the young **bull,**
  Hannah, his mother, approached **Eli** and said:
  "**Pardon, my lord!**
As you **live**, my lord,
  I am the **woman** who stood **near** you here, **praying** to the Lord. **»**

Margin notes

Hannah prayed earnestly at Shiloh the year before, but longed for a child through many years.

"Samuel" means "asked of God."

Elkanah = el-KAY-nah. You start a new beat here, so renew your energy.

Hannah has a plan but will keep the child close for now.

Nazarite = NAZ-uh-right
Hannah is resolved, but it does not come without effort and pain.
These items ("bull," "flour," "wine") are sacrificial offerings, not traveling supplies.
Ephah = EE-fah

Shiloh = SHĪ-loh

Eli = EE-lī

Hannah identifies herself to Eli who had seen her praying the year before and mistook her for a drunkard, then prophesied her pregnancy.

Today, options are given for the readings. Contact your parish staff to learn which readings will be used.

READING I   **1 Samuel.** The first reading relates the story of Elkanah's family from Ephraim. His two wives compete against each other. Peninah longs for love, Hannah for children. One particular year, when they came on pilgrimage to the shrine of the Ark of the Covenant, Hannah, the barren, beloved wife, prayed earnestly before the Ark, begging God for a son, which she would offer to the Lord in return for lifting the scourge of infertility. Eli, the priest, blessed her, and then she withdrew, satisfied that her prayer was answered. Indeed it was: God remembered Hannah, who conceived a son, Samuel. In keeping with her vow, when Samuel was weaned, the parents brought their son back to the sanctuary and consecrated him to the Lord. Here is a family with ups and downs, but whose faith puts them in sync with God's providence and will.

Psalm 84, which may follow this reading, echoes Hannah's faith: "Blessed are they who dwell in your house, O Lord." Hannah came to the sanctuary, prayed to God, and left, witnessing to the truth of the psalm's beatitude: happy those who trust in God, who find refuge in God, who dwell in God's house.

Sirach. Ben Sira addresses the relationship between parents and children, and gives it a religious dimension. "Honoring" and "obeying" the parent is like obeying God, who protects the family; because of this, God places in the parents' hearts love for their children, and in the children's hearts, loving respect towards the parents.

Don't miss the blend of resolve, eloquence, and pain in Hannah's statement to Eli, especially in the poignancy of the final line.

"I **prayed** for this **child**, and **the LORD granted** my request.
Now **I,** in turn, **give him** to the LORD;
   as **long** as he **lives,** he shall be **dedicated** to the LORD."
Hannah **left** Samuel **there.**

Or:

Sirach = SEER-ak
While these are independent proverbs, be sure to avoid a choppy delivery. The assertion of a mother's right is stated with greater force than a father's because, in biblical culture, it was far more significant to rank over "sons" (the "men" in the family) than over "children" (the "boys and girls").

Two distinct ideas here: sins are forgiven; prayers are heard. Stress both.

Slow your pacing on this reference to reverence for one's mother.
A second reminder that "honor" makes for efficacious prayer.

While the first half of the text seems to refer to parents in their prime, these last lines speak of older parents in great need of care.

Here is a warning against prideful neglect.

The last two lines modify "kindness to a father . . . ." Speak those lines as if each began with "It will be . . . ."

READING I   Sirach 3:2–6, 12–14

A reading from the Book of Sirach

  God sets a **father** in **honor** over his **children;**
     a **mother's authority** he **confirms** over her **sons.**
  Whoever **honors** his father **atones** for sins,
     and **preserves** himself from them.
  When he **prays,** he is **heard;**
     he **stores up** riches who **reveres** his mother.
  Whoever **honors** his **father** is **gladdened** by children,
     and, when **he prays,** is **heard.**
  Whoever **reveres** his father will live a **long life;**
     he who **obeys** his father brings **comfort** to his mother.

  My son, take care of your father when he is **old;**
     grieve him not as long as he **lives.**
  Even if his **mind fail,** be **considerate** of him;
     revile him not all the days of his life;
  kindness to a **father** will **not** be **forgotten,**
     firmly planted against the **debt** of your **sins**
     —a house **raised** in **justice** to you.

The sage emphasizes the true meaning of the fourth commandment, which is the only one that includes a reward: Care for our parents, especially when they are elderly. The sage elaborates on the blessings that come from honor to parents: forgiveness, long life, and good children. Parents who are true to their name and vocation deserve honor and respect, even in the decline of old age. Honor to parents is rewarded with life.

Psalm 128, which may follow this reading, proclaims, "Blessed are those who fear the Lord and walk in his ways." In today's feast, the Church directs our attention to the source of happiness. The readings present family life from different angles. The psalmist celebrates healthy daily life: Satisfying work provides prosperity; family life fosters happiness. The poet sings that those who lovingly honor God enjoy the simple and nourishing delights of life and, in the end, the poet enlarges the focus to embrace the nation.

RESPONSORIAL PSALM   Psalm 84:2–3, 5–6, 9–10 (see 5a)

R. Blessed are they who dwell in your house, O Lord.

How lovely is your dwelling place, O LORD
    of hosts!
    My soul yearns and pines for the courts of
    the LORD.
My heart and my flesh cry out for the living
    God.

Happy they who dwell in your house!
    Continually they praise you.
Happy the men whose strength you are!
    Their hearts are set upon the pilgrimage.

O LORD of hosts, hear our prayer;
    hearken, O God of Jacob!
O God, behold our shield,
    and look upon the face of your anointed.

Or:

RESPONSORIAL PSALM   Psalm 128:1–2, 3, 4–5 (1)

R. Blessed are those who fear the Lord and walk in his ways.

Blessed is everyone who fears the LORD,
    who walks in his ways!
For you shall eat the fruit of your handiwork;
    blessed shall you be, and favored.

Your wife shall be like a fruitful vine
    in the recesses of your home;
your children like olive plants
    around your table.

Behold, thus is the man blessed
    who fears the LORD.
The LORD bless you from Zion:
    may you see the prosperity of Jerusalem
    all the days of your life.

READING II   1 John 3:1–2, 21–24

A reading from the first Letter of Saint John

Beloved:
See what **love** the **Father** has **bestowed** on us
    that we may be called the **children of God**.
And **so we are**.
The reason the **world does not know us**
    is that **it did not know him**. »

For meditation and context:

> **TO KEEP IN MIND**
> Don't neglect the Responsorial Psalm just because you aren't proclaiming it. Pray it as part of your preparation.

For meditation and context:

Beloved = bee-LUHV-uhd

The salutation is the key to the tone of the passage.
Let your gratitude for the love of God you've experienced in your life color these lines.

There is a sense of regret in this line.

READING II | **1 John**. John admires the fact of being children of God (the Father), whose love is the origin of believers being God's children. This provides a source of our hope. The goal of hope is to "see" God as he is, which means to participate fully in the divine life. The greatest sign of God's love is the gift of the divine Son, making believers true children of God. This relationship is a reality and also part of the life to come: "We do know that when it is revealed we shall be like

him"—true knowledge of God will ultimately be gained, and we prepare ourselves at the present time by living in imitation of the Son. The living God's presence is within us. We are God's children. If we believe in Jesus and love one another, we remain in God and God in us. Yet this does not guarantee a life without challenges. The world may not recognize us as God's children because we do not recognize each other. John emphasizes the observance of the commandments, especially

insofar as that consists in believing in Christ and loving one another. Faith and charity are inseparable since they are part of a single commandment. The formula "abides in God and God in him," expresses the intimate union between God and the believer.

Colossians. St. Paul places the family in a theological perspective when he shows its source is none other than love. The reading begins with an exhortation to live according to the newness of faith, and Paul presents the example of God's love

Beloved, we are God's children now;
  what we **shall** be has **not yet** been **revealed**.
We **do know** that when it **is revealed** we shall be **like** him,
  for **we** shall **see** him **as he is**.

Beloved, if our **hearts do not condemn** us,
  we have **confidence** in **God** and **receive** from him
      whatever we **ask**,
  because we **keep** his **commandments** and **do** what **pleases** him.
And his **commandment** is **this**:
  we should **believe** in the **name** of his **Son**, Jesus **Christ**,
  and **love** one another just as he **commanded** us.
Those who **keep** his **commandments remain** in him,
    and **he** in **them**,
  and the way we **know** that he **remains** in us
  is from the **Spirit** he **gave** us.

Or:

READING II   Colossians 3:12–21

A reading from the Letter of Saint Paul to the Colossians

[**Brothers** and **sisters**:
Put on, as God's **chosen** ones, **holy** and **beloved**,
  heartfelt **compassion**, **kindness**, **humility**, **gentleness**,
    and **patience**,
  bearing with one another and **forgiving** one another,
  if one has a **grievance** against another;
  as the **Lord** has forgiven **you**, **so must you also do**.
and over **all** these put on **love**,
  that is, the **bond** of **perfection**.
And let the **peace** of **Christ control** your **hearts**,
  the **peace** into which you were also **called** in **one body**.
And be **thankful**.

Margin notes (left column):

What we "are" is joy enough to hold us till we know what more will come!
This is a great truth: We will be like God and know God fully.

Beloved = bee-LUHV-uhd
Let your tone convey the "confidence" of which you speak.

Remember, repetition has a purpose and should never sound like careless redundancy.

Two expectations: believe and love.

Joyfully proclaim the indispensable role of the Spirit in the life of the community of faith.

Colossians = kuh-LOSH-uhnz
Make eye contact as you speak the salutation.
beloved = bee-LUHV-uhd
Speak these admonitions to yourself as much as to your listeners, but don't let them sound like items on a shopping list.

Again, make eye contact as you encourage forgiveness and love.

The energy keeps building from one "and" to the next; each initiates a new idea that requires new energy.

---

and forgiveness perfectly expressed in Christ. If the law of love is imposed on all Christians, it is equally valid for family members. Paul describes the virtues that bring about a happy family life: compassion, kindness, humility, gentleness, and patience. Every member has a right to forgiveness for faults and weakness; each member receives the attention that she or he needs. Husbands and wives strive for mutual love and obedience to each other. Children, too, are in a position to obey; par-

ents instruct them with gentleness and respect. The family that fosters such virtues lives in peace, but healthy family life, in addition to being the result of patience and sacrifice, is God's gift. In this context of writing about love, Paul introduces his indications of family responsibilities (in the longer reading, vv. 18–21): "Wives, be subordinate to your husbands, as is proper in the Lord. Husbands, love your wives, and avoid any bitterness toward them. Children, obey your parents in everything,

for this is pleasing to the Lord. Father, do not provoke your children, so they may not become discouraged."

GOSPEL Today's Gospel is another of a series of unusual experiences that, as Luke describes them, Mary and Joseph undergo in raising their remarkable child. The family was holy, but not without its challenges.

The first visitors to the birthplace were nomads, rough people who lived on the

Your pace can slow a bit, but don't let the energy and enthusiasm wane.

Speak "do everything . . . " with conviction that says it's worth whatever price it costs.

You address three distinct groups within your congregation with three distinct messages. Pause before each sentence to focus and consider before you speak.

Take a three-beat pause before announcing the end of the reading.

Let the **word** of Christ **dwell** in you **richly**,
  as in all **wisdom** you **teach** and **admonish** one another,
  singing **psalms**, **hymns**, and **spiritual songs**
  with **gratitude** in your **hearts** to **God**.
And whatever you do, in **word** or in **deed**,
  do **everything** in the **name** of the **Lord Jesus**,
  giving **thanks** to **God** the **Father** through **him**.]

Wives, be subordinate to your **husbands**,
  as is **proper** in the **Lord**.
Husbands, love your **wives**,
  and avoid **any bitterness** toward them.
Children, obey your **parents** in **everything**,
  for this is **pleasing** to the **Lord**.
Fathers, do **not** provoke your **children**,
  so they may not become **discouraged**.

[Shorter: Colossians 3:12–17 (see brackets)]

GOSPEL   Luke 2:41–52

A reading from the holy Gospel according to Luke

The family faithfully observes the annual festival. At this point, this is just a prosaic family story of unremarkable events.

Your tone should suggest the unusual nature of this decision and the implication for the parents.
Your tone suggests their innocent assumption that all is well.

Here their concern is switched on. Quicken your pace on this sentence.

Each **year** Jesus' **parents** went to **Jerusalem** for the feast
  of **Passover**,
  and when he was **twelve** years **old**,
  they went **up** according to festival **custom**.
After they had **completed** its days, as they were **returning**,
  the boy **Jesus** remained **behind** in **Jerusalem**,
  but his **parents** did not **know** it.
Thinking that he was in the **caravan**,
  they **journeyed** for a **day**
  and **looked** for him among their **relatives** and **acquaintances**,
  but **not finding** him,
  they **returned** to **Jerusalem** to **look** for him. »

periphery of civilized society. Luke wanted his well-read audience to review their own values and presumptions about the evangelical life.

Days after the birth, old Simeon warned the parents, "This child is destined for the fall and rise of many in Israel, and to be as sign that will be contradicted (and you yourself a sword will pierce) so that the thoughts of many hearts may be revealed"

Soon after, on account of a neurotic king embroiled in his lust for power, the

family had to emigrate, with all the dangers involved in crossing a border, and in a hazardous trip with a mother and her newborn, exposed to the elements, to fears, and to uncertainty. Where would they find a home in Egypt? Would Joseph find work? How would the women at the well receive Mary, a foreigner, a migrant?

Finally, in today's Gospel, Luke reports a Passover pilgrimage to Jerusalem, where the child Jesus, now twelve years old, did not join the return caravan, but remained in

the Temple, without informing his parents. After three days—an anticipation of the three days of Jesus, lost during another Passover, his disappearance in death, and his reunion in the Resurrection—the distraught parents worried themselves sick, and the Blessed Virgin uttered a slight scolding: "Why have you done this?"

Everything human is part of the family repertoire; family life can bring out the best and worst in its members. Our families and our other communities—parishes,

This scene is a flash-forward into his future, but his parents can't possibly know this, and they marvel along with the elders.

Consider the likely tone of Mary's voice: anger, disappointment, hurt, relief?

Jesus acknowledges no responsibility for her distress; instead he assumes the role of teacher even with his mother.

Don't rush this final section; all the information is important: Jesus obediently returned home, Mary held many things in her heart, Jesus advances toward his destiny.

TO KEEP IN MIND

In a narrative, find an emotion or point of view for each character, keeping in mind that these might change during the reading.

After three days they **found** him in the **temple,**
  sitting in the **midst** of the **teachers,**
  listening to them and **asking** them **questions,**
  and all who **heard** him were **astounded**
  at his **understanding** and his **answers.**
When his **parents saw** him,
  they were **astonished,**
  and his **mother** said to him,
  "Son, why have you **done** this to **us?**
Your father and I have been **looking** for you with **great anxiety."**
And **he** said to **them,**
  "Why were you looking for **me?**
Did you not **know** that I must be in **my Father's house?"**
But they did not **understand** what he said to them.
He went **down** with them and came to **Nazareth,**
  and was **obedient** to them;
  and his **mother kept all these things** in her **heart.**
And **Jesus advanced** in **wisdom** and **age** and **favor**
  before **God** and **man.**

---

religious communities, schools—are not perfect. But to our benefit and favor is the faith in Jesus—truly God and truly human, a member of a truly human family—that sustains us, in sickness and in health, for better or for worse, for richer or poorer, in time of conflict and peace. That is the Church's faith.

There is an image of the Holy Family, painted by an artist of the Cuzco school, a Catholic artistic tradition founded in Peru in the sixteenth century to evangelize and catechize, that connects the Holy Family with the Holy Trinity. In the lower part, the Blessed Virgin and Joseph frame the Child Jesus; in the upper part, the Holy Spirit, shaped like a dove and, above, the heavenly Father, with arms outstretched, as if he were embracing the family on earth. The vertical axis is formed by the Holy Trinity, Father and Son and, in the middle, the Holy Spirit. The horizontal axis is drawn by the figures of the Holy Family, holding each other's hands. In photos of our families, if we concentrate on the horizontal, we may be disappointed. The picture may be incomplete. We need another perspective. The Cuzco artist invites us to set our eyes on high and appreciate the work of God the Father, the Son, and the Holy Spirit, both within the portrait and in the frame of our real family. K.S.

MARY, THE HOLY MOTHER OF GOD

LECTIONARY #18

READING I   Numbers 6:22–27

A reading from the Book of Numbers

The LORD said to **Moses**:
"**Speak** to **Aaron** and his sons and **tell** them:
This is how you shall **bless** the **Israelites**.
Say to them:
The LORD **bless** you and **keep** you!
The LORD let his face **shine** upon
you, and be **gracious** to you!
The LORD look upon you **kindly** and
give you **peace**!
So shall they invoke my **name** upon the **Israelites**,
and I will **bless** them."

As always, take extra time with such a short reading. Don't rush the introduction, and distinguish the Lord, Moses, and Aaron and his sons.

You have two lines to introduce the blessing; take more time with the first line, speak faster on the second, and then slower again on the blessing itself.

Each invocation is a separate petition; don't run them together.

The key word here is "name," not "my." Remember, you are teaching us to pray. Do it prayerfully!

For meditation and context:

RESPONSORIAL PSALM   Psalm 67:2–3, 5, 6, 8 (2a)

R. May God bless us in his mercy.

May God have pity on us and bless us;
may he let his face shine upon us.
So may your way be known upon earth;
among all nations, your salvation.

May the nations be glad and exult
because you rule the peoples in equity;
the nations on the earth you guide.

May the peoples praise you, O God;
may all the peoples praise you!
May God bless us,
and may all the ends of the earth
fear him!

READING I The Book of Numbers continues the great story of the Exodus journey, beginning with the departure from Sinai and ending with the arrival at the border of the Promised Land. As the book opens, the people prepare to move forward in their desert passage, and the author reviews rules and practices to ensure they maintain the purity of a community dedicated to the Lord.

This passage is commonly called "the priestly blessing," which was to be pronounced at the end of an act of ritual worship. In the Bible, a blessing is understood to transmit a beneficial power to the person or community receiving it. The Lord is the sole source of the blessing and its potency, so it is forever effective, and the blessing becomes effective when accompanied by some act that confirms the blessing. This act of blessing invokes God's name upon the people. In ancient Israel, a name expressed and conveyed the person's character, so the name of God often represents the actual presence of God. Invoking God's name over the people calls upon the divine source of every blessing to bestow positive power upon them.

READING II Paul wrote his letter to the Galatians about twenty-five years after the Resurrection. In this still-new Christian movement there were some conflicting interpretations of Christ and what God accomplished through him. In this letter, Paul clarifies his views of Christ in the face of those who opposed his preaching. Points of disagreement included salvation through the Law or through grace in Christ, and whether Gentiles could be included in Israel's final age of salvation.

Paul upholds both the divinity and humanity of Jesus the Messiah: "God sent

READING II Galatians 4:4–7

Galatians = guh-LAY-shunz

A reading from the Letter of Saint Paul to the Galatians

Brothers and sisters:
When the **fullness** of time had **come**, **God** sent his **Son**,
  born of a **woman**, born under the law,
  to **ransom** those under the law,
  so that **we** might receive **adoption** as **sons**.
As **proof** that you are sons,
  God sent the **Spirit** of his **Son** into our **hearts**,
  crying out, "**Abba, Father!**"
So you are no longer a **slave** but a **son**,
  and if a **son** then also an **heir**, through **God**.

You can add weight to this text by surrounding it with silence. Pause after the salutation, after "Abba, Father," and at each comma in the final sentence.
The parenthetical phrases make important statements about Jesus. Stress them.

Share this truth with gratitude for what the "Son" did for us.
Quicken your pace, then increase your energy, but not your volume, on "Abba, Father" using the same inflection for both words.

Make eye contact as you tell your listeners they are heirs of the promises of God.

GOSPEL Luke 2:16–21

A reading from the holy Gospel according to Luke

The **shepherds** went in **haste** to **Bethlehem** and found **Mary**
    and **Joseph**,
  and the **infant** lying in the **manger**.
When they saw this,
  they made **known** the message
  that had been **told** them about this child.
All who **heard** it were **amazed**
  by what had been **told** them by the **shepherds**.
And **Mary** kept all these things,
  reflecting on them in her **heart**.
Then the **shepherds** returned,
  glorifying and **praising** God
  for all they had **heard** and **seen**,
  just as it had been told to them.

When **eight** days were completed for his **circumcision**,
  he was named **Jesus**, the name given him by the **angel**
  before he was **conceived** in the womb.

Let your tone suggest the haste and excitement of the shepherds.

They are filled with amazement and can't contain their enthusiasm.

A quieter tone tells us Mary is somewhat detached from the shepherd's exhilaration and turns inward to reflect.
The shepherd's joy won't be abated!

Employ slower pacing on this final section. This one sentence focuses us on both Jesus' humanity (circumcision) and his divine origin ("the name given him by the angel").

his Son, born of a woman." The Christ came to free those bound by the Law of Moses and offer a relationship to God like his own. Through Christ, believers are adopted into God's own family as sons and daughters. As proof of this filial relationship, he points out that Christians participate in the powerful presence of the Crucified and Resurrected Christ, the Spirit, and so with Christ can address God as he did: "Abba, Father!" Further, the adopted sons and daughters of God then also share in Christ's inheritance: the fullness of life of the final age of salvation.

GOSPEL In this final scene in Luke's account of the annunciation to the shepherds, we see their joyful response to the Good News. They immediately seek out the infant Jesus, telling Mary and Joseph of their revelation from heaven. Mary responds with a Jewish understanding of God's Word; it is to be received even if it cannot be understood in the moment. Then slowly, with time and reflection, the full meaning will unfold. Mary had surrendered to the message of Gabriel in this way, and now she receives confirmation of his words from a most unlikely source: shepherds, despised as unclean sinners. She continues to hold the words in her heart. Trusting even when she cannot yet fully know, she names her son Jesus, which means "God saves." In time, the meaning of that powerful name and the character of her son as the One in whom God acts to save all humankind, will be revealed to her.

Meanwhile, the shepherds continue to rejoice, praising God. Luke thus raises up a theme he will repeat often: God has come in Jesus to save, first of all, to the lowly, the poor, the outcast, and the despised, including women and sinners. M.F.

THE EPIPHANY OF THE LORD

LECTIONARY #20

READING I   Isaiah 60:1–6

Isaiah = ī-ZAY-uh

You are reading poetry that conveys joy enough to celebrate the end of war, the coronation of a king, and the cure of a dread disease.

Each couplet repeats or develops in the second line what was said in the first. This characteristic of biblical poetry adds texture and color. Enjoy the repetitions and increase energy from the first line to the second. Dark and gloom give way to light! IMagine the countless visitors, from paupers to royalty, who have traveled to this land that Isaiah extols.

Isaiah addresses Jerusalem as if it were a person. Let your tone convey that intimacy.

Now, it is we, Christ's Body, who must radiate the light of his glory.

"Dromedaries" are single-humped camels.

Midian = MID-ee-uhn
Ephah = EE-fah
Sheba = SHEE-buh

"Gold and frankincense" will echo again in today's Gospel. The reading ends as it began, praising God.

A reading from the Book of the Prophet Isaiah

> **Rise up** in **splendor**, **Jerusalem**! Your **light** has **come**,
>   the **glory** of the **Lord shines** upon you.
> **See**, **darkness** covers the earth,
>   and **thick clouds** cover the **peoples**;
> but upon **you** the LORD **shines**,
>   and **over you** appears his **glory**.
> **Nations** shall **walk** by your **light**,
>   and **kings** by your **shining** radiance.
> Raise your **eyes** and **look about**;
>   they all **gather** and **come** to you:
> your **sons** come from **afar**,
>   and your **daughters** in the arms of their **nurses**.
>
> Then you shall be **radiant** at what you see,
>   your **heart** shall **throb** and **overflow**,
> for the **riches** of the sea shall be emptied **out before** you,
>   the **wealth** of nations shall be **brought** to you.
> **Caravans** of **camels** shall **fill** you,
>   **dromedaries** from **Midian** and **Ephah**;
> all from **Sheba** shall come
>   bearing **gold** and **frankincense**,
>   and **proclaiming** the **praises** of the LORD.

READING I | Isaiah offers the people hope as they rebuild after the exile, and he paints a marvelous picture of a new Jerusalem, resplendent with a pilgrimage of peoples who "have gathered, come to you"—to Jerusalem—earlier humiliated, now radiant with joy, because the Lord dawns in her and "his glory shall appear upon you." The prophet combines the exaltation of Jerusalem and her universal destiny. God's light shining upon it, within it, makes the city light for the nations. The exiles begin to return; countless people stream toward the city; an abundance of good things flows in for their benefit. Jerusalem, bearing the marks of Babylon's devastation, is really a poor reality for all the wealth described. God's power has a predilection for the weak and the small. The prophet focuses on the theological city of Jerusalem, home to all peoples. He personifies Jerusalem as a woman who radiates light, while darkness and clouds envelop other nations. Jerusalem, like a mother, gladly welcomes all people as her returning children.

READING II | The image of the ideal king preserved by the chosen people becomes God's plan for the realization of the hopes of all creation to unite all peoples. The author expresses the breadth of this unity by coining words with the prefix *syn* – ("together" or "co-"). The Gentiles are now "co-heirs" with the Jews, members of the same body ("co-bodies"), "partners" in the promise. The reign is more marvelous than people iMagined. Ephesians presents revelation as a unifying process initiated by the Father, realized by Jesus Christ, and developed by the Spirit in the

For meditation and context:

RESPONSORIAL PSALM Psalm 72:1–2, 7–8, 10–11, 12–13 (11)

R. Lord, every nation on earth will adore you.

O God, with your judgment endow the king,
  and with your justice, the king's son;
he shall govern your people with justice
  and your afflicted ones with judgment.

Justice shall flower in his days,
  and profound peace, till the moon
    be no more.
May he rule from sea to sea,
  and from the River to the ends of
    the earth.

The kings of Tarshish and the Isles shall
    offer gifts;
  the kings of Arabia and Seba shall bring
    tribute.
All kings shall pay him homage,
  all nations shall serve him.

For he shall rescue the poor when he cries out,
  and the afflicted when he has no one to
    help him.
He shall have pity for the lowly and the poor;
  the lives of the poor he shall save.

READING II Ephesians 3:2–3a, 5–6

A reading from the Letter of Saint Paul to the Ephesians

The language here is somewhat obscure.
Paul is declaring that he was given a special "revelation," but what that is won't be shared until the end of the text.

Brothers and sisters:
You have **heard** of the **stewardship** of God's **grace**
  that was **given** to me for your **benefit**,
    namely, that the **mystery** was made **known** to me by **revelation**.
It was not made known to people in **other** generations
  as it has **now** been revealed

What was revealed to Paul was also kept hidden from former generations.
Stress the role of the Spirit in enlightening the "apostles and prophets."

  to his **holy apostles** and **prophets** by the **Spirit**:

Here we have the truth formerly hidden but now revealed! You tell us four things: Gentiles are "coheirs," "members," and "copartners," and it's the "gospel" that makes that possible.

  that the **Gentiles** are **coheirs**, **members** of the **same body**,
  and **copartners** in the **promise** in Christ **Jesus** through
    the **gospel**.

GOSPEL Matthew 2:1–12

A reading from the holy Gospel according to Matthew

This is a suspenseful story of menace averted through God's providence.
Don't rush the important details that provide the story's context.

When **Jesus** was born in **Bethlehem** of **Judea**,
  in the days of King **Herod**,
    behold, **Magi** from the **east** arrived in **Jerusalem**, saying,
  "**Where** is the newborn **king** of the **Jews**?

They've traveled far based solely on the testimony of a star.

Church. The Father initiates the plan of salvation, and he has entrusted to the apostle "the stewardship of God's of grace . . . for your benefit," which is ultimately "the mystery . . . which has now been revealed by the Spirit." Gentiles are joint heirs of the inheritance, members of the same body and beneficiaries of Jesus' promise.

GOSPEL The evangelist tells of a star that appears in the night, disappears, and then reappears. He tells of a dream that warns the Magi of the danger of returning to their homeland by the same

route. A star and a dream. What is more tenuous than a dream or a star upon which to fix a project of life? After the angel of the Annunciation and the dream of Joseph, God's wonders continue, so we can fix our faith on the one who comes, on the basis of the testimony of a guiding star and a dream. God addresses humanity, even as God respects human freedom. The signs God sends have a character of light and clarity but, at the same time, of subtlety. Throughout the Gospels, from the Annunciation to the Resurrection, there is always room for uncertainty and the chal-

lenge of faith. What would the Apostle Thomas answer to the report of the Bethlehem star, he who said, "If I do not put my finger in the wound of the nails, if I do not put my hand in the wound open in his side, I will not believe"? Yes, God reveals himself with fine distinction, but we still need an individual to welcome and offer him shelter.

The report of the Magi instructs us. How can wise women and men abandon everything—safety, home, and comfort—and set out on the road to who-knows-where, expose themselves to dangers and

Herod's fear soon turns to threat.

"And all Jerusalem with him": Does the city sense the upheaval Jesus will bring?

Is this the voice of an authority simply sharing expertise, or of a devout believer speaking with reverence?

Let your tone convey the conspiratorial plans Herod is brewing.

Herod laces his poison with honey.

The "star" brings comfort and reassurance.

Note, they enter a house, not a cave or stable. The child is not mentioned without his mother.

First they pay him homage on their knees, then by opening their "treasures." Don't rush the naming of the three precious gifts.

Let your tone suggest the ominous nature of the dream that warned them.

We saw his **star** at its **rising**
  and have **come** to do him **homage**."
When King **Herod heard** this,
  he was greatly **troubled**,
  and **all Jerusalem** with him.
Assembling all the chief **priests** and the **scribes** of the people,
  he **inquired** of them where the **Christ** was to be **born**.
They said to him, "In **Bethlehem** of **Judea**,
  for **thus** it has been **written** through the **prophet**:
    And **you**, **Bethlehem**, land of **Judah**,
      are by no means **least** among the **rulers** of **Judah**;
    since from you shall **come** a **ruler**,
      who is to **shepherd** my people **Israel**."
Then Herod **called** the **Magi secretly**
  and **ascertained** from them the **time** of the star's **appearance**.
He sent them to **Bethlehem** and said,
  "**Go** and search **diligently** for the **child**.
When you have **found** him, **bring** me **word**,
  that I **too** may go and **do** him **homage**."
After their **audience** with the **king** they **set out**.
And **behold**, the **star** that they had **seen** at its **rising**
    preceded them,
  until it **came** and **stopped** over the place where the **child** was
They were **overjoyed** at seeing the **star**,
  and on entering the **house**
  they saw the **child** with **Mary** his **mother**.
They **prostrated** themselves and did him **homage**.
Then they **opened** their **treasures**
  and **offered** him gifts of **gold**, **frankincense**, and **myrrh**.
And having been **warned** in a **dream not** to **return** to **Herod**,
  they **departed** for their **country** by another **way**.

mishaps, on the basis of the testimony of a star? This question raises another one, more to the point. How could the Magi see something unnoticed by so many others? Before we follow the star, we need to recognize it. Another characteristic of God's signs: they are only visible in the dark. At night, when the noise of words diminishes, when the frenzy is calm, when the business slows down, then God manages to speak to the heart. The night strips us of certain pretensions and protections, disguises and distractions—both cosmic night and the soul's dark night. The prophets stress this: God speaks in the silent crack-

ling of a burning bush or in the delicate eloquence of the gentle breeze. To capture the message, we need to enter the night, when silence can be eloquent. Matthew teaches, through the Magi's experience, that God is not found without leaving the routine and following something as tenuous as a star and a dream. After their journey, just when the Magi thought they had reached their goal, they suddenly lost sight of the guiding star. Then they turned to the experts of Jerusalem to ask about what direction to continue. Far from being self-assured, the search has made them wise seekers; their finding has made them more humble.

It is in the stillness of night, when everything is quiet, that the Magi discover the child with his mother, prostrate before him, open the coffers of their hearts and offer precious gifts. They arrived because they had been led by a star, because they had taken the road with simplicity of heart, which allowed them to recognize in that child God's presence in the world. God's signs are finally understood by people who are transformed throughout their search, by the testimony of a star in the night sky.
K.S.

THE BAPTISM OF THE LORD

LECTIONARY #21

READING I   Isaiah 40:1–5, 9–11

A reading from the Book of the Prophet Isaiah

> **Comfort**, give **comfort** to my **people**,
>   says your God.
> Speak **tenderly** to Jerusalem, and **proclaim** to her
>   that her **service** is at an **end**,
>   her **guilt** is **expiated**;
> **indeed**, she has **received** from the **hand** of the LORD
>   **double** for all her **sins**.
>
>   A **voice** cries out:
> In the desert **prepare** the **way** of the LORD!
>   Make **straight** in the wasteland a **highway** for our **God**!
> **Every valley** shall be **filled** in,
>   **every mountain** and **hill** shall be **made low**;
> the **rugged land** shall be made a **plain**,
>   the **rough country**, a **broad valley**.
> **Then** the **glory** of the LORD shall be **revealed**,
>   and **all people** shall see it **together**;
>   for the **mouth** of the LORD has **spoken**.
>
> Go **up** on to a **high** mountain,
>   **Zion**, **herald** of glad **tidings**;
> **cry out** at the **top** of your **voice**,
>   **Jerusalem**, **herald** of **good news**!

Isaiah = ī-ZAY-uh

Begin as instructed: with tenderness and comfort!

Speak as if to wrongdoers who can't believe their crimes have been expunged.

This section calls for greater intensity. The prophet speaks God's command that we clear the clutter and throw open the doors of our hearts!

Keep in mind these are metaphors—images of the terrain in our hearts that must be cleared.

Paint clearly this ideal picture of what will be when our will and God's are one.

"Zion . . . Jerusalem" are just another way of addressing your own assembly.

Today, options are given for the readings. Contact your parish staff to learn which readings will be used.

READING I   **Isaiah 40.** God the Creator, the restorer of life, inspires hope in the exiled people. The Creator has the power to recreate them and the compassion to alleviate their sadness. God calls Isaiah to proclaim mercy to the people. The scene unfolds in two stages: first in Babylon, where the announcement of liberation and the invitation to prepare for the great journey resounds among the exiles (verses 1–5); the prophet then moves to Jerusalem and, from a high place, a herald contemplates the column of those who return home and broadcasts the long-awaited news (verses 9–11).

All creation will rejoice in God's deliverance of the people whose city, Jerusalem, will rise to announce God's arrival. The prophet announces the arrival of salvation: God issues the order to console Jerusalem, to publicize that her "servitude"—referring to her exile in foreign Babylon—is over and that her infidelity has been compensated. A messenger, "a voice," gives the order to pave the highway for the arrival of the king on his return from battle. The joyful descendants of the deportees, those whom he has released from their detention, accompany him. God comes like an attentive shepherd to tend the flock, renew the people's life, and protect them with loving kindness so they do not fall again into the hands of mercenaries.

Isaiah 42. In this first "Song of the Servant," the prophet presents a mysterious individual, the Lord's Anointed. He may represent the chosen people or perhaps a

Fear not to cry out
    and **say** to the cities of **Judah**:
    Here is your **God**!
Here comes with **power**
    the Lord **God**,
    who **rules** by his **strong arm**;
here is his **reward** with him,
    his **recompense** before him.
Like a **shepherd** he **feeds** his **flock**;
    in his **arms** he **gathers** the **lambs**,
carrying them in his **bosom**,
    and **leading** the **ewes** with **care**.

Or:

READING I   Isaiah 42:1–4, 6–7

A reading from the Book of the Prophet Isaiah

Thus says the **Lord**:
Here is my **servant** whom I **uphold**,
    my **chosen one** with whom I am **pleased**,
upon whom I have put my **spirit**;
    he shall bring forth **justice** to the **nations**,
not **crying out**, not **shouting**,
    not making his **voice heard** in the street.
A **bruised reed** he shall not **break**,
    and a **smoldering wick** he shall **not quench**,
until he establishes **justice** on the **earth**;
    the **coastlands** will wait for his **teaching**.

I, the **Lord**, have called **you** for the victory **of justice**,
    I have grasped **you** by the **hand**; »

You must speak these lines from the depth of your own conviction that God is indeed a God of mercy and redemption!

Though shepherds live a hard and rugged life, their lambs and sheep survive only because of their care and even tenderness.

Isaiah = ī-ZAY-uh

The Lord's proud voice introduces the servant. Speak these lines as a blessing that will become a self-fulfilling prophecy.

He won't be like the prophets of old who often made a spectacle of themselves.

His ministry will incarnate gentleness and compassion. "Reed" and "wick" are metaphors for the bruised and faint-hearted among us.

Note the shift to speaking to the servant rather than about him. IMagine speaking these encouraging words to a young person in need of reassurance.

notable person of Israel, such as Jeremiah or another prophet, perhaps Isaiah himself. The servant is fulfilling his mission to restore the covenant with God and return the exiled people to their homeland. His characteristic attitude is humility and kindness; he will be valiant in time of trial and will suffer, and the tools of his craft will be those of peace, not war. He is king, priest, and prophet. As a king, he will redefine the law and establish "justice," which is spelled "salvation," from God. As priest, he will fulfill his mission by being the guarantee of the covenant; as prophet, he will communi-

cate God's will and be the "light of the nations." His mission, enlivened by the Spirit, is to free the human being from every evil, even to the innermost part of our humanity. The physically and spiritually blind will recover their sight to resume the right path to true life and dignity; prisoners will regain the freedom of the redeemed and beloved children of God.

READING II | **Titus.** The first portion of this reading constitutes the heart of the letter to Titus. It may be a confession of faith used in the Baptismal lit-

urgy of the early Church. It contains the main themes of Christian faith and morality —moderation, justice, honesty, piety, hope. The second portion sings of God's saving love through Jesus. Baptism "regenerates and renews" the lives of believers. The term *justified* means "put on the right track," conforming to the divine plan to transform the children into heirs of eternal life and happiness. Our Savior's goodness and his love for all people definitively manifested itself in Jesus, who gave his life for us. That plan of salvation is accomplished through Baptism, by which God regenerates

It is God's grace working through the servant that will cause such transformative effects.

I formed you, and **set you**
  as a **covenant** of the **people**,
  a **light** for the **nations**,
to **open** the **eyes** of the **blind**,
  to **bring out prisoners** from **confinement**,
  and from the **dungeon**, those who live in **darkness**.

For meditation and context:

RESPONSORIAL PSALM   Psalm 104:1b–2, 3–4, 24–25, 27–28, 29–30 (1)

R. O bless the Lord, my soul.

O LORD, my God, you are great indeed!
  You are clothed with majesty and glory,
robed in light as with a cloak.
  You have spread out the heavens like
    a tent-cloth.

You have constructed your palace upon
    the waters.
  You make the clouds your chariot;
you travel on the wings of the wind.
  You make the winds your messengers,
and flaming fire your ministers.

How manifold are your works, O LORD!
  In wisdom you have wrought them all—
the earth is full of your creatures;
  the sea also, great and wide,
in which are schools without number
  of living things both small and great.

They look to you to give them food in
    due time.
  When you give it to them, they gather it;
when you open your hand, they are filled
    with good things.

If you take away their breath, they perish
    and return to the dust.
  When you send forth your spirit,
    they are created,
and you renew the face of the earth.

Or:

RESPONSORIAL PSALM   Psalm 29:1–2, 3–4, 3, 9–10 (11b)

For meditation and context:

R. The Lord will bless his people with peace.

Give to the LORD, you sons of God,
  give to the LORD glory and praise,
give to the LORD the glory due his name;
  adore the LORD in holy attire.

The voice of the LORD is over the waters,
  the LORD, over vast waters.
The voice of the LORD is mighty;
  the voice of the LORD is majestic.

The God of glory thunders,
  and in his temple all say, "Glory!"
The LORD is enthroned above the flood;
  the LORD is enthroned as king forever.

us and makes us daughters and sons through the Spirit. Jesus' baptism is the sign and the first step of Christian Baptism.

Acts. In his speech to Cornelius, Peter clarifies that Jesus went about doing good and healing those oppressed by the devil, because God was with him. Through him God has proclaimed peace, the *šalôm* (total well-being) that guarantees that every person will receive what is needed to live a full life. We who share Baptism into Christ's death, the immersion into the floodwaters of death, are commissioned to complement

Christ's service of bringing justice and peace to the earth.

GOSPEL   The baptism of Jesus puts the finishing touch on the Christmas mystery and reminds us of our own Baptism. Just before creation, the Spirit of God hovered over the waters of chaos. After the creation of man and woman, the sacred author tells about the abundance of water: "In Eden was born a river that watered the garden and then divided into four arms" (Genesis 2:10). God, full of goodness, beauty, power, and

knowledge, lavished his goodness on earth and fertilized it with water. We might listen for God's voice in this creation scene in paradise, addressed to the "image and likeness": "You are my son, you, my daughter, my favorites; in you I am pleased." In Genesis the brand new human being is presented in the midst of the waters of paradise.

When the feet of Jesus of Nazareth touched the waters of the Jordan River so the Son of God might receive the baptism of conversion, those waters did not stop, as they did when Israel, freed from slavery,

READING II   Titus 2:11–14; 3:4–7

A reading from the Letter of Saint Paul to Titus

Beloved:
The **grace** of **God** has **appeared**, **saving all**
    and **training** us to reject **godless** ways
        and **worldly** desires
    and to live **temperately**, **justly** and **devoutly** in **this** age,
as we **await** the **blessed hope**,
the **appearance** of the **glory** of our great **God**
and **savior Jesus Christ**,
who **gave himself** for **us** to **deliver us** from **all lawlessness**
and to **cleanse** for **himself** a **people** as his **own**,
eager to do what is **good**.

    When the **kindness** and **generous love**
        of **God** our **savior appeared**,
    not because of any **righteous deeds** we had done
        but because of his **mercy**,
    he saved us through the **bath** of **rebirth**
        and **renewal** by the **Holy Spirit**,
    whom he **richly poured out** on us
        through **Jesus Christ** our **savior**,
    so that **we** might be **justified** by his **grace**
        and become **heirs** in **hope** of **eternal life**.

Or:

READING II   Acts 10:34–38

A reading from the Acts of the Apostles

Peter proceeded to **speak** to those gathered
    in the house of **Cornelius**, **saying**:
"In **truth**, I see that **God** shows **no partiality**. **»**

Titus = TĪ-tuhs

Beloved = bee-LUHV-uhd

Let the first word set your tone.

The "grace of God" appeared in Christ Jesus.

blessed = BLES-uhd

Be sure to distinguish the sinful ways and the virtues enumerated here. Each is distinct.

Our "blessed hope" is the "appearance" of Christ at his second coming.

Jesus' willing sacrifice is remembered here.

Renew your energy for this section that glows with gratitude.

This point requires extra emphasis: we were saved because of God's "mercy," not because we merited it.

These final lines encapsulate an entire theology of salvation. Through Baptism we received the Spirit and received justification and the promise of eternal life! Slowly progress from one concept to the next.

Remember that Peter is in the home of a Gentile where he has experienced a powerful and unexpected manifestation of the Holy Spirit.

---

crossed the Jordan, the boundary to the Promised Land (Joshua 3:16). At his birth in the flesh, Jesus of Nazareth had crossed another boundary, that which separates the divine from the human, heaven from earth. At the Jordan thirty years later, the Son of God stood in line with sinners, awaiting the ritual that signified a change of life. He who came to take away the sin of the world knew why he was standing in that line; his plan was not to redeem humankind from a distance, but rather to mingle, to be identified with sinners, "becoming like men, becoming obedient unto death" (Philippians 2:7–8). That is why the waters of the Jordan continued their course and carried with them the mystery of what had just happened: the baptism of God's Son, which for the moment went unrecognized by his brothers and sisters. At that time, nobody on the bank of the Jordan who accompanied Jesus was aware of anything unusual, until the radiant light of the Passover—the outcome of this first baptism—revealed the meaning of what had happened at the moment of his baptism. Jesus' baptism was a Trinitarian epiphany in which the Son of God was presented to the world by the Father and the Holy Spirit with the words "You are my Son, my beloved, I delight in you," accompanied by the Spirit's hovering like a dove over the place where the Son was baptized.

We hear in the Gospel: "It happened that among the people who were being baptized, Jesus was also baptized." The presence of the people was not fortuitous; it places his baptism in the context of the Incarnation. Jesus, before taking this plunge in the River Jordan, entered the life of the common people. The Son of God, before being baptized, was incarnate like

Peter has gone through a conversion experience; let us hear that what he's saying is something he never expected to say.

Rather, in **every** nation whoever **fears** him and **acts uprightly**
    is **acceptable** to him.
You know the word that he **sent** to the **Israelites**
    as he proclaimed **peace** through **Jesus Christ**, who is **Lord** of **all**,
    what has **happened all over Judea**,
    beginning in **Galilee** after the **baptism**
    that John **preached**,
    how God **anointed Jesus** of **Nazareth**
    with the **Holy Spirit** and **power**.
He went about doing **good**
    and **healing all** those **oppressed** by the **devil**,
    for **God** was **with him**."

Paint these scenes of Jesus' ministry with vivid energy.

Jesus conquered the prince of this world, therefore the whole world belongs to him.

GOSPEL   Luke 3:15–16, 21–22

A reading from the holy Gospel according to Luke

The people were **filled** with **expectation**,
    and **all** were **asking** in their **hearts**
    whether **John** might be the **Christ**.
John **answered** them all, saying,
    "**I** am **baptizing** you with **water**,
    but **one mightier** than **I** is coming.
I am **not worthy** to **loosen** the **thongs** of his **sandals**.
He will **baptize** you with the **Holy Spirit** and **fire**."

You begin in the middle, so don't rush the mention of the people's suspicions about John.

John speaks with deliberate intent to dispose of the people's misguided speculation.

Even without knowing who the Christ will be, John intuits the nature of his God-given ministry.
"And was praying" is a significant detail that must be heard. Pause first, then share that information.
The real, not metaphoric, nature of this event is highlighted by the word "bodily."
beloved = bee-LUHV-uhd
In Matthew the voice addresses the crowd, but here we have an intimate moment between Father and Son. Consider an encouraging and gentle tone for the divine voice.

After **all** the **people** had been **baptized**
    and **Jesus also** had been **baptized** and was **praying**,
    heaven was **opened** and the **Holy Spirit**
      descended upon him
    in **bodily form** like a **dove**.
And a **voice** came from **heaven**,
    "**You** are my beloved **Son**;
    with **you I** am well **pleased**."

everybody else, was bathed in the common life of the people, sharing the human condition. In Baptism, the eternal Word descends and passes through the midst of sinful people. From the human condition, he who had no sin shared in the human search for meaning in life, the pressing desire for a change, the aspiration for something new. After that immersion in the flesh in the common people, after standing in line with the people, Jesus is submerged in the water of conversion. And immediately after his baptism, Luke writes, Jesus immerses himself in prayer; that is when the sky opened, the Holy Spirit appeared and a voice was heard, attesting to his sonship. The Incarnation of God's Son opened a place in humanity to make way for divinity; Jesus' baptism and prayer open a breach in the sky so that, through the action of the Spirit, our life will ascend to its true dignity.

By Baptism we become sons and daughters of God and partakers of the mission of Christ. Thus, as the Son of God mingled with the people, lived as a brother, reconciled humanity with God and restored our dignity, so we are called to live: in reconciliation, with our true dignity of children of the same Father, sisters and brothers with each other. Is not this what pleases God? As we recall Jesus' baptism, we remember our own Baptism and renew our confession of faith in the Son of God and our commitment to the Gospel. It is the continuation of Jesus' mission in the world today. K.S.

SECOND SUNDAY IN ORDINARY TIME

LECTIONARY #66

READING I   Isaiah 62:1–5

Isaiah = ī-ZAY-uh

Declare newness and joy from the first lines!

A reading from the Book of the Prophet Isaiah

For **Zion's sake** I will **not** be **silent**,
    for **Jerusalem's sake** I will **not be quiet**,
until her **vindication shines** forth like the **dawn**
    and her **victory** like a **burning torch**.

The sound of the words is as important as the words themselves. Make this announcement personal, intended for each member of your assembly.

Nations shall **behold** your **vindication**,
    and all the **kings** your **glory**;
you shall be **called** by a **new name**
    pronounced by the **mouth** of the **Lord**.
You shall be a **glorious crown** in the **hand** of the **Lord**,
    a **royal diadem** held by your **God**.

When an idea is stated twice ("silent"/"quiet," "crown"/"diadem") greater energy goes to the second term. That's what we call "build."

No more shall people call you "**Forsaken**,"
    or your land "**Desolate**,"
but you shall be called "**My Delight**,"
    and your land "**Espoused**."

Again, the key is to make this a personal message directed at your listeners. It is a message for both the nation and the individual.

For the LORD **delights** in you
    and makes your land his **spouse**.
As a **young man marries a virgin**,
    your **Builder** shall **marry you**;
and as a **bridegroom rejoices** in his **bride**
    so shall your **God rejoice** in **you**.

Slow down and soften your tone for this very intimate imagery. Convey the love, not just the words.

READING I   The exile is officially over, and the Jews returning to their home country expect the restoration of the sovereignty of Judah promised by the prophets. The return was not immediately accompanied by joy, however. The once-defeated Jerusalem, slow to recover from the recent disaster, remains a palpable sign of God's distance. But the prophet is not carried away by sorrow; on the contrary, he announces the salvation that God will soon fulfill among his people: justice and salvation will shine brightly, and this will happen in the sight of all peoples; Jerusalem will be a precious jewel, in which God himself will be pleased. The relationship between God and the people will imitate the true love that unites wife and husband. The prophetic voice infuses hope. The people, personified by their capital city, Jerusalem, is God's beloved fiancée. He will not abandon her. The prophet instills confidence in the changing times and the celebration of a wedding feast between God and his people.

READING II   Paul displays the character of the charisms, or spiritual gifts, highlighting how they flow from the grace of the one Spirit. The accent on "the same Spirit," "the same Lord," "the same God," contrasts with the diversity of "gifts," which are manifestations of the Spirit for the common good. Far from being exclusive rights, everyone shares in the gifts, because "one and the same Spirit produces all of these, distributing them individually to each person as he wishes," for the good of the community. As the gifts and services have their origin in the Holy Spirit, who grants them for the good of all, we are urged to recognize them, give thanks, and accept them in other persons. The body of

47

RESPONSORIAL PSALM   Psalm 96:1–2, 2–3, 7–8, 9–10 (3)

R. Proclaim his marvelous deeds to all the nations.

Sing to the LORD a new song;
   sing to the LORD, all you lands.
Sing to the LORD; bless his name.

Announce his salvation, day after day.
Tell his glory among the nations;
   among all peoples, his wondrous deeds.

Give to the LORD, you families of nations,
   give to the LORD glory and praise;
   give to the LORD the glory due his name!

Worship the LORD in holy attire.
   Tremble before him, all the earth;
Say among the nations: The LORD is king.
   He governs the peoples with equity.

TO KEEP IN MIND
Repetition of the same word or phrase over the course of a reading emphasizes a point. Make each instance distinct, and build your intensity with each repetition.

READING II   1 Corinthians 12:4–11

A reading from the first Letter of Saint Paul to the Corinthians

Brothers and sisters:
There are **different** kinds of **spiritual gifts** but the **same Spirit**;
   there are **different** forms of **service** but the **same Lord**;
   there are **different workings** but the **same God**
   who **produces all** of them in **everyone**.
To **each** individual the **manifestation** of the **Spirit**
   is **given** for some **benefit**.
To **one** is given through the **Spirit** the expression of **wisdom**;
   to **another**, the expression of **knowledge** according
      to the **same Spirit**;
   to another, **faith** by the same **Spirit**;
   to another, **gifts** of **healing** by the **one Spirit**;
   to another, mighty **deeds**;
   to another, **prophecy**;
   to another, **discernment** of **spirits**;
   to another, **varieties** of **tongues**;
   to another, **interpretation** of **tongues**.
But **one** and **the same Spirit** produces **all** of these,
   distributing them **individually** to **each person** as **he wishes**.

Corinthians = kohr-IN-thee-uhnz

The salutation helps set the conciliatory tone of Paul's teaching.

Be aware of the reasons for sharing this teaching: to foster appreciation of each other's gifts and to heal division.

This summary sentence ends the opening section. Speak it with authority. Then elaborate with what follows.

In the listing of gifts, you need not emphasize "another" each time it recurs. However, the new gift named in each line must be stressed.

Speak each "gift" as a treasure that adds to the community's storehouse of grace. Don't rush the naming of gifts, but varying your pace can be helpful.

Pause before this important closing summary. Speak with awareness of Paul's authority to share this instruction.

Christ is no place for envy or ill will about gifts, distributed and received according to God's will. Recognizing and accepting the diversity of charisms opens the door to union in the Body of Christ.

GOSPEL Two scenes help us grasp the meaning of the wedding of Cana. The first goes back to Genesis and the couple at the point of leaving paradise, where abundant water fertilized and refreshed the garden, with four rivers flowing to all parts. In this departure from paradise, nothing is cheerful. In another scene,

woman and man again meet. The woman stands facing the cross, contemplating her Son's death. The voice from the cross, "Woman, there is your son," echoes his voice at Cana, "Woman, what can we do?" Just as Cana abounds in water, transformed into an exquisite wine, two fountains, water and blood, spring forth from the pierced body of the Crucified.

Just so, Cana becomes a perfect setting for the formation of a new family. But, as the evangelist neglects to report on the identity of the bride and groom, a symbolism resounds. John informs us, "Jesus did

this as the beginning of his signs." Cana represents the marriage covenant between God and his people (Isaiah's prophecy), the marriage consummated in the sacrifice of the bridegroom on the cross. In the New Testament, marriage continues to be a symbol of the love between God and the Church.

The abundant water transformed into wine symbolizes the effervescent joy that flows from this union. It is a sign of the vitality of the wedding feast that has no end. Wine—happiness—runs dry when the sense of God is lost, when we abandon our

GOSPEL   John 2:1–11

A reading from the holy Gospel according to John

Speak these details with energy.

There was a **wedding** at **Cana** in **Galilee**,
and the **mother** of **Jesus** was there.

Mention of Jesus signals this will be no ordinary wedding feast.

Jesus and his **disciples** were **also** invited to the wedding.
When the **wine** ran **short**,

Mary's tone suggests her concern and her expectations.

the **mother** of **Jesus** said to him,
"They have no **wine**."
And **Jesus** said to her,

"Woman" is in no way disrespectful.

"**Woman**, how does **your** concern affect **me**?
My **hour** has **not yet come**."

Mary does not hear a "no" in his response. Her words contain a deeper level of meaning.

His mother said to the **servers**,
"**Do whatever** he **tells** you."
Now there were **six** stone **water** jars there for Jewish
ceremonial **washings**,
each holding **twenty** to **thirty gallons**.
Jesus **told** them,
"**Fill** the jars with **water**."
So they **filled** them to the **brim**.
Then he told them,

Move briskly through this narration and speak with an upbeat tone.

"**Draw** some out **now** and **take** it to the **headwaiter**."
So they **took** it.
And when the **headwaiter tasted** the **water** that had become **wine**,
without knowing where it **came** from

IMagine the headwaiter drawing the groom aside for this hushed dialogue.

—although the **servers** who had **drawn** the water **knew**—,
the **headwaiter** called the **bridegroom** and said to him,
"**Everyone** serves **good wine first**,
and **then** when **people** have **drunk freely**, an **inferior** one;
but **you** have **kept** the **good wine** until **now**."

A "sign" designates something that has greater witness value than Jesus' various miracles.
The belief of the disciples is a key outcome of this unique event.

Jesus did this as the **beginning** of his **signs** at **Cana** in **Galilee**
and so **revealed** his **glory**,
and his **disciples began** to **believe** in him.

---

first love. The transformation of water from the stone jars into a wine of superior quality is the quality of life we find in and with Christ. The Cana wedding shows how God gives his consent to our happiness, to life without end. The excess of wine anticipates how Christ, the spouse, in his sacrifice on the cross, offers his own blood, the price of salvation for his spouse, the Church.

We no longer feel "abandoned," and our land is no longer "devastated" (first reading), because we are espoused to God, who cares about human life, sadness, and joy. God gets involved in our life and enters it to share the little and big joys, from this time forth, for richer or poorer, in sickness and health, all the days to eternal life. The first reading and the Gospel share the prophetic theme of the wedding between God and his people as a covenant of love. Despite our infidelities, God constantly renews his covenant. The portrait of the Cana wedding points the reader to the "hour" of Jesus, to his Cross and Passover to the Father, his hour of glory: "When I am lifted up from the earth, I will draw all to me." The present "sign" is the beginning of the era of the Messiah, when new wine in abundance—emblematic of irrepressible joy—abounds. K.S.

THIRD SUNDAY
IN ORDINARY TIME

LECTIONARY #69

READING I   Nehemiah 8:2–4a, 5–6, 8–10

A reading from the Book of Nehemiah

Nehemiah = nee-huh-MĪ-uh

Begin with a solemn tone that suggests the exalted nature of this event.

Don't rush the details of how long he read and how many people listened.

The repetition of "men . . . women . . . children" is a mantra-like formula that lends greater dignity to the telling.

The scroll becomes a sign of God's presence and love, so the people show great reverence.

Take time with the telling of this sacred moment.

Ezra the **priest** brought the **law** before the **assembly**,
   which consisted of **men**, **women**,
   and those **children** old enough to **understand**.
Standing at one end of the open place that was before
      the Water **Gate**,
   he **read** out of the **book** from **daybreak** till **midday**,
   in the **presence** of the **men**, the **women**,
   and those **children** old enough to **understand**;
   and **all** the **people listened attentively** to the **book** of **the law**.
Ezra the scribe stood on a wooden **platform**
   that had been made for the occasion.
He **opened** the **scroll**
   so that **all** the **people** might **see** it
   —for he was standing **higher up** than any of the people—;
   and, as he **opened** it, **all** the people **rose**.
Ezra blessed the Lord, the **great God**,
   and **all** the **people**, their **hands** raised **high**, **answered**,
   "**Amen, amen!**"
Then they **bowed** down and **prostrated** themselves
      before the Lord,
   their faces to the **ground**.
Ezra read **plainly** from the **book** of the **law** of **God**,
   interpreting it so that **all** could **understand** what was **read**.

READING I   The first reading recalls a key scene in the rebuilding of the people upon their return from Babylonian captivity: the scribe Ezra presents the book of the law. This ceremony represents the culminating moment of Ezra's effort to unify the returnees from exile and restore the consciousness of the covenant with God, which had always been the foundation of Israel's life. What remains of the Jewish people once their land is annexed to the Persian Empire? The rebuilding of the temple has been delayed, the monarchy disappeared, and the properties of the exiles were occupied by squatters. A single institution remains, one that fostered the unity of God's people for centuries: God's Law transmitted by Moses. To mark the covenant renewal and the birth of Judaism, the priest Ezra solemnly proclaims this law, and the people agree to its conditions. Who cares if the city fortifications have not yet been rebuilt; "rejoicing in the Lord must be your strength." Thanks to this law, faithful followers look ahead with hope. The public proclamation of the Word of God with its catechetical explanation is the essential element that will evolve into the synagogue service. For the first time after the exile, Israel gathers as a people, celebrates the proclamation of the word, and shares in a festive meal.

You are describing a unified experience of proclamation and preaching. "His excellency" = governor.

Then **Nehemiah**, that is, His **Excellency**, and **Ezra**
    the **priest-scribe**
and the **Levites** who were **instructing** the **people**
said to **all** the **people**:
"**Today** is **holy** to the Lord your **God**.
Do **not** be **sad**, and do **not weep**"—
    for **all** the **people** were **weeping** as they **heard** the **words**
        of the **law**.
He said further: "**Go**, **eat** rich **foods** and **drink** sweet **drinks**,
    and **allot portions** to those who had **nothing prepared**;
    for **today** is **holy** to our Lord.
Do **not** be **saddened** this **day**,
    for **rejoicing** in the Lord must be your **strength**!"

Speak these words with compassion, as you might address someone who's apologizing for arriving late to your wedding.

As always, first believe what you are saying, then proclaim it boldly.

For meditation and context:

RESPONSORIAL PSALM   Psalm 19:8, 9, 10, 15 (see John 6:63c)

R. Your words, Lord, are Spirit and life.

The law of the Lord is perfect,
    refreshing the soul;
the decree of the Lord is trustworthy,
    giving wisdom to the simple.

The precepts of the Lord are right,
    rejoicing the heart;
the command of the Lord is clear,
    enlightening the eye.

The fear of the Lord is pure,
    enduring forever;
the ordinances of the Lord are true,
    all of them just.

Let the words of my mouth and the thought
        of my heart
    find favor before you,
O Lord, my rock and my redeemer.

READING II   1 Corinthians 12:12–30

Corinthians – kohr-IN-thee-uhnz

Start slowly using the first sentence to set the stage for the theological point you will make. You're saying: What's true of our bodies is true of Christ and his Body the Church.

A reading from the first Letter of Saint Paul to the Corinthians

[**Brothers** and **sisters**:
As a **body** is **one** though it has **many parts**,
    and **all** the **parts** of the **body**, though **many**, are **one** body,
    so also **Christl**. »

READING II   The central theme of today's readings is the Word of God proclaimed to the people. Ezra reorganizes the believing community after their exile by announcing God's Law. In the Gospel Jesus begins his public activity by commenting on sacred Scripture in the synagogue of Nazareth. In this reading, Paul explains how the Word of God shapes the Body of Christ and is manifest in the diverse charisms, gifts granted by God for the good of the community of believers. He employs the analogy of the body to illustrate the function of the charisms—"As the body is one though it has many parts . . . so also Christ"—to affirm that the Church is "the body of Christ." The body incorporates both the uniqueness of each member and the uniformity of everyone together. Each member, in its singularity and uniqueness, is a part the body.

Paul stresses that Christ is one, as the human body is one, even though it comprises diverse members. Baptism inserts the Christian into Christ's resurrected and glorious Body, and the Church, the assembly of the baptized, is the manifestation and extension of his Body in the world. Therefore, the spiritual gifts and the diverse functions do not impair the unity of Christians; rather, they are a manifestation of the Church's inalienable wealth.

Stress the oneness that results from Baptism, which makes our differences less important than unity.

Be aware of the inherent humor in Paul's vivid analogy.

Varying your pace will help hold the listeners' attention. The details of the analogy ("If the ear should say . . . I am not an eye") can be spoken at a faster pace than Paul's points and conclusions: "there are many parts, yet one body . . . . Indeed, the parts of the body . . . . But God has so constructed the body."

Use eye contact to assure your listeners Paul is speaking about them as well.

Here Paul speaks of the "private" parts of the body that we cover with greater care. Don't belabor the point and keep the pace brisk.

Take a breath and renew your energy on this important line. You are reminding us that the seemingly less honorable parts can take on great importance.

This sentence requires a slower, more sober tone.

For in **one Spirit** we were **all baptized** into **one body**,
   whether **Jews** or **Greeks**, **slaves** or **free** persons,
   and **we** were **all** given to **drink** of **one Spirit**.

Now the **body** is not a **single part**, but **many**.]
If a **foot** should say,
   "**Because I** am **not** a **hand I** do **not belong** to the **body**,"
   it does **not** for this reason **belong any less** to the body.
Or if an **ear** should say,
   "**Because I** am **not** an **eye I** do **not belong** to the **body**,"
   it does **not** for this reason **belong any less** to the body.
If the **whole body** were an **eye**, where would the **hearing** be?
If the **whole body** were **hearing**, where would the **sense**
      of **smell** be?
But as it **is**, **God** placed the **parts**,
   each one of them, in the **body** as he **intended**.
If they were **all one** part, **where** would the **body** be?
But as it **is**, there are **many parts**, yet **one** body.
The **eye** cannot say to the **hand**, "**I** do not **need** you,"
   nor again the **head** to the **feet**, "**I** do not **need** you."
Indeed, the **parts** of the body that seem to be **weaker**
   are all the more **necessary**,
   and those **parts** of the **body** that we consider less **honorable**
   we surround with **greater honor**,
   and our less **presentable** parts are treated with **greater propriety**,
   whereas our **more** presentable parts do not **need** this.
But **God** has so **constructed** the **body**
   as to give **greater honor** to a part that is **without** it,
   so that there may be **no division** in the body,
   but that the **parts** may have the **same concern** for **one another**.
If **one** part **suffers**, **all** the parts **suffer** with it;
   if **one** part is **honored**, **all** the parts **share its joy**.

Only through God's presence among us are we able to take this Word into our lives. Paul relates the amazing news that God's presence is not only with us, but within us. Through Baptism we have become the one body of Christ. We have been given to drink the one Spirit that gives the body life. Together as one, we are the sign of God's presence in the world. We have not only listened to the Word of life; through Baptism God's Word has taken up residence within us, and it is our life. The Word that became flesh and lived among us is now visible to the world in the Body of Christ that we are.

GOSPEL After Jesus reads from the scroll in the synagogue, he announces that he is the fulfillment of Isaiah's prophecies. The poor will be the privileged beneficiaries of the good news of the arrival of the messianic era. The Spirit rests on Jesus, who will announce the Gospel to the poor, just as in Ezra's time the Jews expected a release, understood not as political emancipation, but freedom in the Spirit, which is the theological impact of Jesus' healings.

Paul's reflection on the body of Christ, formed by diverse members, is an image of the unity achieved in one Baptism. Another reason for unity is found in God's Word that nourishes and inspires us. Today's first

A faster pace is appropriate for this listing of roles, but don't lose a sense of the dignity of these God-given offices.

Now [**you** are **Christ's body**, and **individually parts** of it.]
Some people **God** has designated in the **church**
    to be, **first**, **apostles**; **second**, **prophets**; **third**, **teachers**;
    then, **mighty deeds**;
    then **gifts** of **healing**, **assistance**, **administration**,
    and **varieties** of **tongues**.

One idea is communicated through these multiple rhetorical questions. Use a brisk pace, but slow down for the final question and give it a tone of finality.

Are **all apostles**? Are **all prophets**? Are **all teachers**?
Do **all** work **mighty deeds**? Do **all** have **gifts** of **healing**?
Do **all** speak in **tongues**? Do **all interpret**?

[Shorter: 1 Corinthians 12:12–14, 27 (see brackets)]

GOSPEL   Luke 1:1–4, 4:14–21

A reading from the holy Gospel according to Luke

Luke's prologue is one long sentence comprised of several main and subordinate clauses. Keep in mind where you're headed as you vary your pacing and your emphasis.

Luke's careful research is an important assertion.

Here, the text jumps from chapter 1 to chapter 4 of Luke. Renew your energy as you begin this section and emphasize the influence of the Spirit.

Since **many** have **undertaken** to **compile** a **narrative** of the **events**
    that have been **fulfilled** among us,
    just as those who were **eyewitnesses** from **the beginning**
    and **ministers** of the **word** have **handed them down** to **us**,
    I too have **decided**,
    after **investigating everything** accurately **anew**,
    to **write** it down in an **orderly sequence** for you,
    most **excellent Theophilus**,
    so that you may **realize** the **certainty** of the teachings
    you have received.

Jesus' initial acclaim and the spread of his fame are important to Luke.

Jesus returned **to Galilee** in the **power** of the **Spirit**,
    and **news** of him **spread** throughout the **whole region**.
He **taught** in their **synagogues** and was **praised** by **all**. »

---

reading emphasizes the assembly's attention to the Word. It recalls a dark period of history, when the people had lost the sense of the transcendence of their life. From among the ruins, in order to rebuild themselves as God's people, they opened to a plan of life that is not sketched out of reasons and projects, but of the attention to the Word of God. Nehemiah's assembly, hearing the Word of God, became sad. Ezra advised those who led the assembly,

"Do not be sad, and do not weep. . . . Go, eat rich food and drink sweet drinks, and allot portions to those who had nothing prepared; for today is holy to our Lord." The fruit of having heard the Word of God is a joyful life, because it is the extension of God's joy, a generous, fruitful life, because it is molded by the strong subtlety of the Word.

How many times in our lives, in moments of crisis or celebration, do we

allow ourselves to be questioned and enlivened by God's Word? Sometimes we get discouraged by the tremendous distance that separates the truth of God's Word and the condition of our lives. Tears flow freely because we feel so small in the face of the friendship with God and the coherent life we long for. But great work takes constancy and patience. Water by nature is soft and stone is hard, but when a water falls drop by drop on the stone, over time, it

Several significant details here: Nazareth is home for Jesus; he regularly attends synagogue; it's the Sabbath day.

Jesus does not seem to choose the scroll, but he does select the passage.

Pause before narrating that he rolled up the scroll.

The narrative creates suspense as Jesus sits and all fix their eyes on him waiting for what will happen next. Jesus does not disappoint. Speak his final dialogue as Jesus' effort to make them understand what just happened.

He came to **Nazareth**, where he had grown **up**,
and went according to his **custom**
into the **synagogue** on the **sabbath** day.
He **stood up** to **read** and was handed **a scroll** of the prophet **Isaiah**.
He **unrolled** the **scroll** and found the **passage** where it was **written**:
*The **Spirit** of the **Lord** is **upon** me,*
*because he has **anointed me***
*to bring **glad tidings** to the **poor**.*
*He has **sent me** to **proclaim liberty** to **captives***
*and **recovery** of **sight** to the **blind**,*
*to let the **oppressed** go **free**,*
*and to **proclaim** a year **acceptable** to the **Lord**.*
Rolling up the **scroll**, he handed it back to the attendant
and sat **down**,
and the **eyes** of **all** in the **synagogue** looked **intently** at **him**.
He said to them,
"**Today this** Scripture passage is **fulfilled** in your **hearing**."

will be smoothed and sculpted. This is similar to what happens in *lectio divina* and daily attention to the Word of God. The divine Word is also soft and the hearer of the Word often hard-hearted, but if an individual listens to this Word, over time the heart will be transformed and will open to God's love. The heart becomes softer, more humane, less stone, with the action of the Word of God, drop by drop.

Luke begins his Gospel, addressing "most excellent Theophilus." Theophilus means "loved by God" or "friend of God." It is not by accident that he calls his reader by a name that could be applied to anyone who wishes to be God's friend. The evangelist addresses anyone who lets him or herself be examined by the Word, and gives thanks that, like Mary the sister of Martha, they had chosen the essential part, which is attention to the Word of life. K.S.

FOURTH SUNDAY IN ORDINARY TIME

LECTIONARY #72

READING I   Jeremiah 1:4–5, 17–19

A reading from the Book of the Prophet Jeremiah

The **word** of the LORD came to me, saying:
  Before I formed you in the **womb** I **knew you**,
    before you were **born** I **dedicated you**,
    a **prophet** to the **nations** I **appointed** you.

But **do** you **gird** your **loins**;
    stand up and **tell** them
    all that I **command** you.
Be **not crushed** on their account,
    as **though** I would **leave** you **crushed** before **them**;
for it is **I** this **day**
    who have made **you** a **fortified city**,
a **pillar** of **iron**, a **wall** of **brass**,
    against the **whole land**:
against Judah's kings and **princes**,
    against its **priests** and **people**.
They will **fight** against **you** but **not prevail** over you,
    for **I** am **with you** to **deliver** you, says the LORD.

Jeremiah = jayr-uh-MĪ-uh

Only the first line is the prophet's. The balance is spoken by the Lord.

Always begin slowly; here it's especially important so these key declarations are clearly heard.

The text jumps ahead to God's "pep talk." Don't rush, and speak like a teacher, coach, or parent encouraging an insecure youth who faces a great challenge.

"This is what I've done for you," God says. "I've made you like a city with thick walls and strong defenses."

Listed here are all those who will oppose Jeremiah.
Speak this promise with the love of a parent or spouse sending a loved one off to battle.

READING I The account of Jeremiah's vocation tells of the prophet's twofold conviction. He is conscious of being an ambassador to foreign nations, even while his own people reject him. The prophet's first task is to trust in God's Word, taught to him from his youth. Throughout his life, he will contend with civil authorities who endanger the people's freedom and with religious authorities who place their trust in the temple and external cult, while Jeremiah preaches a religion of the heart. But he remains faithful to his vocation in the face of adversity. He will doubt, but the

believer in him stands up and speaks; when the "prophet to the nations" complains, God reassures him: "Before I formed you in the womb, I knew you," who made him "a fortified city . . . against the whole land."

READING II Paul's hymn to love adds another layer to this Sunday's themes. No other gift, not even faith or hope, outshines love that will never pass away, because it shares in and expresses God's very life. Love, the foundation of all, never fails; it is patient and enduring. Love allows Jeremiah and Jesus

to endure suffering and persecution. Knowledge of God's love, even though seen as "in a mirror," inspires trust in God's rescue and praise of God's justice. Love is what really counts in the end.

Writing about love, Paul does not use the word *eros*, understood as possessive desire that seeks its own good; he spells out another word, *agápē*, understood as charity or compassion, that is, love that spreads outwards and does not grab or keep for itself. It is the most excellent gift, not possessive, envious, angry, or begrudging. *Agápē* is comprehensive love that pardons,

For meditation and context:

TO KEEP IN MIND
Don't neglect the Responsorial
Psalm just because you aren't
proclaiming it. Pray it as part of
your preparation.

RESPONSORIAL PSALM   Psalm 71:1–2, 3–4, 5–6, 15, 17 (see 15ab)

R. I will sing of your salvation.

In you, O LORD, I take refuge;
    let me never be put to shame.
In your justice rescue me, and deliver me;
    incline your ear to me, and save me.

Be my rock of refuge,
    a stronghold to give me safety,
    for you are my rock and my fortress.
O my God, rescue me from the hand of the
    wicked.

For you are my hope, O Lord;
    my trust, O God, from my youth.
On you I depend from birth;
    from my mother's womb you are my
    strength.

My mouth shall declare your justice,
    day by day your salvation.
O God, you have taught me from my youth,
    and till the present I proclaim your
    wondrous deeds.

READING II   1 Corinthians 12:31—13:13

A reading from the first Letter of Saint Paul to the Corinthians

[**Brothers** and **sisters**:]
Strive **eagerly** for the **greatest** spiritual gifts.
But I shall **show** you a **still more excellent** way.

If I speak in **human** and **angelic** tongues,
    but do **not** have **love**,
    I am a resounding **gong** or a clashing **cymbal**.
And if I have the **gift** of **prophecy**,
    and **comprehend all mysteries** and **all knowledge**;
    if I have **all faith** so as to move **mountains**,
    but do **not have love**, I am **nothing**.
If I give away **everything** I **own**,
    and if **I hand** my **body over** so that I may **boast**,
    but do **not have love**, I **gain nothing**.

[Love is **patient**, love is **kind**.
It is not **jealous**, it is not **pompous**,
    it is not **inflated**, it is not **rude**,
    it does **not** seek its own **interests**,
    it is not **quick-tempered**, it does not **brood** over **injury**,
    it does not **rejoice** over **wrongdoing**
        but **rejoices** with the **truth**.

Corinthians = kohr-IN-thee-uhnz

From the start, let your tone suggest that this message will be extraordinary.

Pause after "excellent way" to breathe and renew your energy. Then launch into his exhortation.

Because he's speaking in the first person, he can use dismissive language about how these things amount to nothing.

In each successive example the level of excellence grows, and yet it all still amounts to nothing.

This section speaks truth to all our self-delusions, so deliver the lines with authority and conviction.

tolerates, and hopes without limits, while erotic love seeks to preserve itself, and thus becomes a jealous desire, which seeks to seize the good for the self rather than for the common good.

GOSPEL   In the Gospel we hear how Jesus' compatriots do not tolerate that he, citing Scripture, places himself among the prophetic line of Elijah and Elisha, who spared outsiders from starvation and healed a foreigner's leprosy. This provokes a violent reaction that evokes his expulsion from the city, his death on Calvary, and his Resurrection: "Jesus passed through the midst of them" and went away. Throughout his ministry, Jesus will face Israel's disbelief; he will not heed to social pressure, and thus he will extend the Gospel beyond the people's customary boundaries. The prophets Elijah and Elisha had already experienced such a rejection, and the outcome was of benefit to the Gentiles, who would welcome the Good News. Luke's account of the Gospel and the Acts of the Apostles are the story of how far afield the Good News reaches.

There is a parallel between the first reading and the Gospel. Jeremiah and Jesus speak against the tide, as they emphasize the extent of God's goodness; yet they experience rejection by much of their audience because they do not flatter them, because they do not say what people like to hear. Both will cross the borders of the chosen people and open the message of salvation to all nations. Both dealt with opposition from the authorities. Jeremiah's confidence resonates in Jesus' trust in his Father: "Not my will but yours be done." Jesus knows that God will restore life to the dead. His adversaries tried to silence him by throwing him over the cliff, but Jesus, the risen, escaped their death trap.

It **bears all** things, **believes all** things,
   hopes all things, **endures all** things.

Love never fails.
If there are **prophecies**, they will be brought to **nothing**;
   if **tongues**, they will **cease**;
   if **knowledge**, it will be **brought** to **nothing**.
For we **know partially** and we **prophesy partially**,
   but when the **perfect** comes, the **partial** will pass **away**.
When **I** was a **child**, I used to **talk** as a **child**,
   think as a **child**, **reason** as a **child**;
   when I became a **man**, I put **aside childish** things.
At **present** we see **indistinctly**, as in a **mirror**,
   but **then face to face**.
At **present** I know **partially**;
   then I shall know **fully**, as I am **fully known**.
So **faith**, **hope**, **love** remain, these **three**;
   but the **greatest** of these is **love**.]

[Shorter: 1 Corinthians 13:4–13 (see brackets)]

GOSPEL   Luke 4:21–30

A reading from the holy Gospel according to Luke

Jesus began speaking in the **synagogue**, saying:
   "**Today** this **Scripture** passage is **fulfilled** in your **hearing**."
And **all** spoke **highly** of him
   and were **amazed** at the **gracious** words that came
      from his **mouth**.
They **also asked**, "Isn't this the **son** of **Joseph**?" »

Margin notes:

Don't shy from these repetitions, but emphasize only the new verb in each phrase.

After slowly asserting that "Love never fails," move quickly through the listing of what will cease.

Prophesy = PROF-uh-sī

Make the case here with energy and brisk pacing.

This is a continuation of the point just made.

Pause before this climactic final line. Establish eye contact and then speak these compelling words with great sincerity.

Since there is no introduction to the scene, let your solemn tone suggest the impression Jesus has made on them.
Contrast the praise in this line with the skepticism implicit in the question that follows.

The people of Jesus' hometown applauded him for what he had done in Capernaum, and now they received the "son of Joseph" because they desired to profit from his extraordinary gifts. When Jesus announced "Today this Scripture passage is fulfilled in your hearing," his neighbors considered only their own well-being and expected some miracle, but he referred to a more astonishing fulfillment of the prophetic text.

In the synagogue, Jesus explained that the ministry of the prophets Elijah and Elisha, in addition to responding to their fellow citizens, extended also to foreigners; by the same token, Jesus' attentions were not limited to his own race. He was sent to free the prisoners, attend the poor and helpless, and announce joyful news that culminates in the gift of his life, surrendered for the love of all humanity. Jesus does not seek his own interest, but offers every person the freedom and life that has its source in God's love.

God, in Jesus, embodies love (*agápē*) and calls us to do the same. Since the creation of the world there was water that refreshed the whole garden, but the original family rejected the gift by their disobedience. During the exodus, God offered the bread in the desert, manna, but the people were not satisfied and longed for the food of their enslaved life. We were hungry and thirsty, but we rejected the provisions that would restore us. We became weak, wounded by the thorn of selfishness, yet we shunned the life offered to us. When the gracious Word of God, always attentive to his creature, saw that we were not going to reach him, he came to us, assumed the form of daily bread, and became weak to rescue us from weakness, to transform our selfish instincts into love that nourishes the life of others. The Bread of Life gave us the recipe for a full and happy existence.

Sensing the doubt that's welling in their hearts ("Where does this son of Joseph get such wisdom?") Jesus launches into a strong rebuttal.

Capernaum = kuh-PER-nay-*m.

This much-quoted line should not be rushed.

No question that these words of his are provocative. He's challenging Israel's exclusive claim on God.

Jesus never fails to teach; his words are more instruction than indictment.
Zarephath = ZAYR-uh-fath
Sidon = SĪ-duhn
Elisha = ee-LĪ-shuh
Naaman = NAY-uh-muhn

Jesus begins to assert the freedom of God to choose and favor whomever God wills.

They're not only angry, but their righteous anger convinces them the law requires that they destroy this heretic.
Let your confident, serene tone suggest the inner power that enabled him to slice through the crowd unharmed.

He said to them, **"Surely** you will quote me this **proverb,**
　'**Physician, cure** yourself,' and say,
　'Do **here** in your **native place**
　the things that we **heard** were **done** in **Capernaum.'"**
And he said, **"Amen**, I say to you,
　no **prophet** is **accepted** in his own **native place.**
Indeed, I tell you,
　there were many **widows** in **Israel** in the days of **Elijah**
　when the **sky** was **closed** for **three** and a **half years**
　and a severe **famine** spread over the entire **land.**
It was to **none** of these that **Elijah** was **sent,**
　but only to a widow in **Zarephath** in the land of **Sidon.**
Again, there were **many lepers** in Israel
　during the time of **Elisha** the prophet;
　yet not **one** of them was **cleansed,** but only **Naaman**
　　the **Syrian."**
When the people in the **synagogue heard** this,
　they were all **filled** with **fury.**
They **rose** up, **drove** him out of the **town,**
　and **led** him to the **brow** of the **hill**
　on which their town had been **built,**
　to **hurl** him down **headlong.**
But Jesus **passed through** the **midst** of them and **went away.**

Before his passion, he was hungry and thirsty, he wept, he was tired, and fell asleep, like us, and he touched our human condition with kindness and compassion. He applied his medicine to cure us of the frailty that was the result of our sin. The eternal Word adopted our condition and put our frailty to work in his own life. The Son of God became the son of Joseph, adopting our humanity to save us from ourselves: see how the Bread of Life feels hunger, the fountain of Living Water is thirsty, the Almighty grows weary, Life falls asleep in death. Now his hunger satisfies us, his thirst refreshes us and even intoxicates us

with joy; his fatigue infuses new strength in us, his death brings us back to life. All this is the work of his love (*agápē*) which he incarnated and by which he showed us how to transform love (*eros*) into *agápē* for the benefit of humanity, so we might sing and live in harmony with our lovely God.

　Today's readings refer to the prophetic vocation. The prophet is one who has an experience of God, so the divine Word possesses him or her to such a degree that nothing prevents them from bearing witness to God's saving plan. As with Jeremiah, as with Jesus, prophetic life brings on persecution, but what triumphs

in the end is *agápē*, selfless love. The citizens of Nazareth just wanted to see miracles, and the Christians of Corinth valued spectacular charisms, so Paul points to the charisms that really matter. In the end, they add up to one: *agápē*. To speak in tongues, to possess great knowledge, to distribute all possessions to the poor—all of it is of no use if *agápē* is absent, because only *agápē* can put us right with each other. While all other gifts are destined to disappear, *agápē* will never end; in it is our guarantee of eternal life. K.S.

FIFTH SUNDAY IN ORDINARY TIME

LECTIONARY #75

READING I   Isaiah 6:1–2a, 3–8

Isaiah = ī-ZAY-uh

Uzziah = yuh-ZĪ-uh. He reigned fifty-two years during a period of prosperity but was struck with leprosy for disobeying the Lord. He died in 740 BC.

Remember, you are about to narrate a unique and mystical experience.

Convey the angels' praise with energy and awe. Isaiah is awed and overwhelmed but unable to turn away.

Smoke is a biblical sign of God's presence.

Because humans are unworthy to stand before God, "seeing" God almost certainly ensured death. Isaiah's fear is real.

Let your tone suggest the remarkable nature of this event.

What is the tone of the angel: reassuring, comforting, rousing?

Pause to transition from hearing the angel to hearing God's own voice.

Try for a blend of determination and humility.

A reading from the Book of the Prophet Isaiah

In the year **King Uzziah** died,
    I **saw** the **Lord seated** on a **high** and **lofty throne**,
    with the **train** of his **garment filling** the **temple**.
Seraphim were stationed **above**.

They **cried** one to the other,
    "**Holy, holy, holy** is the **Lord** of hosts!
All the **earth** is **filled** with his **glory!**"
At the **sound** of that cry, the frame of the door **shook**
    and the house was **filled** with **smoke**.

Then I said, "**Woe** is me, I am **doomed!**
For I am a man of **unclean** lips,
    living among a **people** of **unclean lips**;
    yet my **eyes** have seen the **King**, the LORD of **hosts!**"
Then one of the **seraphim flew** to me,
    holding an **ember** that he had taken with tongs
        from the **altar**.

He **touched** my **mouth** with it, and said,
    "**See**, now that this has **touched** your **lips**,
    your **wickedness** is **removed**, your **sin purged**."

Then I **heard** the voice of the **Lord** saying,
    "**Whom** shall **I send? Who** will **go** for **us?**"
"**Here I** am," I said; "send **me!**"

READING I As he relates his call, the prophet Isaiah emphasizes certain elements. God calls him during a Temple liturgy. Seraphim surround the throne and celebrate God's holiness. The divine presence is symbolized by the train of the garment that fills the Temple and by the earthquake and the smoke, reminiscent of the signs of God's presence at Sinai (Exodus 19:16–19). This thrice-holy God converses with the prophet, who senses his own unworthiness in the divine presence, but God purifies his mouth so he can convey God's word. The prophet freely volunteers for this service: "Here I am; send me." The vocation narrative stresses the contrast between God's holiness and human smallness expressed by an astonished youth, who consents to being overwhelmed by God and receiving a mission.

READING II The second reading is not the story of Paul's call, but rather his witness to the central belief of Christianity, the Resurrection of Christ. As he presents his testimony, the apostle states his qualifications: "the least of the Apostles," not fit to be called an apostle. "But by the grace of God I am what I am." God's power works through his weakness. Paul recognizes that the task of the prophet or apostle is not to announce his own mes-

For meditation and context:

RESPONSORIAL PSALM   Psalm 138:1–2, 2–3, 4–5, 7–8 (1c)

R. In the sight of the angels I will sing your praises, Lord.

I will give thanks to you, O Lord, with all
    my heart,
    for you have heard the words of my
    mouth;
    in the presence of the angels I will sing
    your praise;
I will worship at your holy temple
    and give thanks to your name.

Because of your kindness and your truth;
    for you have made great above all things
    your name and your promise.
When I called, you answered me;
    you built up strength within me.

All the kings of the earth shall give thanks
    to you, O Lord,
    when they hear the words of your mouth;
and they shall sing of the ways of the Lord:
    "Great is the glory of the Lord."

Your right hand saves me.
    The Lord will complete what he has done
    for me;
your kindness, O Lord, endures forever;
    forsake not the work of your hands.

Corinthians = kohr-IN-thee-uhnz

Like Paul's community, yours has need of this reminder of the Gospel they "received" and on which they "stand." Remember, you are reminding them of "good news." Be sure you sound like it.

Nothing is automatic: We are being saved if we practice what we've been taught.

"In vain": let your tone say: You wouldn't be that foolish, would you?

Here is a review of the faith for which many have shed their blood. Make it sound that important.

This listing of appearances is meant to impress his readers.

READING II   1 Corinthians 15:1–11

A reading from the first Letter of Saint Paul to the Corinthians

I am **reminding** you, [**brothers** and **sisters**,]
    of the **gospel** I preached to you,
    which you indeed **received** and in which you also **stand**.
Through it you are also being **saved**,
    if you hold **fast** to the word I **preached** to you,
    unless you **believed** in **vain**.
For [I **handed** on to you as of **first importance** what I also **received**:
    that **Christ died** for our **sins** in accordance with the **Scriptures**;
    that he was **buried**;
    that he was **raised** on the **third day**
        in accordance with the **Scriptures**;
    that he **appeared** to **Cephas**, then to the **Twelve**.
After that, Christ appeared to **more**
        than **five hundred** brothers **at once**,
    most of whom are still **living**,
    though some have **fallen asleep**.

---

sage, but what he has received and experienced personally. At the ground level of a person's Christian faith is not the intuition of her or his own importance, but a historical event: the death and Resurrection of Jesus, a saving event to be announced in its entirety. This is not simply the report of a past event; it has repercussions in the people's lives today: Christ appeared to Cephas, to the Twelve, then was seen by five hundred sisters and brothers . . . and to the least likely Paul himself. Christ is

manifested to every believer who is faithful to the call she or he has received. People today will believe in the Resurrection of Christ not so much on the testimony of yesterday's witnesses, as by the changed and ever-changing lives of today's witnesses.

GOSPEL Jesus engages his disciples in the midst of their daily lives and activities at the lakeshore. At dawn, a tension is felt between t he rising light and the shadows that resist saying

goodbye to the night. On one hand, the rising sun blinds the eyes and does not let us see right; on the other, the eyes are accustomed to the semidarkness. In today's first reading, the prophet Isaiah sees the splendor of the thrice-holy God and perceives his own indignity. God calls him, but he exclaims, "Woe is me! I am doomed! For I am a man of unclean lips." The intense light makes us aware of the shadows of our existence. Something similar happens when Jesus boards Simon's boat: there is a

Paul has already dealt with the incongruity of his past behavior. His focus is not on guilt but on saving grace.

Paul is saying: I'm "unfit" and yet "I am what I am," an apostle. The reality of what he is is greater than his unworthiness.

This might sound like arrogance were Paul not aware that even his labor was made possible by God's mercy.

After that he appeared to **James**,
    then to **all the apostles**.
Last of all, as to one born **abnormally**,
    he appeared to **me**.]
For **I** am the **least** of the apostles,
    not fit to be **called** an apostle,
    because I **persecuted** the church of **God**.
But by the **grace** of God **I am** what **I am**,
    and his **grace** to me has not been **ineffective**.
Indeed, I have **toiled harder** than **all** of them;
    not I, however, but the **grace** of **God** that is **with** me.
[Therefore, whether it be **I** or **they**,
    so we **preach** and so you **believed**.]

[Shorter: 1 Corinthians 15:3–8, 11 (see brackets)]

GOSPEL   Luke 5:1–11

A reading from the holy Gospel according to Luke

The fishermen are just ending their night of work; Jesus is beginning his day of preaching.

Washing of nets signals the night's work is over.

Jesus does not ask to enter Peter's boat.

The metaphoric meaning of "into the deep" is significant.

His tone suggests, "I'm only doing this because you're asking."

While the **crowd** was **pressing** in on **Jesus** and **listening**
    to the **word** of **God**,
    he was standing by the **Lake** of **Gennesaret**.
He saw two **boats** there alongside the **lake**;
    the **fishermen** had **disembarked** and were **washing** their **nets**.
Getting into one of the boats, the one belonging to **Simon**,
    he asked him to **put out** a **short distance** from the **shore**.
Then he sat **down** and **taught** the crowds from the boat.
After he had finished **speaking**, he said to **Simon**,
    "Put out into **deep water** and **lower** your nets for a **catch**."
Simon said in reply,
    "**Master**, we have worked hard **all night** and have
        caught **nothing**,
    but at **your** command I **will** lower the nets." »

miraculous catch of fish, which moves Simon to crouch at the Master's feet and say, "Depart from me, Lord, for I am a sinful man"—a response that echoes Isaiah's vocation, when he, too, felt unworthy in God's presence.

Here Simon's unexpected catch and his encounter with Jesus await the Master's words: "From now on you will be a fisher of human beings." Contrary to the apparent sense, "to catch human beings" is to remove them from the sea, the symbolic place of evil. To fish for people is to save them from the place of evil and participate in the liberating action of Jesus. There is a connection between the miraculous catch and the new identity Simon Peter acquires on his knees before Jesus. Without this encounter and the awareness of his own limitations, the individual is unproductive; in friendship with Christ, the individual becomes alive and fruitful. It was Jesus' Word that filled the nets; the same Word gives Simon Peter his new identity and transforms his life.

Every Christian is challenged by Baptism to live for the salvation of humanity, in accord with Paul's the testimony to the Corinthians: God's grace "to me has not been ineffective. Indeed, I have toiled harder than all of them; not I, however, but the grace of God that is with me." In the light of the Gospel, we ask ourselves whether our knowledge of Christ and being born anew in Baptism fit into the category

Narrate in the awed tone of the fishermen who are struggling with this unexpected haul.

Pause here to suggest the dawning awareness on Peter that he's in the presence of great mystery.

As he will many more times, Jesus has overturned their expectations and they're completely off-balance.

"Do not be afraid" is Jesus' formula for reassurance (especially following the Resurrection.)

Pause first, then announce their decision in a tone that suggests nothing will ever be the same for them.

When they had done this, they caught a **great number** of fish
and their **nets** were **tearing**.
They signaled to their **partners** in the **other** boat
to come to **help** them.
They came and **filled both** boats
so that the boats were in danger of **sinking**.
When **Simon Peter** saw this, he **fell** at the **knees** of Jesus and said,
"Depart from me, **Lord**, for I am a **sinful man."**
For **astonishment** at the catch of fish they had made **seized** him
and **all** those with him,
and **likewise James** and **John**, the sons of **Zebedee**,
who were **partners** of **Simon**.
Jesus said to **Simon**, "Do **not** be **afraid**;
from now on you will be **catching men."**
When they brought their **boats** to the **shore**,
they **left everything** and **followed him**.

of Good News. We wonder whether our new identity is a consequence of Jesus visiting us, like Peter and the disciples, because that is the root of all authentic human and ecclesial life. Only through friendship with God can we live with and for others, like Paul, after having experienced the Resurrection in his own life, the triumph over death.

An encounter with God does not leave human beings in the same condition as they were before the catch; it changes them, makes them more aware of their dignity. What happens to Isaiah with the vision of the Lord's glory is replicated with Peter and companions when they encounter Jesus. On one hand, they feel confused, for they recognize themselves as "sinners"; on the other, they are fascinated and discover their vocation to follow Jesus and announce his saving work. The first reading and the Gospel present us with portraits of vocations that are born of a living experience of the Lord and result in the new perception of a mission to be fulfilled, even as those who are called are aware of their own limitations. K.S.

SIXTH SUNDAY IN ORDINARY TIME

LECTIONARY #78

READING I Jeremiah 17:5–8

Remember that this is a study in contrasts. Stress those words that convey desolation and emptiness, and don't hold back on the word "Cursed."

The images of "barren bush," "lava waste," and "salt and empty earth" are meant to be jarring. Your tone should convey both distress and warning.

Your tempo and tone on phrases like "stretches out its roots," "leaves stay green," and "shows no distress" contrast with what went before because now you are speaking with the enthusiasm of flowing, surging life that "still bears fruit."

A reading from the Book of the Prophet Jeremiah

Thus says the **Lord**:
Cursed is the one who **trusts** in **human beings,**
 who **seeks** his **strength** in **flesh,**
 whose **heart** turns **away** from the **Lord.**
He is like a **barren bush** in the **desert**
 that **enjoys no change** of **season,**
but **stands** in a **lava** waste,
 a **salt** and **empty** earth.
Blessed is the one who **trusts** in the **Lord,**
 whose **hope** is the **Lord.**
He is like a **tree** planted beside the **waters**
 that stretches out its **roots** to the **stream:**
It fears not the **heat** when it comes;
 its **leaves** stay **green;**
in the year of **drought** it shows **no distress,**
 but **still** bears **fruit.**

READING I Adopting the language of the wise, Jeremiah sketches opposite postures in life: the senseless, who trust in the things of the passing world, and the wise, who trust in the Lord. True security is placing oneself in God's hands. The prophet finds his contemporaries, beginning with the king, behaving like senseless people, relying on the fragile, passing things rather than on the Word of the Lord as the source of life. The contrasting images are poignant: the person who trusts in things of the passing world are "like a barren bush in the desert that enjoys no change of season." The description reminds one of the destruction of Sodom and Gomorrah: a lava waste, "a salt and empty earth." On the other hand, the one who trusts in God "is like a tree planted beside the waters . . . it fears not the heat when it comes." Even in a year of drought, it bears fruit.

READING II Paul points to the center of our hope: the Resurrection of Christ, without which we are lost. We are the most pitiable of people if we place our trust in what has no saving value. Christ, by his Resurrection from the dead, is the first fruits of salvation. The rest of the harvest is to follow. But if we believe in Christ Jesus, whose Resurrection is the pledge of our hope, we are also healthy fruit for eternal life.

For meditation and context:

RESPONSORIAL PSALM   Psalm 1:1–2, 3, 4, 6 (40:5a)

R. Blessed are they who hope in the Lord.

Blessed the man who follows not
    the counsel of the wicked,
nor walks in the way of sinners,
    nor sits in the company of the insolent,
but delights in the law of the LORD
    and meditates on his law day and night.

He is like a tree
    planted near running water,
that yields its fruit in due season,
    and whose leaves never fade.
    Whatever he does, prospers.

Not so the wicked, not so;
    they are like chaff which the wind drives
    away.
For the LORD watches over the way of the
    just,
    but the way of the wicked vanishes.

READING II   1 Corinthians 15:12, 16–20

A reading from the first Letter of Saint Paul to the Corinthians

Brothers and sisters:
If **Christ** is preached as **raised** from the **dead**,
    how can **some** among you say there **is** no Resurrection
        of the dead?
If the dead are **not** raised, neither has **Christ** been raised,
    and if **Christ** has not been raised, your faith is **vain**;
    you are still in your **sins**.
Then those who have fallen **asleep** in Christ have **perished**.
If for **this** life **only** we have hoped in Christ,
    we are the most **pitiable** people of **all**.

But now Christ **has** been raised from the dead,
    the **firstfruits** of those who have fallen **asleep**.

Paul's is an urgent agenda. Don't let this sound unimportant.

"Vain" comes as a surprise after the triple use of "raised." Stress it, and then build in intensity to "you are still . . . ."

Paul is arguing his case. Do the same. The third "if . . . then" clause requires the most intensity. Don't waste the word "pitiable."

There is a shift in tone here. This is the good news that contrasts with earlier arguments.

GOSPEL   Jesus, standing on a level stretch, is within earshot of many disciples, including foreigners. He addresses all who suffer misfortune—poverty, hunger, sorrow, and persecution. The Reign of God transforms human reality, but it also implies a change of status for those who reject it: Jesus does not curse them, but laments their lot in life. The punchline of Jesus' discourse of the Beatitudes and the "bad-attitudes," like the image from Jeremiah, is either happiness or grief, spoken of in terms of blessed or cursed. No one is excluded from God's Reign, but the present world's standards are reversed: the formerly wretched, "you poor," become the privileged in God's Reign.

From his prayer on the mountain, Jesus descended and encountered the crowd. He "came down": his descent leads to the Beatitudes. The Incarnation of the Son of God is traced by his descent and entrance into communion with humanity, and finally by his descent to death, only to ascend in the Resurrection and Ascension. Jesus came down the mountain, and looking at his disciples he said, "Blessed are you who are poor," and then "Woe to you who are rich." Thus, Jesus affirms the need for us to descend and assess our own poverty, so that we might claim the inestimable wealth of God's Reign.

The first word, "Blessed," sets the tone. Who does not want to receive this beatitude? Jesus names the poor, the hungry, the weeping, and the mistreated—in a word, the miserable according to worldly standards—"blessed" and affirms that God's Reign belongs to them. His words clash with our instincts. He declares that, right there, in the place where misery

GOSPEL   Luke 6:17, 20–26

A reading from the holy Gospel according to Luke

Jesus came down with the **Twelve**
   and stood on a stretch of **level ground**
   with a **great** crowd of his **disciples**
   and a **large number** of the **people**
   from all **Judea** and **Jerusalem**
   and the coastal region of **Tyre** and **Sidon.**

And raising his **eyes** toward his **disciples** he said:
"**Blessed** are you who are **poor**,
   for the **kingdom** of **God** is **yours.**
Blessed are you who are now **hungry**,
   for you will be **satisfied.**
Blessed are you who are now **weeping**,
   for you will **laugh.**
Blessed are you when people **hate** you,
   and when they **exclude** and **insult** you,
   and **denounce** your name as **evil**
   on account of the **Son** of **Man.**
Rejoice and **leap** for **joy** on that **day!**
Behold, your **reward** will be **great** in **heaven.**
For their **ancestors** treated the **prophets** in the same **way.**
But **woe** to you who are **rich**,
   for you have **received** your **consolation.**
Woe to you who are **filled** now,
   for you will be **hungry.**
Woe to you who **laugh** now,
   for you will **grieve** and **weep.**
Woe to you when **all speak well** of you,
   for their **ancestors** treated the **false prophets** in this **way.**"

Margin notes:

Take time with these details, emphasizing how many came to hear Jesus.

Tyre = tīr

Sidon = SĪ-duhn

The repetition is intentional. Like a refrain, it draws us in and deepens our experience of what's shared. So stress each "blessed" and each "woe."
Remember that you are naming as "blessed" those the world sees as pitiable. Keep your tone hopeful and consoling.

Make eye contact here. Your energy and joy should peak on the first two lines.
The third is more sober.

Don't overdo the somber tone. Remember that these lines are directed at those who are already disciples.

Emphasize the word "false." Pause before announcing "The Gospel of the Lord."

---

accumulates, he will establish his Reign. On another occasion he teaches that the poor and insignificant are the sacrament of his presence. There is no other place that Jesus visits and privileges more than poverty in any of its forms. To welcome the stranger, feed the hungry, clothe the naked, is to put oneself in touch with Jesus: "Whatever they did to one of the least brothers of mine, you did for me" (Matthew 25:40).

How does God's Reign present itself in poverty? The encounter between Jesus and the world's helplessness becomes the sacrament of salvation; in other words, poverty is the place of the marvelous encounter between the rich, yet poor, God and sinful humanity. St. Paul explains it well: "For your sake he became poor although he was rich, so that by his poverty you might become rich" (2 Corinthians 8:9). God, rich in mercy, looked upon our helplessness and sent his Son to be born in our

flesh to walk side by side with us, poor among the poor. So great was divine love that God not only identified with poverty, but affirmed that the poor are the privileged citizens of God's Reign. If Jesus, the Son of the divine Rich-in-Mercy, became poor, then coming to grips with poverty and the poor is to touch God's Son. Doubly blessed, then, are the poor who allow Jesus to reach them and enter their lives. K.S.

SEVENTH SUNDAY
IN ORDINARY TIME

LECTIONARY #81

READING I   1 Samuel 26:2, 7–9, 12–13, 22–23

A reading from the first Book of Samuel

Ziph = zif

In those days, **Saul** went down to the desert of **Ziph**
   with three thousand picked men of **Israel**,
   to search for **David** in the desert of **Ziph**.

Abishai = AH-bi-shai

So **David** and **Abishai** went among **Saul's soldiers** by night
   and found **Saul** lying asleep within the barricade,
   with his **spear** thrust into the **ground** at his head
   and **Abner** and his men sleeping around him.

Speak softly (but not so softly that you cannot be heard), as in a conspiratorial tone.

Abishai whispered to **David**:
   "God has delivered your **enemy** into your **grasp** this day.
Let me **nail** him to the ground with one **thrust** of the **spear**;
   I will **not need** a second thrust!"

Speak David's words more forcefully.

But David said to Abishai, "Do not harm him,
   for who can lay hands on the Lord's **anointed**
      and remain **unpunished**?"
So **David** took the **spear** and the **water jug** from their place
      at Saul's head,
   and they got away **without** anyone's **seeing** or **knowing**
      or **awakening**.
All remained **asleep**,
   because the Lord had put them into a **deep slumber**.

Pause before proceeding.

Going across to an opposite slope,
   David stood on a remote **hilltop**
   at a **great distance** from **Abner**, son of **Ner**, and the **troops**.
He said: "Here is the king's **spear**.

READING I In today's Gospel we hear Jesus' invitation: "Be merciful, just as your Father is merciful." An example of such compassion is David. King Saul, consumed by jealousy of David's rising popularity, has driven the youth from court and pursues him in the Judean desert. Given the opportunity, David refuses to take revenge against his persecutor. One night he and Abishai enter unimpeded into the king's camp and find Saul and Abner, his military general, asleep and unguarded. Abishai proposes to kill Saul. David stops him and instead steals the insignia of his

royal person to prove that he had the opportunity to eliminate Saul but declined. David was compassionate toward an unjust persecutor, submitting to God, "Merciful and gracious . . . , slow to anger and abounding in kindness" (Psalm 103:8). He did not deal with his enemy according to the unjust attack against himself. However, David adds: "The Lord will reward every person according to the terms of righteousness and faithfulness," words that foreshadow how David will succeed Saul. Here the book of Samuel anticipates Jesus' teaching on forgiveness, but it does not yet

appreciate the value of nonviolence and forgiveness of enemies. For the present, David's respect for the king puts the matter in God's hands.

READING II Paul writes that just as we resemble Adam, made from the earth, so also we resemble Christ, formed in his image. Like Adam, we are fashioned according to God's image, but we also inherit Adam's weakness. Through Baptism, however, we bear the imprint of Christ, share in his Resurrection, and receive from God the gift of his life-giving

Let an attendant come over to get it.
The LORD will reward each man for his **justice** and **faithfulness**.
Today, though the LORD **delivered** you into my **grasp**,
　　I would **not** harm the LORD's **anointed**."

For meditation and context:

RESPONSORIAL PSALM   Psalm 103:1–2, 3–4, 8, 10, 12–13 (8a)

R. The Lord is kind and merciful.

Bless the LORD, O my soul;
　　all my being, bless his holy name.
Bless the LORD, O my soul,
　　forget not all his benefits.

He pardons all your iniquities,
　　heals all your ills.
He redeems your life from destruction,
　　crowns you with kindness and
　　compassion.

Merciful and gracious is the LORD,
　　slow to anger, and abounding in kindness.
Not according to our sins does he deal with us,
　　nor does he requite us according to
　　our crimes.

As far as the east is from the west,
　　so far has he put our transgressions from us.
As a father has compassion on his children,
　　so the LORD has compassion on those who
　　fear him.

READING II   1 Corinthians 15:45–49

A reading from the first Letter of Saint Paul to the Corinthians

Brothers and **sisters**:
It is **written**, *The first man, **Adam**, became a **living being,***
　　the last **Adam a life-giving spirit**.
But the **spiritual** was not **first**;
　　rather the **natural** and **then** the **spiritual**.
The **first man** was from the **earth**, **earthly**;
　　the **second man**, from **heaven**.
As was the **earthly one**, so also are the **earthly**,
　　and as is the **heavenly one**, so also are **the heavenly**.
Just as we have borne the **image** of the **earthly one**,
　　we shall also bear the **image** of the **heavenly one**.

Speak slowly in order to make Paul's argument clear. Stress "spiritual."

This is a key line. Read clearly and slowly.

Speak solemnly and with assurance of what awaits us.

GOSPEL   Luke 6:27–38

Jesus said to his disciples:
"To you who **hear** I say, ≫

---

spirit. We sometimes excuse ourselves by claiming to be "only human." Jesus encourages us to realize our true, lasting human dignity: the image and likeness of God, who is forever merciful and gracious.

GOSPEL | In this Gospel passage, sometimes called the Discourse on the Plain, Jesus formulates the ethics of the Reign of God, emphasizing the forgiveness and love for one's enemies. Jesus wants his disciples to conduct ourselves according to the divine essence: "Be merciful, just as your Father is merciful."

The good news of salvation is the bestowal of grace, and Jesus' followers are agents of that free gift. That God is good to the deserving does not surprise us. That the Son of God would die for a righteous person is understandable. That our heavenly Father makes the sun rise on the worthy, who could object? But that God shows goodness and mercy to the rude, the mean, the swindler, the untrustworthy, and the wicked, that his Son would die for people while they are sinners, that God shines the same sun on the those who love him and

those who despise him, that is more than we can fathom.

According to secular criteria, God's governance is not just. Equity, equality, democracy, and leadership are measured by a different value system in God's Reign. Jesus tells how a wasteful son squandered his inheritance and how his responsible brother fulfilled all his duties, yet the indulgent father did not reward and punish each one as we might expect. On a certain occasion, an infamous sinner is forgiven and washes the feet of Jesus with her tears and wipes them with her hair, while Simon the

Pause before "love," then let the full force of this surprising statement come through strongly. Perhaps a bit of astonishment in your voice can convey your own reaction to Jesus' words.

love your **enemies**, do **good** to those who **hate** you,
bless those who **curse** you, **pray** for those who **mistreat** you.
To the person who **strikes** you on **one cheek**,
   offer the **other** one as **well**,
   and from the person who **takes** your cloak,
   do not **withhold** even your tunic.

Do not rush through these instructions, but give each its due emphasis.

Give to **everyone** who **asks** of you,
   and from the one who **takes** what is yours **do not demand**
     it back.
Do to **others** as **you** would have **them** do to **you**.
For if you **love** those who **love** you,
   what **credit** is that to you?

The "golden rule" is a traditional teaching found in many cultures. Pause before changing to a questioning tone.

Even **sinners love** those who **love** them.
And if you do **good** to those who do **good** to you,
   what **credit** is that to you?
Even **sinners** do the same.
If you **lend money** to those from whom you **expect** repayment,
   what **credit** is that to you?

This line is intentionally insulting.

Even **sinners** lend to **sinners**,
   and get back the **same** amount.
But rather, **love** your **enemies** and do **good** to them,
   and **lend** expecting nothing back;
   then your **reward** will be **great**

Again, speak with solemnity, urging your listeners to respond by doing more than what seems reasonable.

   and you will be **children** of the **Most High**,
   for he himself is kind to the **ungrateful** and the **wicked**.
Be **merciful**, just as your Father is **merciful**.

This is an important line. Pause before and after it, and proclaim it with both compassion and urging in your voice.

"**Stop judging** and you will **not** be **judged**.
Stop condemning and you will **not** be **condemned**.
Forgive and you will be **forgiven**.
Give and gifts will be **given** to you;

These words are a promise. Proclaim them as such.

   a good measure, packed together, shaken down,
     and overflowing,
   will be **poured** into your lap.

Express your astonishment at the greatness of God's love.

For the **measure** with which you **measure**
   will in return **be measured** out to you."

Pharisee, the host of the dinner where this happened, a man scrupulous in fulfilling his religious duties, runs the risk of not being pardoned. According to one parable, the people who were hired in the final hour receive the same daily wage as those who worked all day under the hot sun.

In the Gospel, details like these do not astonish us. We almost expect them. It does not surprise us that the last come in first, that the more ambitious will be the servant of all, that God prefers the sick, the lame, the migrant and the orphan to the so-called winners in society. Nor is it striking that God pities the repentant sinner.

What is striking is that Jesus expects his followers to do likewise. He reminds us that the standard of our action and attitude is none other than God himself. "Be merciful just as your Father is merciful." However, this high standard of the Christian life does not reduce the resentment that sometimes invades and eats away at our hearts. It seems an inexorable law of nature to feel offended in the face of what seems like injustice in our eyes. Yet the Gospel clarifies that we will be judged as we judge others: "Stop judging and you will not be judged. . . . For the measure with which you measure will in return be measured out to you." So, once and for all, let us leave resentment behind. May our hearts be the exact reflection of God's heart of mercy, as we respond with compassion, just as we have received compassion from our loving God. K.S.

EIGHTH SUNDAY IN ORDINARY TIME

LECTIONARY #84

READING I   Sirach 27:4–7

A reading from the Book of Sirach

> When a **sieve** is shaken, the **husks** appear;
> > so do one's **faults** when one **speaks**.
> As the test of what the potter **molds** is in the **furnace**,
> > so in **tribulation** is the test of the **just**.
> The **fruit** of a tree shows the **care** it has had;
> > so too does one's **speech** disclose the bent of one's **mind**.
> Praise **no** one before he **speaks**,
> > for it is **then** that people are **tested**.

RESPONSORIAL PSALM   Psalm 92:2–3, 13–14, 15–16 (see 2a)

R. Lord, it is good to give thanks to you.

It is good to give thanks to the LORD,
    to sing praise to your name, Most High,
to proclaim your kindness at dawn
    and your faithfulness throughout
        the night.

The just one shall flourish like the palm tree,
    like a cedar of Lebanon shall he grow.
They that are planted in the house of
        the LORD
    shall flourish in the courts of our God.

They shall bear fruit even in old age;
    vigorous and sturdy shall they be,
declaring how just is the LORD,
    my rock, in whom there is no wrong.

sieve = siv

Pause after the first line of each sentence, then lower your voice solemnly as you continue.

Slow down a bit for the last line.

For meditation and context:

READING I   Ben Sira proposes how to measure a person's character, which comes down to how the person talks. To listen carefully before judging is the proof of wisdom; the way a person talks reveals their interior life. Just as the fiery kiln is the proof of the clay pot and the fruit is the proof of the tree from which it is picked, so conversation is the proof of a person's character. This wisdom regarding testing the just and the wicked by their speech challenges us to reflect on how we talk, which is the evidence of our interior lives, our consciences, attitudes, intentions, and affections. Our speech reveals where we have allowed ourselves to be planted and take root. In today's Gospel Jesus will warn us against judging others and justifying ourselves. Jesus, too, projects the image of the fruit tree, analogous to a person's virtue. A good person produces goodness; evil produces evil. Ben Sira is realistic as he assesses how people talk.

READING II   1 Corinthians 15:54–58

A reading from the first Letter of Saint Paul to the Corinthians

Brothers and sisters:
When this which is **corruptible** clothes itself with **incorruptibility**
    and this which is **mortal** clothes itself with **immortality**,
    then the word that is **written** shall come **about**:
        Death is swallowed up in *victory*.
        Where, O *death*, is your *victory?*
        Where, O *death*, is your *sting?*
The **sting** of death is **sin**,
    and the **power** of sin is the **law**.
But **thanks** be to God who gives us the **victory**
    through our **Lord** Jesus **Christ**.

Therefore, my beloved brothers and sisters,
    be **firm**, **steadfast**, always fully **devoted** to the **work** of the **Lord**,
    knowing that in the **Lord** your labor is not in **vain**.

Read slowly in order to make the point clear. Pause after each line.

Allow your voice to ring out as you proclaim Christ's victory over death.

Speak solemnly but briefly.

Again, raise your voice, this time with gratitude.

End on a quiet, encouraging note.

GOSPEL   Luke 6:39–45

A reading from the holy Gospel according to Luke

Jesus told his disciples a **parable**,
    "Can a **blind** person guide a **blind** person?
Will not **both** fall into a **pit**?
No **disciple** is superior to the **teacher**;
    but when fully **trained**,
    every disciple will be **like** his **teacher**.
Why do you notice the **splinter** in your **brother's** eye,
    but do not perceive the wooden **beam** in your **own**?

Pause before moving on to the next example. Although the guide and the teacher clearly refer to the same type
of person, the images are distinct.

Pause again before continuing, then speak with incredulity and perhaps some indignation.

This is a strong condemnation. Do not try to soften it.

READING II | Paul also reflects on the harvest of our sinful nature or of our virtue. Those who are embedded in a life of sin and corruption are destined for death. For those who are "steadfast and persevering," death wins no definitive victory; the harvest is eternal life. The good people, who are "fully engaged in the work of the Lord," know their toil is not in vain. They shall bear fruit for eternal life.

GOSPEL | Jesus speaks in parables. He warns those who are in a position to guide others to take care to correct themselves, lest they be ridiculed; then he relates the parable of the decayed and good fruit: "every tree is known by its own fruit." The secrets of the heart are revealed by the words of the mouth. The first reading recalls the same adage about the tree known by its fruit: the way a person speaks reflects what is in the heart. Jesus often returns to the teaching about wisdom: at the core of all religion and relationship, below the surface veneer, the heart, the conscience, and the attitude is the font of good or bad things, and only God knows its secrets.

But it is often easier for us to look outward rather than inward. The faults we most staunchly denounce are often those committed by others; the defects we recognize with more accuracy are those of our neighbor. Our most thorough and sincere examinations of conscience are often those

Observe a lengthy pause before continuing in a bit softer tone.

How can you **say** to your **brother**,
　'Brother, let me remove that **splinter** in your **eye**,'
　when you do not even **notice** the wooden **beam** in your
　　own eye?
You **hypocrite**! **Remove** the wooden beam from **your** eye first;
　then you will see **clearly**
　to remove the **splinter** in your **brother's** eye.
A **good** tree does not bear **rotten** fruit,
　nor does a **rotten** tree bear **good** fruit.
For **every** tree is known by its **own** fruit.
For people do not pick **figs** from **thornbushes**,
　nor do they gather **grapes** from **brambles**.
A **good** person out of the store of **goodness** in his **heart**
　　produces **good**,
　but an **evil** person out of a store of **evil** produces **evil**;
　for from the fullness of the **heart** the **mouth** speaks."

Speak encouragingly the words about the good person.

that examine the consciences of others. The temptations we face fearlessly, without yielding at all, are those that threaten the soul of our neighbors. Jesus commented, "Why do you notice the splinter in your brother's eye?" What plank in my eye? I see perfectly well!

Let us learn from the speck in the neighbor's eye, or the flaw in his or her conduct: it is time to get our own eyes checked, to remove the film of distrust, and correct any shortsighted suspicion. Jesus says, "You hypocrite! Remove the wooden beam from your eye first," and then with your own conscience clear, you can offer correction to your neighbor. In the end, he says: "No disciple is superior to the teacher." We have an excellent guide in Jesus, who instructs us with confidence. How and where does he guide? And with what precaution? With mercy, toward understanding and compassion, leading us to forgive ourselves as well as our neighbor. Jesus speaks of mercy, the key to cre-ating a better world inside and out. The excellent teacher tells us that "from the fullness of the heart the mouth speaks."
K.S.

ASH WEDNESDAY

LECTIONARY #219

READING I   Joel 2:12–18

A reading from the Book of the Prophet Joel

Even **now**, says the LORD,
    return to me with your **whole heart**,
    with **fasting**, and **weeping**, and **mourning**;
Rend your hearts, not your **garments**,
    and **return** to the LORD, your God.
For **gracious** and **merciful** is he,
    slow to anger, **rich** in kindness,
    and **relenting** in **punishment**.
Perhaps he will **again** relent
    and leave behind him a **blessing**,
Offerings and **libations**
    for the LORD, your God.

Blow the **trumpet** in Zion!
    proclaim a **fast**,
    call an **assembly**;
Gather the people,
    notify the congregation;
Assemble the elders,
    gather the **children**
    and the **infants** at the **breast**;
Let the bridegroom **quit** his room
    and the bride her **chamber**.

This text consists of three sections that differ in mood. In this first section, the prophet passionately urges the people to abandon sin and return to God.

In the first lines we hear God's own voice urging remorse and conversion.

"Rend your hearts . . . " asks that they convert inwardly, not simply make an outward show.

Any possible threat is balanced with images of God's patience and mercy.

Your optimistic tone should suggest the possibility of God "relenting" and abandoning threats of punishment.

Here begins section two—it is a rousing call to every member of the community to ask forgiveness!

The tempo and energy are swelling as you give one command after another.

Neither children, nor infants, nor honeymooners are exempt from this call to repentance.

READING I   A calamity that had fallen on the land of Judah gave the prophet cause to call the people to conversion, for which external rites and customs are not enough. Conversion means turning to God with the whole self—conscience, intention, speech, and conduct. The conversion of heart does not focus on external practices or habits, but it puts our ways of thinking and acting in harmony with transcendent values. "Return to me with all your heart," implies a revision of our way of thinking and judging, attention to attitudes and behavior, both per-

sonal and collective, in family and Church, social and political life. Joel urges the people faced with a crisis to an interior renewal: "Rend your hearts, not your garments," "return to the Lord, your God," which is to be accompanied by penance —fasting, weeping, and mourning. While both internal and external aspects are necessary, the prophet insists on the urgency of the interior change over the exterior gestures. The Lord's attributes, "gracious and merciful is he, slow to anger, rich in kindness," confirm the divine willingness to act always in the people's favor. God's mercy is

not a trade-off or a requirement, but a gift freely offered. A person of deep faith and hope, Joel is not just content to console his audience; he awakens our conscience, inviting us to face the future and open ourselves to hope.

READING II   Paul stresses the necessity of reconciliation with God, and the time is now. Christ is the mediator of this reconciliation in his sacrifice of atonement for sins The word *reconciliation*, in biblical language, also can be expressed as "atonement," which describes the action

Even the priests should be moved to tears.

You are telling the people what to say, not actually saying it, so don't overdramatize this line.

The people ask God not to make them a laughingstock among the nations.

The final lines comprise the third section, which is God's response to the people's repentance. Read slowly and imagine God quietly surveying the assembled masses bowed in humble contrition.

For meditation and context:

Between the **porch** and the **altar**
    let the **priests**, the **ministers** of the Lord, **weep**,
And say, "**Spare**, O Lord, your people,
    and make not your **heritage** a **reproach**,
    with the nations **ruling** over them!
Why should they say among the peoples,
    '**Where** is their God?' "

Then the Lord was stirred to **concern** for his land
    and took **pity** on his people.

RESPONSORIAL PSALM   Psalm 51:3–4, 5–6ab, 12–13, 14 and 17 (3a)

R. Be merciful, O Lord, for we have sinned.

Have mercy on me, O God, in your goodness;
    in the greatness of your compassion wipe
        out my offense.
Thoroughly wash me from my guilt
    and of my sin cleanse me.

For I acknowledge my offense,
    and my sin is before me always:
"Against you only have I sinned,
    and done what is evil in your sight."

A clean heart create for me, O God,
    and a steadfast spirit renew within me.
Cast me not out from your presence,
    and your Holy Spirit take not from me.

Give me back the joy of your salvation,
    and a willing spirit sustain in me.
O Lord, open my lips,
    and my mouth shall proclaim your praise.

Corinthians = kohr-IN-thee-uhnz

Like Joel, Paul makes a passionate plea to get our attention and produce a response.
Through our words and our lives, we are to call others to reconciliation with God.

Christ not only became like the rest of sinful humanity, he assumed all human sin upon himself.
Worse than never knowing Christ is knowing him in vain; that is, seeing the light and then turning from it.

READING II   2 Corinthians 5:20—6:2

A reading from the second Letter of Saint Paul to the Corinthians

Brothers and sisters:
We are **ambassadors** for **Christ**,
    as if **God** were **appealing** through us.
We **implore** you on behalf of Christ,
    be **reconciled** to God.
For **our** sake he made him to **be** sin who did not **know** sin,
    so that we might become the **righteousness** of God in him.

Working **together**, then,
    we **appeal** to you not to receive the grace of God in **vain**. »

of "making one," as we can see by dissecting the word into syllables, at-one-ment. In this section of his letter, Paul writes about reconciliation, a concept rarely used in the New Testament, yet it sinks its roots in the Old Testament. Reconciling has to do with friendship with God and with one's neighbor. The apostolic ministry promotes reconciliation, which is not just a matter of repairing fractured relationships from the past, but of becoming God's ambassadors of peace for the present and future. This reading gives a warning at the beginning of the Lenten journey, and it is urgent. Now is

the right time to be reconciled with God. Now is the right time to apply the confession and petition of Psalm 51, today's Responsorial Psalm, to our own lives ("Against you only have I sinned, / and done what is evil in your sight. . . . A clean heart create for me, O God, and a steadfast spirit renew within me"). We are not alone; the Holy Spirit breathes grace and graciousness to us. The time is right to confess our guilt, to be created anew, and to become ministers of reconciliation.

GOSPEL   Jesus' words remind us that the cosmetic cover of vanity, which encourages ostentation and hypocrisy, deprives justice of its selflessness and purity of intention rooted in God. The person who does honorable things only to be seen by others becomes a comic figure of justice, playing the role of generous, pious, and self-giving on the stage of vanity. Such an actor does not seek justice, only a very poor replica of the divine self. The proof Jesus offers his disciples regarding the practices of penance and conversion is

For he says:

> In an **acceptable** time I **heard** you,
>   and on the day of **salvation** I **helped** you.

Behold, **now** is a very **acceptable** time;
    behold, **now** is the **day** of **salvation**.

This is Lent's main message: now—today—is the time to respond, before it's too late!

GOSPEL   Matthew 6:1–6, 16–18

A reading from the holy Gospel according to Matthew

Jesus said to his **disciples**:
    "Take care not to perform righteous deeds
    in order that people may **see** them;
        otherwise, you will have no **recompense** from your heavenly
            Father.
When you give **alms**,
    do not blow a **trumpet** before you,
        as the **hypocrites** do in the **synagogues** and in the **streets**
    to win the praise of **others**.
Amen, I say to you,
    they have **received** their reward.
But when **you** give alms,
    do not let your **left** hand know what your **right** is doing,
        so that your almsgiving may be **secret**.
And your **Father** who sees in secret will **repay** you.

The contrast throughout is between the "hypocrites" and "you." When a discipline is introduced (giving alms, praying, fasting) stress the verb, but on the second mention of the discipline, stress the pronoun "you." Our good deeds are to be for the glory of God, not for our own glorification.

Don't over-articulate these instructions as if they were complicated directives. It's a simple message spoken in common sense tones.

There is a dismissive tone in these judgments pronounced by Jesus.

You will repeat this line twice more; employ the same inflection each time.

---

that they be visible only to God, and not done to gratify the self or entertain others.

According to myth, the phoenix bird raises a funeral pyre in her own nest, intones her enchanting song, and is immolated as she bursts into flame and is reduced to ashes. But every time she dies, she rises again from the ashes. What about us during this season of Lent? What thoughts, feelings, and behaviors might be reduced to ashes? What do we need to change in attitude and conduct so that true and lasting happiness can rise from the ashes? Repent! May we be changed from

the inside out, so God's grace may penetrate our lives.

If the prophet Joel lived at the present time, how might he warn us? Change the direction of our lives and return to God, our first love; fast from selfishness and ill temperament. As for alms, create a space where sister, brother, and neighbor can live with dignity. And prayer? Be consistent in our single-hearted friendship with our loving God. The prophet defines what is worth more than anything else in our life: Turn to the Lord with penitential practices that really have weight, that are born in the inte-

rior life and register their effect in our conduct, and bring us closer—reconcile us—to God and one another. That is the aim of our fasting, almsgiving, and prayer.

If you are going on a trip, you cannot take everything along with you. You have to choose from what you have and pack your luggage with care. We reduce our baggage to the essentials, packing according to the place and climate we are travelling to. When embarking on a journey, one must fast, deprive oneself of some things that we are used to having with us. Secondly, when you are going on a trip, you think

This is less mockery of their puffed-up arrogance and more a deep sense of regret over their self-deception.

Jesus' tone is rather ominous.

Even fasting must be done in joy if we understand rightly why and for whom we're doing it.

Again, regret over their blindness.

Speak with an energetic, upbeat tone.

Go slowly on this final iteration; your punctuated stress should signal that this line culminates the reading.

"When **you** pray,
do not be like the **hypocrites**,
who love to stand and pray in the **synagogues** and on **street**
corners
so that others may **see** them.
Amen, I say to you,
they have **received** their reward.
But when **you** pray, go to your **inner** room,
close the door, and pray to your Father in **secret**.
And your Father who **sees** in secret will **repay** you.

"When **you** fast,
do not look **gloomy** like the **hypocrites**.
They **neglect** their appearance,
so that they may **appear** to others to be **fasting**.
Amen, I say to you, they have **received** their reward.
But when **you** fast,
anoint your head and **wash** your face,
so that you may not **appear** to be fasting,
except to your **Father** who is **hidden**.
And your Father who **sees** what is hidden will **repay** you."

ahead, anticipate some possible need or unexpected event; just in case, you take some medication or something else that would be difficult to acquire along the way, or maybe a gift for the friend who is going to pick you up. When embarking on a journey, there is an aspect of almsgiving, charity. Thirdly, before embarking on the trip, it is necessary to communicate and arrange the arrival in advance, reserve a place in a hotel. When preparing for a trip, there is an aspect of prayer, which is like making contact with the persons on the other end of the trip, to alert them to your arrival.

This is an analogy of the journey we undertake today as we travel toward the Paschal Mystery, toward the Resurrection and new life. As prepare the gifts for the Eucharist today we pray: "We entreat you, O Lord, / that, through works of penance and charity, / we may turn away from harmful pleasures / and, cleansed from our sins, may become worthy / to celebrate devoutly the Passion of your Son." K.S.

FIRST SUNDAY
OF LENT

LECTIONARY #24

READING I   Deuteronomy 26:4–10

Deuteronomy = doo-ter-AH-nuh-mee; dyoo-ter-AH-nuh-mee

A reading from the Book of Deuteronomy

Moses spoke to the **people**, saying:
 "The **priest** shall **receive** the **basket** from **you**
 and shall set it in front of the **altar** of the Lord, your **God**.
Then you shall **declare** before the Lord, your **God**,
 'My **father** was a **wandering Aramean**
 who went down to **Egypt** with a **small household**
 and **lived** there as an **alien**.
But **there** he became **a nation**
 great, **strong**, and **numerous**.
When the **Egyptians maltreated** and **oppressed** us,
 imposing **hard labor upon** us,
 we **cried** to the **Lord**, the **God** of our **fathers**,
 and he **heard** our **cry**
 and **saw** our **affliction**, our **toil**, and our **oppression**.
He brought us **out** of **Egypt**
 with his **strong hand** and **outstretched arm**,
 with **terrifying power**, with **signs** and **wonders**;
 and **bringing** us into **this country**,
 he gave us **this land flowing** with **milk** and **honey**.

Name Moses with the tone of dignity and respect his memory should evoke.

This procedural detail is followed by a dignified and lofty recitation of a very sacred history.
A shift in tone should signal the quote within a quote.
Aramean = ayr-uh-MEE-uhn

Recalling the enslavement in Egypt requires a different tone.

Let gratitude fill your voice as you describe God's mercy.

Part of what's remembered is God's awesome power and dignity.

"Milk and honey" does not imply a lack of hardship.

READING I | Each year, during the Feast of Weeks (Pentecost), the Israelite farmer was to offer God the first-fruits of the harvest in thanksgiving for the gift of the land. On this occasion, he pronounced a liturgical formula, the creed that began, "My father was a wandering Aramean . . . " This formula, found in the first reading, expresses three articles of the Hebrew faith: the vocation of the patriarchs, the freedom from Egyptian slavery, and the gift of the land flowing with milk and honey. This creedal statement highlights the historical dimension of the Hebrew and Christian faith. God is not the result of a private revelation or an abstract ideology, but a real presence, incarnate in the complicated and often fragile plot of human experience. God's existence and continual presence is revealed in the people's history. In her liturgy, Israel recites this creed, the fundamental core of her faith.

Deuteronomy portrays the people at a critical time, the exodus and journey through the wilderness, when God delivered them from Egypt and fed them in the desert. Even now God continues to accompany and protect us along the way ("for to his angels he has given command about you, / that they guard you in all your ways," Psalm 91:11, the Responsorial Psalm). Deuteronomy describes the ritual for offering the firstfruits of the harvest and the recital of God's saving deeds. The words and actions testify that our provident God cares about the people's suffering and devises new ways of setting us free and fostering a more human and congenial life. Deuteronomy promotes unceasing trust that God will continue to protect and provide for the people. Coming to know God creates in the individual, and in the believ-

"'Therefore, I have now brought . . .'" should communicate deep gratitude for God's mercy. The quote within a quote ends here.

This is both a liturgical instruction and a call to humble worship.

Therefore, I have now brought you **the firstfruits**
   of the **products** of the **soil**
   which **you**, O Lord, have **given** me.'
And having **set** them before the Lord, your **God**,
   you shall **bow down** in his **presence**."

For meditation and context:

RESPONSORIAL PSALM   Psalm 91:1–2, 10–11, 12–13, 14–15 (see 15b)

R. Be with me, Lord, when I am in trouble.

You who dwell in the shelter of the
   Most High,
   who abide in the shadow of the Almighty,
say to the Lord, "My refuge and fortress,
   my God in whom I trust."

No evil shall befall you,
   nor affliction come near your tent,
for to his angels he has given command
   about you,
   that they guard you in all your ways.

Upon their hands they shall bear you up,
   lest you dash your foot against a stone.
You shall tread upon the asp and the viper;
   you shall trample down the lion and
   the dragon.

Because he clings to me, I will deliver him;
   I will set him on high because he
   acknowledges my name.
He shall call upon me, and I will
   answer him;
   I will be with him in distress;
I will deliver him and glorify him.

READING II   Romans 10:8–13

A reading from the Letter of Saint Paul to the Romans

Brothers and **sisters**:
What does **Scripture** say?
The **word** *is* **near** *you,*
   in your **mouth** *and in your* **heart**
   —**that** is, the **word of faith** that we **preach**—,
for, if you **confess** with your **mouth** that **Jesus** is **Lord**
   and **believe** in your **heart** that **God raised** him from the **dead**,
you **will** be **saved**. ❯❯

Begin with energy and ask the question with an upbeat tone.

Here is the answer to Paul's own question. Announce it with joy.

Slow down to enunciate Paul's careful reasoning.

ing community, two important attitudes: gratitude and adoration, which are manifest in our communal life.

 The second reading puts us in direct relation to Easter. It announces the center of the Church's faith, that is, the decisive historical event of Christ's Resurrection. This brief profession of faith expresses two aspects of the Easter message. The first proclaims that "Jesus is Lord," the result of the glorification of Jesus in the Paschal Mystery. The second phrase formulates the Paschal

Mystery in terms of the Resurrection: "God raised him from the dead." This faith, open to all, is to be professed with the lips and believed in the heart, so that it bears witness in action.

The message from Romans puts us in the position of the believers in Deuteronomy. We are called upon to bear witness to God's saving deed of raising Christ and to rejoice in our confidence that God will save us along with him. We find ourselves in the middle between Christ's final victory and our own struggle with evil, but we trust in God's power to save us. The

joyful confidence of the psalm revives our spirits: "Everyone who calls on the name of the Lord will be saved" (Romans 10:13; see Psalm 91:14).

GOSPEL   After his baptism, Jesus, "filled with the Holy Spirit," was "led by the Spirit" into the desert of temptation. Thus the evangelist describes two currents in Jesus' life. In his baptism, the Holy Spirit descended upon him, and he heard the Father's voice naming him his beloved Son. Now that same Spirit leads him to the desert to be tempted by the

Be sure to contrast "believes" / "confesses" and "mouth" / "heart."

> For one **believes** with the **heart** and so is **justified**,
>   and one **confesses** with the **mouth** and so is **saved**.
> For the **Scripture** says,

Declare this scriptural truth with conviction.

>   *No* one who **believes in him** *will be put to* **shame**.
> For there is **no distinction** between **Jew** and **Greek**;
>   the **same Lord** is **Lord** of **all**,

The generosity of God is emphasized in these closing lines. That Christ's salvation is available to all is a revolutionary declaration. Proclaim it persuasively.

>   enriching **all** who **call upon** him.
> For "**everyone** who **calls** on the name of the **Lord will be saved**."

GOSPEL   Luke 4:1–13

A reading from the holy Gospel according to Luke

Let the *end* of the opening sentence suggest your tone; the seriousness of what's to unfold should be heard from the start.

> **Filled** with the **Holy Spirit**, **Jesus returned** from the **Jordan**
>   and was **led** by the **Spirit** into the **desert** for **forty days**,
>   to be **tempted** by the **devil**.

Without overdoing it, keep in mind the physical state of Jesus and the barren desert context.
Avoid a stereotypical devil who drips with malice. Instead, make him reasonable, intelligent, and persuasive.

> He ate **nothing** during those days,
>   and when they were **over** he was **hungry**.
> The **devil said** to him,
> "**If** you are the **Son** of **God**,
>   **command** this **stone** to become **bread**."

Don't rush any of Jesus' replies. Suggest, instead, his effort to come to his conclusions.

> **Jesus answered** him,
> "It is **written**, *One does* **not live** *on* **bread alone**."
> Then he took him up and **showed** him
>   **all** the **kingdoms** of the **world** in a **single instant**.

Don't fail to convey the settings to which the devil transports Jesus.

> The **devil said** to him,
> "I shall **give** to you **all** this **power** and **glory**;
>   for it has been **handed over to** me,
>   and **I** may give it to **whomever** I **wish**.
> **All this** will be **yours**, **if** you **worship** me."

Pause after the devil's dialogue before giving Jesus' response.

> **Jesus** said to him in **reply**,
> "It is **written**:
>   *You shall* **worship** *the* **Lord**, *your* **God**,
>   *and* **him alone** *shall you* **serve**."

---

devil. Recall Israel's temptations in the desert, when God's chosen people, bound for the Promised Land, were tempted to turn away from their friendship with God. Temptation has a deep root in our history, in a garden, when Eve and Adam failed the primordial test and short-circuited their first and best friendship.

The devil, tempting the Son of God, introduces something new into the history of temptation. Not that this present temptation was subtler or gentler, or that Jesus was less shaken by the test. Yes, he was hungry; he tasted the intoxicating thirst for

saving the world. As humans do, Jesus hungered for power; he feared having to face death alone. The extreme sensitivity of Jesus, Son of God and human, made him more susceptible to all temptation and the pain it causes. We, tempted, have some protection; our habitual falling into temptation forms a kind of callus in the soul that protects us from the brutality of sin and dulls the sour aftertaste. Jesus, innocent of sin, had no calluses. His experience reveals something new about temptation: his love. Jesus loves the Father, with a degree of love that neither Adam nor Eve nor anyone

else had achieved. He never betrayed his first love. (Temptation always offers an alternative to true love; it bargains with what is most precious in life.) The friendship Jesus enjoys with the Father strengthens him against all temptation. Think about it. More than any other human, the Son of Man was besieged by temptation, even to his last hour, when the devil tempted him in the person of the spectators mocking him with words that echoed the early temptations in his adult life, "If you are the Messiah, the King of the Jews, the elect, save thyself." Jesus suffered temptation to

The heart of this temptation is "*If* you are the Son of God . . . " He wants to sow doubt in Jesus' heart that would require a sign from God to dispel.

Is Jesus informing the devil or warning him?

The end is not the end, for the devil will seek another opportunity.

Then he led him to **Jerusalem**,
  made him **stand** on the **parapet** of the **temple**, and said to him,
"If you are the **Son** of **God**,
  throw yourself down from here, for it is **written**:
    *He will **command** his **angels** concerning you, to **guard** you,*
  and:
    *With their **hands** they will **support** you,*
    *lest you **dash** your **foot** against a **stone**."*
Jesus said to him in **reply**,
  "It **also** says,
    *You **shall not put** the **Lord**, your **God**, to the **test**."*
When the **devil** had finished **every temptation**,
  he **departed** from him **for a time**.

the point of death, and the ultimate triumph over temptation was his death for the love of the Father and our humanity, expressed in his last hour when he intoned the psalm: Father, "into your hands I commend my spirit" (Luke 23:46).

We, the family of Eve and Adam, and by Baptism, the newly formed family in Jesus, know that temptation has not ceased. It is present constantly, it crouches just around the corner to assault us, but we have a choice in its regard, as sons and daughters of Adam and Eve and members of the family of Jesus. In the Our Father, we

do not ask that all temptation be removed from our lives, but rather that we not fall into it. Dodging temptation, which is part of our lives, is not an option; rather we pray to respond with a firm no in its face. We pray to pass the test. The key to not failing and falling into temptation is love, which fortified Jesus throughout his life. In the hour of temptation, in the midst of anguish similar to that of Jesus, we learn to what degree the Father loves and welcomes us, as he welcomed his Son Jesus at his Passover. Temptation can be met with the same

words of Jesus dying on the cross: "Father, into your hands I commend my spirit." K.S.

SECOND SUNDAY
OF LENT

LECTIONARY #27

READING I   Genesis 15:5–12, 17–18

A reading from the Book of Genesis

The **Lord God** took **Abram outside** and said,
  "Look up at the **sky** and count the **stars**, if you can.
Just so," he added, "shall **your descendants** be."
Abram put his **faith** in the LORD,
  who **credited** it to him as an act of **righteousness**.

He then **said** to him,
  "I am the LORD who brought you from **Ur** of the **Chaldeans**
  to give you **this land** as a **possession**."
"O **Lord God**," he asked,
  "how am I to **know** that I shall **possess** it?"
He **answered** him,
  "Bring me a three-year-old **heifer**, a three-year-old **she-goat**,
  a three-year-old **ram**, a **turtledove**, and a young **pigeon**."
Abram brought him **all** these, **split** them in **two**,
  and placed **each half opposite** the **other**;
  but the **birds** he did **not** cut up.
Birds of prey **swooped** down on the carcasses,
  but Abram **stayed** with them.
As the **sun** was about to **set**, a **trance** fell upon Abram,
  and a **deep**, **terrifying darkness enveloped** him.

When the sun had **set** and it was **dark**,
  there **appeared** a **smoking fire pot** and a **flaming torch**,
  which **passed between** those pieces.

Genesis = JEN-uh-sis

Keep in mind that Abram has just whined to the Lord that he has no son to inherit his wealth. God is saying, "Look. THAT'S how many 'sons' you will have!"
Pause before announcing this significant line. God immediately crowns him with "righteousness."

Abram is being reminded that this is the same God who called him to leave his homeland. Don't make Abram sound demanding. In the intimacy of the relationship, it is alright to ask.

The specifics are less important than the elaborateness and seriousness of the ritual.

The "birds of prey" require a negative tone that suggests they are omens of threat.

The "fire pot" and "torch" contrast with the "terrifying darkness" of the scene.

READING I The first reading describes the covenant between God and Abram. God had already promised Abram that he would have descendants, an improbable promise to an elderly man and his equally elderly wife. God reassures Abram, whose faith in the face of the impossible is credited to him as righteousness. God now seals the covenant with a ritual in which animals are split and the covenanting parties commit themselves to fidelity by an oath. As the covenant part-ners pass between the split animals, each calls down on himself the same fate if he were to be unfaithful. At sunset, a terrifying darkness overwhelms Abram; then God appears in smoke and fire to pass between the carcasses. Thus the covenant is sealed; God is forever committed to be faithful to his people, even those yet to be born.

READING II Many are those who wish to dissuade Paul from faith in Christ crucified and focus him on the external practices of Jewish law, such as dietary practices and circumcision. To Paul, these are mere "earthly things," practices of little concern for one who is destined for eternal life. Paul exhorts us to raise our eyes of faith, to fortify our hope. We try to be responsible with regard to our citizenship in the present world and its values, which are conditioned by time and everyday concerns. At the same time, we are called to keep valid our passport to an eternal Kingdom, where God reigns. Paul

Speak the divine promise slowly, with dignity and authority.

It was on **that** occasion that the LORD made a **covenant**
    with **Abram**,
  saying: "To **your descendants** I **give** this **land**,
  from the **Wadi** of **Egypt** to the **Great River**, the **Euphrates**."

For meditation and context:

RESPONSORIAL PSALM   Psalm 27:1, 7–8, 8–9, 13–14 (1a)

R. The Lord is my light and my salvation.

The LORD is my light and my salvation;
  whom should I fear?
The LORD is my life's refuge;
  of whom should I be afraid?

Hear, O LORD, the sound of my call;
  have pity on me, and answer me.
Of you my heart speaks; you my glance seeks.

Your presence, O LORD, I seek.
  Hide not your face from me;
do not in anger repel your servant.
  You are my helper: cast me not off.

I believe that I shall see the bounty
  of the LORD
  in the land of the living.
Wait for the LORD with courage;
  be stouthearted, and wait for the LORD.

READING II   Philippians 3:17—4:1

Philippians = fih-LIP-ee-uhnz

A reading from the Letter of Saint Paul to the Philippians

This is an unusual opening declaration. Make sure it's heard, but put the stress on "imitators," not "me."

Join with **others** in being **imitators** of **me**, [brothers and sisters,]
  and **observe those** who thus **conduct** themselves
  according to the model you have in **us**.
For many, as I have **often told** you
  and **now** tell you even in **tears**,
  conduct themselves as **enemies** of the **cross** of **Christ**.
Their **end** is **destruction**.

"Enemies of the cross" are those who think belief in Christ is not enough and require adherence to the old Law.
He fears for the salvation of those who deny the efficacy of the cross and weeps for them.

Their **God** is their **stomach**;
  their **glory** is in their "**shame**."
Their **minds** are occupied with **earthly** things.
But [**our** citizenship is in **heaven**,
  and from **it** we **also** await a **savior**, the **Lord Jesus Christ**.

You need a shift in tone to contrast with what went before. You're saying: "*This* is who we are."
Let this sound like the Good News it is!

He will change our **lowly** body
  to **conform** with his **glorified** body
  by the **power** that enables him **also**
  to bring **all things** into **subjection** to **himself**. »

encourages his beloved Philippian community to keep firm in the Lord, who "will change our lowly body to conform with his glorified body." To do so, he invites the community to follow his example and embrace the cross with trust. Our citizenship is in God's Kingdom, and Christ glorified will save us, even from the death that has a hold on our present existence.

GOSPEL   In the transfiguration Jesus is bathed in light; his face is

radiant, his garments dazzling white. Elijah and Moses also shine in glory as Jesus converses with them about his "exodus that he was going to fulfill in Jerusalem." His "exodus" refers to the freedom from sin that Jesus will achieve for us through his cross and Resurrection. How do his companions, Peter, James, and John, react? While Jesus prayed, they had become drowsy with fatigue and the sun's heat. It is not the only time they will have trouble staying awake as Jesus in prays. Shortly before Jesus'

betrayal in the garden of olives, as he is overwhelmed by sadness, the apostles will fall asleep. Today, in the Transfiguration, Moses and Elijah attend Jesus; soon, in Gethsemane, an angel will attend him. These two moments embrace the ecstasy and agony of Jesus, and in both scenes the disciples are caught in the pendulum. At times the intensity of life with Jesus gets to be too much. The disciples had the best intentions to share these moments with him, but they only half understood their

Pause before this closing statement and look at your own assembly, then speak to them with the love Paul felt for the Philippians.

Therefore, my **brothers** and **sisters**,
   whom I **love** and **long for**, my **joy** and **crown**,
   in **this way stand firm** in the **Lord**.]

[Shorter: Philippians 3:20—4:1 (see brackets)]

GOSPEL   Luke 9:28b–36

A reading from the holy Gospel according to Luke

Since there are few words of narration, take extra time to suggest the special and sacred nature of this ascent.
Highlight the fact that Jesus is in the midst of prayer.
Let your tone suggest the significance of these giants of Israel's history.

Jesus took **Peter**, **John**, and **James**
   and went up the **mountain** to **pray**.
While he was **praying**, his **face changed** in **appearance**
   and his **clothing** became **dazzling white**.
And **behold**, **two men** were **conversing** with him, **Moses**
      and **Elijah**,
   who **appeared** in **glory** and spoke of his **exodus**
   that he was going to **accomplish** in **Jerusalem**.
Peter and his **companions** had been **overcome** by **sleep**,
   but becoming **fully awake**,
   they saw his **glory** and the **two men standing** with him.

Don't overdramatize, but let us hear the very special nature of this event.

As they were about to **part** from him, **Peter** said to **Jesus**,
   "**Master**, it is **good** that we are **here**;
   let us make **three tents**,
   one for **you**, one for **Moses**, and one for **Elijah**."

Peter is eager to extend this sacred, privileged moment.

But he did **not know** what he was **saying**.
While he was **still speaking**,
   a **cloud came** and **cast** a **shadow** over them,
   and they became **frightened** when they **entered** the **cloud**.

This is no ordinary "cloud." It signifies God's presence. See Exodus 24:16–18.

Only Jesus is left to embody both the Law and the Prophets.

Then from the cloud came a **voice** that said,
   "**This** is my **chosen Son**; listen to **him**."
After the **voice** had **spoken**, **Jesus** was found **alone**.

Let your slowed delivery and your tone suggest the powerful impact made on the disciples.

They fell **silent** and did not at that time
   tell **anyone** what they had **seen**.

---

teacher, and they flagged in their endurance. They said senseless things like, "Master, it is good that we are here." Perhaps they really mean, "Why continue on to the capital? Life is good on the mountain. With three tents, we might bask in present glory and prolong this pleasant retreat." Later, in Gethsemane, Jesus will address those well-intentioned three, once again overwhelmed: "Why are you sleeping? Wake up and pray that you may not be subjected to the trial."

Jesus prayed with few words and formulas. When he prays, his Father embraces him. His words are direct: "Remove this cup from me," and he ends: "Let not my will but yours be done," a simple prayer, placing himself at the Father's disposition. Prayer is a conscious opening up to the Father, who never stops loving us. When Jesus prayed, he let himself be carried away by true love. Do we expect anything different when we pray? But our experience is often different, when the prayer is diluted by distraction,

inner noise, drowsiness, and ambition. Let us be awake and attentive to the glory of Christ. K.S.

THIRD SUNDAY OF LENT

LECTIONARY #30

READING I   Exodus 3:1–8a, 13–15

A reading from the Book of Exodus

Moses was tending the flock of his **father**-in-law **Jethro**,
   the **priest** of **Midian**.
Leading the flock across the **desert**, he came to **Horeb**,
   the **mountain** of **God**.
There an **angel** of the Lord **appeared** to **Moses** in **fire**
   flaming out of a **bush**.
As he **looked on**, he was **surprised** to see that the **bush**,
   though on **fire**, was **not consumed**.
So **Moses** decided,
   "I must go **over** to **look** at this **remarkable sight**,
   and see why the **bush** is **not burned**."

When the Lord saw him **coming over** to **look** at it more **closely**,
   God **called** out to him from the **bush**, **"Moses! Moses!"**
He answered, **"Here** I am."
God said, **"Come no nearer**!
Remove the **sandals** from your **feet**,
   for the **place** where you **stand** is **holy ground**.
I am the **God** of your **fathers**," he continued,
   "the God of **Abraham**, the God of **Isaac**, the God of **Jacob**."
Moses hid his **face**, for he was **afraid** to **look** at God.
But the Lord said,
   "I have **witnessed** the **affliction** of **my people** in **Egypt** »

Exodus = EK-suh-duhs

Though the opening events are unremarkable, let your tone suggest something special is about to happen.
Jethro = JETH-roh
Midian = MID-ee-uhn
Horeb = HOHR-ebb

Communicate the bizarre nature of this sight.

He wants to solve this mystery.

The second "Moses" receives more emphasis.

God is making Moses aware of who has reached out to him.

Remember, God is reasserting his intimate relationship with the patriarchs. Speak of them tenderly.

No human could survive looking upon God.

These lines reveal the merciful compassion of God.

READING I God prepares Moses for the theophany, God's manifestation. He is to take off his shoes as a sign of respect for a sacred place. When Moses asks God's name, the unusual response expresses the living reality of the divine nature, "I AM"—essentially different from idols, which amount to nothing. This name indicates the nearness of the "God-with-us" and is an invitation to come closer, to know God truly, which takes time and effort. The revelation of the divine name brings Moses—who upon presenting himself before the burning bush, responded "Here I am"—into lasting friendship with God. Moses delves into the reality of the burning bush and discovers God's concern for his oppressed people: "I have witnessed the affliction of my people in Egypt. . . . I know well what they are suffering." God who sees commits himself to them: "I have come down to rescue them . . . and lead them out of that land into a good and spacious land." God directs Moses along the path to freedom that passes through detachment from oneself and requires trust in God and personal effort, as well as the ability to relate to one another with mutual respect, which is the basis of the Ten Commandments. God is patient, but expects change, as the attitude of the caretaker of the fig tree indicates, in today's Gospel. But first we must remove the sandals from our feet, and recognize that the place where we stand is holy.

and have **heard** their **cry** of **complaint**
  against their **slave drivers**,
so I **know well** what they are **suffering**.
Therefore I have come down to **rescue** them
  from the **hands** of the **Egyptians**
  and **lead** them **out** of **that** land into a **good** and **spacious** land,
  a land **flowing** with **milk** and **honey**."

Moses said to **God**, "But when I **go** to the **Israelites**
  and say to them, 'The **God** of your **fathers** has **sent** me to you,'
  if they **ask** me, '**What** is his **name?**' **what** am I to **tell** them?"
God replied, "**I am who am**."
Then he added, "**This** is what you shall tell the **Israelites**:
  I AM sent me to **you**."

God spoke **further** to **Moses**, "**Thus** shall you **say**
  to the **Israelites**:
The **LORD**, the **God** of your **fathers**,
  the God of **Abraham**, the God **of Isaac**, the God of **Jacob**,
  has **sent me** to **you**.

"**This** is my **name forever**;
  thus am I to be **remembered** through **all generations**."

"I have come down" is a biblical figure of speech that signals an extraordinary divine intervention.

This special knowledge will give Moses confidence to approach his kinsmen.

This is a turning point in the history of salvation. Don't rush the moment.

Speak with authority and dignity. First God is "Lord," then God is the one who was in relationship with Abraham, Isaac, and Jacob!

Look directly at your assembly and let your tone stress the divine relationship God is asserting.

For meditation and context:

TO KEEP IN MIND
Pray the text, using your favorite method of praying with Scripture.

RESPONSORIAL PSALM   Psalm 103:1–2, 3–4, 6–7, 8, 11 (8a)
R. The Lord is kind and merciful.

Bless the LORD, O my soul;
  and all my being, bless his holy name.
Bless the LORD, O my soul,
  and forget not all his benefits.

He pardons all your iniquities,
  heals all your ills.
He redeems your life from destruction,
  crowns you with kindness and
    compassion.

The LORD secures justice
  and the rights of all the oppressed.
He has made known his ways to Moses,
  and his deeds to the children of Israel.

Merciful and gracious is the LORD,
  slow to anger and abounding in kindness.
For as the heavens are high above the earth,
  so surpassing is his kindness toward
    those who fear him.

READING II   Paul describes to the Christians of Corinth how Israel's experience of the exodus prefigures their salvation in Christ. By evoking "our ancestors," he identifies the Church of Christ with the people of Israel; this is the basis of Paul's reinterpretation of the exodus. The former slaves—who by their "baptism" in the Red Sea became a new, free people, and who were nourished with the "spiritual food" of the manna and the "spiritual drink" of water from the rock—grumbled against the Lord and turned to fictitious gods to save them. For Paul this page of biblical history prefigures the Christian experience: "These things happened to them as an example, and they have been written down as a warning to us, upon whom the end of the ages has come" (v. 11). Like our ancestors, the Christian also traverses the desert, a place of temptation, which offers false deities more comfortable and made to our liking. The reference to the tragic fate of some faithless Israelites justifies the final appeal to the Christian community: "Whoever thinks he is standing secure should take care not to fall."

GOSPEL   Today, just as the people in the Gospel did, we ask ourselves about the calamities that happen in places near and far: Where was God among the losses? Earthquakes and hurricanes that leave thousands dead and hundreds of thousands without the basics to live, raise the question: Why now Syria or Haiti,

READING II   1 Corinthians 10:1–6, 10–12

A reading from the first Letter of Saint Paul to the Corinthians

I do **not** want you to be **unaware**, **brothers** and **sisters**,
    that our **ancestors** were **all under** the **cloud**
    and all **passed through** the **sea**,
    and **all** of them were **baptized** into **Moses**
    in the **cloud** and in the **sea**.
All **ate** the **same spiritual food**,
    and all **drank** the **same spiritual drink**,
    for they **drank** from a **spiritual rock** that **followed** them,
    and the **rock** was the **Christ**.
Yet God was **not pleased** with **most** of them,
    for they were **struck down** in the **desert**.

These things **happened** as **examples** for **us**,
    so that **we** might not **desire evil** things, as **they** did.
Do not **grumble** as some of **them** did,
    and **suffered death** by the **destroyer**.
These things **happened** to **them** as an **example**,
    and they have been **written down** as a **warning** to **us**,
    upon whom the **end** of the **ages** has **come**.
Therefore, whoever **thinks** he is **standing secure**
    should **take care** not to **fall**.

GOSPEL   Luke 13:1–9

A reading from the holy Gospel according to Luke

Some people told **Jesus** about the **Galileans**
    whose **blood Pilate** had mingled with the **blood**
    of their **sacrifices**. »

Margin notes (Reading II)

Corinthians = kohr-IN-thee-uhnz

The opening calls for clear eye-contact and strong delivery. During the Exodus, a cloud and a pillar of fire led the Israelites through the desert.

Your tone is upbeat, for these are all positive experiences.

"All passed through . . . all . . . were baptized . . . all ate . . . all drank . . . ": *stress* these repetitions.

Paul links the rock that produced water in the desert to Christ, the source of living water.

"Yet" is the fulcrum on which your tone takes a turn.

Paul is very deliberate in drawing out his analogy. Let your tone do the same.

The Israelites, to their peril, grumbled mightily in the desert!

Here "us" also includes your assembly!

This last sentence is a blunt statement of warning. Don't dilute it.

Margin notes (Gospel)

Jesus' point will be based on the details narrated in these opening lines. Share them simply but clearly.

Galileans = gal-ih-LEE-uhnz

---

already crushed for centuries by injustice and misery? Jesus, facing such questions, shifts the focus toward the audience: "If you do not repent, you will perish in the same way." We are not mice in a laboratory where God suspects and surprises sinners to punish them or rewards the good with nice things. Jesus is clear on this point: the victims of Pilate or the earthquake are no worse sinners than we are. Every person is admonished to change her or his way of thinking and respond to God's grace. Jesus pointed the finger when he warned, "If you do not repent, you will all perish like they did."

It is true that the loving Father of Jesus watches over us, but not to catch us in sin and penalize us. He cares for us like the gardener in the parable of the fig tree that seems only to take up space. Thanks to the insightful gardener, the barren tree is given one last chance. The gardener, who cultivates hope, knows his profession and is well aware that sometimes it takes several years for a tree to bear fruit. So he recommends a good dose of patience: "Sir, leave it for this year also, and I shall cultivate the ground around it and fertilize it; and it may bear fruit in the future. If not you can cut it down." As the gardener considers the tree and hopes for a change, so God watches each of us, looks into our heart, and awaits the change of attitude and conversion. To this end, he gives an extension, since conversion requires patience. What does Jesus mean by the parable? We enjoy the care of

Jesus' question is rhetorical; his tone makes a "no" response quite apparent.

The call for repentance is paramount.

Jesus uses a second illustration to reinforce his point.

Jerusalem = juh-ROO-suh-lem; juh-ROO-zuh-lem

The dialogue at the end of the second example is identical to that in the first. Don't waste it.
Pause and take a breath before launching into the parable.

The owner is both disappointed and angry.

Our sins affect more than just ourselves!

The gardener's call for mercy ends with a sober warning.

This final option should not sound vindictive.

Jesus said to them in reply,
   "Do you **think** that because these **Galileans suffered**
     in **this way**
   they were **greater sinners** than **all other** Galileans?
By no means!
But I **tell** you, if **you** do **not repent**,
   you will **all perish** as **they** did!
Or those **eighteen people** who were **killed**
   when the tower at **Siloam fell** on them—
   do you **think** they were **more guilty**
   than **everyone else** who lived in **Jerusalem?**
By no means!
But I **tell you**, if you do **not repent**,
   you will **all perish** as **they** did!"

And he told them this **parable**:
   "There once was a person who had a **fig tree** planted
     in his **orchard**,
   and when he **came** in search of **fruit** on it but found **none**,
   he said to the **gardener**,
   'For **three years** now **I have come** in search of **fruit**
     on this **fig tree**
   but have found **none**.
So **cut** it **down**.
Why should it **exhaust** the **soil?**'
He said to him in **reply**,
   '**Sir**, **leave** it for **this** year **also**,
   and I shall **cultivate** the ground around it and **fertilize** it;
   it **may** bear **fruit** in the **future**.
If not you can **cut** it **down**.'"

an excellent gardener who applies his hand to cultivate souls. He loosens the soil, applies the fertilizer of grace, prunes and encourages us to put into practice what is in our nature. These interventions, sometimes drastic, are proof of love; what may seem like injury to us is his work to heal us, so we may rejoice with him, who never abandons us, even in pain.

Where is God in the face of human misery today? It is healthy for us to ask such a question, and with our eyes on the crucifix, we ask, where was God on Good Friday? Thus we acknowledge that God is in the thick of it, in the wounds and pains of human life. Patient God, suffering on the cross, identifies with his loved one at all times, even to death, to raise us up to the fullness of life. The meaning of the Christian life is to walk the path of conversion, to encourage each other to seek and follow Jesus. We hope that no one strays, that no one will delay. The compassionate gardener, who begs that we not be cut down and trashed, is Jesus, who intercedes for us until the end of time: "Wait a little, while I will attend to you with greater care." For now, let us intercede for each other, as we join our efforts to those of the loving gardener, so nobody placed in our charge and in our environment is lost. K.S.

THIRD SUNDAY OF LENT, YEAR A

LECTIONARY #28

READING I   Exodus 17:3–7

A reading from the Book of Exodus

In those days, in their **thirst** for **water**,
  the people **grumbled** against Moses,
  saying, "**Why** did you ever make us **leave** Egypt?
Was it just to have us **die** here of **thirst**
  with our **children** and our **livestock**?"
So Moses **cried** out to the LORD,
  "What shall I **do** with this people?
A little **more** and they will **stone** me!"
The LORD **answered** Moses,
  "Go over there in front of the **people**,
  along with some of the **elders** of Israel,
  holding in your hand, as you go,
  the **staff** with which you struck the **river**.
I will be **standing** there in front of you on the rock in **Horeb**.
Strike the rock, and the **water** will flow from it
  for the people to **drink**."
This Moses **did**, in the presence of the **elders** of Israel.
The place was called **Massah** and **Meribah**,
  because the Israelites **quarreled** there
  and **tested** the LORD, saying,
  "Is the LORD in our **midst** or **not**?"

Start slowly. "Thirst for water" sets up the whole reading.

Like a frustrated parent, angry at first but then melting into a tone of loving reassurance.

"Staff . . . river" is a reference to the plague that changed the Nile river to blood. The staff that deprived Egypt of water will provide for Israel. The words, "in front of the people" convey the public nature of God's reassurance made "in the presence of the elders" who witness the saving miracle. Speak the words "This . . . did" in a tone that suggests the miracle occurred.

Massah = MAH-sah; Meribah = MAYR-ih-bah.

Massah means "the place of the test," and Meribah means "the place of the quarrelling." The question can be read with the anxiety of the people or with the narrator's regret at their apparent lack of faith.

READING I The episode of Massah (meaning "temptation" or "test") and Meribah (meaning "grumbling" or "protest") is emblematic. After the first stretch of the journey through the desert, a place of trial and purification, the people are exhausted and thirsty. What is their attitude? The verbs are significant: they *grumble* against Moses for having led them to freedom, they *quarrel* and *put the Lord to the test*. They mistrust God and doubt that Moses had been sent to save them; hence their skepticism: "Is the Lord in our midst or not?" Moses, at his wits' end —"What shall I do with this people? A little more and they will stone me!"—turns to God, who instructs him to respond to the people's need. Moses, as intercessor, invokes the help of God, who responds by ordering him to strike the rock with the same staff with which earlier he had struck the waters of the Nile. This demonstrates to the faithless people God's continued presence before and after their deliverance from slavery. Moses obeyed, and thus the episode ends. This event will be recalled as an example of how the lack of faith on the people's part redounds on Moses, who, in solidarity with the exodus generation, will die without entering the Promised Land. Thus he becomes a figure of Christ, who, sinless, bore the effects of the sin of humanity.

For meditation and context:

RESPONSORIAL PSALM   Psalm 95:1–2, 6–7, 8–9 (8)

R. If today you hear his voice, harden not your hearts.

Come, let us sing joyfully to the LORD;
　let us acclaim the Rock of our salvation.
Let us come into his presence with
　　thanksgiving;
　let us joyfully sing psalms to him.

Come, let us bow down in worship;
　let us kneel before the LORD who
　　made us.
For he is our God,
　and we are the people he shepherds, the
　　flock he guides.

Oh, that today you would hear his voice:
　"Harden not your hearts as at Meribah,
　　as in the day of Massah in the desert.
Where your fathers tempted me;
　they tested me though they had seen
　　my works."

READING II   Romans 5:1–2, 5–8

Don't read this like abstract theology, for the text announces hope, love, and joy!
Paul describes the workings of faith, hope, and love, moving effortlessly from one to the other: faith brings peace and access to grace; this leads to a hope which will not disappoint. Note: we don't "speak" of hope; instead, we "boast" of it!

A reading from the Letter of Saint Paul to the Romans

Brothers and sisters:
Since we have been **justified** by **faith**,
　we have **peace** with God through our Lord Jesus **Christ**,
　through whom we have gained **access** by faith
　to this **grace** in which we stand,
　and we boast in **hope** of the glory of **God**.

And hope does not **disappoint**,
　because the **love** of God has been poured out into our **hearts**
　through the Holy **Spirit** who has been **given** to us.
For **Christ**, while we were still **helpless**,
　died at the appointed time for the **ungodly**.
Indeed, only with **difficulty** does one die for a **just** person,
　though perhaps for a **good** person one might even find **courage**
　　to die.
But God **proves** his love for us
　in that while we were still **sinners** Christ **died** for us.

It would be unusual to willingly die for a righteous person, but more unusual is what God did—dying for us while we were still in sin! With joy and awe.

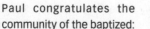 Paul congratulates the community of the baptized: "we have peace with God through our Lord Jesus Christ." He reflects on the experience of being saved in Christ Jesus. Once a believer has been justified, salvation follows. This is manifested by the peace that is undeniable and by the person's hope and confidence. This peace is characterized by the confidence that the baptized person has: that human life indeed has transcendent value, that they have responded to the

challenge of living, and that they participate now in the purpose of life. The second effect of salvation: "we boast in the hope of the glory of God." We are not disappointed in our hope "because the love of God has been poured out into our hearts through the Holy Spirit who has been given to us." The baptized look forward to that time when we experience this salvation—and not only us, but when all people are caught up in God's saving activity and so participate in God's glory. The believer realizes

that this saving activity is possible only because of the gratuitous action of Christ's life. There was nothing inherent in human beings that necessitated such an action. None of us dares boast of his or her own merit. While we were sinners Christ died for us: "For Christ, while we were still helpless, died at the appointed time for the ungodly" (Romans 5:6, 8). Just so is the tender care of the Creator who has poured love "into our hearts through the Holy Spirit

GOSPEL　John 4:5–42

A reading from the holy Gospel according to John

[**Jesus** came to a town of **Samaria** called **Sychar**,
　near the plot of land that **Jacob** had given to his son **Joseph**.
Jacob's **well** was there.
Jesus, **tired** from his journey, sat down there at the well.
It was about **noon**.

A **woman** of Samaria came to draw **water**.
Jesus **said** to her,
　"Give me a **drink**."
His **disciples** had gone into the **town** to buy **food**.
The **Samaritan** woman said to him,
　"How can **you**, a **Jew**, ask me, a **Samaritan woman**, for a **drink**?"
—For **Jews** use nothing in **common** with Samaritans.—
Jesus **answered** and said to her,
　"If you knew the **gift** of God
　and **who** is saying to you, 'Give me a drink,'
　you would have asked **him**
　and he would have given you **living** water."
The woman **said** to him,
　"**Sir**, you do not even have a **bucket** and the cistern is **deep**;
　where then can you **get** this living water?
Are you **greater** than our father Jacob,
　who **gave** us this cistern and drank from it himself
　with his **children** and his **flocks**?"
Jesus **answered** and said to her,
　"Everyone who drinks **this** water will be **thirsty** again;
　but whoever drinks the water **I** shall give will **never** thirst;
　the water I shall give will become in him
　a **spring** of water **welling** up to eternal **life**."
The **woman** said to him,
　"Sir, **give** me this water, so that I may not be **thirsty**
　or have to keep **coming** here to draw water."] ❯❯

Narrate as if you were one of the Samaritans who is converted at the end of the story. It's your own town that you're describing; the woman is your neighbor, and this incident changed your life.

Samaria = suh-MAYR-ee-uh; Sychar = SĪ-kahr.

Slower pacing helps suggest his tiredness.

She is stunned that he would ask her for a favor.

She bluntly challenges him and his boldness.

She's eager for this amazing water.

---

who has been given to us." How can we fail to trust?

 GOSPEL　It was a sultry Friday afternoon, and the air weighed heavy in festival Jerusalem, packed with pilgrims. During the holidays, many people, entering and leaving the city gate, passed in front of the spectacle on the little hill. Amid so much noise and hollering, only one voice is remembered. A criminal nailed to a cross spoke: "I'm thirsty." This cry echoed

what that same young man had said on another stifling afternoon in a different city, when he addressed a woman at a well, "Give me a drink." She also was thirsty for what every human desires: affection and love. Was this young intruder who crossed the barrier of good manners and addressed a lady alone at a well thirsty for the Samaritan woman? Yes, Jesus is thirsty for her, with a divine thirst that is implied in his request: "Give me a drink." Jesus was thirsty, for the salvation of that woman, who

ignored the true object of her thirst. So, now, Jesus' love for humanity as it is meant to be, stirred the thirst in her interior life.

Yes, God thirsts for her and craves her thirst. To satisfy the thirst of each one, his own and that of the Samaritan, Jesus has one remedy: to reveal her most basic thirst and not waste it on secondary desires, to join her thirst with that of Jesus, who is the font of Living Water. This lady had suffered tremendous thirst in an attempt to love and be loved: she confessed to having five

Is her tone wholly transformed, or is this a final brusque reply?

Jesus said to her,
   "**Go** call your **husband** and come **back**."
The woman **answered** and said to him,
   "I do not **have** a husband."

Jesus is blunt here, but not harsh.

Jesus answered her,
   "You are **right** in saying, 'I do not have a **husband**.'
For you have had **five** husbands,
   and the one you have **now** is not your **husband**.
What you have said is **true**."

His prescient knowledge impresses her, but she abruptly changes subjects.

Here, too, despite the teaching, maintain a conversational tone.

The woman said to him,
   ["Sir, I can see that you are a **prophet**.
Our **ancestors** worshiped on this **mountain**;
   but you people say that the place to worship is in **Jerusalem**."
Jesus said to her,
   "**Believe** me, woman, the hour is **coming**
   when you will **worship** the Father
   neither on this mountain **nor** in Jerusalem.
You people worship what you do not **understand**;
   we worship what we **understand**,
   because **salvation** is from the **Jews**.
But the hour is **coming**, and is now **here**,
   when **true** worshipers will worship the Father in **Spirit**
      and **truth**;
   and **indeed** the Father **seeks** such people to worship him.
God is **Spirit**, and those who **worship** him
   must worship in **Spirit** and **truth**."

She begins to sense who she's talking to.

The woman **said** to him,
   "I know that the **Messiah** is coming, the one called the **Christ**;
   when he **comes**, he will tell us **everything**."
Jesus said to her,

His self-identification is a gesture of love to the woman.

   "I am **he**, the one **speaking** with you."]

At that moment his disciples **returned**,
   and were **amazed** that he was talking with a **woman**,
   but still no one said, "What are you **looking** for?"
   or "Why are you **talking** with her?"

> **TO KEEP IN MIND**
> A narrative has characters, dialogue, a setting, and action. Help your listeners see the story unfold, keep characters distinct, and be clear about shifts in setting.

husbands and at least one additional man. Little by little, scorched by her own desires, she ends up still tortured by thirst, alone by the well of Sychar. Jesus' attitude toward her catches her attention. He does not wield the Decalogue of Moses; neither does he judge or condemn her. He cares not about the vicious chain of gossip that might have trailed her. He shows compassion, speaks to her in such a way that she discovers a thirst she had ignored up to this point in life. She has drunk much, but of water that does not quench the thirst. "If you knew the gift of God and who is saying to you, 'Give me a drink,' you would have asked him and he would have given you living water" (v. 10).

Physical thirst is inevitable, but it is a sign of a deeper desire incubated in the heart. Like the Samaritan woman, many of us ignore our deepest thirst until Jesus comes and awakens our true desire. Jesus is, at one and the same time, our thirst and our satisfaction. The person who drinks of the water he gives will no longer thirst. Experience teaches us that thirst and satisfaction are repeated throughout life, but the encounter with Jesus opens another horizon. He awakens our deepest desire; he reveals our thirst for true life, which is only satisfied in our friendship with Jesus, the savior of the world. The well where that water is drawn, where Jesus is sitting to minister to us, is not far away. It is inside us, in the depths of our being: "the water I shall give will become in [whoever drinks] a

The woman **left** her water jar
and went into the town and said to the people,
"**Come** see a man who told me **everything** I have done.
Could he possibly be the **Christ**?"
They went out of the town and **came** to him.
Meanwhile, the disciples **urged** him, "Rabbi, **eat**."
But he said to them,
"I have **food** to eat of which you do not **know**."
So the disciples **said** to one another,
"Could someone have **brought** him something to eat?"
Jesus said to them,
"My **food** is to do the will of the one who **sent** me
and to **finish** his work.
Do you not **say**, 'In four months the **harvest** will be here'?
I tell you, look up and see the fields **ripe** for the harvest.
The reaper is **already** receiving **payment**
and gathering crops for eternal **life**,
so that the **sower** and **reaper** can rejoice **together**.
For here the saying is verified that 'One **sows** and another **reaps**.'
I sent you to **reap** what you have not **worked** for;
others have done the work,
and **you** are sharing the **fruits** of their work."

[Many of the **Samaritans** of that town began to **believe** in him
because of the word of the **woman** who testified,
"He told me **everything** I have done."
When the Samaritans **came** to him,
they invited him to **stay** with them;
and he stayed there two **days**.
Many **more** began to believe in him because of his word,
and they **said** to the woman,
"We no longer believe because of **your** word;
for we have heard for **ourselves**,
and we **know** that this is **truly** the savior of the **world**."]

[Shorter: John 4:5–15, 19b–26, 39a, 40–42 (see brackets)]

The second act begins here. The return of disciples shatters the mood. They seem suspicious.

The woman undertakes her missionary journey. Speak the phrase "Could he possibly be . . . ?": with expectant joy.

They're prodding: "Rabbi, eat!" His response summarizes his ministry.

Note the ample harvest imagery.

This is the final act. Maintain high energy when speaking "the word of the woman."

They are urging him to remain with them.

There should be joy and gratitude in their comment to the woman who is responsible for their faith. Place special emphasis on the title given to Jesus.

---

spring of water welling up to eternal life" (v. 14). This means we will never be without thirst, but neither will we ever be short of water. Our desire and satisfaction are found in the source, in our own interior, Jesus' life within us. There, desire and refreshment coincide; they bear fruit in the love, peace, and joy in the Holy Spirit.

Along the strenuous road of life, we say with Jesus: "I thirst" and "Give me a drink." The human being, destined for the infinite, is tormented by the arid finitude all around, and we ache from insatiable desires. Thirsty, we are aware of the need for the living water that refreshes, vivifies us, and instills meaning in our days. Jesus, the divine pilgrim who travels the dusty roads of human life with us, shares our thirst and makes us aware that the thirst for unlimited love cannot be satisfied by any of the many drinks we are offered in the present life. Only Jesus pours into the heart the water that springs forth for eternal life, the Holy Spirit, the inexhaustible joy of God.

Even so, we find ourselves thirsty again. So Jesus meets us again under the midday sun, where he unmasks the false thirst that moves us every day to return to the well, carrying with us the heavy jars and pitchers that momentarily refresh us but do not quench the real thirst. The Lord comes to the well of our heart; to each one he will arrive on an unforgettable sultry afternoon, when our own journey will cross with his. There he always awaits us, at the sixth hour, hanging from the cross: "I am thirsty," I thirst for you, for your salvation, for your love. Let us rest in God's thirst for us, which wells up as a spring that gives eternal life. K.S.

FOURTH SUNDAY OF LENT

LECTIONARY #33

READING I   Joshua 5:9a, 10–12

A reading from the Book of Joshua

The LORD said to **Joshua**,
  "**Today** I have **removed** the **reproach** of **Egypt** from you."

While the **Israelites** were encamped at **Gilgal** on the plains
    of **Jericho**,
  they celebrated the **Passover**
  on the evening of the **fourteenth** of the **month**.
On the day **after** the **Passover**,
  they **ate** of the **produce** of the **land**
  in the form of **unleavened cakes** and **parched grain**.
On that **same day after** the **Passover**,
  on which they ate of the **produce** of the **land**, the **manna ceased**.
No **longer** was there **manna** for the **Israelites**,
  who **that** year ate of the yield of the land of **Canaan**.

Pause briefly after "Today." Removal of "reproach" is an announcement of joy.

Gilgal = GIL-gahl
Jericho = JAYR-ih-koh

Speak of the Passover with reverence.

Eating food they've grown is occasion for joy.

The cessation of manna signifies the end of an era, but it is not sad news.

With God's help, Israel will now fend for herself; speak with a mix of pride and gratitude.

Canaan = KAY-n*n

For meditation and context:

RESPONSORIAL PSALM   Psalm 34:2–3, 4–5, 6–7 (9a)

R. Taste and see the goodness of the Lord.

I will bless the LORD at all times;
  his praise shall be ever in my mouth.
Let my soul glory in the LORD;
  the lowly will hear me and be glad.

Glorify the LORD with me,
  let us together extol his name.
I sought the LORD, and he answered me
  and delivered me from all my fears.

Look to him that you may be radiant
    with joy,
  and your faces may not blush with shame.
When the poor one called out, the
    LORD heard,
  and from all his distress he saved him.

READING I The people are encamped at Gilgal, their first stop in the Promised Land, and their Passover celebration enlivens their hope for the future. It is the beginning of a new stage in Israel's history. Egypt and the desert hardships are things of the past. They crossed the Jordan and performed the rite of circumcision, which signifies the people's intimate commitment to the Lord. The provision of manna has ceased; from now on, they will feed on the fruits of the Promised Land, which the Lord has given. There is no need to fear the enemy; the Lord's words indicate a rupture with the past: "Today I have removed the reproach of Egypt from you." The reading highlights three things that are required: obedience to the law, the liturgy, and cultivation of the land for food.

READING II In today's passage from the Second Letter to the Corinthians we learn the extent of God's gift. God has reconciled us through Christ, who gave his own life to save us from sin, but it is up to us to accept that reconciliation and return to the house of the loving Father in our real, everyday lives. We have received the ministry of reconciliation. Paul's mandate is precise: "entrusting to us

READING II   2 Corinthians 5:17–21

Corinthians = kohr-IN-thee-uhnz

Use the greeting to win everyone's attention; then announce the joyous good news that follows.
You will need to believe this about yourself to proclaim with conviction.
Take time with this significant declaration of God's benign initiative.

That ministry is now ours!

Only if we believe that our "trespasses" are not held against *us* can we become true "ambassadors."

Don't ignore the strong word, "implore."

Pause before starting this final sentence. You are sharing a profound truth that, for us, is joyful good news. Stress the words "be" and "know."

A reading from the second Letter of Saint Paul to the Corinthians

Brothers and **sisters**:
Whoever is in **Christ** is a **new creation**:
   the **old** things have **passed away**;
   behold, **new** things have **come**.
And **all this** is from **God**,
   who has **reconciled** us to **himself through Christ**
   and given us the **ministry** of **reconciliation**,
   namely, God was **reconciling** the **world** to **himself** in **Christ**,
   not counting their **trespasses against** them
   and **entrusting** to **us** the **message** of **reconciliation**.
So we are **ambassadors** for **Christ**,
   as if **God** were appealing **through** us.
We **implore** you on **behalf** of **Christ**,
   be reconciled to **God**.
For **our sake** he made **him** to be **sin** who did **not know** sin,
   so that **we** might become the **righteousness** of **God** in **him**.

GOSPEL   Luke 15:1–3, 11–32

Jesus tells the story in the midst of the righteous and the outcast. He addresses the parable to the complainers: is he trying to chasten or to change hearts?

Pharisees = FAYR-uh-seez
The pacing of the dialogue should be brisk.

This too-soon division of property must be painful for the father.
You might narrate this with the naïve bravado of the son.

A reading from the holy Gospel according to Luke

Tax collectors and **sinners** were **all drawing near** to **listen** to **Jesus**,
   but the **Pharisees** and **scribes** began to **complain**, saying,
   "**This** man **welcomes sinners** and **eats** with them."
So to **them** Jesus addressed **this parable**:
"A man had **two sons**, and the **younger** son said to his father,
   '**Father** give me the **share** of your **estate** that should **come**
      to me.'
So the father **divided** the property **between** them.
After a few **days**, the **younger** son collected **all** his **belongings** »

---

the message of reconciliation . . . on behalf of Christ, be reconciled to God." He urges us to a response that imitates and prolongs God's gift of reconciliation in our own lives. Reconciliation is envisioned, above all, as a re-creation of the believer, a "new creation," resurrected in Christ. Paul's "brothers and sisters," having been reconciled to Christ and to whom the ministry of reconciliation has been entrusted, are sent to the whole world as "ambassadors for Christ."

GOSPEL   For a time, one son is carried away by his foolish inclinations and departs from the paternal home. The loving father exercises patience toward this youth. When the father's patience is rewarded with the foolish son's return, the other, elder son separates himself from the family on a principle of mistaken righteousness. Of the three, the eldest son is unable to enjoy the fruits of the family home; instead, he ponders his own virtue, meditating on the kid goat he

never requested of his father, to celebrate with his friends. Rather than rejoice that his father's dearest hope has been fulfilled, he clings to his resentment and refuses to enter his brother's welcome home celebration. In that house, we find not only a prodigal brother, but also and above all, a father prodigal in his love, who lavishes mercy and forgiveness on the strayed sheep. This the elder son cannot tolerate. How can he live in a house where the heart is more important than order and discipline, where

The tone shifts here. Pick out the words that convey the son's degradation: "squandered," "dissipation," "longed," and especially "pods" and "swine."

The prodigal's humiliation is now complete.

His conversion has begun and he is willing to admit his selfishness.

His rehearsal is sincere, but leave out the emotion here and save it for his actual dialogue with the father.

This is a classic and critical line. God is always looking for us while we are still "a long way off."

The father won't even let him finish his rehearsed contrition. He is focused on welcome, healing, and celebration. The "ring" signifies household authority.

Another classic and revered line.

Here begins an unexpected new act of the drama. Your tone can signal the coming confrontation.

and **set off** to a **distant country**
  where he **squandered** his inheritance on a life of **dissipation**.
When he had **freely spent everything**,
  a **severe famine struck** that country,
  and he found himself in **dire need**.
So he **hired** himself **out** to one of the local **citizens**
  who **sent** him to his **farm** to **tend** the swine.
And he **longed** to eat his **fill** of the **pods** on which the **swine fed**,
  but **nobody gave** him any.
Coming to his **senses** he thought,
  'How many of my father's hired **workers**
  have **more** than enough food to eat,
  but here am **I**, **dying** from **hunger**.
I shall **get up** and go to my **father** and I shall **say** to him,
  "**Father**, I have **sinned** against **heaven** and against **you**.
I no longer **deserve** to be called your **son**;
  treat me as **you** would **treat** one of your **hired workers**."'
So he **got up** and **went back** to his **father**.
While he was still a **long way off**,
  his **father** caught **sight** of him, and was **filled** with **compassion**.
He **ran** to his son, **embraced** him and **kissed** him.
His **son said** to **him**,
  '**Father**, I have **sinned** against **heaven** and against **you**;
  I no longer **deserve** to be called your **son**.'
But his **father** ordered his **servants**,
  '**Quickly** bring the **finest robe** and put it **on** him;
  put a **ring** on his **finger** and **sandals** on his **feet**.
Take the **fattened calf** and **slaughter** it.
Then let us **celebrate** with a **feast**,
  because this **son** of mine was **dead**, and has come to **life** again;
  he was **lost**, and has been **found**.'
Then the **celebration began**.
Now the **older** son had been out in the **field**
  and, on his way **back**, as he neared the **house**,
  he heard the sound of **music** and **dancing**.

mercy surpasses justice, where the sinner receives forgiveness without reproach?

The parable is above all the story of the boundless love of a Father, who offers his repentant child the gift of reunion and unconditional reconciliation. The prodigal son, in his anxiety over conversion, in his longing to return to the family home and to be forgiven, represents those who long for reconciliation on all levels and without reserve. He represents all who realize that such a repair is possible only insofar as it derives from a fundamental reconciliation, one that bridges the gap between God and the human person, the reconciliation that receives a person into the family of God, whose mercy is boundless.

Nevertheless, the parable illustrates, by spotlighting the elder son's divisive selfishness, the condition of the human family. The elder son's attitude, which mirrors that of the Pharisees and scribes who complain about the tax collectors and sinners drawing near to Jesus, throws light on the difficulty involved in satisfying the desire and efforts for one reconciled, united family. The elder boy, jealously choosing to stay outside the party, reminds us of the need for a change of heart and mind through the rediscovery of the Father's mercy, the need for laying aside misunderstanding and hostile feelings. The sad story of the elder son is an incentive to look inside ourselves and consider to what extent we may block the unity and reconciliation in the family.

The servants, unaware of his displeasure, are in full celebration mode.

He **called** one of the **servants** and **asked** what this might **mean**.
The servant said to him,
    'Your **brother** has **returned**
    and your **father** has **slaughtered** the **fattened calf**
    because he has him **back safe** and **sound**.'
He became **angry**,
    and when he **refused** to enter the **house**,
    his **father** came **out** and **pleaded** with him.
He said to his father in reply,

Stress the father's initiative. The angry son holds nothing back.

    '**Look**, **all these years** I **served** you
    and **not once** did I **disobey** your **orders**;
    yet you **never** gave me even a young **goat**
       to **feast** on with my **friends**.
But when **your son** returns

For this boy, the "far country" was in his own resentful heart.

    who **swallowed** up your **property** with **prostitutes**,
    for **him** you **slaughter** the **fattened calf**.'
He **said** to him,
    '**My son**, **you** are here with me **always**;
    everything I have is **yours**.

The father understands the son's complaint but won't compromise his love and mercy. Remember, most of those in church are more like this son than the prodigal. Don't rush.

But **now** we must **celebrate** and **rejoice**,
    because your brother was **dead** and has come to **life** again;
    he was **lost** and has been **found**.'"

Speak the last line sustaining eye contact with the assembly.

THE 4 STEPS OF *LECTIO DIVINA* OR PRAYERFUL READING

1. *Lectio:* Read a Scripture passage aloud slowly. Notice what phrase captures your attention and be attentive to its meaning. Silent pause.

2. *Meditatio:* Read the passage aloud slowly again, reflecting on the passage, allowing God to speak to you through it. Silent pause.

3. *Oratio:* Read it aloud slowly a third time, allowing it to be your prayer or response to God's gift of insight to you. Silent pause.

4. *Contemplatio:* Read it aloud slowly a fourth time, now resting in God's word.

I, you, each one of us is at the same time prodigal son and elder brother. In light of the inexhaustible mercy that wipes out sin, the Church and the sacraments work, with and in imitation of the heavenly Father, his beloved Son, and their Holy Spirit, for the conversion of hearts, for the reconciliation of people with God and with one another—these being two realities that are intimately connected.

The first reading reports the celebration of Passover in the Promised Land. The itinerary of the exodus has ended; from now on, we must be attentive to what the heart seeks, reconciliation. In the Gospel, the younger son is reconciled with his father. Paul reminds us that God "reconciled us to himself through Christ." The focus of the liturgy is the entrance into the Promised Land, return to the father's house. But not everybody wants to enter.
K.S.

FOURTH SUNDAY OF LENT, YEAR A

LECTIONARY #31

READING I   1 Samuel 16:1b, 6–7, 10–13a

A reading from the first Book of Samuel

The voice of God is authoritative and resolute.

The LORD said to **Samuel**:
    "Fill your horn with **oil**, and be on your way.
I am sending you to **Jesse** of **Bethlehem**,
    for I have chosen my **king** from among his **sons**."

As Jesse and his sons came to the **sacrifice**,
    Samuel looked at **Eliab** and thought,
    "**Surely** the LORD's anointed is here before him."

Speak of Eliab with Samuel's conviction that this is God's anointed.

Eliab = ee-LĪ-uhb.

But the LORD said to Samuel:
    "Do not judge from his **appearance** or from his lofty **stature**,
    because I have **rejected** him.
Not as **man** sees does **God** see,
    because man sees the **appearance**
    but the LORD looks into the **heart**."

Give God's dialogue the tone of a patient teacher rather than a disciplinarian. God uses this opportunity to teach a valuable lesson about God's ways and ours.

Suggest the tediousness of this lengthy process. Stress "seven."

In the **same** way Jesse presented **seven** sons before Samuel,
    but Samuel said to Jesse,
    "The LORD has not chosen any **one** of these."
Then Samuel **asked** Jesse,
    "Are these **all** the sons you have?"

Samuel is confused, perhaps worried, and somewhat exasperated.

Jesse is not hopeful that his youngest will be the one.

Jesse replied,
    "There is still the **youngest**, who is tending the **sheep**."
Samuel said to Jesse,
    "**Send** for him;
    we will not **begin** the sacrificial banquet until he **arrives** here."

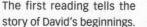 The first reading tells the story of David's beginnings. Samuel, having reported God's rejection of Saul as king, has been sent by God to anoint a king from Jesse's house, for God has seen among Jesse's boys a king of his choosing. Samuel is certain that the eldest, a tall, handsome man, is God's choice. It is not so. Samuel looks at the qualities of the young men, and finds among them the qualities that he considers are appropriate for a king of Israel, "appearance" and "lofty stature," qualities found in Saul. But God rejects these candidates for the royal, messianic throne. The reason is theological: "Not as man does God see, because man sees the appearance but the Lord looks into the heart." Seven candidates pass before Samuel without God's approving any of them. Finally, Jesse sends for his youngest, "who is tending the sheep"— just what one would expect of a future king. When David arrives, Samuel anoints him in the presence of his family; "and from that day on, the spirit of the Lord rushed upon David."

Speak with great respect and admiration for David.

Jesse **sent** and had the young man **brought** to them.
He was **ruddy**, a youth **handsome** to behold
   and making a **splendid** appearance.

God is pleased with this choice!

The LORD said,
   "**There**—**anoint** him, for **this** is the one!"

Describe the anointing in a slow, stately way, but then emphasize the force of the Spirit that "rushed" upon David..

Then Samuel, with the horn of **oil** in hand,
   anointed David in the presence of his **brothers**;
   and from **that** day **on**, the **spirit** of the LORD **rushed**
      upon David.

For meditation and context:

RESPONSORIAL PSALM   Psalm 23:1–3a, 3b–4, 5, 6 (1)

R. The Lord is my shepherd; there is nothing I shall want.

The LORD is my shepherd; I shall not want.
   In verdant pastures he gives me repose;
beside restful waters he leads me;
   he refreshes my soul.

You spread the table before me
   in the sight of my foes;
you anoint my head with oil;
   my cup overflows.

He guides me in right paths
   for his name's sake.
Even though I walk in the dark valley
   I fear no evil; for you are at my side
with your rod and your staff
   that give me courage.

Only goodness and kindness follow me
   all the days of my life;
and I shall dwell in the house of the LORD
   for years to come.

READING II   Ephesians 5:8–14

Ephesians = ee-FEE-zhuhnz

The Good News of the opening and closing sentences undergirds the teaching tone in the body of the reading.

Speak one line at a time. You must not blur these ideas..

"Goodness," "righteousness," and "truth" are three distinct virtues.

"Try" sets the tone of this line: exhortation softened by an understanding that doing right is not an easy process to learn.

Imagine speaking these words to a beloved young person in your charge.

A reading from the Letter of Saint Paul to the Ephesians

Brothers and sisters:
You were once **darkness**,
   but now you are **light** in the **Lord**.
Live as **children** of light,
   for **light** produces every kind of **goodness**
      and **righteousness** and **truth**.
Try to learn what is **pleasing** to the Lord.
Take no part in the fruitless works of **darkness**;
   rather **expose** them, for it is shameful even to **mention**
      the things done by them in secret; **»**

READING II Paul exhorts the Christians to live as children of light, because Christ has enlightened us. *Light* is an allusion to Baptism, the sacrament of enlightenment. Through Baptism, Christians become daughters and sons of light, members of Christ, the light of the world. By this transformation, a new life is gained; our deeds are the fruit of the anointing we received; and we are the fragrant perfume of Christ that fills the earth. With the words "goodness and righteousness and truth," derived from the light, the apostle emphasizes the benefits to the community's life: benevolence, respect for the rights of others, and sincerity in word and action. Christian behavior is a ray of light that does not merely offset the deeds of darkness, it transforms them. The true disciple of Christ is an apostle of light to the world.

but everything **exposed** by the light becomes **visible**,
for everything that **becomes** visible is **light**.
Therefore, it says:
  "**Awake**, O sleeper,
  and **arise** from the **dead**,
  and **Christ** will give you **light**."

GOSPEL   John 9:1–41

A reading from the holy Gospel according to John

[As **Jesus** passed by he **saw** a man **blind** from **birth**.]
His **disciples** asked him,
  "**Rabbi**, who **sinned**, **this** man or his **parents**,
  that he was born **blind**?"
Jesus answered,
  "Neither **he** nor his **parents** sinned;
  it is so that the works of **God** might be made **visible**
    through him.
We have to do the works of the one who sent me while it is **day**.
Night is coming when **no** one can work.
While I am in the **world**, I am the **light** of the world."
When he had said this, [he **spat** on the ground
  and made **clay** with the saliva,
  and **smeared** the clay on his **eyes**, and said to him,
  "Go **wash** in the **Pool** of **Siloam**"—which means **Sent**—.
So he **went** and **washed**, and came back able to **see**.

His **neighbors** and those who had **seen** him earlier
    as a **beggar** said,
  "Isn't this the one who used to sit and **beg**?"
Some said, "It **is**,"
  but **others** said, "**No**, he just **looks** like him."
He said, "I **am**."]
So they said to him, "How were your eyes **opened**?"

Hear the cadence in this line. Speak it with joyous hope.

Stress "blind from birth" for it is later questioned.

Jesus' answer is unexpected and new. Don't rush.

Enjoy the graphic details!

Siloam = sih-LOH-uhm
Relate the miracle with a sense of awe. Pause, to shift to a new scene.

The man is insistent: "I am!"

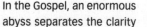 GOSPEL   In the Gospel, an enormous abyss separates the clarity of the blind and the Pharisees' confusion. Jesus, the light of the world, announced: "I came into this world for a judgment, so that those who do not see might see, and those who do see might become blind" (v. 39). The blindest blind are those who choose not to see. Instead of recognizing the light of Christ, the Pharisees argued about the mud Jesus had made with his saliva on the Sabbath; they criticized and condemned the insightful blind man as well as Jesus, the healer. They stayed in the dark, preferring their habitual blindness to the transformation of life that comes with a new vision.

The blind man never asked Jesus to grant him sight, nor did Jesus ask him whether he wanted to see, but gradually, as he approached the Light of the World, he received the light of faith. With the mud on his face, he obeyed without understanding: "Go wash yourself in the Pool of Siloam," and when he returned he was able to see. Even then, he did not know who had healed

He relates the details joyfully.

It suddenly dawns on him that he doesn't know Jesus' whereabouts. Pause. New scene.

As you read "So then the Pharisees," your tone hints at where they're going with this.

Proclaim "He put clay . . . " in a matter-of-fact way, but joyfully.

One of the Pharisees is angry, the other reasonable.

He must decide if he will make this confession of faith, and he does it boldly.

Their speech is guarded. They say only what they must.

He replied,
"The man called **Jesus** made **clay** and **anointed** my eyes
and told me, 'Go to **Siloam** and **wash**.'
So I went there and **washed** and was able to **see**."
And they said to him, "Where **is** he?"
He said, "I don't **know**."

[They brought the one who was once blind to the **Pharisees**.
Now Jesus had made clay and opened his eyes on a **sabbath**.
So then the Pharisees **also** asked him how he was able to see.
He **said** to them,
"He put **clay** on my eyes, and I **washed**, and now I can **see**."
So some of the **Pharisees** said,
"This man is not from **God**,
because he does not keep the **sabbath**."
But **others** said,
"How can a **sinful** man do such **signs**?"
And there was a **division** among them.
So they said to the blind man **again**,
"What do **you** have to say about him,
since he opened **your** eyes?"
He said, "He is a **prophet**."]

Now the Jews did not **believe**
that he had been **blind** and gained his **sight**
until they summoned the **parents** of the one who had gained
his sight.
They **asked** them,
"Is this your **son**, who you say was **born** blind?
How does he now **see**?"
His parents answered and said,
"We **know** that this is our **son** and that he was born **blind**.
We do **not** know how he **sees** now,
nor do we know **who** opened his eyes.
Ask **him**, he is of **age**;
he can speak for **himself**." »

him. To the Pharisees he confessed that the one who had brought light into his life was a prophet. While his parents, constrained by social pressure, were timid about recognizing Jesus as a prophet, their formerly blind son challenged his accusers, "Do you want to become his disciples, too?" And they excommunicated him from the community. Finally, when the formerly blind man met Jesus, he knelt down before him, left behind his limitations, and entered the light, by virtue of a grace he had not even requested. Meanwhile, critics gradually withdrew from the light and locked themselves inside their preferred darkness.

The Gospel of the healing of the blind man ends with an alternative: a person who acknowledges that she or he owes sight to Christ comes to the light, but the one who believes that they see is blind. To the Pharisees who ask Jesus, "Surely we are not also blind, are we?" Jesus responds, "If you were blind, you would have no sin; but now you are saying, 'We see,' so your sin remains." Jesus diagnoses a blindness more malignant than that of the eyes: selfishness, stubbornness, and arrogance. For

Offer this aside as an excuse for the parents' behavior.

His parents said this because they were **afraid**
of the Jews, for the Jews had already **agreed**
that if anyone **acknowledged** him as the **Christ**,
he would be **expelled** from the **synagogue**.
For this reason his **parents** said,
"He is of **age**; question **him**."

They feel they've been duped, so they look further.

So a **second** time they called the man who had been **blind**
and said to him, "Give **God** the praise!
We **know** that this man is a **sinner**."

The tone here should be: "Don't entangle me in your politics. All I know is that I'm healed!"

He replied,
"If he is a **sinner**, I do not **know**.
One thing I **do** know is that I was **blind** and now I **see**."
So they said to him,
"What did he **do** to you?
How did he open your eyes?"

Speak the narration as if through clenched teeth, suggesting the exasperation of the leaders.

He answered them,
"I told you **already** and you did not **listen**.
Why do you want to hear it **again**?

He's becoming impatient, and bold!

Do **you** want to become his disciples, **too**?"

The leaders' anger is mounting.

They **ridiculed** him and said,
"**You** are that man's disciple;
we are disciples of **Moses**!
We **know** that God spoke to **Moses**,
but we do **not** know where this one is from."
The man answered and said to them,
"This is what is so **amazing**,
that you do not know where he is **from**, yet he opened my **eyes**.
We **know** that God does not listen to **sinners**,
but if one is **devout** and does his **will**, he **listens** to him.
It is **unheard** of that anyone ever **opened** the eyes of a person
born blind.

First he mocks them, and then he instructs them.

If this man were not from **God**,
he would not be able to **do** anything."

our part, we can do little to alleviate it, but Jesus gives the remedy.

When Paul writes of Baptism in today's second reading, he exhorts us to behave like "children of light." On our journey of faith, we replicate the pattern of the man born blind: "You were once darkness, but now you are the light in the Lord." We have been enlightened by the Lord, the light of the world. That is why Paul enjoins us, "Live as children of light." As a generation of light, following the pattern of the one born blind, we are led from darkness into light and thus transformed. The darkness is illuminated; it becomes light. In Ephesians, as in the Gospel, it is clear the light of Christ not only illuminates but transforms the believer into something that mirrors Christ and shines together with him. It is not enough, however, to become daughters and sons of light; we must behave as such, and produce the fruits of light, which are "every kind of goodness and righteousness and truth" (Ephesians 5,10).

In the end, the challenge for Jesus is not giving a blind person sight. The real challenge is to open the eyes of those who

They take refuge in the false assumption that his blindness was the result of sin. Pause before the final scene with Jesus.

As yet, he has not seen Jesus. He's anxious to "see" him.

Pause after the words "he said" to suggest his moment of decision.

Jesus' tone attracts the attention of the Pharisees.

This is strong, uncompromising language, but it's motivated by his desire that they truly "see."

[They answered and said to him,
  "You were born totally in **sin**,
  and are you trying to teach **us**?"
Then they **threw** him out.

When Jesus **heard** that they had thrown him out,
  he **found** him and said, "Do you **believe** in the Son of Man?"
He answered and said,
  "Who **is** he, sir, that I may **believe** in him?"
Jesus said to him,
  "You have **seen** him,
  and the one **speaking** with you is **he**."
He said,
  "I **do** believe, Lord," and he **worshiped** him.]
Then Jesus said,
  "I came into this world for **judgment**,
  so that those who do **not** see **might** see,
  and those who **do** see might become **blind**."

Some of the **Pharisees** who were with him **heard** this
  and said to him, "Surely **we** are not also blind, **are** we?"
Jesus said to them,
  "If you **were** blind, you would have no **sin**;
  but now you are saying, 'We **see**,' so your sin **remains**."

[Shorter: John 9:1, 6–9, 13–17, 34–38 (see brackets)]

say they see, but close their eyes to the truth. Today's Gospel reading opens with a single blind man on stage; it closes with a crowd of incurable, guilty, blind judges who pretend to see and even put blinders on others. They deny the miracle in front of them because it calls their knowledge and authority into question; they do not want to see it. The presence of the formerly blind is intolerable for those who do not want to see. Jesus cures, enlightens, and gives life, while the supposed religious experts insist on discussing, interpreting, investigating, and presenting objections. We face the challenge of letting ourselves see, flourish, and bear fruit in the light of Christ. The words of the special preface for this Eucharist sum up the teaching of the readings: "By the mystery of the Incarnation, he has led the human race that walked in darkness into the radiance of faith." K.S.

FIFTH SUNDAY
OF LENT

LECTIONARY #36

READING I   Isaiah 43:16–21

Isaiah = Ī-ZAY-uh

Remember, these are not questions but poetic lines that describe how God saved Israel and destroyed Pharaoh's army. Stress the verbs "opens" and "leads."

Your tone should signal that now we hear the voice of the Lord instead of the prophet. Use a slower, more solemn tone.

These words are meant to rouse hearts and engender hope.

All of nature will respond to God's saving initiative.

The natural response of a person of faith to God's mercy is overflowing praise.

A reading from the Book of the Prophet Isaiah

Thus says the Lord,
   who opens a **way** in the **sea**
   and a **path** in the **mighty waters**,
who **leads** out **chariots** and **horsemen**,
   a **powerful army**,
till they lie **prostrate** together, **never** to **rise**,
   snuffed out and **quenched** like a **wick**.
Remember **not** the events of the **past**,
   the things of **long ago** consider **not**;
see, I am doing something **new**!
   Now it **springs forth**, do you not **perceive** it?
In the **desert** I make a **way**,
   in the **wasteland**, **rivers**.
Wild beasts honor me,
   jackals and **ostriches**,
for I put **water** in the **desert**
   and **rivers** in the **wasteland**
   for my **chosen people** to **drink**,
the people whom I **formed** for **myself**,
   that they might **announce** my **praise**.

READING I The first reading encourages the chosen people to look forward to the day of their liberation from exile in Babylon. It evokes the liberation of Egypt, mentioning the tempestuous waters of the sea and the Egyptian cadavers washed ashore. But the story of salvation does not stop with the exodus from Egypt, a glorious event of the past. God's voice sets the present generation on the road to Jerusalem and the future. The new exodus will be even more marvelous than the previous one; God will again pave a highway, and the wilderness will be transformed into a paradise, where wild animals will honor their creator and the chosen people will drink from abundant streams and praise God. Isaiah shines the light on "something new" on the horizon, as he recalls the past, and projects a present oriented towards the bright future. He encourages the exiled people to trust that God will restore them to their homeland in a more wondrous exodus than before.

102

For meditation and context:

RESPONSORIAL PSALM   Psalm 126:1–2, 2–3, 4–5, 6 (3)

R. The Lord has done great things for us; we are filled with joy.

When the LORD brought back the captives
   of Zion,
   we were like men dreaming.
Then our mouth was filled with laughter,
   and our tongue with rejoicing.

Then they said among the nations,
   "The LORD has done great things
   for them."
The LORD has done great things for us;
   we are glad indeed.

Restore our fortunes, O LORD,
   like the torrents in the southern desert.
Those that sow in tears
   shall reap rejoicing.

Although they go forth weeping,
   carrying the seed to be sown,
they shall come back rejoicing,
   carrying their sheaves.

READING II   Philippians 3:8–14

A reading from the Letter of Saint Paul to the Philippians

Brothers and **sisters**:
I consider **everything** as a **loss**
   because of the **supreme good** of knowing **Christ Jesus** my **Lord**.
For **his** sake I have **accepted** the loss of **all things**
   and I **consider** them so much **rubbish**,
   that I may **gain Christ** and be **found** in **him**,
   not having any **righteousness** of my **own** based on the **law**
   but that which comes through **faith** in **Christ**,
   the **righteousness** from **God**,
   depending on **faith** to **know** him and the **power**
      of his **Resurrection**
   and the **sharing of** his **sufferings** by being **conformed**
      to his **death**,
   if **somehow** I may **attain** the **Resurrection** from the **dead**.

It is **not** that I have **already** taken hold of it
   or have already **attained perfect maturity**,
   but I **continue** my pursuit in **hope** that I **may possess** it,
   since I have **indeed been taken** possession **of** by **Christ Jesus**.
Brothers and **sisters**, **I** for **my** part
   do **not** consider **myself** to have **taken** possession. »

Philippians = fih-LIP-ee-uhnz

The Letter to the Philippians is known as the "Letter of Joy." Let that color your tone. "Everything" refers to his earlier efforts to achieve righteousness through the Law, which has lost its power and meaning for him.

Christ is the only prize worth seeking.

Paul can't speak of "Resurrection" without also speaking of the necessary path there: "sufferings" and "death."

Paul speaks honestly of the progress he still must make. "Taken hold of it" refers to the resurrected life that comes only after death.

He has not yet reached the "goal," but nothing in his past (nor anything in ours!) will prevent further progress.

READING II The event on the Damascus road (recounted in Acts 9) transformed Paul. Elsewhere he stresses the power of God's grace; here he gives his personal assessment: "I consider everything as a loss because of the supreme good of knowing Christ Jesus my Lord." He is referring to the intimacy of biblical knowledge by which one enters into communion with Christ, by knowing "him and the power of his Resurrection and the sharing of his sufferings by being conformed to his death." Paul desires to be fully identified with Christ, conscious that he will not achieve this by his own efforts but by God's grace and "righteousness" or "justice." This justice is illustrated in today's Gospel, which tells of grace extended to the adulterous woman, who is a figure of God's people. The new justice to which Paul refers is exercised through the restored relationship that springs from merciful love. Adhering to Christ means giving up self-sufficiency "that I may gain Christ and be found in him, not having any righteousness of my own based on the law but that which comes through faith in Christ." Our knowledge of

The "goal" and "prize" is eternal life with Christ.

Just one thing: **forgetting** what lies **behind**
but **straining forward** to what lies **ahead**,
I **continue** my **pursuit** toward the **goal**,
the **prize** of God's upward **calling**, in **Christ Jesus**.

GOSPEL   John 8:1–11

As proclaimer, you are a faith-filled storyteller. Tell the story simply and naturally, aware that Jesus has love for *all* the players in this tense drama.

Jesus has probably been praying before this encounter.

Don't rush the details of how the crowds flocked to him.

Emphasize the treatment of the woman, exposed and humiliated before the crowd.

The leaders play their cards close so as all the better to snare Jesus.

This aside reveals your attitude as narrator—protective of Jesus or contemptuous of the leaders.

Slow your delivery as you share this enigmatic behavior.

Let Jesus speak without anger. The witnesses to the sin were to be the first to throw a stone.

Jesus' words and actions have undone them, so they cower away.

A reading from the holy Gospel according to John

Jesus went to the **Mount** of Olives.
But **early** in the **morning** he arrived again in the **temple** area,
    and **all** the **people** started **coming** to him,
    and he **sat** down and **taught** them.
Then the **scribes** and the **Pharisees** brought a **woman**
    who had been **caught** in **adultery**
    and made her **stand** in the **middle**.
They said to him,
    "Teacher, **this woman** was **caught**
    in the **very act** of committing **adultery**.
Now in the **law**, **Moses** commanded us to **stone** such women.
So what do **you** say?"
They said this to **test** him,
    so that they could have some **charge** to bring against him.
Jesus bent down and began to **write** on the **ground** with his **finger**.
But when they continued **asking** him,
    he **straightened up** and said to them,
    "Let the **one among you** who is **without sin**
    be the **first** to throw a **stone** at her."
Again he **bent** down and **wrote** on the **ground**.
And in **response**, they went **away one** by **one**,
    beginning with the **elders**.
So he was left **alone** with the **woman before** him.

---

and sharing with Christ is always imperfect; Christian existence is characterized not by having reached a goal but by "straining forward to what lies ahead" in pursuit of knowing Christ. Paul reminds us that we depend on God to restore us; he knows that righteousness cannot be claimed on one's personal merit; it is an ongoing gift from God.

GOSPEL On Mount Sinai God engraved the Ten Commandments on two stone tablets. In today's Gospel, the evangelist tells how the Son of God writes on the Palestinian soil. Both inscriptions are interventions of grace. Hoping to trap Jesus, some Pharisees and scribes present a woman caught in adultery to Jesus, insisting, "Now in the law, Moses commanded us to stone such women. So what do you say?" They were right. The law condemns the woman and her partner to death. Jesus does not argue with them, but raises the argument to another level. On the limestone ground of Judea, he reinterprets what God wrote on the tablets of the law: "Jesus bent down and began to write on the ground with his

Shift tone for this new beat in the drama.

The woman must be mystified at all this.

Then **Jesus straightened up** and **said** to her,
   "Woman, **where are** they?
Has **no one condemned** you?"
She replied, **"No one**, sir."
Then Jesus said, **"Neither** do **I condemn** you.
Go, and from now **on** do **not sin** any **more**."

finger." Jesus traces in the thin topsoil the new law of grace. What did Jesus write? A list of sins? A cast of adulterers present? Or, the new law: "Love your neighbor as yourself" or "Do not judge and you will not be judged" (see Luke 6:37).

In the woman brought before him, Jesus recognized the people he came to save. She is Israel of yesterday, the prophet Hosea's wife, the figure of the people covenanted but not always faithful to God; and she is the Church of tomorrow, whom Jesus loves and for whom he will sacrifice himself, to release her from slavery to sin. Jesus came not to judge but to forgive and save: "Let the one among you who is without sin be the first to throw a stone at her," and thus he opens the way to grace, even as he reminds us that we are all sinners, even the Pharisees, and we all need mercy. K.S.

FIFTH SUNDAY OF LENT, YEAR A

LECTIONARY #34

READING I   Ezekiel 37:12–14

A reading from the Book of the Prophet Ezekiel

Thus says the LORD God:
  O my **people**, I will **open** your **graves**
  and have you **rise** from them,
  and bring you **back** to the land of **Israel**.
Then you shall **know** that I am the LORD,
  when I **open** your graves and have you **rise** from them,
  O my people!
I will put my **spirit** in you that you may **live**,
  and I will **settle** you upon your land;
  thus you shall know that I am the LORD.
I have **promised**, and I will **do** it, says the LORD.

Ezekiel = ee-ZEE-kee-uhl

"Thus says the Lord" is meant to get our attention. Speak it with authority. Pause briefly before narrating the intense vision.

The same idea is stated twice, with word order reversed. This is a poetic technique meant to give emphasis. Enjoy the repetition and speak it boldly.

Use a quieter tone here. This is God's promise of restoration. The fulfillment of the promise will persuade Israel of God's great love for them. "And I will do it" must be spoken with strength and conviction.

For meditation and context:

RESPONSORIAL PSALM   Psalm 130:1–2, 3–4, 5–6, 7–8 (7)

R. With the Lord there is mercy and fullness of redemption.

Out of the depths I cry to you, O LORD;
  LORD, hear my voice!
Let your ears be attentive
  to my voice in supplication.

If you, O LORD, mark iniquities,
  LORD, who can stand?
But with you is forgiveness,
  that you may be revered.

I trust in the LORD;
  my soul trusts in his word.
More than sentinels wait for the dawn,
  let Israel wait for the LORD.

For with the LORD is kindness
  and with him is plenteous redemption;
and he will redeem Israel
  from all their iniquities.

READING I   Ezekiel's message is that God will bring new life to exiled and scattered people; God will restore them to their own land. In the extended version of the vision of the field of dry bones (Ezekiel 37:1–14), the Lord asks if these bones can return to life, and the prophet answers, "You alone know that." The answer opens the door to hope. He commands the bones to hear God's word, which created all things in the beginning and now re-creates flesh and sinews over the bones. The prophet summons the wind to breathe into the bodies (recalling Genesis 2:7), which come alive and stand up. Finally, the prophet is instructed to interpret the vision for the people: "I will open your graves and have you rise from them. . . . I will put my spirit in you that you may live, and I will settle you upon your land." God will give new life to the nation that has been reduced to dry bones.

This liturgy presents the Resurrection in a crescendo that reaches back to Ezekiel's oracle and forward to Christ's definitive victory over death. Through the prophet's mouth, God announces the opening of the tombs; this is a promise of the return to Israel of the children of those who went into exile in Babylon. Some fifty years

READING II   Romans 8:8–11

A reading from the Letter of Saint Paul to the Romans

Brothers and sisters:
Those who are in the **flesh** cannot **please** God.
But **you** are not in the flesh;
  on the **contrary**, you are in the **spirit**,
    if only the Spirit of God **dwells** in you.
Whoever does not **have** the Spirit of Christ does not **belong**
    to him.
But **if** Christ is **in** you,
  although the **body** is dead because of **sin**,
    the **spirit** is **alive** because of **righteousness**.
If the **Spirit** of the one who raised Jesus from the dead **dwells**
    in you,
  the **One** who raised Christ from the **dead**
  will give life to **your** mortal bodies also,
    through his **Spirit dwelling** in **you**.

GOSPEL   John 11:1–45

A reading from the holy Gospel according to John

Now a man was **ill**, **Lazarus** from **Bethany**,
  the village of **Mary** and her sister **Martha**.
Mary was the one who had **anointed** the Lord with perfumed **oil**
  and dried his **feet** with her **hair**;
  it was her **brother** Lazarus who was ill.
So [the sisters sent **word** to Jesus saying,
  "**Master**, the one you **love** is **ill**."
When Jesus **heard** this he said,
  "This illness is **not** to end in **death**,
  but is for the **glory** of **God**,
  that the **Son** of God may be **glorified** through it." »

Margin notes (left column):

A short text calls for a slow reading. Paul's logic is filled with joy.

The negative tone of "Those who are in the flesh . . . " immediately turns positive on "But you are not . . . ."

The negative tone of "does not belong to him . . . " immediately turns positive on "But if Christ . . . ."
Contrast "dead/sin" with "alive/righteousness."
This is an "if-then" clause with an implied "then." Proclaim these words with joy.

For the narrator, these are familiar names and places. Speak of the anointing with tenderness.
Bethany = BETH-uh-nee

Say the word "Master" with anxiety in your tone.

Don't get philosophical here. Keep the tone low-key and conversational.

---

before, the people had been deported, and discouragement had gripped their depressed spirits, but now God will restore life to the people, who are dying in a foreign land. That day will be like a new creation. Ezekiel's images anticipate the salvation of humanity in the Resurrection of Jesus.

READING II   The second reading complements the others as Paul applies their wisdom to the Christian community. "If the Spirit of the One who raised Jesus from the dead dwells in you, the One who raised Christ from the dead will give life to your mortal bodies also, through his Spirit dwelling in you." The same Spirit, who breathed new life into the disheartened community during the exile, will raise us to eternal life. The same Jesus who restored Lazarus to life wins eternal life for us through his death and Resurrection.

Paul rereads Ezekiel's oracle and applies it to the present generation: the Spirit of God "dwells in you." It is a source of security, peace, and joy, because it constitutes the unshakable foundation of his belonging to Christ. Therefore, fidelity to

Proclaim the words "Jesus loved" slowly. Everything else builds on this.

Now Jesus **loved** Martha and her sister and Lazarus.
So when he **heard** that he was ill,
   he **remained** for two **days** in the place where he was.
Then **after** this he said to his disciples,
   "Let us go back to **Judea**."]

The disciples are immediately anxious and incredulous.

The disciples said to him,
   "**Rabbi**, the Jews were just trying to **stone** you,
   and you want to go **back** there?"

Again, avoid a lofty tone and keep it conversational.

Jesus answered,
   "Are there not **twelve** hours in a day?
If one walks during the **day**, he does not **stumble**,
   because he sees the **light** of this world.
But if one walks at **night**, he **stumbles**,
   because the light is not **in** him."

Here, speak as if you were really going to wake a sleeping friend.

He said this, and then told them,
   "Our friend **Lazarus** is **asleep**,
   but I am going to **awaken** him."

The tone here should be "Master, you're not making sense!"

So the disciples said to him,
   "Master, if he is **asleep**, he will be **saved**."
But Jesus was talking about his **death**,
   while **they** thought that he meant **ordinary** sleep.
So then Jesus said to them **clearly**,

Speak with some gravity, but not sadness.

   "**Lazarus** has **died**.
And I am **glad** for you that I was not there,
   that you may **believe**.
Let us **go** to him."

He's willing to pay the price of discipleship.

So **Thomas**, called **Didymus**, said to his fellow disciples,
   "Let us **also** go to **die** with him."

"Four days" reflects the Jewish belief that the spirit left the body after three days: hence Lazarus is "fully" dead.

[When Jesus **arrived**, he found that Lazarus
   had already been in the **tomb** for **four days**.]
Now Bethany was **near** Jerusalem, only about two miles away.
And many of the **Jews** had come to Martha and Mary
   to **comfort** them about their brother.
[When Martha **heard** that **Jesus** was coming,
   she went to **meet** him;
   but **Mary** sat at home.

the Lord is not only possible, but a reality: "You are not in the flesh; . . . although the body is dead because of sin, the spirit is alive." The duel between death and life has ended on the cross, and for every Christian, victory is won in Baptism. Therefore, we put our Baptism into action every day, every moment, not in living according to the flesh but in accord with the definitive victory. So then, Christians are encouraged

to be led by the Spirit of God who lives within us and gives us the strength to live, free from enslavement by the desires of the flesh and the principles of the present world. The same Spirit who raised Jesus from the dead is at work to raise us up to live according to the design of God in Christ.

GOSPEL   Lazarus has fallen sick, but his friend Jesus does not rush to the family home to visit, and Lazarus falls asleep and dies. Three days later, his friend Jesus sets out on the road to Bethany to visit the family. Martha, sister of the deceased, goes to meet Jesus, and voices a gentle reprimand, "Lord, if you had been here my brother would not have died." But he did die, four days ago.

Martha exhibits mixed emotions: disappointment and hopefulness.

Martha has missed his point. Jesus' explanation and self-identification are the key points of this Gospel passage.

Speak slowly here. This parallels the "light of the world" pronouncement in last week's Gospel.

Martha's confession is sincere and unreserved.

Use a quieter tone here. Martha may have been coaxing Mary to go, but now Mary goes eagerly.

Her line echoes Martha's, but vary the delivery for variety.

Martha said to Jesus,
　"Lord, if you had **been** here,
　my brother would not have **died**.
But even **now** I know that **whatever** you ask of God,
　God will **give** you."
Jesus said to her,
　"Your brother will **rise**."
Martha said to him,
　"I **know** he will rise,
　in the **Resurrection** on the last **day**."
Jesus told her,
　"**I** am the Resurrection and the **life**;
　whoever **believes** in me, even if he **dies**, will **live**,
　and everyone who **lives** and believes in me will **never** die.
Do **you** believe this?"
She said to him, "**Yes**, Lord.
I have come to believe that you are the **Christ**, the Son of **God**,
　the one who is **coming** into the **world**."]

When she had **said** this,
　she went and called her sister Mary **secretly**, saying,
　"The **teacher** is here and is **asking** for you."
As soon as she **heard** this,
　she rose **quickly** and **went** to him.
For Jesus had not yet come into the **village**,
　but was still where Martha had **met** him.
So when the Jews who were with her in the house **comforting** her
　saw Mary get up quickly and go out,
　they **followed** her,
　presuming that she was going to the **tomb** to **weep** there.
When Mary came to where **Jesus** was and **saw** him,
　she fell at his **feet** and said to him,
　"**Lord**, if you had **been** here,
　my brother would not have **died**."
When Jesus saw her **weeping** and the **Jews** who had come with
　her weeping, »

His sisters attended him when he lay sick and dying, and they prepared the body for burial, carefully washing his body as they wrapped it in the burial cloths. For days after they received the seemingly endless parade of friends, relatives, and neighbors who stopped in to pay their respects and express condolences. It had been an unkind illness, and now the grueling first days of death. Lazarus would surely still be alive had Jesus not stalled, had he come on time. For surely, every place that

Jesus is, there is life. Life was born at the Jordan, where Jesus' first disciples had met him, when their lives took on greater meaning. Life was enhanced in Cana in Galilee, at a wedding party, when Jesus, his mother, and the disciples drank of the new wine. There was liveliness and even scandal in Jerusalem around when Jesus visited the temple and cleansed it of the graft and commerce there. Once, in a visit with Jesus at night, Nicodemus found light and rebirth. A Samaritan woman heard from Jesus the

secret to the source of living water welling up within her. A paralytic felt new vigor and strength in his lifeless, withered limbs. More than five thousand ate the picnic of the bread and fish. Light entered the blind man's eyes as he came to see also with the eyes of faith, and pronounce Jesus the Lord. Where Jesus was, there was life.

　Martha chided Jesus gently, but her delicate reprimand voices her perplexity. If only Jesus had been here, his friend, my

Jesus experiences genuine sorrow here.

[he became **perturbed** and deeply **troubled**, and said,
"Where have you **laid** him?"
They said to him, "**Sir**, come and **see**."
And Jesus **wept**.
So the Jews said, "See how he **loved** him."
But some of them said,

Convey the contrasting moods of the crowd.

This should be a very gentle reproach.

"Could not the one who opened the eyes of the **blind** man
have **done** something so that this man would not have **died**?"

Proclaim these simple but dramatic statements slowly.

So Jesus, perturbed **again**, came to the **tomb**.
It was a **cave**, and a **stone** lay across it.
Jesus said, "Take away the **stone**."
Martha, the dead man's **sister**, said to him,

Concern about the stench is a very practical one.

"Lord, by **now** there will be a **stench**;
he has been dead for **four days**."
Jesus said to her,
"Did I not tell you that if you **believe**
you will see the **glory** of **God**?"
So they **took** away the stone.
And Jesus raised his **eyes** and said,
"**Father**, I **thank** you for **hearing** me.

Jesus prays for others here, not himself.

I know that you **always** hear me;
but because of the **crowd** here I have said this,
that they may believe that you **sent** me."
And when he had **said** this,
he cried out in a **loud** voice,

Use great authority here, calling "Lazarus" as if it were the name of those most in need of renewed life.

Witness the event so that the assembly will see and feel it with you. Read slower than you've ever read.

"**Lazarus**, come **out**!"
The **dead** man **came** out,
tied **hand** and **foot** with **burial** bands,
and his face was wrapped in a **cloth**.
So Jesus said to them,
"**Untie** him and let him **go**."

Pause slightly before delivering this conclusion. Hearing this Gospel should arouse deeper faith in the assembly.

Now **many** of the Jews who had come to Mary
and **seen** what he had done began to **believe** in him.]

[Shorter: John 11:3–7, 17, 20–27, 33b–45 (see brackets)]

---

brother, would not have died. But he did die. Because Jesus' hour had not yet come.

Martha's experience of Jesus around her brother's death is now transferred to another time. The clock turns ahead to today: sadness, uncertainty, and fear, generated by concerns for daily bread, the bread of life, and the threat of a society that doesn't provide all the security and answers that are needed for a healthy, whole, peaceful life. Sickness, doubt, and sadness invade hopeful, good, and whole-

some hearts. We feel that if the Lord were here, we would not be distressed, navigating the rivers of tears in darkness. And we hear the words, in our own mouths and hearts, born of loving memories, hopeful but not yet whole in their confession of faith, "I know he will rise, in the Resurrection on the last day" (11:24).

Just as Martha and her sister Mary had to hunt in their hearts for truth, search their memory for faith in Jesus, touch the love they had for Jesus, alive and real

before them, so must we also examine our hearts. We are Martha and Mary, grieving; we are disciples, perplexed; we are Lazarus, dead and buried. And the final day has arrived, the day of a faithful encounter with Jesus; it is a day of dying to one way of contemplating the world, and rising to a new vision, opening our eyes to the light of Easter. K.S.

PALM SUNDAY OF THE PASSION OF THE LORD

LECTIONARY #37

GOSPEL AT THE PROCESSION   Luke 19:28–40

A reading from the holy Gospel according to Luke

Jesus proceeded on his **journey** up to **Jerusalem**.
As he drew near to **Bethphage** and **Bethany**
   at the place called the **Mount** of **Olives**,
   he sent **two** of his **disciples**.
He said, **"Go** into the **village opposite** you,
   and as you **enter** it you will **find** a **colt tethered**
   on which **no one** has **ever sat**.
Untie it and **bring** it here.
And if anyone should **ask** you,
   'Why are you **untying** it?'
   you will answer,
   'The **Master** has **need** of it.'"
So those who had been **sent** went **off**
   and found **everything just** as he had **told** them.
And as they were **untying** the **colt**, its **owners** said to them,
   "Why are you **untying** this **colt?"**
They answered,
   "The **Master** has **need** of it."
So they **brought** it to **Jesus**,
   threw their **cloaks** over the colt,
   and helped **Jesus** to **mount**. **»**

Jerusalem = juh-ROO-suh-lem;
juh-ROO-zuh-lem
Bethphage = BETH-fuh-jee
Bethany = BETH-uh-nee

Suggest the fuller meaning of the movement toward Jerusalem.

His confident tone regarding the "colt" can be spoken with strength or with such matter-of-factness that no one would think to question it.

"Found everything . . . told them": is this what they expected or are they surprised? The owners' question could be either a challenge or a non-threatening request for an explanation.
"The Master has need of it": delivered with *confidence* in the adequacy of the rehearsed response, or parroted with *uncertainty* about its efficacy

---

PROCESSION GOSPEL   The procession was organized. Some people laid their cloak on the donkey's back; others, running ahead, made a carpet with their jackets and cloaks for the privileged donkey to walk over them; still others scattered greens along the road and waved olive and palm branches cut from the trees along the road. Who were they who proclaimed Jesus their king? Among them, perhaps, the once-blind Bartimaeus of Jericho; Martha and Mary, Jesus' Bethany hostesses; his first disciple, his mother; other disciples, caught up in the festive atmosphere; beneficiaries of his miracles, former lepers and demoniacs; people that had eaten of the loaves and fish; a one-time paralytic; pickpockets, which are never lacking in large crowds. And Jerusalem would not be Jerusalem without the vendors of trifles and trinkets. Residents of the neighborhood of the Mount of Olives left their houses to greet the pilgrims. From this crowd rose the cry "Hosanna" and "Blessed is he who comes." Some people whose lives had been changed by Jesus cried out; others, curious spectators, joined in the chorus. In the midst of the hubbub is Jesus, mounted on a donkey: the Messiah Sovereign takes possession of his reign.

As he **rode along**,
   the people were spreading their **cloaks** on the **road**;
   and **now** as he was approaching the **slope** of the **Mount**
     of **Olives**,
   the **whole multitude** of his **disciples**
   began to **praise God aloud** with **joy**
   for **all** the **mighty deeds** they had seen.
They proclaimed:
   "**Blessed** is the **king** who **comes**
     in the **name** of the **Lord**.
   Peace in **heaven**
     and **glory** in the **highest**."
Some of the **Pharisees** in the crowd said to him,
   "**Teacher**, **rebuke** your **disciples**."
He said in reply,
   "I **tell** you, if **they keep silent**,
   the **stones** will **cry out**!"

READING I Isaiah 50:4–7

A reading from the Book of the Prophet Isaiah

The **Lord God** has **given** me
   a **well-trained tongue**,
that I might know how to **speak** to the **weary**
   a **word** that will **rouse** them.
Morning after **morning**
   he **opens** my **ear** that I may **hear**;
and I have **not rebelled**,
   have **not turned back**.
I **gave** my **back** to those who **beat** me,
   my **cheeks** to those who **plucked** my **beard**;
my **face** I did **not shield**
   from **buffets** and **spitting**. »

Margin notes:

Express the mounting excitement and joy. They spread "cloaks," not "palms."

Blessed = BLES-uhd

"Peace in heaven" is Luke's version of "hosannah."

They are fearful.

Jesus is saying: This is out of my hands. With energy.

Isaiah = i-ZAY-uh

The Lord's servant is speaking with gratitude despite much suffering.

Be aware of the multivalent meaning of "weary" as you speak the word.

God has been persistent and faithful.

Communicate pride and gratitude for the God-given strength to endure.

Don't gloss over these graphic details. Give them their due. "Plucked my beard" is a grave insult in that culture. The past tense lessens the intensity of the pain described.

Jesus, who entered the holy city days before his passion, desires today to enter triumphant in our lives. The humble mount is different now: it is our very heart, which we clothe with the testimony of our faith. The carpet of cloaks, capes, and branches consists of simplicity, our Baptismal promises, our joy, and our compassion for the afflicted. Throughout the circumstances of our lives, Jesus' entrance into the heart anticipates our entrance into the heavenly Jerusalem. What about us, his faithful followers, believers, and some others who join in the festal procession by chance or curiosity? For whatever reason, Jesus wants to enter intimately into our lives and take possession of his rightful inheritance. With pleasure and holy fear, let us accompany him to Jerusalem.

On that original Palm Sunday, the liveliness of Jesus' entry into Jerusalem was short-lived for many who were present. The supple green boughs soon dried and stiffened. The enthusiastic "Hosanna" was transposed to the chaotic cry of the manipulated rabble: "Crucify him, crucify him!" How different are the fresh, green branches, and the cruel, dry, and rigid crossbeam, the soft flowers and the brittle

Here is the voice of hope in the face of adversity.

Speak with rock-like confidence and strength.

The **Lord God** is **my** help,
   therefore I am **not disgraced**;
I have **set** my **face** like **flint**,
   knowing that I shall **not** be put to **shame**.

For meditation and context:

RESPONSORIAL PSALM   Psalm 22:8–9, 17–18, 19–20, 23–24 (2a)

R. My God, my God, why have you abandoned me?

All who see me scoff at me;
   they mock me with parted lips, they wag
      their heads:
"He relied on the Lord; let him deliver him,
   let him rescue him, if he loves him."

Indeed, many dogs surround me,
   a pack of evildoers closes in upon me;
they have pierced my hands and my feet;
   I can count all my bones.

They divide my garments among them,
   and for my vesture they cast lots.
But you, O Lord, be not far from me;
   O my help, hasten to aid me.

I will proclaim your name to my brethren;
   in the midst of the assembly I will
      praise you:
"You who fear the Lord, praise him;
   all you descendants of Jacob, give glory
      to him;
   revere him, all you descendants of Israel!"

READING II   Philippians 2:6–11

A reading from the Letter of Saint Paul to the Philippians

Philippians = fih-LIP-ee-uhnz

Begin slowly, but with solid energy.
Speak the name of the Lord with reverence.

Christ Jesus, though he was in the **form** of **God**,
   did not regard **equality** with **God**
   something to be **grasped**.

"Rather" signals a shift. As important as what he rejected, what Christ humbly embraced is even more important.

Rather, he **emptied** himself,
   taking the **form** of a **slave**,
   coming in **human likeness**;
   and found **human** in **appearance**,
he **humbled** himself,
   becoming **obedient** to the point of **death**,
   even **death** on a **cross**.

Speak with gratitude that Christ became one of us, also of the great pain he endured.

Another significant shift: tempo quickens. You can get louder, or softer but more intense.

Because of this, God **greatly exalted** him
   and **bestowed** on him the name
   which is **above every name**,
   that at the **name** of **Jesus** »

---

thorns of his passion! We spread before him a lush carpet, then strip him naked and cast lots for his tunic. In our interior lives, we are shocked by our own contradictory nature: capable of the best and the worst, one day fearless and the next a coward. We cultivate the virtue that leads to life eternal, and we are stuck in the mire that separates us from God. Who does not want to have Jesus Christ as their true King? But not just

yet. The triumphal entrance to Jerusalem challenges each one of us to consistency and perseverance, so the good intentions are not just lights that shine momentarily, like fireworks that burst into flame and rapidly burn out. The celebration of the Paschal Mystery that we begin today contains the two aspects: life and death, failure and success. The ritual spirals around two axes: the applause that receives the Christ

in our city and the weeping that accompanies him to the tomb. To carry a palm frond in the hand is to say to Jesus: "Come, Lord, welcome to our city. Whatever you ask, I will put into practice in life, because I believe that you are the only God, who has come to take me with you, to live with you forever in eternal Jerusalem."

    The first two readings also emphasize the tension in this liturgy. The third poem of

every knee should **bend,**
of those in **heaven** and on **earth** and **under** the earth,
and **every tongue confess** that
Jesus Christ is **Lord,**
to the **glory** of **God** the **Father.**

Slowly—stress "heaven," "earth," and "under the earth." The hymn is citing Isaiah 45:23.

Your greatest energy goes to the acclamation of Christ, followed by a slightly lower key delivery of the final line.

PASSION   Luke 22:14—23:56

The Passion of our Lord Jesus Christ according to Luke

When the **hour came,**
  Jesus took his **place** at **table** with the **apostles.**
He **said** to them,
  "I have **eagerly desired** to eat this **Passover** with **you**
    before I **suffer,**
  for, I **tell you,** I **shall not eat** it **again**
  until there is **fulfillment** in the **kingdom** of **God."**
Then he took a **cup,** gave **thanks,** and said,
  "**Take this** and **share** it among yourselves;
  for I **tell** you that from **this time on**
  I shall **not drink** of the **fruit** of the **vine**
  until the **kingdom** of **God comes."**
Then he took the **bread,** said the **blessing,**
  broke it, and **gave** it to them, saying,
  "**This** is my **body,** which will be **given** for **you;**
  do this in **memory** of me."
And likewise the **cup** after they had **eaten,** saying,
  "**This cup** is the **new covenant** in my **blood,**
  which will be **shed** for **you.**

"And yet **behold,** the **hand** of the one who is to **betray** me
  is **with** me on the **table;**
  for the **Son of Man indeed goes** as it has been **determined;**
  but **woe to that man** by **whom** he is **betrayed."**
And they began to **debate** among themselves
  who among them would **do** such a **deed.**

"Hour" refers to the hour of Jesus' Death, not the time of the meal. In other words, the time of fulfillment has been inaugurated.

Only Luke includes this line. Jesus anticipates the suffering ahead.

Intimate, yet solemn mood.

Take time with these sacred words. Don't speak them as a formula, but convey the love they embody.

The sense of betrayal is deep.

Shatter the mood.

---

the Lord's servant (first reading) is the mysterious, prophetic presentation of the savior, Christ the King. But he does not achieve salvation by military victory, but by suffering and surrender to adverse forces. The two poles of this poem are his purifying suffering and final liberation. The same antithesis serves as the basis for the second text, the Christological hymn in Philippians. The servant, who surrenders to death on a cross, receives "the name which is above every name," that reveals his true reality as Savior and Son of God. Already on the cross, Jesus offers the example of the forgiveness of sinners to us who contemplate the scene.

READING I Isaiah describes a mysterious Servant, called by God, whose suffering will win the life of the people. The Servant is not identified; he may be the people Israel, or a prophet like Moses or Jeremiah, or a person yet to come. The Servant speaks of his mission at the service of the Word and his terrible suffering. Maltreated, the target of insults, faced with apparent failure, he performs his service

The Apostles' insensitivity turns into self-absorption.

Jesus continues his teaching ministry to the end.

Don't rush past this significant line.

Jesus speaks with gratitude and hope.

A sudden shift, as if Jesus responds to seeing Peter with this urgent caution.

A solemn instruction to Peter.

Peter is fully sincere.

Not judgmental. Jesus will forgive.

Mood shift. Instructing, but more urgent.

Then an **argument** broke out among them
  about **which** of them should be **regarded** as the **greatest**.
He said to them,
  "The **kings** of the **Gentiles lord** it **over** them
  and those in **authority over** them are addressed as
      '**Benefactors**';
  but among **you** it shall **not be so**.
Rather, let the **greatest** among you be as the **youngest**,
  and the **leader** as the **servant**.
For **who** is **greater**:
  the one **seated** at table or the one who **serves**?
Is it not the **one seated** at **table**?
I am among you as the one who **serves**.
It is **you** who have **stood by** me in my **trials**;
  and I **confer** a **kingdom** on you,
  just as my **Father** has conferred **one** on **me**,
  that you may **eat** and **drink** at my **table** in my **kingdom**;
  and you will **sit** on **thrones**
  judging the **twelve** tribes of **Israel**.

"**Simon**, **Simon**, **behold Satan** has demanded
  to **sift** all of you like **wheat**,
  but I have **prayed** that your **own faith** may **not fail**;
  and once you have **turned back**,
  you must **strengthen** your **brothers**."
He said to him,
  "**Lord**, I am prepared to go to **prison** and to **die** with you."
But he replied,
  "I **tell** you, **Peter**, before the **cock crows this day**,
  you will deny **three times** that you **know** me."
He said to them,
  "When I **sent you forth** without a **money bag** or a **sack**
    or **sandals**,
  were you in **need** of anything?"
"**No**, **nothing**," they replied.
He said to them, »

patiently, confident of God's triumph in his life. His fate prefigures that of the humble Christ, who did not resist the Father's will and was not excused from suffering evil, and he remained confident even to the sacrifice on the cross. In the Christian appreciation of this text, we recognize the Servant as Jesus of Nazareth, the Lamb of God, sacrificed to take away the sin of the world. Obedient to the end, he fulfills

God's will; he shines light and infuses life into God's people.

The suffering of the Servant anticipates the Paschal Mystery of Christ, the humiliation that is an essential part of the exaltation: the Servant surrenders to a sacrificial death to seal the new covenant and serve as the redeemer of the family of God. Jesus is aware that his death will issue in triumph and glorification.

In dying on the cross, Christ reveals what his divinity consists of. The image of the patient Servant does not mean only that Jesus assumes his human condition as faithfully as possible; the Servant reveals the nature of God, who, not content with being almighty and distant, identifies with his people. The humanity of Jesus, projected in the image of the Servant, is not an accident or a parenthesis in his life as Son

He's urging them to be ready for anything, including hostile opposition.

"But **now** one who has a **money bag** should **take** it,
and likewise a **sack**,
and one who does **not** have a **sword**
should **sell** his **cloak** and **buy** one.
For I **tell** you that **this Scripture** must be **fulfilled** in me,
namely, *He was counted among the* **wicked**;
and **indeed** what is written about **me** is coming to **fulfillment**."
Then they said,
"**Lord, look**, there are **two** swords here."
But he replied, "**It is enough!**"

As if saying: Lord, we're ready to fight! Jesus says, That's enough! They've missed his point.

The garden is a familiar place of prayer.

Then going **out**, he **went**, as was his **custom**, to the Mount
of **Olives**,
and the **disciples followed** him.
When he **arrived** at the place he **said** to them,
"**Pray** that you may **not undergo** the **test**."
After withdrawing about a **stone's throw** from them and **kneeling**,
he **prayed**, saying, "**Father**, if you are **willing**,
take this cup away from me;
still, not **my** will but **yours** be done."
And to **strengthen** him an **angel from heaven appeared** to him.

Jesus is not in anguish here.

He was in **such agony** and he **prayed** so **fervently**
that his **sweat** became like **drops** of **blood**
falling on the **ground**.
When he **rose** from **prayer** and **returned** to his **disciples**,
he found them **sleeping** from **grief**.
He **said** to them, "**Why** are you **sleeping**?
Get up and **pray** that you may **not undergo** the **test**."

Now the agony begins in earnest.

Luke makes excuses for disciples' lack of vigilance. Jesus is forceful in his urging.

While he was **still speaking**, a **crowd** approached
and in **front** was **one** of the **Twelve**, a man named **Judas**.
He went up to **Jesus** to **kiss** him.
Jesus said to him,
"**Judas**, are you **betraying** the **Son** of **Man** with a **kiss**?"
His disciples **realized** what was about to happen, and they asked,
"**Lord**, shall we **strike** with a **sword**?"

The pain of betrayal is palpable.

Eager to defend.

of God. It is, rather, the perfect manifestation of God's heart, communicating God's universal love for humanity to the point of renouncing the self even to the point of death. Through the service of Christ, God comes into personal contact with all aspects of our poverty and offers the complete sacrifice of loving service.

By our Baptism and identification with Christ, every Christian is challenged to be the servant of others, to promote human life, and to embody the love that transcends the self and the limits imposed by sin. Our service of humankind is explicitly the work of divine transcendence and not reduced to philanthropy or humanism; it is directly linked to our confession of faith and thus to Christ.

READING II This Christological hymn presents the contrast between Jesus' humiliation to death and his exaltation above every other name. Christ did not hold on to divine privilege for himself. Rather, he was born in human flesh and became the servant of his sisters and brothers, selfless to the point of accepting an unjust, dishonorable death on the cross. The hymn presents him in three moments:

Jesus says: Don't interfere. Only Luke records this compassionate healing.

There is judgment in his voice.

And **one** of them struck the high priest's **servant**
  and **cut** off his right **ear**.
But **Jesus** said in reply,
  "Stop, **no more** of this!"
Then he **touched** the servant's ear and **healed** him.
And Jesus said to the **chief priests** and **temple guards**
  and **elders** who had **come** for him,
  "Have you come out as against a **robber**, with **swords**
    and **clubs**?
Day after **day** I was **with** you in the **temple** area,
  and you did **not seize** me;
  but **this** is **your hour**, the time for the **power** of **darkness**."

After **arresting** him they **led** him **away**
  and took him into the **house** of the **high priest**;
  Peter was following at a **distance**.
They lit a **fire** in the **middle** of the **courtyard** and **sat around** it,
  and **Peter** sat down **with** them.

She's too loud to ignore.

When a **maid** saw him **seated** in the **light**,
  she looked **intently** at him and said,
  "This man too was with him."
But he **denied** it saying,
  "Woman, I **do not know** him."

Peter still remains calm.

A short while **later** someone **else** saw him and said,
  "You too are **one** of them";
  but Peter answered, "My **friend**, I am **not**."

Hostile. Through clenched teeth.

About an hour **later**, still **another** insisted,
  "Assuredly, this man **too** was **with** him,
  for he **also** is a **Galilean**."
But **Peter** said,
  "My **friend**, I do **not know** what you are **talking** about."
Just as he was **saying** this, the **cock crowed**,
  and the **Lord turned** and **looked** at **Peter**;
  and **Peter remembered** the **word** of the **Lord**,
  how he had **said** to him,
  "Before the **cock crows** today, you will **deny** me
    three times." **»**

divine preexistence, debasement and death on the cross, and glorious exaltation. The first part traces a downward movement: Jesus Christ, Son of God, descended, "taking the form of a slave"; in the second, the Incarnation plunges him to obedience to the point of death, the ultimate self-surrender; finally, he advances upward when God intervenes to exalt him and give him the Name above every other name.

One interpretation is that here Christ is the replica of Adam. Christ is the image of God as was Adam, but, unlike Adam, he did not work that privilege to his own advantage. According to this interpretation, the hymn draws a parallel between the pride and disobedience of Adam and the humility and service of the Son of God. Thus the hymn praises Jesus for being faithful to his human condition up to the end, even in death, while Adam was unfaithful in grasping after what was not properly his and trying to elude death. Between the two, the one who is equal to God is the one who is true to his status of a human being.

GOSPEL In Luke's account of the passion, Jesus demonstrates what he taught throughout his

Jesus' look releases bitter tears. Luke alone relates this detail.

Pause.

As narrator, you are angered by this treatment of Jesus.

Prophesy = PROF-uh-sī

He **went out** and **began** to **weep bitterly**.

The men who held Jesus in **custody** were **ridiculing** and
　　beating him.
They **blindfolded** him and **questioned** him, saying,
　"**Prophesy! Who is it** that **struck** you?"
And they **reviled** him in saying **many other things against** him.

"Sanhedrin" = san-HEE-druhn. There is tension throughout the scene.

When **day** came the council of **elders** of the people **met**,
　　both **chief priests** and **scribes**,
　and they brought him **before** their **Sanhedrin**.
They said, "If **you are** the **Christ, tell us**,"
　but he **replied** to them, "If I **tell you**, **you** will **not believe**,
　and if I **question**, you will **not respond**.
But from **this time on** the **Son** of **Man** will be **seated**
　at the **right hand** of the **power** of **God**."
They all asked, "**Are** you then the **Son** of **God**?"
He replied to them, "**You** say that I am."
Then they said, "What further **need** have **we** for **testimony**?
We have **heard** it from his **own mouth**."

Pilate comes across as sympathetic. His interest in Jesus grows steadily.

[Then the **whole assembly** of them **arose** and **brought** him
　　before **Pilate**.
They brought **charges** against him, saying,
　"We found this man **misleading** our people;
　he **opposes** the payment of **taxes** to **Caesar**
　and **maintains** that **he** is the **Christ**, a **king**."
Pilate asked him, "**Are you** the **king** of the **Jews**?"
He said to him in reply, "**You** say so."
Pilate then addressed the **chief priests** and the **crowds**,
　"I find this man **not guilty**."
But they were **adamant** and said,
　"He is **inciting** the **people** with his **teaching**
　　throughout **all Judea**,
　from **Galilee** where he **began even** to **here**."

He's a blasphemer!

On the offensive, they accuse him of political crimes.

"Galilean" = gal-ih-LEE-uhn. Pilate is eager to be rid of Jesus.

ministry. Thus, at the Last Supper, the total gift of his person in the bread and wine is the proof of his humble service. To the prediction of Peter's denial Jesus adds the prayer that, once recovered, he can support the brothers in the faith. The passion is presented as the final struggle against Satan, who returns after the third temptation following his baptism in the Jordan. Jesus teaches that this struggle will also fall

on the disciples, and those who persevere in the test or by repentance will triumph. The agony of Gethsemane must be understood as an intense struggle and prayer, as well as a complete expression of abandonment to the Father's will.

In the shadow of his redemptive work was his friend Judas Iscariot, who started the chain of events that led to the arrest, the mock trial, the way of the cross, and

death. Without the hand of Judas, would the Father's plan for our salvation have been achieved?

Jesus is the faithful witness, strong in his declarations before the Sanhedrin and humble before the mockery, the blows, and the bitter hatred against him. He shows himself to be a compassionate prophet to the daughters of Jerusalem, he is the merciful intercessor on behalf of his enemies,

Herod is expecting to be entertained.

On hearing **this** Pilate asked if the **man** was a **Galilean**;
and upon learning that he was under **Herod's** jurisdiction,
he sent him to **Herod**, who was in **Jerusalem** at that time.
Herod was **very glad** to see **Jesus**;
he had been **wanting** to see him for a **long time**,
for he had **heard** about him
and had been **hoping** to **see** him perform some **sign**.
He **questioned** him at **length**,
but he gave him **no answer**.
The **chief priests** and **scribes**, meanwhile,
stood by **accusing** him **harshly**.

Again, you are not an impartial narrator.

Herod and his **soldiers** treated him **contemptuously**
and **mocked** him,
and after **clothing** him in **resplendent garb**,
he **sent** him back to **Pilate**.

Don't rush this detail.

Herod and **Pilate** became **friends that very day**,
even though they had been **enemies** formerly.
Pilate then summoned the **chief priests**, the **rulers**
and the **people**
and said to them, **"You** brought **this man** to **me**
and **accused** him of **inciting** the **people** to **revolt**.

Pilate makes his best effort, arguing logically and convincingly.

I have conducted my investigation in **your presence**
and have **not found** this man **guilty**
of the **charges** you have brought **against** him,
nor did **Herod**, for **he** sent him **back** to us.
So **no capital crime** has been **committed** by him.
Therefore I shall have him **flogged** and then **release** him."

The crowd turns ugly.

But **all together** they **shouted out**,
"Away with this man!
Release Barabbas to us."

Barabbas offers a glimmer of hope. Read as if hoping Pilate might persuade them.

—Now **Barabbas** had been **imprisoned** for a **rebellion**
that had taken place in the **city** and for **murder**.—
Again Pilate **addressed** them, **still wishing** to **release** Jesus,
but they **continued** their **shouting**,
"Crucify him! **Crucify** him!"

and he is the Savior who welcomes a criminal into his Kingdom. It is on the cross that Jesus' earthly ministry is fulfilled; there he surrenders his life into the Father's hands, the perfect sacrifice for the conversion and salvation of the world.

The Palm Sunday liturgy celebrates opposite poles of the human heart. On one side, the choir chants, "Blessed is the king who comes in the name of the Lord." On the other, the rabble holler, "Crucify him, crucify him!" Jesus is the protagonist, greeted with festivity and outrage. Both scenes take place in the same city: the people who accompany their king with praise are the ones who betray and deny him, and finally allow him to be put to death. No wonder it is like this. We know too well the tug-of-war within the human heart. On the one hand, my heart is able to sense a reality beyond what is obvious, to pray and praise the King, Jesus, and submit to his reign. Peter is our spokesman: "Lord, I am prepared to go to prison and to die with you." A few hours later, the same heart is able to reject Jesus, with the voice of the same Peter: "I do not know him, woman."

The human role in the story of our redemption is not only one of betrayal,

Pilate more emotional now.

Their anger persuades him.
A very reluctant decision.

"Cyrenian" = sī-REE-nee-uhn

Blessed = BLES-uhd

TO KEEP IN MIND
Proclamation cannot be effective
unless it is expressive. As you
prepare your proclamation, make
choices about emotions. Some
choices are already evident in the
text.

Pilate addressed them a **third** time,
   "**What evil** has this man **done**? »
   I found him **guilty** of **no capital crime**.
Therefore I shall have him **flogged** and then **release** him."
With **loud shouts**, however,
   they **persisted** in calling for his **crucifixion**,
   and **their** voices **prevailed**.
The **verdict** of **Pilate** was that their **demand** should be **granted**.
So he **released** the man who had been **imprisoned**
   for **rebellion** and **murder**, for whom they **asked**,
   and he **handed Jesus over** to them to **deal** with as they **wished**.

As they **led him away**
   they took hold of a certain **Simon**, a **Cyrenian**,
   who was coming in from the **country**;
   and after **laying** the **cross** on him,
   they **made** him **carry** it **behind Jesus**.
A **large crowd** of people **followed Jesus**,
   including **many women** who **mourned** and **lamented** him.
Jesus **turned** to them and **said**,
   "**Daughters** of **Jerusalem**, do **not** weep for **me**;
   weep instead for **yourselves** and for your **children**
   for **indeed**, the **days are coming** when **people** will **say**,
   '**Blessed** are the **barren**,
   the **wombs** that never **bore**
   and the **breasts** that never **nursed**.'
At **that time** people will say to the **mountains**,
   '**Fall upon us**!'
   and to the **hills**, '**Cover us**!'
   for if these things are done when the **wood** is **green**
   what will **happen** when it is **dry**?"
Now **two others**, **both criminals**,
   were **led** away **with** him to be **executed**.

---

however. In the plan of the new creation in Christ crucified and resurrected, there are also several actors who accompany the divine savior. As he approached Jerusalem, Jesus sent two disciples to fetch his transport; he made use of a donkey and the foal of a donkey as a symbol of his reign of peace. A few days later, the majestic provider of everything depended on the provisions of other people in the preparation for the Passover meal, which was an advance of the sacrifice on the cross. Hours later, in Gethsemane, he requested that Peter and the Zebedee sons accompany him in his solitude: "Stay here and watch with me." Jesus needed Caiaphas, the high priest, to interrogate him and examine his identity as Messiah and the Son of God. As Simon Peter was denying him, Pilate's wife recognized and declared that the accused Jesus was a righteous man. On the way to Golgotha, Jesus needed the strength of Simon of Cyrene to carry his cross. Jesus heard the confession of a thief crucified with him, and who pleaded for entry into his Reign. When he was thirsty, Jesus voiced his thirst, and someone offered him a sponge soaked in vinegar to drink. Jesus, once dead, received the verdict of the executioners: "Truly, this one was innocent."

Jesus ministers even as he goes to his death.
Speaking through exhaustion and pain.
Slowly.
Pause briefly after this poignant line.

When they came to the **place** called the **Skull**,
   they **crucified** him and the **criminals** there,
   one on his **right**, **the other** on his **left**.
Then **Jesus** said,
   "Father, **forgive** them, they **know not** what **they do."**
They **divided** his **garments** by **casting lots**.

People watch. It's the leaders and soldiers who jeer; speak with their voices.

The **people stood** by and **watched**;
   the **rulers**, meanwhile, **sneered** at him and said,
   "He **saved others**, let him **save himself**
   if he is the **chosen** one, the **Christ** of **God."**
Even the **soldiers** jeered at him.
As they **approached** to **offer** him **wine** they called **out**,
   "If **you** are King of the **Jews**, **save yourself."**

Emphatic. Spoken in Pilate's voice.

Above him there was an **inscription** that read,
   "This is the **King** of the **Jews."**

Now **one** of the **criminals** hanging there **reviled** Jesus, saying,
   "Are you **not** the **Christ**?
   Save yourself and us."
The **other**, however, **rebuking** him, said in reply,
   "Have **you no fear** of **God**,
   for **you** are subject to the **same condemnation**?
And **indeed**, **we** have been **condemned justly**,
   for the sentence **we received corresponds** to our **crimes**,
   but **this** man has done **nothing criminal**."

Remember, he too is exhausted and dying, but sincere.
A prayer. As if murmured over and over.
Take time with this.

Then he said,
   "Jesus, **remember** me when you **come** into your **kingdom**."
He replied to him,
   "Amen, **I say** to **you**,
   today you will be **with** me in **Paradise**."

The powers of darkness are raging.

It was **now** about **noon** and **darkness** came
     over the **whole land**
   until **three** in the **afternoon**
   because of an **eclipse** of the **sun**.
Then the **veil** of the **temple** was **torn** down the **middle**. »

And he made use of a centurion with a spear, who opened the font of living water and blood of salvation.

The author of life needed the women who accompanied him in his ministry in Galilee, who observed the funeral and wept, and who later verified the site of the tomb. He required Joseph of Arimathea to take care of the funeral arrangements, and Nicodemus, who earlier had interviewed with Jesus at night, and who after the death and before sunset, anointed the body of Jesus with costly perfumes. On Resurrection day he depended on his friends; Mary Magdalene, the other Mary, Salome, and Joanna, who rose early to visit and mourn at the gravesite, and there received the announcement of the angel of the Resurrection.

The central character of the drama of Holy Week enlists numerous supporting players to bring to fulfillment the creation of a new world, our redemption. Among them, we count ourselves. We may accompany Jesus in his Gethsemane, or with Ms. Pilate, to confess him innocent, or with the soldiers, to proclaim, "Truly, he was Son of God." We deal with the preparations and details to receive Jesus in our small world,

"Father / into your hands / I commend my spirit." Deliberate and peaceful.

Jesus cried out in a **loud voice**,
  "**Father**, into **your hands** I **commend** my **spirit**";
and when he had **said** this he **breathed** his **last**.

[Here all kneel and pause for a short time.]

Jesus' innocence declared again. Crowd experiences change of heart. Women watch prayerfully.

The **centurion** who **witnessed** what had **happened glorified God**
    and said,
  "**This man** was **innocent beyond doubt**."
When **all** the **people** who had **gathered** for this spectacle **saw**
    what had **happened**,
  they returned **home beating** their **breasts**;
  but **all** his **acquaintances stood** at a **distance**,
  including the **women** who had **followed** him from **Galilee**
  and **saw** these events.]

Joseph is obviously a believer.

Now there was a **virtuous** and **righteous** man
    named **Joseph**, who,
  though he was a **member** of the **council**,
  had **not consented** to their plan of action.

"Arimathea" = ayr-ih-muh-THEE-uh

He came from the **Jewish** town of **Arimathea**
  and was **awaiting** the **kingdom** of **God**.
He went to **Pilate** and **asked** for the **body** of **Jesus**.
After he had taken the **body down**,

Don't rush these many details.

  he **wrapped** it in a **linen cloth**
  and **laid** him in a **rock-hewn tomb**
  in which **no one** had **yet** been **buried**.
It was the **day** of **preparation**,
  and the **sabbath** was about to **begin**.

It is the women who take notice and prepare.

The **women** who had come from **Galilee** with him
    followed behind,
  and when they had **seen** the **tomb**
  and the **way** in which his **body** was **laid** in it,
  they **returned** and **prepared spices** and **perfumed oils**.
Then they **rested** on the **sabbath** according to the **commandment**.

[Shorter: Luke 23:1–49 (see brackets)]

in the heart of our family or community, in our workplace, at our meals and fiestas. Our shadowy service consists in offering our sins and faults, which spark mercy at the dawn of the new world. At other times, we serve Jesus like Simon of Cyrene, bearing his cross, or we play the part of the donkey, who chauffeured the king into his reign, and on the back of whom Jesus was proclaimed sovereign. The drama of passion, which we contemplate throughout this Holy Week of our redemption, celebrates that life which in all its details serves a transcendent purpose in the plan of God—all powerful yet in need of us. In the course of this week, we have ample opportunity to know ourselves better, to hear the sad and joyful cries and the contrary songs of our own heart, to accompany with faith and love the one who died for our sins, by whose blood we have been washed. K.S.

HOLY THURSDAY: MASS OF THE LORD'S SUPPER

LECTIONARY #39

READING I   Exodus 12:1–8, 11–14

A reading from the Book of Exodus

The LORD said to **Moses** and **Aaron** in the land of **Egypt**,
  "This **month** shall stand at the **head** of your **calendar;**
  you shall reckon it the **first** month of the year.
Tell the whole **community** of **Israel:**
  On the **tenth** of this month every one of your families
  must procure for itself a **lamb**, one apiece for each **household**.
If a family is too **small** for a whole lamb,
  it shall **join** the **nearest** household in procuring one
  and shall **share** in the lamb
  in **proportion** to the number of persons who **partake** of it.
The lamb must be a year-old **male** and without **blemish**.
You may **take** it from either the **sheep** or the **goats**.
You shall **keep** it until the **fourteenth** day of this month,
  and **then**, with the whole assembly of Israel **present**,
  it shall be **slaughtered** during the evening **twilight**.
They shall take some of its **blood**
  and apply it to the two **doorposts** and the **lintel**
  of every **house** in which they **partake** of the lamb.
That same **night** they shall **eat** its roasted **flesh**
  with **unleavened** bread and bitter **herbs**. »

Through these many details regarding a ritual meal, you evoke the roots of our faith and help us be present to that original event and experience it tonight.
This sacred meal has bonded the Jewish people and united them to their ancestors for thousands of years. What you describe is of great significance.
Your tone must suggest these are not fussy details, but a means of sustaining the nation.

God is aware of the needs and the limits of his people.

This offering to the Lord must not be flawed, but the finest they have to offer.

The ritual draws the people together in community.

This blood will become a life-saving sign.

All is done in haste: no time for dough to rise, so "*unleavened* bread" is required. Bitter herbs will remind them of their bitter enslavement.

READING I   In the account of the Passover meal in Exodus, the details can be applied to the life of the baptized Christian. The first requirement, a lamb, "a year-old male and without blemish . . . from either the sheep or the goats," to be slaughtered on the late afternoon of the fourteenth day, that is, the night of the full moon of the first month of springtime, with "the whole assembly of Israel present." Some of the victim's blood is painted "on the doorposts and the lintel of every house in which they partake of the lamb." The supper, of "roasted flesh with unleavened bread and bitter herbs," is eaten "with your loins girt, sandals on your feet and your staff in hand," as if the dinner guests were in a hurry to leave on a journey. In Christian terms, this means that the faithful be prepared to leave the passing world, to take the road to the promised land and so live with provident God, not to accommodate ourselves too comfortably in the present world without concern for our life with God. The crucified and resurrected Christ is the Lamb who saves us from death. The blood on the doorposts and lintels is the Eucharist that preserves our life and saves us from death. The blood of Christ will deliver us from judgment, because the sacrificed Lamb takes away the sin of the world, reconciles us with God, and delivers us from the slavery to sin.

READING II   Paul narrates the Eucharistic memorial of God's deliverance in Christ. Like the Passover, this memorial is a festal meal that features the cup of "the new covenant" in Christ's blood, both poignant signs of life shared between the two covenant partners. Paul reminds the Corinthians of

Speak in an authoritative tone that culminates in the weighty pronouncement: "It is the Passover . . . ."

Don't shy from these hard images of destruction: Israelites and Egyptians are in the hands of the all-powerful God.
"I, the LORD" is a declaration of God's singular sovereignty.
Again, blood, the sign of death, becomes a sign of new life.

In these lines we hear God's voice saying to Israel, I have chosen you and will let no harm come to you.
This is a solemn pronouncement; observing this commandment will help ensure Israel's future.

For meditation and context:

> "This is **how** you are to **eat** it:
> with your loins **girt**, **sandals** on your feet and your **staff**
> in **hand**,
> you shall eat like those who are in **flight**.
> It is the **Passover** of the LORD.
> For on this **same** night I will go through **Egypt**,
> **striking** down every **firstborn** of the land, both **man** and **beast**,
> and executing **judgment** on all the **gods** of Egypt—I, the LORD!
> But the **blood** will mark the houses where **you** are.
> **Seeing** the blood, I will pass **over** you;
> **thus**, when I **strike** the land of Egypt,
> **no** destructive blow will come upon **you**.
>
> "**This** day shall be a **memorial feast** for you,
> which all your generations shall **celebrate**
> with **pilgrimage** to the LORD, as a **perpetual** institution."

RESPONSORIAL PSALM   Psalm 116:12–13, 15–16bc, 17–18
(see 1 Corinthians 10:16)

R. Our blessing-cup is a communion with the Blood of Christ.

How shall I make a return to the LORD
for all the good he has done for me?
The cup of salvation I will take up,
and I will call upon the name of the LORD.

Precious in the eyes of the LORD
is the death of his faithful ones.
I am your servant, the son of your
handmaid;
you have loosed my bonds.

To you will I offer sacrifice of thanksgiving,
and I will call upon the name of the LORD.
My vows to the LORD I will pay
in the presence of all his people.

TO KEEP IN MIND
Don't neglect the Responsorial Psalm just because you aren't proclaiming it. Pray it as part of your preparation.

the tradition of the Lord's Supper. Jesus, "on the night he was handed over," pronounced the words over the bread that interpret and make present his sacrifice: "This is my body that is for you." At the end of the meal, the words over the cup inaugurate the New Covenant. The words of institution over the bread and those over the wine announce the death of the Lord until he returns. The Eucharist is celebrated between Jesus' death and his final coming, that is, "until he returns." This Eucharist, the memorial of the New Covenant, will nourish and unify the participants with

each other and with our Lord, who has given his life for us.

GOSPEL The Gospel begins slowly, introducing Jesus' mindset before the Passover, and thus his Passion: he knew his hour had come, he loved his own, and he was confident that God had given him everything. Thus the evangelist draws out the description of Jesus' last supper with his disciples. It is the hour we have been waiting for since the marriage at Cana, the hour of Jesus' proof of love and power.

The slow beginning is in contrast with the moving picture that follows. Jesus rose, stripped himself of his outer garment, wrapped a towel around his waist, poured water in a basin, and began to wash the disciples' feet. Do we not hear the echo of Paul's hymn in Philippians about Jesus: being of divine condition, he divested himself of his greatness (took off his cloak) and assumed the condition of a slave (girded a towel)? The love and power of God's Son is portrayed in the actions of a servant! This gesture takes on special meaning because

Corinthians = kohr-IN-thee-uhnz

This short text is a precious condensation of Christ's institution of the Eucharist. Each detail is chosen, so all are significant.

Paul was not there, so his narrative came to him through revelation from Christ. Don't miss the poignant detail that it's "the night he was betrayed."
Note the verbs: "took," gave thanks, "broke."

Only Paul and Luke relate the command to "Do this . . . in remembrance of me."

This is an intimate moment of self-giving. It's Jesus' voice we hear.
Paul's voice returns underscoring the great significance of the ritual we are privileged to celebrate.

READING II   1 Corinthians 11:23–26

A reading from the first Letter of Saint Paul to the Corinthians

Brothers and sisters:
I **received** from the Lord what I also handed on to **you**,
    that the Lord **Jesus**, on the **night** he was handed **over**,
    took **bread**, and, after he had given **thanks**,
    broke it and said, "This is my **body** that is for **you**.
Do this in **remembrance** of me."
In the **same** way also the **cup**, after supper, saying,
    "This cup is the new **covenant** in my **blood**.
Do this, as often as you **drink** it, in **remembrance** of me."
For as often as you **eat** this bread and **drink** the cup,
    you proclaim the **death** of the **Lord** until he **comes**.

First you set the context—it is "before . . . the Passover" and when "his hour had come."
This reminder of his enduring love for them will be enacted shortly.
Don't miss the assertion of the devil's role in the imminent betrayal.

In John, Jesus is always fully aware and in control of what is happening around him.

Used to caring for and waiting on him, the disciples are thrown by this role-reversal.

GOSPEL   John 13:1–15

A reading from the holy Gospel according to John

Before the feast of **Passover**, Jesus knew that his hour had **come**
    to pass from **this** world to the **Father**.
He loved his **own** in the world and he loved them to the **end**.
The **devil** had already induced **Judas**, son of Simon the **Iscariot**,
    to hand him **over**.
So, during **supper**,
    fully **aware** that the Father had put **everything** into his power
    and that he had **come** from God and was **returning** to God,
    he **rose** from supper and took off his outer **garments**.
He took a **towel** and **tied** it around his **waist**.
Then he poured **water** into a **basin**
    and began to **wash** the disciples' **feet**
    and **dry** them with the towel around his waist. »

---

of the time it takes place: the day before his death.

After washing his disciples' feet, Jesus instructs them to do the same: "If I, . . . the master and teacher, have washed your feet, you ought to wash one another's feet." How eloquent a teacher, whose example speaks louder than words! To present himself at our feet is what the Son of God does by stripping himself of his divinity, putting on the clothing of our humanity, placing himself at the service of our health and salvation, and inviting us to identify with him by doing the same. "I have

given you a model to follow, so that what I have done for you, you should also do." Here the lesson is acted out: stripping ourselves of our pretensions, lending ourselves to mutual service, offering unassuming gestures, as conscious and loving as a mother or father, divested of particular interests or desirous of applause in the service of the family.

At the Last Supper, Jesus instituted the Eucharist, the priesthood, and the commandment of love. In addition, he gives us an example of humility and service, teaching what it means to be his disciple. He

took the place of the servant, recognized the greater dignity of his neighbor, and forgot his own dignity in favor of the other. What Jesus will do in the following hours will be an even greater lesson: he will love us to death, renounce himself for our sake.

The evangelist introduces the last supper with these words: "Before the feast of the Passover, Jesus knew that his hour had come to pass from this world to the Father. He loved his own in the world and he loved them to the end." Everything is related under the heading of love: the Passover supper, the foot washing, the farewell

Peter's discomfort is genuine.

Jesus responds gently and fails to persuade Peter.

Again, Peter is sincerely asserting, "I can never let you humiliate yourself this way."

Jesus' stronger, clearer response causes a complete reversal in Peter.

Jesus' gentle tone returns, assuring Peter he is already "clean."

"But not all . . ." must have elicited a twinge of pain in Jesus.

Jesus' question is rhetorical and he immediately shares his prepared answer.

Jesus' emphatic speech signals an awareness that this will be a hard teaching to adopt.

Here is yet more emphasis from Jesus to do as he has done.

He came to Simon **Peter**, who said to him,
 "**Master**, are you going to wash **my** feet?"
Jesus **answered** and said to him,
 "What I am **doing**, you do not understand **now**,
 but you **will** understand **later**."
Peter said to him, "You will **never** wash my **feet**."
Jesus answered him,
 "Unless I **wash** you, you will have no **inheritance** with me."
Simon Peter said to him,
 "**Master**, then not only my **feet**, but my **hands** and **head**
  as well."
Jesus said to him,
 "Whoever has **bathed** has no **need** except to have his
  feet washed,
 for he is clean all **over**;
 so **you** are clean, but not **all**."
For he knew who would **betray** him;
 for this **reason**, he said, "Not **all** of you are clean."

So when he had **washed** their **feet**
 and put his **garments** back on and reclined at **table** again,
 he **said** to them, "Do you **realize** what I have **done** for you?
You call me '**teacher**' and '**master**,' and **rightly** so, for indeed I **am**.
If **I**, therefore, the **master** and **teacher**, have washed **your** feet,
 you ought to wash one **another's** feet.
I have given you a **model** to follow,
 so that as **I** have done for **you**, you should **also** do."

speech. To be Jesus' disciple is to abide in his love, which moves him to serve and to give us life. Following Jesus, communing with him, involves walking the path he opened for us: attaining glory by the loving surrender of our own lives.

In this same supper, Jesus instituted the Eucharist. Once again, the atmosphere of love and self-surrender permeates the moment of the institution: my body for you, the new covenant in my blood. Here he teaches that the meaning of the Eucharist is inseparable from his death and Resurrection. He offers himself as the means of our holy communion with God and with one another. Just as his love for humanity achieved salvation for humankind, communion with his body and blood teaches us to live and put into practice this unconditional love. K.S.

GOOD FRIDAY: CELEBRATION OF THE LORD'S PASSION

LECTIONARY #40

READING I   Isaiah 52:13—53:12

A reading from the Book of the Prophet Isaiah

Isaiah = ĭ-ZAY-uh

The voice of God, strong and proud.

Sudden mood shift to narrating the suffering of God's servant.

The sense of this verse is: In the way that many were amazed at him—because he was so disfigured he didn't even look human—in that same way others will be startled and astonished.

New voice: that of the people.

Much lamenting here. People hid their faces because he was not pleasing to look at.

See, my servant shall **prosper**,
  he shall be raised **high** and greatly **exalted**.
Even as many were **amazed** at him—
  so **marred** was his look beyond human **semblance**
  and his **appearance** beyond that of the sons of **man**—
so shall he **startle** many **nations**,
  because of him **kings** shall stand **speechless**;
for those who have not been **told** shall **see**,
  those who have not **heard** shall **ponder** it.

Who would **believe** what we have heard?
  To **whom** has the **arm** of the Lord been **revealed**?
He grew up like a **sapling** before him,
  like a **shoot** from the parched **earth**;
there was in him no **stately** bearing to make us **look** at him,
  nor **appearance** that would **attract** us to him.
He was **spurned** and **avoided** by people,
  a man of **suffering**, accustomed to **infirmity**,
one of those from whom people **hide** their faces,
  spurned, and we held him in no **esteem**.

Yet it was **our** infirmities that he bore,
  our **sufferings** that he endured,
while we thought of him as **stricken**,
  as one **smitten** by God and **afflicted**. »

READING I This canticle is one reason the prophet Isaiah could be called the fifth evangelist. The Servant of the Lord, like an innocent lamb burdened with the sins of his people, is led in silence to the altar of sacrifice. Initially, God announces the nobility of his ill-treated servant, who humbled himself, and did not open his mouth; the servant desired that God take these sufferings into account and bring good out of the pain. The people express surprise at the exaltation of such a person, one who endured our sufferings and humiliation. Finally, God welcomes this righteous servant who bore our guilt and, through suffering, made others righteous. This innocent servant, who took upon himself everybody's sin, was counted among sinners and gave his life for them. In response, God enriches him who took on the sins of all people, so that they may live to the full. This understanding of vicarious suffering is unique in the Old Testament. From the time of the Gospels Christians have interpreted the Servant songs to refer to Jesus' passion and death.

"Stripes" meaning the marks left behind from a whipping.

> But he was **pierced** for our **offenses**,
>   **crushed** for our **sins**;
> upon **him** was the chastisement that makes us **whole**,
>   by his **stripes** we were **healed**.
> We had all gone astray like **sheep**,
>   each following his **own** way;
> but the LORD laid upon **him**
>   the guilt of us **all**.

Softer tone. The two images—"lamb," "sheep"—make the same point so the pace can be a bit quicker, though intensity should not wane.

> Though he was **harshly** treated, he **submitted**
>   and opened **not** his mouth;
> like a **lamb** led to the **slaughter**
>   or a **sheep** before the **shearers**,
>   he was **silent** and opened not his mouth.

"Oppressed" and "condemned" are *two* distinct words; don't rush them together. Perhaps anger and regret over this indignity.

> **Oppressed** and **condemned**, he was taken **away**,
>   and who would have thought any more of his **destiny**?
> When he was cut **off** from the land of the living,
>   and **smitten** for the sin of his people,
> a **grave** was assigned him among the **wicked**
>   and a **burial** place with **evildoers**,
> though he had done **no wrong**
>   nor spoken any **falsehood**.

Resignation.

> But the LORD was **pleased**
>   to **crush** him in **infirmity**.

Voice of God returns—Energetic, proud, and proclaiming.

> If he gives his **life** as an offering for **sin**,
>   he shall see his **descendants** in a **long** life,
>   and the **will** of the LORD shall be **accomplished**
>   through him.

Quieter now, but persuasive.

> Because of his **affliction**
>   he shall see the **light** in fullness of days;
> through his **suffering**, my servant shall justify **many**,
>   and their **guilt** he shall **bear**.
> **Therefore** I will give him his **portion** among the **great**,
>   and **he** shall divide the **spoils** with the **mighty**,

High point of the reading; Servant is honored; but notice *why*: he suffered willingly!

Omnipotence renounces itself and becomes impotence, but Jesus lives the apparent failure and defeat, the fruit of his surrender to God and people, with confidence in God's parental care. From his pierced side springs the blood with which those who belong to the new people are mysteriously marked. Christ is crucified, our Passover lamb has been sacrificed, the covenant is sealed by the lamb's blood, and the people are freed from slavery to sin and ushered into the Promised Land of life eternal with God.

Because of his suffering, the Servant is repulsive to those who look upon him. Yet his suffering is intimately tied up with our own, for it is the consequence of our sins. His silent suffering wins justification for many, and thus the suffering servant on the cross is the emblem of our triumph.

Ritardando (slowing toward the end): "and win pardon . . . offenses."

because he **surrendered** himself to **death**
and was counted among the **wicked**;
and he shall take **away** the sins of **many**,
and win **pardon** for their **offenses**.

For meditation and context:

RESPONSORIAL PSALM   Psalm 31:2, 6, 12–13, 15–16, 17, 25 (Luke 23:46)

R. Father, into your hands I commend my spirit.

In you, O LORD, I take refuge;
   let me never be put to shame.
In your justice rescue me.
Into your hands I commend my spirit;
   you will redeem me, O LORD,
     O faithful God.

For all my foes I am an object of reproach,
   a laughingstock to my neighbors, and a
     dread to my friends;
   they who see me abroad flee from me.
I am forgotten like the unremembered dead;
   I am like a dish that is broken.

But my trust is in you, O LORD;
   I say, "You are my God.
In your hands is my destiny; rescue me
   from the clutches of my enemies and my
     persecutors."

Let your face shine upon your servant;
   save me in your kindness.
Take courage and be stouthearted,
   all you who hope in the LORD.

READING II   Hebrews 4:14–16; 5:7–9

A reading from the Letter to the Hebrews

Brothers and sisters:
Since we have a great high **priest** who has passed through
   the **heavens**,
   Jesus, the Son of **God**,
   let us hold **fast** to our **confession**.
For we do not have a high priest
   who is unable to **sympathize** with our **weaknesses**,
   but one who has similarly been tested in every way,
   yet without **sin**.
So let us **confidently** approach the throne of **grace**
   to receive **mercy** and to find grace for timely **help**.

In the days when Christ was in the **flesh**,
   he offered **prayers** and **supplications** with loud
     cries and **tears** »

Begin with confident rejoicing.

He was one of us. He can sympathize and knows our pain.

Confidently persuade us of his sinlessness.

Christ truly suffered: That's why he understands our suffering.

READING II   Jesus has been glorified and has entered in God's presence, and so, with his help, our faith is in a safe place. Jesus is the faithful and compassionate high priest, "who has passed through the heavens." He identifies with us through his trials and thus welcomes us into God's presence. Christ, the eternal priest, understands us because he was tested as we are. He suffered hunger and thirst, weariness, sadness, and temptations; he suffered humiliation and torture, and thus he can sympathize with us in our weaknesses. The result is that, thanks to Christ, we can "approach with confidence the throne of grace." Here the term "confidence" [in Greek, *parresia*] expresses not just a subjective feeling but a freedom of access which is ours by right. What made Jesus the perfect priest was the lesson of obedience that he taught by his life and service; the author alludes to the scene of Gethsemane. Thus, "he became the author of eternal salvation for all who obey him."

to the one who was able to **save** him from **death**,
  and he was **heard** because of his **reverence**.
Son though he **was**, he learned **obedience** from what he suffered;
  and when he was made **perfect**,
  he became the **source** of eternal **salvation** for all who **obey** him.

GOSPEL   John 18:1—19:42

The Passion of our Lord Jesus Christ according to John

Jesus went out with his **disciples** across the Kidron **valley**
  to where there was a **garden**,
  into which he and his disciples entered.
Judas his **betrayer also** knew the place,
  because Jesus had **often** met there with his disciples.
So Judas got a band of **soldiers** and **guards**
  from the chief **priests** and the **Pharisees**
  and went there with **lanterns**, **torches**, and **weapons**.
Jesus, knowing **everything** that was going to happen to him,
  went out and said to them, "Whom are you **looking** for?"
They **answered** him, "**Jesus** the **Nazorean**."
He said to them, "**I AM**."
Judas his betrayer was **also** with them.
When he said to them, "**I AM**,"
  they turned away and fell to the **ground**.
So he **again** asked them,
  "**Whom** are you looking for?"
They said, "**Jesus** the **Nazorean**."
Jesus answered,
  "I **told** you that **I AM**.
So if you are looking for **me**, let these men **go**."
This was to **fulfill** what he had said,
  "I have not lost **any** of those you gave me."

Margin notes:

Note: Jesus "learned" obedience through his suffering.

Jesus modeled obedience. We imitate him and find salvation. Ritardando (slowing toward the end): "for . . . obey him."

Kidron = KID-ruhn. The garden is a peaceful, familiar place.

The shadow of Judas suddenly shifts the mood.

"Lanterns" are symbolic of the hour of darkness.
Jesus moves forward fully aware and in charge of his destiny.

Jesus' power overwhelms the guards. He'll be taken only when he permits it.

GOSPEL   The passion according to John is a historical and theological treatise framed by the mention of the garden at the beginning and the end—the olive orchard known by its Hebrew name Gethsemane and the orchard or garden of the gravesite. This report unfolds in five scenes: the arrest of Jesus in the garden; Jesus before Annas, framed by Peter's first and second denials; Jesus before Pilate; the crucifixion; and the death and burial. What is surprising is the presentation of Jesus, who, different from the portrait of the suffering servant (Isaiah 53, the first reading), is characterized by his mastery of the situation throughout the arrest to the crucifixion. In John's passion, Jesus' kingship manifests itself in a special way in the trial before Pilate, where Jesus is proclaimed as sovereign of a kingdom not of this world. Another unique feature of John's passion is the emphasis on the Son's obedience to the Father. The quotes from the Old Testament are an expression of the Father's will, and they are designed to lead to faith in Christ. John 19:26–27, in which Jesus gives his mother to the care of the

Violence expressed with "struck" and "cut off."

Malchus = MAL-kuhs

Jesus rebukes Peter.

Annas = AN-uhs; Caiaphas = KĪ-uh-fuhs. This is a significant quote attributed to Caiaphas.

Is Peter kept out or staying out from fear?

Peter doesn't want to be overheard denying Jesus.
New scene. Renew energy.

Jesus is strong in his self-defense, showing the weakness of their "case."

Then Simon **Peter**, who had a **sword**, **drew** it,
　　struck the high priest's slave, and **cut** off his right ear.
The slave's name was **Malchus**.
Jesus said to Peter,
　　"Put your sword into its **scabbard**.
Shall I not **drink** the cup that the Father gave me?"

So the band of **soldiers**, the **tribune**, and the Jewish **guards**
　　　　seized Jesus,
　　bound him, and brought him to **Annas** first.
He was the **father-in-law** of **Caiaphas**,
　　who was high **priest** that year.
It was **Caiaphas** who had **counseled** the Jews
　　that it was better that **one** man should die rather than
　　　　the **people**.

Simon **Peter** and **another** disciple **followed** Jesus.
Now the **other** disciple was **known** to the high **priest**,
　　and he entered the **courtyard** of the high priest with **Jesus**.
But **Peter** stood at the gate **outside**.
So the other **disciple**, the **acquaintance** of the high priest,
　　went out and spoke to the **gatekeeper** and brought Peter **in**.
Then the **maid** who was the gatekeeper said to Peter,
　　"You are not one of this man's **disciples**, are you?"
He said, "I am **not**."
Now the slaves and the **guards** were standing around a char-
　　　　coal **fire**
　　that they had made, because it was **cold**,
　　and were **warming** themselves.
Peter was **also** standing there keeping warm.

The high priest **questioned** Jesus
　　about his **disciples** and about his **doctrine**.
Jesus **answered** him,
　　"I have spoken **publicly** to the world.
I have always taught in a **synagogue**
　　or in the **temple** area where all the Jews **gather**,
　　and in **secret** I have said **nothing**. Why ask **me**? ≫

beloved disciple, has no parallel in the other three Gospels. His hour has come, and his mother accompanies him along with the beloved disciple, who represents the true believers; Mary represents the Church and accentuates her spiritual maternity. Jesus' death is his glorification, and his burial emphasizes the high price of his passion and death.

Jesus dies at the hour when the paschal lambs in the temple were sacrificed. The difference is that his sacrifice is once and for all because the perfect sacrifice makes all other victims unnecessary. From his pierced side flows the Blood that cleanses those who belong to the new people of God and receive salvation. Christ crucified is the "true Passover lamb,"

sacrificed (see 1 Corinthians 5:7), and perfectly fulfilling the motive of all previous sacrifices: thus he seals the covenant with God that brings salvation. Jesus' suffering is a "glorious passion," for the Father has already given his answer that transforms defeat into triumph and the place of sacrifice of an innocent servant becomes the center of universal attraction: "When I am

Deliver line like a slap—fast and hard.

Jesus holds his ground.

New scene.

Peter gets angry.

The denials are brief, but with this line suggest the lasting impact on Peter.

A spat among political adversaries. Each is annoyed with the other.

Ask those who **heard** me what I said to them.
They know what I said."
When he had **said** this,
one of the temple guards standing there **struck** Jesus and said,
"Is this the way you answer the high **priest**?"
Jesus answered him,
"If I have spoken **wrongly**, **testify** to the wrong;
but if I have spoken **rightly**, why do you **strike** me?"
Then Annas sent him **bound** to **Caiaphas** the high priest.

Now Simon **Peter** was standing there keeping warm.
And they **said** to him,
"**You** are not one of his disciples, **are** you?"
He **denied** it and said,
"I am **not**."
One of the **slaves** of the high priest,
a **relative** of the one whose **ear** Peter had cut **off**, said,
"Didn't I see you in the **garden** with him?"
Again Peter denied it.
And **immediately** the **cock** crowed.

Then they brought Jesus from **Caiaphas** to the **praetorium**.
It was **morning**.
And they themselves did not **enter** the praetorium,
in order not to be **defiled** so that they could eat the **Passover**.
So **Pilate** came out to **them** and said,
"What **charge** do you bring against this man?"
They **answered** and said to him,
"If he were not a **criminal**,
we would not have handed him over to you."
At this, **Pilate** said to them,
"Take him **yourselves**, and **judge** him according to your **law**."
The Jews **answered** him,
"We do not have the right to **execute** anyone,"
in order that the word of Jesus might be **fulfilled**
that he said indicating the kind of **death** he would die.

lifted from the earth, I will attract all people to me "(John 12:32). In the slain lamb's flesh "all things were fulfilled" (John 19:30), the Father's plan to gather all God's children previously dispersed by sin (John 11:52). Through the Lamb's blood, God reconciles humankind with himself once and for all, so we can enter into a communion of life with him (second reading). At his death, Jesus shares perfectly the Spirit with the Father, and at the same time, he pours his Spirit, the source of new life, into our humanity.

Central to this liturgy is the contemplation of the crucifix, and we hear the acclamation "Behold, the wood of the Cross, on which hung the salvation of the world." Two thousand years ago the cross of Jesus was hoisted upright outside the Jerusalem walls during a festival. Today, just as long ago, we behold the cross. And what is our reaction? Many pass by, glancing out of curiosity. Others stop and look, or hurriedly turn away in horror. Many persons pass by, almost without realizing what has gone on at Golgotha, and they continue on their way. They may turn momentarily toward the sight of the con-

Scene shift. Pilate is "starting over." Pilate is not presented as a villain.

Stressing "are" or "king" changes the meaning of the question.

Jesus speaks with confidence.

So **Pilate** went back into the **praetorium**
and **summoned** Jesus and said to him,
"Are you the **King** of the **Jews**?"
Jesus answered,
"Do you say this on your **own**
or have **others** told you about me?"
Pilate answered,
"I am not a **Jew**, am I?
Your own **nation** and the chief **priests** handed you over to me.
What have you **done**?"
Jesus answered,
"My **kingdom** does not belong to **this** world.
If my kingdom **did** belong to this world,
my attendants would be **fighting**
to **keep** me from being handed over to the Jews.
But as it **is**, my kingdom is not **here**."
So Pilate said to him,
"Then you **are** a king?"
Jesus answered,
"**You** say I am a king.
For this I was **born** and for **this** I came into the **world**,
to **testify** to the **truth**.
Everyone who **belongs** to the truth **listens** to my voice."
Pilate said to him, "What is **truth**?"

When he had **said** this,
he **again** went out to the Jews and said to them,
"I find no **guilt** in him.
But you have a custom that I release one **prisoner** to you
at **Passover**.
Do you want me to release to you the **King** of the **Jews**?"
They cried out again,
"Not **this** one but **Barabbas**!"
Now Barabbas was a **revolutionary**. »

Seeking a quick resolution. Is he trying to put words in their mouths?

Barabbas = buh-RAB-uhs

demned criminals before they return to their business, as their lives have little to do with a man hanging on a cross. It would be impossible to help such a person, and what is the use? What can be done for somebody whose hands are nailed to a cross? There really is little that a person can do to take away the pain. The result is, for so many that do not stop, that the cruci-

fied is just another person, perhaps a victim of society's wrongs. So people pass by; perhaps they turn and look back once more, for death by crucifixion is not the usual way to die. Perhaps some shake their heads, insult the crucified, or pity him. Some might wonder what that criminal might have done to deserve such a death sentence.

Some onlookers may be saddened to behold the cross, but they keep on their way because they cannot see beyond the surface. If we were looking for a figure to embody our hopes and dreams, a gold medal athlete, a movie star, or a wealthy entrepreneur would be more attractive than a crucified man would. Some people pass by and feel cheated, like Cleopas: "We

A greatly understated scene, but the pain
is real.

Then Pilate took Jesus and had him **scourged**.
And the soldiers wove a **crown** out of **thorns** and placed it
    on his **head**,
    and clothed him in a **purple** cloak,
    and they came to him and said,
    "**Hail**, **King** of the **Jews**!"
And they **struck** him **repeatedly**.
Once **more** Pilate went out and said to them,
    "**Look**, I am bringing him out to you,
    so that you may **know** that I find no **guilt** in him."
So Jesus came out,
    wearing the crown of **thorns** and the purple **cloak**.

Perhaps he is saying: Look at what you made
me do!

When a phrase is repeated, give greater
stress to second utterance.

And he said to them, "**Behold**, the man!"
When the chief priests and the guards saw him they **cried** out,
    "**Crucify** him, **crucify** him!"
Pilate said to them,
    "Take him **yourselves** and crucify him.
I find no **guilt** in him."
The Jews **answered**,
    "We have a **law**, and according to that law he ought to **die**,
    because he made himself the **Son** of **God**."
Now when Pilate **heard** this statement,
    he became even **more** afraid,
    and went back into the praetorium and said to **Jesus**,
    "Where are you **from**?"
Jesus did not **answer** him.
So Pilate said to him,
    "Do you not speak to **me**?

Pilate's frustration turns on Jesus.

Do you not know that I have power to **release** you
    and I have power to **crucify** you?"
Jesus answered him,
    "You would have **no** power over me
    if it had not been **given** to you from **above**.
For this reason the one who handed me **over** to you
    has the **greater** sin."

hoped that he would be the deliverer of Israel." Many pass by, with only a nod to what is happening on Golgotha. Am I one of them, passing by and ignoring the Gospel of life that comes from death? Do I pass by without realizing the effect of what is happening on this little hill outside Jerusalem?

Many passersby actually pause because there under the cross they feel at home, because there with the Crucified, they find meaning for their life. Some persons linger awhile, perhaps bow or kneel, embrace the corpse, and kiss the wounds. Who are they if not the sinners who embrace this cross? We ourselves bow or kneel, because we crucified him. He bore our sins; our faults brought on this death. Now we kiss the wounds we inflicted. Who

are we who bow or kneel before the cross? Sinners, crucified in our own guilt. We join the chorus lead by the repentant thief: "Jesus, remember me, when you enter your Reign."

Little children pause before the cross of Jesus, and they are not sure how to respond. The Crucified One is their advocate, for he loves them; he insisted they be

"Friend of Caesar" is a title of honor bestowed by Rome on high-ranking officials—which Pilate might lose if he mishandles this situation.

Gabbatha = GAB-uh-thuh

A last effort to forestall.

New scene. Slowly.

Golgotha = GOL-guh-thh

Proclaim the inscription.

"What I have written, I / have / written!"

Consequently, Pilate tried to **release** him; but the **Jews** cried **out**,
  "If you **release** him, you are not a **Friend** of **Caesar**.
Everyone who makes himself a **king** opposes Caesar."

When Pilate heard these words he brought Jesus out
  and **seated** him on the **judge's** bench
  in the place called **Stone Pavement**, in **Hebrew**, **Gabbatha**.
It was **preparation** day for **Passover**, and it was about **noon**.
And he said to the **Jews**,
  "**Behold**, your **king**!"
They **cried** out,
  "**Take** him away, **take** him away! **Crucify** him!"
Pilate said to them,
  "Shall I crucify your **king**?"
The chief priests answered,
  "We have no king but **Caesar**."
Then he **handed** him over to them to be **crucified**.

So they **took** Jesus, and, **carrying** the cross **himself**,
  he went out to what is called the **Place** of the **Skull**,
  in **Hebrew**, **Golgotha**.
There they **crucified** him, and with him two **others**,
  one on either **side**, with Jesus in the **middle**.
Pilate also had an **inscription** written and put on the cross
It read,
  "**Jesus** the **Nazorean**, the **King** of the **Jews**."
Now many of the Jews **read** this inscription,
  because the place where Jesus was crucified was near the **city**;
  and it was written in **Hebrew**, **Latin**, and **Greek**.
So the chief **priests** of the Jews said to Pilate,
  "Do not write 'The **King** of the Jews,'
  but that he **said**, 'I am the King of the **Jews**.'"
Pilate answered,
  "What I have **written**, I have **written**." »

allowed to come to him, and he saw in them a sign of God's reign. Children are amazing; maybe they don't understand, but they know—perhaps better than their parents—that here is something important that is very close to the human heart.

Before the Crucified One, elderly people stop and bend down, old women and men who have little more to expect from the present life than today, and many of them have no more guarantee in the present life than death itself. Old people embrace their dying Lord. They know that the greatest grace and hardest task of their lives still awaits them; they believe the crucified Lamb of God is their shepherd, and they will lack nothing in the eternal feast that awaits them.

Before the Crucified, the homeless, migrants, and undocumented come and kneel. They stare at the deceased victim, their brother, abandoned by his people near the road outside the city—after a difficult life where he did not even have a place to rest his head, one poorer than foxes with burrows and birds with nests. Widows and mothers who have lost their

Tone shift: quoting scripture.

New scene. Women are much grieved. *Four* women are identified: "his mother's sister" is different from "Mary the wife of Clopas." Clopas = KLOH-puhs; Magdala = MAG-duh-luh

When the soldiers had **crucified** Jesus,
    they took his **clothes** and **divided** them into four **shares**,
    a share for each **soldier**.
They also took his **tunic**, but the tunic was **seamless**,
    woven in one **piece** from the top down.
So they said to one another,
    "Let's not **tear** it, but cast **lots** for it to see whose it will be,"
    in order that the passage of **Scripture** might be **fulfilled**
        that says:
        *They divided my **garments** among them,*
            *and for my **vesture** they cast **lots**.*
This is what the soldiers **did**.
Standing by the **cross** of Jesus were his **mother**
    and his mother's **sister**, **Mary** the wife of **Clopas**,
    and Mary of **Magdala**.
When Jesus **saw** his mother and the **disciple** there whom
        he **loved**
    he said to his mother, "**Woman**, behold, your **son**."
Then he said to the **disciple**,
    "Behold, your **mother**."
And from that hour the disciple took her into his **home**.

New scene. Stress Jesus' awareness and control. Hyssop = HIS-uhp

After this, aware that everything was now **finished**,
    in order that the Scripture might be **fulfilled**,
    Jesus said, "I **thirst**."
There was a **vessel** filled with common **wine**.
So they put a sponge **soaked** in wine on a sprig of **hyssop**
    and put it up to his **mouth**.
When Jesus had **taken** the wine, he said,
    "It is **finished**."
And bowing his **head**, he handed over the **spirit**.

Jesus' "spirit" is the Holy Spirit, the spirit of the new creation. Jesus' Death is the giving of the Spirit.

[Here all kneel and pause for a short time.]

Now since it was **preparation** day,
    in order that the bodies might not **remain**
    on the cross on the **sabbath**,

sons and daughters approach and bow before the Crucified, and weep—because the eyes of the crucified still gaze with tenderness, as he addresses his own mother whom he leaves in the care of the beloved disciple. Engaged and married couples, and those who love each other, bow down before the Crucified One, because in him is all the power that turns sentimentality into a love stronger than death. Here on the cross, is displayed God's unique love that burns but does not consume the heart, but rather replenishes the interior life and becomes more fertile.

Before the cross, scholars and wise counselors kneel. They learn from the school of the cross that all wisdom that is not tested by love is vain; they learn the logic of the cross, that God saved the world by the craziness of the cross, before which every mouth is silent and all the wisdom of the world is mute. Such is the intelligent madness of divine love.

Who are we who stand or kneel before the cross? Anyone who has ever known God's mercy. We fall silent, prostrate, weep perhaps, and worship the Crucified. We

for the sabbath day of that week was a **solemn** one,
the Jews asked Pilate that their legs be **broken**
and that they be taken **down**.
So the **soldiers** came and **broke** the legs of the **first**
and then of the **other** one who was crucified with Jesus.
But when they came to Jesus and saw that he was already **dead**,
  they did **not** break **his** legs,
  but **one** soldier thrust his **lance** into his **side**,
  and immediately **blood** and **water** flowed out.
An **eyewitness** has **testified**, and his testimony is **true**;
  he **knows** that he is speaking the **truth**,
  so that you **also** may come to **believe**.
For this happened so that the **Scripture** passage might
    be **fulfilled**:
  *Not a **bone** of it will be **broken**.*
And again **another** passage says:
  *They will **look** upon him whom they have **pierced**.*

After this, **Joseph** of **Arimathea**,
  secretly a **disciple** of Jesus for **fear** of the **Jews**,
  asked Pilate if he could **remove** the body of Jesus.
And Pilate **permitted** it.
So he came and **took** his body.
Nicodemus, the one who had first come to him at **night**,
  also came bringing a mixture of **myrrh** and **aloes**
  weighing about one hundred **pounds**.
They took the **body** of Jesus
  and bound it with **burial** cloths along with the **spices**,
  according to the Jewish burial custom.
Now in the place where he had been crucified there was
    a **garden**,
  and in the garden a **new tomb**, in which no one had yet
    been **buried**.
So they laid Jesus **there** because of the Jewish **preparation** day;
  for the tomb was close by.

Breaking legs assured quicker death, by asphyxiation.

Blood and water: important symbols.

With conviction.

With tender respect for Joseph and, later, Nicodemus.

Arimathea = ayr-lh-muh-THEE-uh

Nicodemus – nik-oh-DEE-muhs

myrrh = mer

aloes = AL-ohz

Slow pacing.

kiss and embrace the death that gave us life. We are amazed at his love to the limit, the obedience stronger than death on the cross. We contemplate the one before us and realize our debts are now settled by this improbable sacrifice. We contemplate Christ with his arms always open to welcome us. We desire to be close to the Son of the Father, our brother who sacrificed for us. We want to knock on that one door that opens to true life. We long to hear how he, in his agony, pronounces absolution: "Father, forgive them." K.S.

HOLY SATURDAY: EASTER VIGIL

LECTIONARY #41

READING I   Genesis 1:1—2:2

A reading from the Book of Genesis

[In the **beginning**, when God created the **heavens** and the **earth**,]
    the earth was a formless **wasteland**, and **darkness** covered
        the **abyss**,
    while a mighty **wind** swept over the **waters**.

Then God **said**,
    "Let there be **light**," and there **was** light.
God saw how **good** the light was.
God then **separated** the light from the **darkness**.
God called the light "**day**," and the darkness he called "**night**."
Thus **evening** came, and **morning** followed—the **first** day.

Then God said,
    "Let there be a **dome** in the **middle** of the waters,
        to **separate** one body of water from the **other**."
And so it **happened**:
    God **made** the dome,
    and it separated the water **above** the dome from the water
        below it.
God called the dome "the **sky**."
Evening came, and **morning** followed—the **second** day.

Then God said,
    "Let the **water** under the sky be gathered into a single **basin**,
        so that the dry **land** may appear."

Speak the first three words with all that is in you.

Notice the five-part pattern of each day. Use the repeated refrains to draw your listeners deeper into the pattern of God's creative work. The *pattern* should be obvious, so it is better to *stress* the repetitions than to hide them with novel readings on each day.

The declaration that creation is "good" and the accomplishment of God's command are stressed each time they recur.

Renew your energy with each "Then God said."

TO KEEP IN MIND
Words in bold are significant words about which you must make a choice to help their meaning stand out. You may (or may not) choose to stress them.

Today, options are given for the readings. Contact your parish staff to learn which readings will be used.

READING I The account of creation reads like a liturgy that celebrates the creative force of God's Word, the excellence of God's work, and the per-fection of the human being, "image and likeness" of God. The writer takes special care in this preamble to the Torah and the whole Bible, evidenced in the repetitions that advance the description. The seven-day Jewish week inspired the framework. In the first three "days" of creation, God's word arranges the spaces; in the next three, these are adorned, furnished, and populated. The message of this master-piece is clear: our home, the world, was designed and created with a view to beauty and order. Humans are entrusted with endowing this beautiful world with an even greater integration: "Be fertile and multiply; fill the earth and subdue it." Our Jewish and Christian faith teaches us to live in the here and now, conscious that God is our creator

Identify each creation—"the earth . . . the sea"—with tenderness.

There is much detail here: use the words marked for emphasis to guide you in placing your stress. Every word isn't important. Here it's the energy and enthusiasm that matter most.

Here as before, it's important to convey a sense of joy and wonder rather than overemphasize details.

Proclaim "and he made the stars" quickly, with excitement, or slowly, with amazement. Note that the purpose of each of the lights somehow serves humanity.

Each time it recurs, this refrain should convey the end of an epoch of time and creation. Speak with a sense of accomplishment, joy, and peace.

And so it **happened**:
   the water under the sky was **gathered** into its basin,
   and the dry **land** appeared.
God called the **dry land** "the **earth**,"
   and the **basin** of the **water** he called "the **sea**."
God saw how **good** it was.
Then God said,
   "Let the **earth** bring forth **vegetation**:
   every kind of **plant** that bears **seed**
   and every kind of **fruit** tree on earth
   that bears fruit with its **seed** in it."
And so it **happened**:
   the earth brought forth every kind of plant that bears **seed**
   and every kind of **fruit** tree on earth
   that bears fruit with its **seed** in it.
God saw how **good** it was.
Evening came, and morning **followed**—the **third** day.

Then God said:
   "Let there be **lights** in the dome of the sky,
   to separate **day** from **night**.
Let them mark the fixed **times**, the **days** and the **years**,
   and serve as **luminaries** in the dome of the sky,
   to shed **light** upon the earth."
And so it **happened**:
   God made the **two** great lights,
   the **greater** one to govern the **day**,
   and the **lesser** one to govern the **night**;
   and he made the **stars**.
God set them in the **dome** of the sky,
   to shed **light** upon the earth,
   to **govern** the day and the night,
   and to separate the **light** from the **darkness**.
God saw how **good** it was.
Evening came, and **morning** followed—the **fourth** day. »

and provider. As God's image and likeness, we are charged with sustaining the life and the beauty of our home, the world we live in, and the people who inhabit this home.

READING II The guiding thread of Genesis 12—24 is the promise of a descendant for Abraham, to which faith is the acceptable response.

Abraham starts out by obeying a mandate to move into the future, becoming a migrant in a foreign country without the benefit of citizenship. In return, he receives the implausible promise of a family to be born to him and Sarah, both well past the usual age for starting a family. As the story unravels, Abram—or Abraham—considers his options to acquire a male heir: by legal adoption, or through the surrogate maternity by the Egyptian servant, Hagar. However, the promise is clear; it is to be the child of the elderly Sarah. At first, Abraham hesitated and chuckled over the improbability of such a promise, but finally he believed, and his son Isaac was born. Once the child reached adolescence, his father received God's blood-chilling challenge: how far does

This "day" teems with life; there is much excitement and energy in this narration.

Then God said,
   "Let the water **teem** with an **abundance** of living **creatures**,
   and on the **earth** let **birds** fly beneath the **dome** of the sky."
And so it **happened**:
   God created the great **sea** monsters
   and all kinds of **swimming** creatures with which the
      water **teems**,
   and all kinds of winged **birds**.
God saw how **good** it was, and God **blessed** them, saying,
   "Be **fertile**, **multiply**, and **fill** the water of the seas;
   and let the birds **multiply** on the earth."
Evening came, and morning **followed**—the **fifth** day.

Notice God "blesses" the creatures. End this section with calm satisfaction.

Renew energy once again with joy at the thrill of creating life.

Then God said,
   "Let the **earth** bring forth all kinds of living **creatures**:
   cattle, **creeping** things, and wild **animals** of all kinds."
And so it **happened**:
   God made all kinds of wild **animals**, all kinds of **cattle**,
   and all kinds of **creeping** things of the earth.
God saw how **good** it was.

The reading reaches a subclimax here. *All creation is good!*

Then [God said:
   "Let us make **man** in our **image**, after our **likeness**.
Let them have **dominion** over the **fish** of the sea,
   the **birds** of the air, and the **cattle**,
   and over all the wild **animals**
   and all the creatures that crawl on the **ground**."
God created **man** in his **image**;
   in the image of **God** he created him;
   male and **female** he created them.
God **blessed** them, saying:
   "Be **fertile** and **multiply**;
   fill the earth and **subdue** it.
Have **dominion** over the fish of the **sea**, the birds of the **air**,
   and all the **living** things that move on the earth."

A nobler, slower pacing. Humans are made in God's own likeness! Use, don't rush, the repetitions. They deepen our sense of these great truths.

Speak this as a blessing. All the beauty and good God has created is entrusted to humanity.

---

your faith reach? "Take your son Isaac, your only one, whom you love, and . . . offer him up as a holocaust." The sentimental implications of this theological text may disconcert the reader. How dare a father sacrifice his own child? But there is more to the text than what appears on the surface. The expression, God "put Abraham to the test," indicates the divine intention: even as

God rejects human sacrifice, God desires that the chosen people place their future in God's hands. The lesson is profound: the human being who is responsive to God's Word cannot harvest its fruits without having experienced the sacrifice of the sowing, the renunciation of the self that opens the way for the grace of God in our lives.

READING III The Book of Exodus presents the passage through the Red Sea as the nucleus of the divine pedagogy that moved Israel's faith from God the Savior to faith in God the Creator. Having come to believe that God liberates Israel from slavery, the people reasoned, in faith, that God who saved, was, since the beginning of all time, the creator of all

God **also** said:
  "**See**, I give you every **seed**-bearing plant all over the earth
    and every **tree** that has seed-bearing **fruit** on it to be your **food**;
    and to all the **animals** of the land, all the **birds** of the air,
    and all the living creatures that crawl on the **ground**,
    I give all the **green** plants for food."
And so it **happened**.
God looked at **everything** he had made, and he found it
    very good.]
Evening came, and **morning** followed—the **sixth** day.

Thus the **heavens** and the **earth** and all their array
    were **completed**.
Since on the **seventh** day God was **finished**
  with the work he had been doing,
    he **rested** on the seventh day from all the work he
    had undertaken.

[Shorter: Genesis 1:1, 26–31a (see brackets)]

This is the summary statement: God's creation is very *good!*

With a sense of accomplishment and pride. Pause after "completed."

"Rested" suggests more than not working; it means delighting in the "work," that is, the beloved creation God has now completed.

For meditation and context:

RESPONSORIAL PSALM Psalm 104:1–2, 5–6, 10, 12, 13–14, 24, 35 (30)

R. Lord, send out your Spirit, and renew the face of the earth.

Bless the LORD, O my soul!
  O LORD, my God, you are great indeed!
You are clothed with majesty and glory,
  robed in light as with a cloak.

You fixed the earth upon its foundation,
  not to be moved forever;
with the ocean, as with a garment, you
    covered it;
  above the mountains the waters stood.

You send forth springs into the watercourses
  that wind among the mountains.
Beside them the birds of heaven dwell;
  from among the branches they send forth
    their song.

Or:

You water the mountains from your palace;
  the earth is replete with the fruit
    of your works
You raise grass for the cattle,
  and vegetation for man's use,
producing bread from the earth.

How manifold are your works, O LORD!
  In wisdom you have wrought them all—
the earth is full of your creatures.
  Bless the LORD, O my soul!

---

things. This reading closes the first part of Exodus. The decisive event happens at the sea. The Hebrews, pursued by Egyptian warriors, crossed the sea on foot, a crossing described as a new creation: the waters are separated, dry land appears and opens a path for the rescue; the waters are described as walls on each side, making way for the advance of God's people. The

night passed without incident, and the dawn of liberation followed. The text reads: "In the night watch just before dawn the Lord cast through the column of the fiery cloud upon the Egyptian force a glance that threw it into panic." The walls of water collapse on the Egyptians, and the sea drowns them. By this act of redemption, the people know who they are and who God is. This

deliverance gave both parties their identity: The chosen people are redeemed from slavery by God, their *go'el* (Hebrew for "pay the price for freedom"), the relative who pays a debt or ransom, securing the person's freedom. This story anticipates Jesus' Resurrection, the central event in our life of faith and the gift of our identity. Jesus is our *go'el*, our redeemer, our next-of-kin through

For meditation and context:

RESPONSORIAL PSALM Psalm 33:4–5, 6–7, 12–13, 20 and 22 (5b)

R. The earth is full of the goodness of the Lord.

Upright is the word of the LORD,
  and all his works are trustworthy.
He loves justice and right;
  of the kindness of the LORD the earth
   is full.

By the word of the LORD the heavens
   were made;
  by the breath of his mouth all their host.
He gathers the waters of the sea as in a flask;
  in cellars he confines the deep.

Blessed the nation whose God is the LORD,
  the people he has chosen for his own
   inheritance.
From heaven the LORD looks down;
  he sees all mankind.

Our soul waits for the LORD,
  who is our help and our shield.
May your kindness, O LORD, be upon us
  who have put our hope in you.

READING II Genesis 22:1–18

A reading from the Book of Genesis

[God put **Abraham** to the **test**.
He called to him, "**Abraham**!"
"**Here** I am," he replied.
Then God said:
  "Take your son **Isaac**, your **only** one, whom you **love**,
   and go to the land of **Moriah**.
There you shall **offer** him up as a **holocaust**
   on a **height** that I will point **out** to you."]
Early the next **morning** Abraham saddled his **donkey**,
  took with him his son **Isaac** and two of his **servants** as well,
  and with the **wood** that he had cut for the **holocaust**,
  set out for the place of which God had told him.

On the **third** day Abraham got **sight** of the place from afar.
Then he **said** to his servants:
  "Both of you stay here with the **donkey**,
   while the **boy** and I go on over **yonder**.
We will **worship** and then come **back** to you."

The opening line both introduces and summarizes the entire story. Pause slightly after "Abraham." "Here I am" is eager.

Don't give away what's coming at the end. God's voice is solemn, not stern. Emphasize the gravity of God's command by stressing "only" and "love."

Abraham works hard to hide his pain. Don't let this sound like a trip to the mall.

---

whom God has saved us from the slavery of sin and death. In Baptism we die and are raised to life with him. The canticle of Moses, the responsorial song to this reading, follows this reading in the Paschal Vigil. It is the thanksgiving song for God's intervention in delivering the people from slavery, God's guidance and providence in the desert. In a sense, this is the national anthem of a people who has been liberated from slavery and lives now in the freedom of God's grace.

READING IV The fourth reading is an oracle of God's deliverance from exile, an eloquent page wherein the prophet tells of God's immense, tender love for the people. God is portrayed as a husband who divorced his wife in a moment of anger, but now calls her back because he cannot stop loving her, and he pledges restoration and unfailing love. For a short time he hid his face from the people's infidelity, which brought on all sorts of misfortune. The memory of the oath sworn after Noah's flood emphasizes that God is firm in not repeating such a tactic. The storm-battered

This image foreshadows Jesus' carrying his own Cross. Don't waste it.

This dialogue is poignant: Isaac is sincerely curious and unaware. Abraham speaks intentionally and his words are pained and weighty.

Slowly: the scene grows tense and darker. Share one image at a time. Tying up the boy can't sound like he's buttoning his jacket.

Don't speak like you're describing a "near-miss," but as if you were relating the actual slaughter. "But" breaks the mood; pace is faster. The second "Abraham" is louder, stronger than the first.

"Here I am," has no sense of relief yet, just terror. The "Do not . . . " commands can be spoken with calm and tender compassion. Speak the words "I now know . . . " with solemnity. Pause after "beloved son."

beloved – bee-LUHV-uhd

Here the pace and mood become faster, more upbeat. The "ram" replaces Isaac. Don't rush. Yahweh-yireh – YAH-way—YEER-ay means "The Lord will see [to it]."

In a long passage like this, variety in pacing is urgent. Though it is "God" speaking, you must not adopt a monotone nor an overly slow delivery. Speak like a parent announcing good news to an anxious child—both reassuring and praising.

Thereupon Abraham took the wood for the holocaust
   and **laid** it on his son **Isaac's** shoulders,
   while he himself carried the **fire** and the **knife**.
As the two walked on **together**, Isaac **spoke** to his
   father Abraham:
   "**Father**!" Isaac said.
"**Yes**, son," he replied.
Isaac continued, "Here are the **fire** and the **wood**,
   but where is the **sheep** for the holocaust?"
"**Son**," Abraham answered,
   "God **himself** will provide the sheep for the holocaust."
Then the two **continued** going forward.

[When they **came** to the place of which God had told him,
   Abraham built an **altar** there and arranged the **wood** on it.]
Next he **tied** up his son **Isaac**,
   and put him on **top** of the wood on the altar.
[Then he **reached** out and took the **knife** to **slaughter** his son.
But the LORD's **messenger** called to him from **heaven**,
   "**Abraham**, **Abraham**!"
"**Here** I am," he answered.
"Do not lay your **hand** on the boy," said the **messenger**.
"Do not do the least **thing** to him.
I **know** now how **devoted** you are to God,
   since you did not **withhold** from me your own beloved **son**."
As Abraham looked **about**,
   he spied a **ram** caught by its horns in the **thicket**.
So he went and **took** the ram
   and offered **it** up as a holocaust in **place** of his son.]
Abraham **named** the site **Yahweh-yireh**;
   hence people now say, "On the mountain the LORD will **see**."

[**Again** the LORD's messenger **called** to Abraham from heaven
   and said:
   "I **swear** by myself, declares the LORD,
   that because you **acted** as you **did** »

city will be splendidly restored, rebuilt on a foundation of precious stones; parapets and gates made of red gems will provide security, beauty, and protection. It is a theological projection of the new Jerusalem. God is not simply going to restore the past, but will create it new in the light of the Lord, who on this night of grace rises from the dead and is the first of

an immense throng that populates the new city. Here Isaiah expounds an important teaching: the new Jerusalem will not subsist on the basis of justice, but only on the grace of God's infallible love. The New Covenant is founded on God's promise to save humanity and make the people, by divine grace, just and free.

READING V The second part of the book of Isaiah, from which this reading comes, announces a new, liberating exodus: a highway open for the exiled people to return to their land, with heavenly food, God's Word, and forgiveness to guide and heal them. As usual, the prophet invites the exiled people in many ways. Calling out as if he is selling goods in

The fulfillment of these promises is what tonight's readings and liturgy are all about.

If you've given proper emphasis and not rushed the preceding, the final line will call us all to obedience.

in not **withholding** from me your beloved **son**,
I will bless you **abundantly**
and make your **descendants** as **countless**
as the **stars** of the **sky** and the **sands** of the seashore;
your descendants shall take **possession**
of the gates of their **enemies**,
and in your **descendants** all the nations of the earth shall
　　find **blessing**—
all this because you **obeyed** my **command**."]

[Shorter: Genesis 22:1–2, 9a, 10–13, 15–18 (see brackets)]

For meditation and context:

RESPONSORIAL PSALM　　Psalm 16:5, 8, 9–10, 11 (1)

R. You are my inheritance, O Lord.

O LORD, my allotted portion and my cup,
　　you it is who hold fast my lot.
I set the LORD ever before me;
　　with him at my right hand I shall not
　　　　be disturbed.

Therefore my heart is glad and my soul
　　rejoices,
　　my body, too, abides in confidence;
because you will not abandon my soul to the
　　netherworld,
　　nor will you suffer your faithful one to
　　　　undergo corruption.

You will show me the path to life,
　　fullness of joys in your presence,
　　the delights at your right hand forever.

READING III　　Exodus 14:15—15:1

A reading from the Book of Exodus

Don't fear the repetitions in this text; have confidence in the power of this story to move your listeners. Be eager to tell it to people eager to hear it again. Begin with the strong voice of God.

"Pharaoh . . . army . . . chariots . . . charioteers": this will become a much repeated refrain. Use all the words each time the line recurs.

The **LORD** said to **Moses**, "**Why** are you crying out to me?
Tell the Israelites to go **forward**.
And **you**, lift up your **staff** and, with hand outstretched
　　over the **sea**,
　　split the sea in **two**,
　　that the Israelites may pass **through** it on dry **land**.
But I will make the **Egyptians** so **obstinate**
　　that they will go in **after** them.

a marketplace, the prophet offers wisdom, the Word of God, as food or drink; the price cannot be better—free of charge. The hearers cannot resist God's offer to quench their thirst—an allusion to the exodus through the desert—and he adds the incentive of milk, which calls to mind "the land flowing with milk and honey." God promises to lead the people in the new exodus. God offers

the people life in the material and theological sense, and this in the form of "the everlasting covenant" (v. 3).

In the second part, the prophet speaks of seeking God, an invitation that runs throughout the Bible. For, "As high as the heavens are above the earth, so high are my ways above your ways and my thoughts above your thoughts." The prophet illus-

trates how God's plan is always fulfilled by using the example of water, which always attains its goal of fertilizing the earth despite its apparent weakness and delay. God's Word is effective: "my word shall not return to me void, but shall do my will, achieving the end for which I sent it."

Then I will receive **glory** through **Pharaoh** and all his **army**,
  his **chariots** and **charioteers**.
The Egyptians shall know that **I am the Lord**,
  when I receive glory through **Pharaoh**
  and his **chariots** and **charioteers**."

"Column of cloud" and the "angel" are manifestations of God's presence and protection. The action intensifies. Build suspense.

The **angel** of God, who had been **leading** Israel's camp,
  now **moved** and went around **behind** them.
The column of **cloud** also, leaving the **front**,
  took up its place **behind** them,
  so that it came **between** the camp of the **Egyptians**
  and that of **Israel**.

Slow your pace to suggest the passage of time over the long night. Pause.

But the cloud now became **dark**, and thus the **night** passed
  without the rival camps coming any closer together all
    night long.

Speak with renewed vigor. See what you describe.

Then Moses **stretched** out his hand over the **sea**,
  and the LORD **swept** the sea
  with a **strong** east **wind** throughout the night
  and so **turned** it into **dry** land.

A marvelous sight.

When the **water** was thus **divided**,
  the **Israelites** marched into the **midst** of the sea on **dry** land,
  with the water like a **wall** to their **right** and to their **left**.

Use a faster pace here.

The Egyptians **followed** in **pursuit**;
  all Pharaoh's **horses** and **chariots** and **charioteers** went
    after them
  right into the **midst** of the sea.
In the **night** watch just before **dawn**
  the LORD **cast** through the column of the fiery cloud
  upon the Egyptian force a **glance** that threw it into a **panic**;
  and he so **clogged** their chariot wheels
  that they could hardly **drive**.

Speak slower and quietly; you are aware that it was God who saved.

With **that** the Egyptians sounded the **retreat** before Israel,
  because the LORD was fighting for them **against** the Egyptians.

Then the LORD told **Moses**, "**Stretch** out your **hand** over the **sea**,
  that the **water** may flow **back** upon the Egyptians,
  upon their **chariots** and their **charioteers**." »

READING VI The sixth reading is a wisdom hymn from Baruch, who personifies wisdom as a woman and equates her with the Law, through which she is God's gift to the people. The text comes from late Hellenism, when the people of Israel, living among foreigners and having suffered terrible setbacks, realized that their greatness and reason for being was not based on any human power, but on God's wisdom, identified here with the Law, which outlines a way of life superior to that of other peoples. To walk by her light is to find life with God. The poet encourages Israel to accept this marvelous gift of life. The poem begins with a variation of the words of the Shema "Hear . . . O Israel," (the basic creed of Israel, Deuteronomy 6:4), a call to the people in exile, so they recognize they have been punished for abandoning the Word of the Law. Wisdom reminds the people that the "fountain of wisdom" is to walk "in the way of God." "Blessed are we, O Israel; for what pleases God is known to us!" (Baruch 4:4). God has taught us the words of everlasting life.

God's justice is uncompromising.

"Dawn" is the moment of liberation.

Narrate these lines without any hint of vindictiveness.

Speak with gratitude and relief.

God's power inspires a reverential fear. Use a hushed tone.

The joy of this song should ring in your voice and show on your face.

So Moses **stretched** out his hand over the sea,
  and at **dawn** the sea flowed **back** to its normal **depth**.
The Egyptians were fleeing head **on** toward the **sea**,
  when the LORD **hurled** them into its midst.
As the water flowed **back**,
  it **covered** the **chariots** and the **charioteers** of Pharaoh's
    whole **army**
which had followed the Israelites into the sea.
Not a single **one** of them escaped.
But the **Israelites** had marched on dry **land**
  through the **midst** of the sea,
  with the water like a **wall** to their **right** and to their **left**.
Thus the LORD **saved** Israel on that day
  from the power of the **Egyptians**.
When Israel **saw** the Egyptians lying **dead** on the **seashore**
  and beheld the great **power** that the LORD
  had shown **against** the Egyptians,
  they **feared** the LORD and **believed** in him and in his
    servant Moses.

Then **Moses** and the **Israelites** sang this **song** to the LORD:
  I will **sing** to the LORD, for he is **gloriously triumphant;**
  horse and **chariot** he has cast into the **sea.**

For meditation and context:

RESPONSORIAL PSALM   Exodus 15:1–2, 3–4, 5–6, 17–18 (1b)
R. Let us sing to the Lord; he has covered himself in glory.

I will sing to the LORD, for he is gloriously
    triumphant;
  horse and chariot he has cast into the sea.
My strength and my courage is the LORD,
  and he has been my savior.
He is my God, I praise him;
  the God of my father, I extol him.

The LORD is a warrior,
  LORD is his name!
Pharaoh's chariots and army he hurled into
    the sea;
  the elite of his officers were submerged
    in the Red Sea.

The flood waters covered them,
  they sank into the depths like a stone.
Your right hand, O LORD, magnificent
    in power,
  your right hand, O LORD, has shattered
    the enemy.

You brought in the people you redeemed
  and planted them on the mountain of
    your inheritance—
the place where you made your seat,
    O LORD,
  the sanctuary, LORD, which your hands
    established.
The LORD shall reign forever and ever.

On this night when Christ appears as the one who fulfills all that has been expressed by the Old Testament, Baruch offers clues that apply to the Easter Vigil. The Old Testament prizes life above all other things. To separate oneself from God is death. Our return to God gives us new life. The experience of the calamities suffered by Israel have taught her that only in the Lord is life (Baruch 3:11–12). The implication of this liturgy is that we rejoice in the full life that Jesus, the Messiah, offers. This joy will fill our hearts, and it is what we will offer others. Jesus is our joy, and he gives meaning to our life.

READING VII   This reading conveys God's promise that the covenant will be renewed and God's people will be restored to their land. God will cleanse them from all their impurities and idols. The nucleus of the promise is the gift of "a new heart" and "a new spirit." There is no use repairing an old heart; we need a new, faithful heart to offer God. The exiles had kept hope alive while the city of Jerusalem and the temple were standing; even after

Isaiah = ī-ZAY-uh

"Husband" and "Maker" are meant to express tenderness and compassion. Persuade us that God can love us this much.

Use a brisk pace with "like a wife forsaken" and increase intensity on "a wife married in youth."

Contrast the regret of "For a brief moment . . . " with the joy of "but with great tenderness . . . ." The same point is made twice. Maintain your energy and conviction throughout.

The exile is compared to Noah's flood. God says: As I swore then, so I swear now never to punish you again.

These words represent the excess of love. Don't hold back.

Spoken directly to Jerusalem. Say this lovingly, as if embracing the one with whom you are reconciling.

Carnelians = kahr-NEEL-yuhnz

Carnelians are reddish quartz; carbuncles are smooth, round, deep-red garnets.

God is making a promise. Speak with reassuring strength and conviction.

READING IV Isaiah 54:5–14

A reading from the Book of the Prophet Isaiah

The One who has become your **husband** is your **Maker**;
  his **name** is the LORD of **hosts**;
your **redeemer** is the **Holy** One of Israel,
  called **God** of all the **earth**.
The LORD calls you **back**,
  like a wife **forsaken** and grieved in **spirit**,
a wife married in **youth** and then cast **off**,
  says your God.
For a brief **moment** I **abandoned** you,
  but with great **tenderness** I will take you **back**.
In an outburst of **wrath**, for a **moment**
  I **hid** my face from you;
but with enduring **love** I take **pity** on you,
  says the LORD, your **redeemer**.
This is for me like the days of **Noah**,
  when I **swore** that the waters of Noah
  should never **again** deluge the earth;
so I have sworn not to be **angry** with you,
  or to **rebuke** you.
Though the mountains **leave** their place
  and the hills be **shaken**,
my **love** shall **never** leave you
  nor my covenant of peace be **shaken**,
  says the LORD, who has **mercy** on you.
O **afflicted** one, **storm-battered** and **unconsoled**,
  I lay your **pavements** in **carnelians**,
  and your **foundations** in **sapphires**;
I will make your **battlements** of **rubies**,
  your **gates** of **carbuncles**,
  and all your **walls** of precious **stones**.
All your **children** shall be taught by the LORD,
  and **great** shall be the **peace** of your children. **»**

the destruction, the ruins refueled the hope for a new beginning in the ancestral land. But the people were painfully reminded of their idolatrous past: "Son of man, when the house of Israel lived in their land, they defiled it by their conduct and deeds" (v. 17). God punished the people and expelled them from their land. But instead of the pagans seeing this punishment as divine

justice, they interpreted it as weakness on God's part. They confused the Lord with the many unreliable, inept gods of the nations. That is why God determines to act differently, for the honor of his name.

In the present oracle the Lord promises something new: "Not for your sakes do I act, house of Israel, but for the sake of my holy name, which you profaned among the

nations to which you came" (v. 22). God will act to defend his name; he will gather the people from the foreign nations and will return them to their own land: "You shall live in the land I gave your fathers; you shall be my people, and I will be your God."

The Baptism that flows from the Resurrection of the Lord gives Christians a whole new life, a law inscribed on the flesh

In **justice** shall you be established,
　　far from the fear of **oppression**,
　　where destruction cannot come **near** you.

For meditation and context:

RESPONSORIAL PSALM　Psalm 30:2, 4, 5–6, 11–12, 13 (2a)
R. I will praise you, Lord, for you have rescued me.

I will extol you, O LORD, for you drew
　　me clear
　and did not let my enemies rejoice
　　over me.
O LORD, you brought me up from
　the netherworld;
　you preserved me from among those
　　going down into the pit.

Sing praise to the LORD, you his faithful ones,
　　and give thanks to his holy name.
For his anger lasts but a moment;
　a lifetime, his good will.
At nightfall, weeping enters in,
　but with the dawn, rejoicing.

Hear, O LORD, and have pity on me;
　O LORD, be my helper.
You changed my mourning into dancing;
　O LORD, my God, forever will I give
　　you thanks.

TO KEEP IN MIND

Pace: The rate at which you read is influenced by the size of your church, the size of the congregation, and the complexity of the text. As each increases, rate decreases.

READING V　Isaiah 55:1–11

Isaiah = ī-ZAY-uh

A reading from the Book of the Prophet Isaiah

Thus says the LORD:
All you who are **thirsty**,
　　come to the **water**!
You who have no **money**,
　　come, receive **grain** and **eat**;
come, without **paying** and without **cost**,
　　drink **wine** and **milk**!
Why spend your money for what is not **bread**,
　　your **wages** for what fails to **satisfy**?
Heed me, and you shall eat **well**,
　　you shall **delight** in **rich** fare.
Come to me **heedfully**,
　　listen, that you may have **life**.
I will **renew** with you the everlasting **covenant**,
　　the benefits assured to **David**.

Note the imperatives, but the tone is as if inviting hungry, homeless children to a feast.

Ignore the comma after "come."

Ask the questions sincerely as if expecting an answer.

To be nourished, it is necessary to heed and listen to the Lord. "That you may have life" is the heart of God's promise. Slower pace.

---

of the heart and with which the Holy Spirit draws us to do good and to avoid evil. Only through behavior attached to the Gospel can we glorify and manifest the oneness of God in our world. Transforming our society will be possible insofar as we allow ourselves to be transformed from inside out by the Spirit, who is the inheritance the Father has given us.

EPISTLE Paul identifies two truths about human life. One is death, the source of which is Adam, and the other is the fullness of life, with Christ as head. Whoever believes in Christ lives her or his life with Christ. This happens every day, in joy and sadness, light and night. How do we know Christ's power in us is real? According to Paul, the believer "lives in the newness of life" (v. 4) by the identity with the death of Jesus in Baptism, an immersion in death from which we rise to new life in Jesus resurrected. In Baptism,

"Him" is David. The nation will be restored.

Renew your energy. Imagine those you are trying to persuade getting up to leave. Your words must catch and hold them.

This is not condemnation, but an earnest call for conversion.

This section explains why God can be so "generous in forgiving." God's plans are not our plans; God's methods not our methods. Slowly, with great dignity.

This is an important teaching about the efficacy of the Word of God: it accomplishes what it sets out to do! Go slowly. This is a long comparison. Speak with conviction and authority.

As I made him a **witness** to the peoples,
    a **leader** and commander of **nations**,
so shall you **summon** a nation you knew **not**,
    and nations that knew you not shall **run** to you,
because of the LORD, your **God**,
    the **Holy** One of Israel, who has **glorified** you.

Seek the LORD while he may be **found**,
    call him while he is **near**.
Let the scoundrel **forsake** his way,
    and the **wicked** man his **thoughts**;
let him **turn** to the LORD for **mercy**;
    to our **God**, who is **generous** in **forgiving**.
For **my** thoughts are not **your** thoughts,
    nor are **your** ways **my** ways, says the LORD.
As high as the **heavens** are above the **earth**,
    so high are **my** ways above **your** ways
    and **my** thoughts above **your** thoughts.

For just as from the **heavens**
    the **rain** and **snow** come down
and do not **return** there
    till they have **watered** the **earth**,
    making it **fertile** and **fruitful**,
giving **seed** to the one who **sows**
    and **bread** to the one who **eats**,
so shall my **word** be
    that goes forth from my mouth;
my **word** shall not return to me **void**,
    but shall do my **will**,
    achieving the end for which I **sent** it.

we descend with Jesus in his death, and we rise from the waters to his resurrected life. Perhaps Paul's language and graphic imagery is clearer if we remember that the Baptismal rite in the early Church called for stripping off the old clothes, stepping into the Baptismal pool, being immersed under water—a reminder of death—stepping out of the pool and being clothed in a white garment to announce the Resurrection of Christ, which is a reality for the newly baptized. Paul is realistic when he takes into account that, although the believer's situation has changed in essence, many appearances still remain. This is why he speaks in the future of life in the Resurrection: "If, then, we have died with Christ, we believe that we shall also live with him." As believers, our humanity is renewed in Christ. Paul encourages Christians to "think of yourselves as being dead to sin and living for God in Christ Jesus."

GOSPEL | After Jesus' death and Resurrection, the world experienced an essential change. Jesus returned to the Father, but he never left us,

RESPONSORIAL PSALM   Isaiah 12:2–3, 4, 5–6 (3)

R. You will draw water joyfully from the springs of salvation.

God indeed is my savior;
  I am confident and unafraid.
My strength and my courage is the LORD,
  and he has been my savior.
With joy you will draw water
  at the fountain of salvation.

Give thanks to the LORD, acclaim his name;
  among the nations make known his
    deeds,
  proclaim how exalted is his name.

Sing praise to the LORD for his glorious
    achievement;
  let this be known throughout all
    the earth.
Shout with exultation, O city of Zion,
  for great in your midst
  is the Holy One of Israel!

READING VI   Baruch 3:9–15, 32—4:4

A reading from the Book of the Prophet Baruch

Hear, O Israel, the **commandments** of **life**:
  listen, and know **prudence**!
How is it, Israel,
  that you are in the land of your **foes**,
  grown old in a **foreign** land,
defiled with the **dead**,
  accounted with those destined for the **netherworld**?
You have **forsaken** the fountain of **wisdom**!
  Had you walked in the way of **God**,
  you would have dwelt in enduring **peace**.
Learn where **prudence** is,
  where **strength**, where **understanding**;
that you may know also
  where are length of **days**, and **life**,
  where light of the **eyes**, and **peace**.
Who has **found** the place of wisdom,
  who has entered into her **treasuries**?

The One who knows **all** things knows **her**;
  he has probed her by his **knowledge**—

Baruch = buh-ROOK

This is exhortation motivated by love.

You are asking: "Do you know why?"

The answer: "I'll tell you why!" Still, love is the motive.

Here is the better way: follow it and find peace! You are cajoling, exhorting, wanting to spur a change in behavior. There is a lilting cadence in these lines. Don't rush them. "Days" and "peace" can be sustained.

There is a dramatic shift in mood here. This is a poetic song of praise to Wisdom.

never deprived us of his presence. In his birth in the flesh, which culminated in his death, Resurrection, and Ascension, human nature recovered our true value. By his Passover, his presence has infiltrated the universe, even to the most remote and resistant domain, which is death. By his death and Resurrection, life and liberation permeate all human places, even the most

inaccessible. Christ touched our flesh, attended our parties, worked alongside us, suffered and died, and in his Resurrection he raised everything to a higher plane. The effects of his Passover are within reach, if a person so disposes herself or himself. That is the key: if one is willing. Jesus' resurrected presence does not convince the believer with incontestable evidence. It is

mysterious, as was the news in the early morning hours of the Resurrection: "Why do you seek the living one among the dead? He is not here, but he has been raised." When the women announced this good news to the Eleven, they had not yet seen him. "Two men" in glowing garments communicated this news to them. The Apostles were incredulous, but Peter has-

"The One" = God. You are retelling the story of creation. Use a faster, joyous tempo.

"Dismisses light" means orders the sun to go down. "Calls it" indicates a sunrise. Maintain high energy here.

Let your voice ring with joy at God's goodness!

This is a new beat. Use a more sober tone. "Given her" indicates understanding. "Jacob" and "Israel" represent the whole people.

beloved: bee-LUHV-uhd

"She has appeared on earth" refers to Wisdom, now personified as the book of the Law.

Use a contrasting tone for those who "live" and those who "die." Pause before next line.

Imagine yourself saying, "Oh, my dear child, turn and receive . . . ." "Glory" indicates the Law. "Privileges" refers to knowing and observing the Law. You are saying: "Don't throw away the riches you've been given." End on a note of joy.
Blessed = BLES-uhd or blesd

For meditation and context:

the One who **established** the earth for all time,
  and **filled** it with four-footed **beasts**;
he who **dismisses** the light, and it **departs**,
  calls it, and it obeys him **trembling**;
before whom the **stars** at their posts
  shine and **rejoice**;
when he **calls** them, they answer, "Here we **are**!"
  shining with **joy** for their Maker.
Such is our **God**;
  no other is to be **compared** to him:
he has traced out the whole way of **understanding**,
  and has given her to **Jacob**, his **servant**,
  to **Israel**, his beloved **son**.

Since then she has **appeared** on earth,
  and **moved** among people.
She is the **book** of the **precepts** of God,
  the **law** that endures **forever**;
all who **cling** to her will **live**,
  but those will **die** who **forsake** her.
Turn, O Jacob, and **receive** her:
  walk by her **light** toward **splendor**.
Give not your glory to **another**,
  your **privileges** to an **alien** race.
Blessed are we, O Israel;
  for what **pleases** God is **known** to us!

RESPONSORIAL PSALM   Psalm 19:8, 9, 10, 11 (John 6:68c)

R. Lord, you have the words of everlasting life.

The law of the LORD is perfect,
  refreshing the soul;
the decree of the LORD is trustworthy,
  giving wisdom to the simple.

The precepts of the LORD are right,
  rejoicing the heart;
the command of the LORD is clear,
  enlightening the eye.

The fear of the LORD is pure,
  enduring forever;
the ordinances of the LORD are true,
  all of them just.

They are more precious than gold,
  than a heap of purest gold;
sweeter also than syrup
  or honey from the comb.

---

tened to verify the report. He investigated the empty grave and the shroud left behind—flimsy evidence, really. He was startled and, disconcerted, returned to the room and bolted the door behind him.

Meanwhile, Jesus was resurrected and gloriously alive. The evangelists describe the strange climate of the first few hours, when doubt finally met certainty. The news

of the Resurrection was based on rumors, and what Jesus had said "while he was still in Galilee, that the Son of Man must be handed over to sinners and be crucified, and rise on the third day." The Apostles did not set out to look for Jesus. Where to look? According to the Gospels, it is always Jesus who appears and lets himself be found, lets himself be felt and seen, at

unexpected times and places—the risen Jesus; but he remains beyond the control of his friends. This is the tension of the Resurrection news, both in the Gospels and in the Church today: Jesus has risen and he lives; he promised to remain with his Church, but his presence remains unnoticed by many. Even most baptized Christians know the risen Christ only based

READING VII   Ezekiel 36:16–17a, 18–28

A reading from the Book of the Prophet Ezekiel

"Their land" is their own land. Ezekiel's tone is blunt. Don't dilute the anger. "Fury," "scattered," "dispersing," "judged," "profane" are all strong words that convey God's wrath. Let them work.

The word of the LORD came to me, saying:
   Son of **man**, when the house of **Israel** lived in their **land**,
   they **defiled** it by their **conduct** and **deeds**.
Therefore I poured out my **fury** upon them
   because of the **blood** that they poured out on the ground,
   and because they defiled it with **idols**.

"Because of the blood . . . " refers to worshiping false idols.

I **scattered** them among the nations,
   dispersing them over **foreign** lands;
   according to their **conduct** and **deeds** I judged them.

The exile is God's punishment for Israel's infidelity.

But the punishment backfired because it gave God a bad name.

But when they came among the nations **wherever** they came,
   they served to **profane** my holy name,
   because it was said of them: "These are the people of the LORD,
   yet they had to **leave** their land."

Speak the taunt in the voice of the foreigners.

So I have **relented** because of my holy name
   which the house of Israel **profaned**
   among the nations where they came.

Pause at this new beat. Frustrated, God reluctantly adopts a new approach. Note that the words "profaned among the nations" is repeated three times.

Therefore **say** to the house of Israel: Thus says the Lord GOD:
   Not for **your** sakes do I act, house of Israel,
   but for the sake of my holy **name**,
   which you **profaned** among the nations to which you came.
I will prove the **holiness** of my great name, profaned among
      the nations,
   in whose midst you have **profaned** it.

God must restore his "good name."

Thus the nations shall **know** that **I** am the LORD, says the
      Lord GOD,
   when in their sight I prove my holiness through **you**.

God's anger slowly yields to mercy and love. Speak this as a promise.

For I will take you **away** from among the nations,
   gather you from all the foreign lands,
   and bring you **back** to your **own** land.

The tone becomes more reassuring and loving here.

---

on rumors. It requires a special insight inspired by faith to perceive it.

   Follow the Gospel plot. For the disciples to identify Jesus, an initiative, a gesture —always unexpected—is needed on his part: the explanation of the Scriptures makes his presence palpable, or a miraculous catch of fish, or, like Thomas, the disciples need to see and come in contact

with his wounds; or, it may be enough for Jesus to pronounce a name: "Mary." Just so, we discover a constant in all the Gospels: it is always Jesus who takes the initiative, allows himself to be recognized, opens our eyes, and kindles our heart like the disciples of Emmaus. Why is it so? Because the news and material evidence of the risen Jesus does not convince us. We

need him to wake us up, to rise in our hearts just as he rose from the grave. Jesus, who by faith lives in the heart, still sleeps. At times it seems we are barely conscious of the Resurrection, and our knowledge is founded only on rumor. We have not yet met him, resurrected and alive, in the center of our lives. For many the heart is like his tomb, once sealed with

God will purify the people. This is an important image of Baptism for tonight's liturgy.

Make eye contact with the assembly for this classic and memorable line. Speak slowly and sincerely.

Imagine saying this to a child whom you love in order to ensure the child's success and prosperity. Say the words "You shall be . . . God" like a spouse vowing fidelity.

I will sprinkle **clean water** upon you
  to **cleanse** you from all your **impurities**,
  and from all your **idols** I will cleanse you.
I will give you a **new** heart and place a new **spirit** within you,
  taking from your bodies your **stony** hearts
  and giving you **natural** hearts.
I will put my **spirit** within you and make you live by my **statutes**,
  careful to observe my **decrees**.
You shall **live** in the land I gave your **fathers**;
  you shall be my **people**, and I will be your **God**.

For meditation and context:

RESPONSORIAL PSALM   Psalm 42:3, 5; 43:3, 4:2

R. Like a deer that longs for running streams, my soul longs for you, my God.

A thirst is my soul for God, the living God.
  When shall I go and behold the face
  of God?

I went with the throng
  and led them in procession to the house
  of God,
amid loud cries of joy and thanksgiving,
  with the multitude keeping festival.

Send forth your light and your fidelity;
  they shall lead me on
and bring me to your holy mountain,
  to your dwelling-place.

Then will I go in to the altar of God,
  the God of my gladness and joy;
then will I give you thanks upon the harp,
  O God, my God!

Or:

For meditation and context:

RESPONSORIAL PSALM   Isaiah 12:2–3, 4bcd, 5–6 (3)

R. You will draw water joyfully from the springs of salvation.

God indeed is my savior;
  I am confident and unafraid.
My strength and my courage is the LORD,
  and he has been my savior.
With joy you will draw water
  at the fountain of salvation.

Give thanks to the LORD, acclaim his name;
  among the nations make known
  his deeds,
  proclaim how exalted is his name.

Sing praise to the LORD for his glorious
  achievement;
  let this be known throughout all
  the earth.
Shout with exultation, O city of Zion,
  for great in your midst
  is the Holy One of Israel!

Or:

stone. One day, when we least expect it, the time will come and the stone will be removed from our heart. Then Christ will reveal himself to us so we can announce to the world what was once only a rumor.

Luke paints the scene of the Resurrection when the women discover that the tombstone was removed. The Resurrection means that the stone that

blocks us is removed, so life does not stay stuck within the sealed off heart. Life is not enclosed in a tomb. But we "live," and often return to visit the tomb. If we want to recognize Jesus, the Risen One, we will not find him in the past or in the programs of death. He will find the one who seeks him and he will offer true and lasting life. To dispose ourselves for this encounter with life, it is fit-

ting for us to go forward, not back. There is no point in looking for the living among the dead.

Tonight, Christ, the Light of the world, rising from the tomb, addresses creation: "I congratulate you, Heaven and Earth and all that is in you, for now you have attained your perfect state!" In the beginning when God created you, God noted that it was

For meditation and context:

RESPONSORIAL PSALM   Psalm 51:12–13, 14–15, 18–19 (12a)

R. Create a clean heart in me, O God.

A clean heart create for me, O God,
  and a steadfast spirit renew within me.
Cast me not out from your presence,
  and your Holy Spirit take not from me.

Give me back the joy of your salvation,
  and a willing spirit sustain in me.
I will teach transgressors your ways,
  and sinners shall return to you.

For you are not pleased with sacrifices;
  should I offer a holocaust, you would not
    accept it.
My sacrifice, O God, is a contrite spirit;
  a heart contrite and humbled, O God, you
    will not spurn.

EPISTLE   Romans 6:3–11

A reading from the Letter of Saint Paul to the Romans

Paul's literary device is a rhetorical question. Let it sound like a question. Make eye contact with the assembly and speak as directly as Paul writes.

Take the time to understand Paul's point: what happened to Christ will happen to us. He died and was buried, then rose. We die and are buried in Baptism; we, too, will rise to new life.

Paul develops the idea: we were made one with Christ by sharing a death (Baptism) like his; so we also will be made one with him by experiencing Resurrection.

Don't let this sound repetitive. Sustain the energy. Contrast "died" and "live."

"We know" means that we are convinced! "Dies no more . . . death no longer has power . . ." is the same idea stated twice: the greater stress goes to the second statement.

Use the contrasts: "his death . . . his life."

Brothers and sisters:
Are you **unaware** that we who were **baptized** into Christ **Jesus**
    were baptized into his **death**?
We were indeed **buried** with him through baptism into death,
    so that, just as Christ was **raised** from the dead
    by the glory of the **Father**,
    we **too** might live in newness of **life**.

For if we have grown into **union** with him through a **death**
    like his,
    we shall also be **united** with him in the **Resurrection**.
We know that our **old** self was **crucified** with him,
    so that our **sinful** body might be done away with,
    that we might no longer be in **slavery** to sin.
For a **dead** person has been **absolved** from sin.
If, then, we have **died** with Christ,
    we believe that we shall also **live** with him.
We know that **Christ**, **raised** from the dead, dies no **more**;
    death no longer has **power** over him.
As to his **death**, he died to sin once and for **all**;
    as to his **life**, he lives for **God**.

good; now that the creative work has received its final touch, we sing in harmony with God: it is an excellent work. God created with his Word. In the new creation the Incarnate Word visits humanity and brings it to perfection.

This night, the hope of the prophets penetrates the walls of the grave and speaks in the person of the Risen One:

"You, Isaiah, who announced that the marriage between God and his people would be repaired, that the house destroyed will be rebuilt: Arise and see how admirably your promises have come true! And you, prophet, who relate that the Word does not return to its origin without effect, behold the return of the Word to God, with all the promises of the Old Testament in his entou-

rage! You, sad Jeremiah, who lamented the day of your birth, arise and rejoice now! It is for this day that you were born, your prophecies have been fulfilled. Ezekiel, do not delay; the Resurrection of the body that you announced is at hand. Rise up."

This Easter night the incarnate Word knocks at the doors of the tombs of the sages, and cries, "Arise and come out of

Make eye contact with the assembly. We are "*dead* to sin and living for God in Christ Jesus"! Announce this joyfully.

Consequently, you **too** must think of yourselves as being **dead** to **sin**
and **living** for **God** in Christ **Jesus.**

For meditation and context:

RESPONSORIAL PSALM   Psalm 118:1–2, 16–17, 22–23

R. Alleluia, alleluia, alleluia.

Give thanks to the LORD, for he is good,
    for his mercy endures forever.
Let the house of Israel say,
    "His mercy endures forever."

The right hand of the LORD has struck
        with power;
    the right hand of the LORD is exalted.
I shall not die, but live,
    and declare the works of the LORD.

The stone which the builders rejected
    has become the cornerstone.
By the LORD has this been done;
    it is wonderful in our eyes.

GOSPEL   Luke 24:1–12

A reading from the holy Gospel according to Luke

Begin with a solemn and sober mood. The women come to do what they could not on Friday: anoint the body with spices and perfume.

The mood is shattered by the discovery of the rolled-back stone. The failure to find the body arouses fear.

The mood intensifies from puzzlement to terror.

The men want to build faith, not reprimand. Give them a soothing, persuasive voice meant to calm the women's fears.

Your energy should be greatest on "he has been raised."

At **daybreak** on the **first day** of the **week**
    the **women** who had come from **Galilee with** Jesus
    took the **spices** they had **prepared**
    and **went** to the **tomb.**
They found the **stone rolled away** from the **tomb**;
    but when they **entered,**
    they did **not** find the **body** of the **Lord Jesus.**
While they were **puzzling** over this, **behold,**
    two men in **dazzling garments appeared** to them.
They were **terrified** and **bowed** their **faces** to the **ground.**
They **said** to them,
    "**Why** do you **seek** the **living** one among the **dead?**
He is **not here,** but he has been **raised.** »

---

the land of death! Come, sit down and eat the bread of life; drink of the living water, the Holy Spirit that springs from the side of the Lamb and floods the nascent Church. You know him, Baruch, because your sentences speak about him, the eternal Word, the true wisdom.

"Miriam with tambourine in hand, sing and lead us in the dance of liberation, together with your sober brother Moses, whom you rescued from the waters.

Abraham, not far behind; intone the song of the long wait along with your son Isaac; and Sarah, now you have every reason to laugh."

Tonight, Christ, the savior of the world, was walking among the dead, looking for someone in particular, his primitive father who ate of the forbidden tree. "Adam, Adam, where are you? And where is she who was born from your side, she who tasted with you the bitter fruit of sin?

The wisdom you desired to savor by your own designs, now I present him to you, Christ, your descendant, who repaired your disobedience in the noblest way, by his obedience." When Christ, the author of new life in the Resurrection, met our first parents, he encouraged them: "Awake! Get up, now. This is what you have been waiting for! It is time, icons of your creator, divine images. Eve and Adam, and all your children, get up and exit this place of

Your intensity dips as they gently remind the women, but rises again on the reference to "third day."

Much is suggested by "they remembered."

Speak excitedly and breathlessly. Take time with the list of women. Your tone suggests their integrity and reputation for reliability, making the Apostles' judgment of "nonsense" a surprise.

Surprise us with Peter's response.

Peter now believes the women's story, but what does it all mean? Your tone must indicate his simultaneous amazement and puzzlement.

Remember what he **said** to you while he was **still** in **Galilee**,
    that the **Son** of **Man** must be **handed over** to **sinners**
    and be **crucified**, and **rise** on the **third day**."
And they **remembered** his words.
Then they **returned** from the **tomb**
    and **announced all these things** to the **eleven**
    and to **all** the **others**.
The women were **Mary Magdalene**, **Joanna**,
    and **Mary** the mother of **James**;
    the **others** who **accompanied** them also told this
        to the *apostles*,
    but their **story** seemed like **nonsense**
    and they did **not believe** them.
But **Peter** got up and **ran** to the tomb,
    bent down, and **saw** the **burial** cloths **alone**;
    then he went **home amazed** at what had **happened**.

TO KEEP IN MIND
Pay attention to the pace of your reading. Varying the pace gives listeners clues to the meaning of the text. The most common problem for proclaimers new to the ministry is going too fast to be understood.

death. Here, take my hand and I will lead you to the long awaited paradise."

Finally, in these shadows of the night, the risen Christ addresses us, and invites us to accompany him in his Passover, which is also ours. He addresses us: "And you, Flesh, wake up! Your long siesta is over. Happy Easter! While you were sleeping, I removed from your breast the heart of stone and gave you a human heart, which has the capacity to love as God loves you.

Wake up, O Flesh; clothe yourself with my Resurrection, where you will find your true human value. I, dead and resurrected, have come for you; take my hand, hold on tight now that we exit the grave and you will regain your true loveliness and the fullness of life, as God intended from the beginning. My sacrifice has freed you from the weight of yourself; I have definitively set you free from the seduction of death."

Wake up, Sleepy Head! Rise from the dead and step out of the darkness and death, out of the tomb, so my light may enlighten you! To those who live in darkness: come out and be enlightened. Rise up, all you prophets and sages, women and men who lived and died for this moment, because Christ, your light, has risen from the tomb. Step up to an authentic life worth dying for and worth living! Happy Easter!
K.S.

EASTER SUNDAY

LECTIONARY #42

READING I   Acts of the Apostles 10:34a, 37–43

A reading from the Acts of the Apostles

Peter proceeded to **speak** and said:
　"You **know** what has happened all over **Judea**,
　beginning in **Galilee** after the baptism
　that **John preached**,
　how God **anointed Jesus** of **Nazareth**
　with the Holy **Spirit** and **power**.
He went about doing **good**
　and **healing** all those **oppressed** by the **devil**,
　for **God** was with him.
We are **witnesses** of all that he **did**
　both in the country of the **Jews** and in **Jerusalem**.
They put him to **death** by hanging him on a **tree**.
This man God **raised** on the **third day** and granted that he
　　be **visible**,
　not to **all** the people, but to **us**,
　the **witnesses chosen** by God in **advance**,
　who **ate** and **drank** with him **after** he rose from the **dead**.
He **commissioned** us to preach to the **people**
　and **testify** that he is the one appointed by God
　as **judge** of the **living** and the **dead**.
To him all the **prophets** bear **witness**,
　that **everyone** who **believes** in him
　will receive **forgiveness** of **sins** through his **name**."

Except for the first six words, the entire reading is spoken in the voice of Peter. Remember that Peter is making a public address.

"Spirit" and "power" are important characteristics of Jesus' ministry.
Jesus' healing ministry and exorcisms are important signs of who he is. Don't rush any of this first paragraph.
Pause to establish eye contact with the assembly. Peter is saying: "I was there!" There is a personal, intimate quality to this entire text.

The announcement of Jesus' crucifixion is followed immediately by the announcement of his Resurrection. Pause after "tree" and again after "This man." Use a more upbeat tone for the balance of the paragraph.

Speak the words "the witnesses chosen by God . . . " humbly. This emphasizes Peter's credibility.

The tone continues to be energetic and earnest. "Preach" and "testify" will be redundant unless you build energy from one to the other.

Today, options are given for the readings. Contact your parish staff to learn which readings will be used.

READING I　In Peter's speech on the occasion of the Baptism of Cornelius, Luke narrates when and how Christianity opened to the Gentiles as well as Jews. During the speech, the Holy Spirit descends upon everybody present. The Jewish believers are astounded that God's gifts are given also to persons who are not of the chosen race. In a style similar to his speeches in Jerusalem (see Acts 2:14–36, 3:11–26), Peter testifies that Jesus was killed "hanging him on a tree" and announces his Resurrection and appearances to the Apostles, commissioned to preach and bear witness. Peter stresses that God's message is first sent to Israel, then to a smaller group of witnesses to reach the people of Israel; the message is universal, Jesus is judge of "the living and the dead"; forgiveness reaches "everyone who believes in him."

READING II　**Colossians.** By Baptism the Christian becomes a sharer in the Lord's death and Resurrection: "your life is hidden with Christ in God." This brings with it not only the commitment to renounce sin and walk in a new life, but also an orientation to the heavenly realities, sustained by the awareness of our own identity as God's daughters and sons. The baptized Christian makes a conscious effort to "seek what is above, where Christ is seated at God's right hand," while adopting an attitude of detachment from merely earthly things. In Baptism the Christian has

For meditation and context:

RESPONSORIAL PSALM　Psalm 118:1–2, 16–17, 22–23 (24)

R. This is the day the Lord has made; let us rejoice and be glad.
or R. Alleluia.

Give thanks to the LORD, for he is good,
　for his mercy endures forever.
Let the house of Israel say,
　"His mercy endures forever."

"The right hand of the LORD has struck
　　with power;
　the right hand of the LORD is exalted.
I shall not die, but live,
　and declare the works of the LORD."

The stone which the builders rejected
　has become the cornerstone.
By the LORD has this been done;
　it is wonderful in our eyes.

READING II　Colossians 3:1–4

Colossians = kuh-LOSH-uhnz

This short text requires a slow reading.

"If then you were raised . . . " means
"because you were raised . . . ."

The tone is firm, yet encouraging.

Tell us two things: who will appear and what
will happen.

A reading from the Letter of Saint Paul to the Colossians

Brothers and sisters:
If then you were **raised** with **Christ**, seek what is **above**,
　where Christ is **seated** at the right hand of **God**.
Think of what is **above**, not of what is on **earth**.
For you have **died**, and your life is **hidden** with Christ in **God**.
When Christ your life **appears**,
　then you **too** will appear with him in **glory**.

Or:

READING II　1 Corinthians 5:6b–8

Corinthians = kor-in-THEE-uhnz

This short text requires a slow reading.

Be more energetic with the second "yeast"
clause. Use ritardando (slowing toward the
end) with the words "of sincerity and truth."

A reading from the first Letter of Saint Paul to the Corinthians

Brothers and sisters:
Do you not **know** that a little **yeast** leavens **all** the **dough**?
Clear **out** the **old** yeast,
　so that you may become a **fresh** batch of dough,
　inasmuch as you are **unleavened**.
For our paschal **lamb**, **Christ**, has been **sacrificed**.

died with Christ and lives now hidden in the One who lives. When Christ is manifested in glory, then the spiritual beauty of those who, acting by faith in adherence to Christ in daily life, find in him the fullness of life: "When Christ our life appears, then you shall appear with him in glory."

　1 Corinthians. The encounter with the risen Christ determines the Christian's moral conduct. Paul draws a parallel with the Hebrew Passover to teach that the sin or virtue of even one community member affects the whole Church. He focuses on two Easter symbols: the unleavened bread

and the immolated lamb, both of which were eaten during the feast. Leaven introduced into the loaf is an image of the sinner who, by her or his conduct, contaminates the community. As long as believers live in communion with Christ, we make every effort to reject anything that corrupts the life we received in Baptism. Recalling the Jewish Passover that Jesus performed as a memorial of his own saving death, the apostle instructs his community: "Get rid of the old yeast to make of yourselves fresh dough, unleavened loaves." He writes that the Corinthians must be pure, new bread

that Christ consecrates in the offering of himself. "Christ our Passover has been sacrificed"—the lamb slain, whose blood, as in Exodus, shields us from the exterminating angel. The Christian, conscious of the implications of this sacrifice, is urged to live the new life in Christ, which requires that they eliminate from their lives the leaven of sin, and present themselves to God in a pure state, as the unleavened bread of the Passover.

| GOSPEL | In this Gospel, there is a "seeing" that does not |

Therefore, let us **celebrate** the feast,
    not with the **old** yeast, the yeast of **malice** and **wickedness**,
    but with the **unleavened** bread of **sincerity** and **truth**.

For meditation and context:

The Easter Sequence is an ancient liturgical hymn that praises Christ, the Paschal victim, for his victory over death. Mary Magdalene recounts her experience at Christ's tomb, proclaiming, "Christ my hope is arisen."

SEQUENCE   Victimae paschali laudes

Christians, to the Paschal Victim
    Offer your thankful praises!
A Lamb the sheep redeems;
    Christ, who only is sinless,
    Reconciles sinners to the Father.
Death and life have contended in that
        combat stupendous:
    The Prince of life, who died, reigns
        immortal.

Speak, Mary, declaring
    What you saw, wayfaring.
"The tomb of Christ, who is living,
    The glory of Jesus' Resurrection;
Bright angels attesting,
    The shroud and napkin resting.
Yes, Christ my hope is arisen;
    to Galilee he goes before you."
Christ indeed from death is risen, our new
        life obtaining.
    Have mercy, victor King, ever reigning!
    Amen. Alleluia.

GOSPEL   John 20:1–9

A reading from the holy Gospel according to John

Magdala = MAG-duh-luh.

On the **first** day of the **week**,
    Mary of **Magdala** came to the **tomb** early in the **morning**,
    while it was still **dark**,
    and saw the **stone removed** from the **tomb**.

Speak slowly here; the mood is a bit melancholy.

So she **ran** and went to Simon **Peter**
    and to the **other** disciple whom Jesus **loved**, and told them,
    "They have taken the **Lord** from the **tomb**,
    and we don't know where they **put** him."

Your pace should quicken here; Mary is fearful and distressed.

So **Peter** and the **other** disciple went out and **came** to the **tomb**.
They **both ran**, but the **other** disciple ran **faster** than Peter
    and arrived at the tomb **first**;
    he **bent down** and saw the **burial** cloths there, but did not go **in**.

Let Peter and John do the racing, not you. Convey their haste without rushing the lines. Say "but the other disciple . . . did not go in": in a hushed tone.

When Simon **Peter** arrived **after** him,
    he went **into** the tomb and **saw** the **burial** cloths there,
    and the cloth that had covered his **head**,
    not with the **burial** cloths but rolled **up** in a **separate place**. »

Stress Peter's activity: he enters, sees, and examines. Speak the words "saw and believed" with quiet reverence.

---

produce faith and another "seeing" that does. The beloved disciple's faith reaches beyond appearances and penetrates the inner dimension and meaning. It is a look of love that enables the disciple to see beyond the material evidence and believe that Jesus rose from the dead.

Today, love takes the initiative, impels us towards the light of faith. Mary Magdalene senses something and goes to the tomb, the place of death. It is proper for love to step outside itself and seek the Beloved. Sometimes life that awaits us seems so far away, so insecure, that we withdraw into the familiar past, to the death of the day before yesterday, rather than opening ourselves to the new life that awaits us today.

The evangelist is clever with details. His report is intriguing, and what it means is eloquent. Magdalene "saw the stone removed from the tomb." The heavy stone, impossible for her to move by herself, no longer presents an obstacle. The stone that would not allow entry into those secret regions of life suddenly is not there. Magdalene did not approach the grave, but ran to report the news. Her report to the Apostles is profound, for John quotes her as saying, "The Lord has been taken from the tomb." Love speaks of a living being, not of an inert, dead body. Talk about friendship for eternity!

AFTERNOON GOSPEL   At Easter, the day death died and true life was born, the disciples in Jerusalem were paralyzed by confusion and fear. Two of them deserted the holy city and took the road to Emmaus. The events of Good Friday had shaken their faith. We do not know the location of Emmaus, some

Take us through the text by allowing us to experience the characters' various emotions: Mary's panic, the disciples' instant anxiety, Peter's confusion before the empty wrappings and folded cloth, and John's silent assent in faith.

Then the **other** disciple **also** went in,
  the one who had arrived at the tomb **first**,
  and he **saw** and **believed**.
For they did not yet **understand** the **Scripture**
  that he had to **rise** from the **dead**.

AFTERNOON GOSPEL   Luke 24:13–35

A reading from the holy Gospel according to Luke

That **very day**, the **first day** of the **week**,
  two of **Jesus' disciples** were going
    to a village seven miles from **Jerusalem** called **Emmaus**,
  and they were **conversing** about **all** the **things**
    that had **occurred**.
And it **happened** that while they were **conversing** and **debating**,
  Jesus himself drew **near** and **walked** with them,
  but their **eyes** were **prevented** from **recognizing** him.
He **asked** them,
  "**What** are you **discussing** as you **walk** along?"
They **stopped**, looking **downcast**.
One of them, named **Cleopas**, said to him in **reply**,
  "Are **you** the **only visitor** to **Jerusalem**
  who does **not know** of the **things**
  that have **taken place** there in these **days**?"
And he **replied** to them, "What **sort** of things?"
They **said** to him,
  "The **things** that **happened** to **Jesus** the **Nazarene**,
  who was a **prophet mighty** in **deed** and **word**
  before **God** and **all** the **people**,
  how our **chief priests** and **rulers** both **handed** him **over**
  to a **sentence** of **death** and **crucified** him.
But **we** were **hoping** that he would be the **one** to **redeem Israel**;
  and **besides** all **this**,
  it is **now** the **third day** since this took **place**.

Let your tone convey the irony of their failure to recognize the very one they're discussing.

Jesus is "playing dumb" here.

It's understandable that they would not yet fully "understand."

Jesus coaxes further. Initially their response might sound like: "How could you not know this?" But soon they are into the story.

We can't help but feel sorry for them and their sense of loss.

seven miles from Jerusalem. If Jerusalem is high in the dorsal mountain range of Palestine, Emmaus is downhill. Could it be that Luke made use of this imprecision to affirm that Emmaus is part of the topography of a person's life, somewhere in the valleys of tears, in the tortuous ravines of doubt, or on the slopes of uncertainty? Yes, the Emmaus road is that of the defeated unbelievers, the perplexed, those stunned by pain or trauma. Two disciples left peaceful Jerusalem and headed toward an unknown place in the valley. As they jour-

neyed, they talked about current events, which they could not comprehend.

A stranger approaches and walks with them. The eyes, accustomed to seeing in a certain way, do not recognize the dead Jesus, now living. Do I feel sorry because I have not recognized Jesus in the people who accompany me? How many times he walks beside us like a stranger! One of the travelers, Cleopas, addresses the stranger: "Are you the only visitor to Jerusalem who does not know . . . ?" Are we not all strangers in transit in the present world? Why is only Cleopas named? Because the

anonymous person who accompanies him and who finally comes to recognize Jesus is us.

We may identify with the travelers to Emmaus. The two disciples expected more positive results from their discipleship, freedom for Israel. But the phrase "redeem Israel" also implies freeing ourselves from corruption and sin. We experience times when Christ's presence seems eclipsed by the brutal facts, when God seems far away, the feeling, the faith, the inspiration, and the friendship reduced to a memory. But history teaches that in times like

The "day" of this occurrence is important. They just can't add two and two: the tomb was empty and angels announced his rising, yet this does not yet add up to Resurrection. Emmaus = eh-MAY-uhs.

Jesus' emotion is real: frustration and some sadness.

This is a new beat; don't rush.

Cleopas = KLEE-oh-puhs.

They plead with him to stay!

He responds with annoyance.
Slowly narrate this Eucharistic scene. Pause after "gave it to them."

Speak these lines with energy and awe.

Use a quickened pace here, but keep it natural and realistic.

Remember this is a story. Tell it as if for the first time, with enthusiasm and suspense.

Are they dismissing the testimony because it came from women?

Some **women** from our **group**, however, have **astounded** us:
　　they were at the **tomb early** in the **morning**
　　and did **not** find his **body**;
　　they came **back** and **reported**
　　that they had **indeed** seen a **vision** of **angels**
　　who **announced** that he was **alive**.
Then **some** of those **with** us **went** to the **tomb**
　　and found things **just** as the **women** had **described**,
　　but **him** they did **not see**."
And he **said** to them, "Oh, how **foolish** you are!
How slow of **heart** to **believe all** that the **prophets spoke**!
Was it not **necessary** that the **Christ** should **suffer** these things
　　and **enter** into his **glory**?"
Then **beginning** with **Moses** and **all** the **prophets**,
　　he **interpreted** to them what referred to **him**
　　in **all** the **Scriptures**.
As they **approached** the village to which they were **going**,
　　he gave the **impression** that he was going on **farther**.
But they **urged** him, "**Stay** with us,
　　for it is **nearly evening** and the **day** is **almost over**."
So he went in to **stay** with them.
And it **happened** that, while he was **with** them at **table**,
　　he took **bread**, said the **blessing**,
　　broke it, and **gave** it to them.
With **that** their **eyes** were **opened** and they **recognized** him,
　　but he **vanished** from their **sight**.
Then they said to each other,
　　"Were not our **hearts burning within us**
　　while he **spoke** to us on the **way** and **opened** the **Scriptures**
　　　　to us?"
So they **set out** at **once** and **returned** to **Jerusalem**
　　where they found **gathered** together
　　the **eleven** and those **with** them who were **saying**,
　　"The **Lord** has **truly** been **raised** and has **appeared** to **Simon**!"
Then the **two recounted**
　　what had taken **place** on the **way**
　　and how he was made **known** to them in the **breaking** of **bread**.

these, Christ is near; the Son of God, whom people had seen killed, now lives; the one whom they imagine lying dead in a tomb approaches and accompanies them on the road to Emmaus.

　　When they arrive, the disciples offer hospitality to the stranger. It strikes us how they convince him to stay the night. Remember Abraham and Sarah who, unknowingly, hosted angels and God (see Genesis 18). Now, the travelers not only open the doors of the house, but they share the table. Here the Gospel reaches its peak, in the breaking of bread, when

they recognize the strange guest turned host. He takes the bread, blesses it, breaks and shares it, and their eyes are opened. The disciples are transformed; their hearts overflow with joy—then suddenly Jesus is not there. Could it be that his physical presence is no longer necessary, because he walks with us at all times, in all places? The Emmaus disciples, because they opened the door of their heart to an outsider, or came to know themselves as guests and strangers in the present world, recognized Jesus, forever at their side. K.S.

SECOND SUNDAY OF EASTER

LECTIONARY #45

READING I   Acts 5:12–16

A reading from the Acts of the Apostles

Begin with an upbeat and joyous tone.

Many **signs** and **wonders** were **done** among the **people**
   at the **hands** of the **apostles**.
They were **all together** in Solomon's **portico**.

A shadow of threat looms over the community, for some did not dare to gather for fear of the authorities.
Accent the "esteem" of the people.

None of the others **dared** to **join** them, but the **people**
      esteemed them.
Yet **more** than **ever**, **believers** in the **Lord**,
   great numbers of **men** and **women**, were **added to** them.

The steady growth of the community is reason for rejoicing.

Thus they **even carried** the **sick** out into the **streets**
      and **laid** them on **cots** and **mats**
      so that when **Peter** came **by**,
   at least his **shadow** might **fall** on **one** or **another** of them.

Relate these events with reverence, as if you had witnessed what you describe.

People gather from other parts of the region as word spreads of the marvels in Jerusalem.

A **large number** of **people** from the **towns**
   in the **vicinity** of **Jerusalem also** gathered,
      bringing the **sick** and those **disturbed** by **unclean spirits**,
      and they were **all cured**.

 READING I   In the beginning of Acts, Luke's summary of the ideal Christian life demonstrates the result of faith in Christ: a community of one heart and one mind. Spiritual needs are cared for in common through the Apostles' teaching, the prayers, the meal, and the common life. Material needs are answered by the sharing of possessions. The apostolic community of the Twelve is a magnet that draws believers, enlivened by the Holy Spirit, to share their experience of the risen Christ.

Luke describes the life of the nascent community and extols the spirit of communion and healing: "they even carried the sick out into the streets and laid them on cots and mats so that when Peter came by, at least his shadow might fall on one or another of them . . . they were all cured." The healings were the proof of the community's identity with Jesus, who, at the beginning of his ministry in the Nazareth synagogue, identified himself as the healer of a world afflicted.

READING II   The theological language of Revelation reveals the Church in struggle throughout history, now rejoicing in the Lord's triumph over the forces of evil. Christ, resurrected and triumphant, infuses the Church with confidence to face difficulties and build a new heaven and a new earth now in the present world. John writes for a persecuted community; he relates how on the Lord's day Jesus Christ appears, whom John envisions as the final Judge and, at the same time, as

For meditation and context:

RESPONSORIAL PSALM   Psalm 118:2–4, 13–15, 22–24 (1)

**R. Give thanks to the Lord for he is good, his love is everlasting.
or R. Alleluia.**

Let the house of Israel say,
  "His mercy endures forever."
Let the house of Aaron say,
  "His mercy endures forever."
Let those who fear the LORD say,
  "His mercy endures forever."

I was hard pressed and was falling,
  but the LORD helped me.
My strength and my courage is the LORD,
  and he has been my savior.
The joyful shout of victory
  in the tents of the just.

The stone which the builders rejected
  has become the cornerstone.
By the LORD has this been done;
  it is wonderful in our eyes.
This is the day the LORD has made;
  let us be glad and rejoice in it.

READING II   Revelation 1:9–11a, 12–13, 17–19

A reading from the Book of Revelation

I, **John**, your **brother**, who **share** with you
  the **distress**, the **Kingdom**, and the **endurance** we have
    in **Jesus**,
  found myself on the **island** called **Patmos**
  because I proclaimed **God's word** and gave **testimony** to **Jesus**.
I was **caught up** in **spirit** on the **Lord's** day
  and **heard behind** me a **voice** as **loud** as a **trumpet**, which said,
  "**Write** on a **scroll** what you **see**."
Then I **turned** to **see whose voice** it **was** that **spoke** to me,
  and when I **turned**, I saw **seven gold lampstands**
  and in the **midst** of the **lampstands** one **like a son** of **man**,
  wearing an **ankle-length robe**, with a **gold sash**
    around his **chest**. »

This is the first of six consecutive weeks we read from the Book of Revelation. Note that the word *Revelation* is singular.

The greeting conveys an intimate connection between John and his readers.

Patmos = PAT-muhs

It is Sunday and the Spirit takes hold of him.

The "voice as loud as a trumpet" is immediately recognized as bearing a divine message.
Remember that throughout you are narrating a divine vision; keep the tone regal and authoritative.
Jesus is seen symbolically as standing in the midst of the seven great Christian communities of that day.

priest ("ankle-length robe") and the King ("a gold sash around his chest"). The words with which Jesus is proclaimed are significant. "I am the first and the last, the one who lives. Once I was dead, but now I am alive forever and ever." In the risen Jesus is all our hope of happiness and salvation. Like the disciples in the Gospel, the visionary is instructed to bear witness, and he is called to record the vision so others may share his experience of the risen Christ and come to believe. The reading presents the

theme of the resurrected Christ's lordship over the whole Church, represented here by the seven churches of Asia Minor, the "seven lampstands." Christ is described as being like the "Son of man," as presented in the book of Daniel (see 7:13–14). He died, and now he lives forever, and he holds in his hand the destinies of all people.

GOSPEL   It is the first day of the week, also the eighth day, one that follows the Sabbath rest and

recalls God's activity during the week of creation. In the Gospel agenda, it is the same day as the marriage at Cana, which overflowed with joy and new wine in the presence of Jesus, the Bridegroom. It is the day after the Sabbath, when the paralytic carried his mat into the temple and caused a scandal among the religious people, the same Sabbath when Jesus made mud and smeared it on a blind person's face. It is the birthday of new life, when Magdalene and the disciples discovered the tomb emptied

"Fell down" is both a response of fear and reverence.

The voice of the "son of man" is both powerful and compassionate.

Remember, these words are meant to comfort those in distress. Fill your voice with hope and blessing.

This is a command that has *three* elements.

When I caught **sight** of him, I **fell down** at his **feet** as though **dead**.
He **touched** me with his **right hand** and said, "Do **not** be **afraid**.
I am **the first** and **the last**, the **one** who **lives**.
Once I was **dead**, but **now** I am **alive forever** and **ever**.
I hold the **keys** to **death** and the **netherworld**.
Write down, therefore, what you have **seen**,
    and what is **happening**, and what **will happen afterwards**."

GOSPEL   John 20:19–31

A reading from the holy Gospel according to John

It's the day of the Resurrection, Sunday, and they're behind locked doors, full of fear, when Jesus comes and wishes peace. Those are a lot of details for a first sentence. Read with hushed reverence.

Jesus' entrance is unexpected and shocking. He speaks with authority and intimacy.

On the **evening** of that **first day** of the **week**,
    when the **doors** were **locked**, where the **disciples** were,
    for **fear** of the **Jews**,
    Jesus came and **stood** in their **midst**
    and said to them, "**Peace** be with **you**."
When he had **said** this, he **showed** them his **hands** and his **side**.
The **disciples rejoiced** when they **saw** the **Lord**.
Jesus said to them **again**, "**Peace** be with **you**.

Not until they see the hands and side do they "rejoice."

Jesus subdues their rejoicing to announce his mission for them.

Don't rush the detail of his breathing on them.

As the **Father** has **sent me**, so **I** send **you**."
And when he had **said** this, he **breathed** on them and **said**
    to them,
    "**Receive** the **Holy Spirit**.
Whose **sins** you **forgive** are **forgiven** them,
    and whose **sins** you **retain** are **retained**."

Pause at the end of this dialogue before introducing Thomas.

Didymus = DID-ih-muhs.

They speak with awed enthusiasm.

Thomas, called **Didymus**, one of the **Twelve**,
    was not **with** them when **Jesus came**.
So the **other** disciples said to him, "We have **seen** the **Lord**."
But **he** said to them,

Don't render Thomas as stubborn or narrow. Without knowing it, Thomas asks for what the others have already received.

    "**Unless I see** the **mark** of the **nails** in his **hands**
    and **put** my **finger** into the **nailmarks**
    and **put** my **hand** into his **side**, I will **not believe**."

---

of death. Today, night has fallen, as it did another time in Genesis, when God saw that all of his creative work was good. But in addition to that assessment, evening may bring fear and uncertainty. Suddenly the assembled disciples heard a familiar greeting: "*Shalom 'alehem." Shalom*, is charged with meaning, wishing the disciples the blessing of full life, well-being, health, prosperity, and everything one might wish for a complete life.

"Jesus came and stood in their midst." He greets them and shows them his hands and his side—the hands of one who fash-

ioned the created world that first week, who had refashioned the clay of human nature, giving us a body and soul, a personal identity. He showed his hands, soiled with our dirt, the calloused hands of a carpenter whom we had nailed to a cross. These hands remind us of six days' work, particularly the sixth day, when he left his fingerprints on the human being, fashioned in his image and likeness. On that evening of the Resurrection day, Jesus also showed us his side, so we could see his heart, pierced for his love. How much God loves us, to death! On this Resurrection evening,

the encounter with his disciples on the first day of the week, Jesus repeats the action of God the creator. He breathes into us his Holy Spirit, just as he had filled our lungs with his life in the moment of our creation in paradise.

But he doesn't stop there, with fashioning us and giving us his life. Now he commissions us for the work of the new creation that consists in the difficult and delicate work of reconciliation, the labor of pardon. Forgiveness recreates the world according to God's design. And we are the dispensers of that pardon and reconcilia-

Here starts a new beat. Sustain your energy and stress the presence of Thomas.

Deliver this "Peace be with you" in a solemn, unrushed manner as before.

Jesus is giving him what he already gave the others—physical proof of his Resurrection.

Try a brief pause between "My Lord . . . " and " . . . and my God."

What Jesus says of Thomas is true of all the Apostles.
Blessed = blesd or BLES-uhd

Don't lose energy on these final lines for they make an important statement of faith: eternal life comes through Jesus Christ.

Now a **week later** his **disciples** were **again** inside
    and **Thomas was with** them.
Jesus came, although the **doors** were **locked**,
    and **stood** in their **midst** and said, "**Peace** be with **you**."
Then he said to **Thomas**, "**Put** your **finger here** and **see** my **hands**,
    and **bring** your **hand** and **put** it into my **side**,
    and **do** not be **unbelieving**, but **believe**."
Thomas **answered** and said to him, "**My Lord and my God!**"
Jesus **said** to **him**, "Have you **come** to **believe**
    because you have **seen** me?
Blessed are **those** who **have not seen** and **have believed**."

Now **Jesus** did **many other signs** in the **presence** of his **disciples**
    that are **not written** in this book.
But **these are written** that you may **come to believe**
    that **Jesus** is the **Christ**, the **Son** of **God**,
    and that **through this belief** you may have **life** in **his name**.

THE **4** STEPS OF *LECTIO DIVINA* OR PRAYERFUL READING

1. *Lectio:* Read a Scripture passage aloud slowly. Notice what phrase captures your attention and be attentive to its meaning. Silent pause.

2. *Meditatio:* Read the passage aloud slowly again, reflecting on the passage, allowing God to speak to you through it. Silent pause.

3. *Oratio:* Read it aloud slowly a third time, allowing it to be your prayer or response to God's gift of insight to you. Silent pause.

4. *Contemplatio:* Read it aloud slowly a fourth time, now resting in God's word.

---

tion in our communities and families, in our world small and great. When we refuse to be instruments of *shalom* and pardon, we deny the grace we received in Baptism.

Thomas catches our attention in this passage with his confession of faith and Jesus' blessing for the person who believes without seeing. Thomas was also called Didymus, the twin, but his twin is never identified in Scripture. One possible twin is Nathanael. At the beginning of the Gospel of John, Nathanael tried to quench the enthusiasm of his friend Philip, who had informed him: "We have found him whom Moses wrote in the law, and the prophets, Jesus of Nazareth," to which Nathanael, in disbelief, answered, "Can anything good come out of Nazareth?" But he finally came to confess, "Master, you are the Son of God, you are the King of Israel." Thomas, too, refused to believe the testimony of his friends, disbelief for which Jesus reproaches him and to which he finally responds with the disciple's finest confession of faith: "My Lord and my God." K.S.

THIRD SUNDAY OF EASTER

LECTIONARY #48

READING I   Acts 5:27–32, 40b–41

A reading from the Acts of the Apostles

When the **captain** and the **court officers** had **brought**
        the **apostles** in
    and made them **stand** before the **Sanhedrin**,
    the **high priest questioned** them,
    "We gave you **strict orders**, did we **not**,
    to **stop teaching** in **that name?**
Yet you have **filled Jerusalem** with your **teaching**
    and want to **bring this man's blood** upon **us**."
But **Peter** and the **apostles** said in reply,
    "We must **obey God** rather than **men**.
The **God** of our **ancestors raised Jesus**,
    though **you** had him **killed** by **hanging** him on a **tree**.
God exalted him at his **right hand** as **leader** and **savior**
    to grant **Israel repentance** and **forgiveness** of **sins**.
We are **witnesses** of these things,
    as is the **Holy Spirit** whom **God** has **given** to those who
        obey him."

The **Sanhedrin ordered** the **apostles**
    to **stop speaking** in the **name** of **Jesus**, and **dismissed** them.
So they **left** the **presence** of the **Sanhedrin**,
    rejoicing that they had been found **worthy**
    to **suffer dishonor** for the **sake** of the **name**.

The high priest has no patience for these righteous zealots.

His anger peaks at the thought that they are implicating him in Jesus' death.

Peter is self-confident. He was freed and ordered by an angel to preach of Jesus.

Even this setting is an opportunity to proclaim "the name" of Jesus.
"Repentance" and "forgiveness" should not be run together. They are distinct concepts.

Note that both the disciples and the Holy Spirit give witness.
Although the flogging is left out of our portion today, let that violence color the announcement of the disciples' brusque dismissal.

It is a sober rejoicing cited here; read slowly, aware of those today who still suffer and die for the sake of the "name."

READING I   In the first reading, Peter and the apostles pay the price of being jailed and interrogated for their witness to God's salvation wrought through Jesus' death and Resurrection. They defend themselves by declaring that such public testimony is more imperative than obedience to human authority, and they rejoice in the ill treatment received. Through Christ they have learned that deliverance from death comes through death.

Death lasts a moment; God's love lasts for life eternal.

READING II   his vision in Revelation offers a dense theology. The slain Lamb, recalling the figures of the suffering Servant (Isaiah 53:6–7) and the paschal lamb of the exodus (Exodus 12:12–13), reveals Christ sacrificed and resurrected, endowed now with the full messianic purpose of saving the world and restoring it to its pristine design. The throne indicates God's absolute sovereignty over history and over all beings, sovereignty now exercised by the risen Christ. The twenty-four elders comprise the ideal Church, including the Old and New Covenant (twelve tribes and twelve Apostles). The four living creatures are the personified sign of the manifold action of God extending in the four cardinal directions, north, south, east, and west. Christ is the slain Lamb who, through his sacrifice, gives his life for many; the Lamb who was

For meditation and context:

RESPONSORIAL PSALM   Psalm 30:2, 4, 5–6, 11–12, 13 (2a)

R. I will praise you, Lord, for you have rescued me.
or R. Alleluia.

I will extol you, O Lord, for you drew me
    clear
    and did not let my enemies rejoice over
    me.
O Lord, you brought me up from the
    netherworld;
    you preserved me from among those
    going down into the pit.

Sing praise to the Lord, you his faithful
    ones,
    and give thanks to his holy name.
For his anger lasts but a moment;
    a lifetime, his good will.
At nightfall, weeping enters in,
    but with the dawn, rejoicing.

Hear, O Lord, and have pity on me;
    O Lord, be my helper.
You changed my mourning into dancing;
    O Lord, my God, forever will I give you
    thanks.

READING II   Revelation 5:11–14

This is the second of six consecutive weeks we read from Revelation.

You are narrating a cosmic vision that should evoke a sense of awe. Try to "see" in your own mind's eye all the images you relate.

"Living creatures" and "elders" symbolize all creation and the Church.

The seven words that characterize the Lamb should suggest *distinct* qualities.

The whole universe gives praise. Distinguish one location from another.

Speak this as your own prayer that fuses gratitude and awe.

Pause after "answered" as if to listen to the "Amen" before you speak it. Imagine the whole Church falling to its knees in adoration.

A reading from the Book of Revelation

I, John, looked and **heard** the voices of **many angels**
    who **surrounded** the **throne**
    and the **living creatures** and the **elders.**
They were **countless** in **number,** and they **cried out**
        in a **loud voice:**
    "**Worthy** is the **Lamb** that was **slain**
        to receive **power** and **riches, wisdom** and **strength,**
        honor and **glory** and **blessing.**"
Then I heard **every creature** in **heaven** and on **earth**
    and **under** the **earth** and in the **sea,**
    everything in the **universe,** cry out:
    "To the **one** who **sits** on the **throne** and to the **Lamb**
        be **blessing** and **honor, glory** and **might,**
        forever and **ever.**"
The **four living creatures** answered, "**Amen,**"
    and the **elders** fell **down** and **worshiped.**

---

slain and is "standing" is Christ, once dead, now risen; the "seven horns" refers to the fullness of divine power; the seven eyes are "the seven spirits of God," the fullness of the Spirit. The attributes of the Lamb (power, wealth . . . praise) are seven, and indicate that the Risen One possesses the fullness of divine virtue. The universal multitude acclaims God's unending reign. Our Eucharistic celebration, at which the slain Lamb of God is present in the Body and Blood on the altar, is replete with joy and

enthusiasm. In the Eucharist we attest to the faith that God is the true Lord of history with its protagonist, Jesus Christ, the immolated Lamb, symbol of humility and self-surrender, triumphant in the resurrection. Humanity and all creation respond to God's salvific intervention with praise: "To the One seated on the throne, and to the Lamb, be praise and honor, glory and might, forever and ever." K.S.

GOSPEL   Fishing may sound to land-dwellers like an appealing trade. Think of the thrill of the catch, the sudden frenzy when the net is full or the bait has been taken. Remember the telling of fish stories and boasting about the size of a catch? But fishing is not as thrilling as it might at first seem. There are drawbacks. Fish do not always bite, a school of fish does not always find its way into the nets. It is a grueling task: the tedious wakefulness, the damp and cold, the rocking discomfort

GOSPEL   John 21:1–19

A reading from the holy Gospel according to John

[At that time, **Jesus revealed** himself **again** to his **disciples**
    at the **Sea** of **Tiberias.**
He **revealed** himself in **this way**.
Together were **Simon Peter, Thomas** called **Didymus,**
    Nathanael from **Cana** in **Galilee,**
    Zebedee's sons, and **two others** of his **disciples.**
Simon Peter said to them, "I am going **fishing.**"
They said to him, "**We also** will **come with** you."
So they **went out** and got into the **boat,**
    but **that night** they caught **nothing.**
When it was already **dawn, Jesus** was **standing** on the **shore;**
    but the **disciples** did not **realize** that it was **Jesus.**
Jesus said to them, "**Children,** have you **caught anything** to **eat?**"
They answered him, "**No.**"
So he said to them, "**Cast** the **net** over the **right side** of the **boat**
    and you will **find** something."
So they **cast** it, and were **not** able to **pull** it **in**
    because of the **number** of **fish.**
So the **disciple** whom **Jesus loved** said to **Peter,** "It is the **Lord.**"
When **Simon Peter heard** that it was the **Lord,**
    he **tucked in** his **garment,** for he was **lightly clad,**
    and **jumped** into the sea.
The **other** disciples **came** in the **boat,**
    for they were **not far** from **shore,** only about a **hundred yards,**
    dragging the **net** with the **fish.**
When they **climbed out** on **shore,**
    they **saw** a charcoal **fire** with **fish** on it and **bread.**
Jesus said to them, "**Bring** some of the **fish** you just **caught.**"
So **Simon Peter** went over and **dragged** the **net ashore**
    full of one **hundred fifty-three large fish.**
Even though there were so **many,** the **net** was **not torn.**

It is here that Jesus previously multiplied the loaves and fishes.
Try telling this story as a believer who is evangelizing others.
Speak the names with familiarity and affection.
Didymus = DID-ih-muhs

The number of disciples, seven, may represent the entire community of disciples.
Peter needs to keep busy, but their whole night is wasted.
Jesus brings the light of day.

Note the tender salutation.

That catch is surprising, as is their willingness to follow this stranger's advice.

The "disciple whom Jesus loved" is the first to recognize Jesus.

Peter "dresses" before jumping into the sea!

Emphasize the size of the catch.

Jesus has anticipated their hunger and met their need.

The number of fish is important. Their labor done, Jesus invites them to breakfast.

---

of cramped boats. And the hazards, like getting snagged on the river or lake bottom, water sloshing into the boat, the bumbling of fellow fishers, the tear or tangle of the net, or the snap of the lines.

Is there any wonder that after a night vigil of fishing the disciples were slow to recognize the curious onlooker on the shore? Or that those whom Jesus made fishers of people may have considered the bystander's greeting as an unwanted interruption, being caught with embarrassingly empty nets?

But one of the fishermen, the beloved disciple, had not been daunted by a long night of toil and watching. His gaze was ever on the lookout for the beloved Lord. So when he recognized the bystander, his heart leapt, and he announced to his fellow fishers, "It is the Lord." Other disciples, their vision blurred by the task at hand, were jolted into frantic response, and one, the skipper, grabbed the clothes he had discarded during the heavy night's toil, and dove into the sea. Meeting the resurrected Jesus, he clothes himself in Baptism.

This story of the resurrected Jesus on the shore highlights the personalities of the fervent, impassioned Peter, as well as the sublime, beloved disciple. Peter, impulsive; the beloved disciple, ever watching and insightful. The beloved disciple was the first to recognize their Lord; Peter, the first to approach the Lord. Didn't it happen just like this on Easter morning, when the two raced to the tomb, having been informed by Magdalene that the Lord had been taken from the tomb to an unknown place. Peter entered the gravesite first and beheld the cloth wrappings that had embraced the

Jesus said to them, "**Come,** have **breakfast.**"
And **none** of the **disciples dared** to **ask** him, "**Who are** you?"
  because they **realized** it was the **Lord.**
Jesus came over and **took** the **bread** and **gave** it to them,
  and in like **manner** the **fish.**
This was now the **third time** Jesus was **revealed** to his **disciples**
  after being **raised** from the **dead.**]

When they had **finished breakfast,** Jesus said to Simon **Peter,**
  "**Simon,** son of **John,** do **you love** me more than **these?**"
Simon Peter answered him, "**Yes,** Lord, you **know** that
    I love you."
Jesus said to him, "**Feed** my **lambs.**"
He then said to **Simon Peter** a **second** time,
  "**Simon,** son of **John,** do **you love** me?"
Simon Peter answered him, "**Yes,** Lord, you **know**
    that **I** love you."
Jesus said to him, "**Tend my sheep.**"
Jesus said to him the **third** time,
  "**Simon,** son of **John,** do **you love** me?"
Peter was **distressed** that Jesus had **said** to him a **third** time,
  "Do **you love** me?" and he **said** to him,
  "**Lord, you know everything;** you **know** that I **love** you."
Jesus said to him, "**Feed** my **sheep.**
Amen, amen, I say to you, when you were **younger,**
  you used to **dress yourself** and **go** where **you wanted;**
  but when you **grow old,** you will **stretch** out your **hands,**
  and **someone else** will **dress** you
  and **lead** you where you do **not want** to **go.**"
He said this **signifying** by what **kind** of **death** he would
    glorify God.
And when he had **said** this, he said to him, "**Follow** me."

[Shorter: John 21:1–14 (see brackets)]

Asking might betray their lack of vision and of faith, so they demur.

Don't overlook the Eucharistic language here.

Again, John stresses the recurrence of Jesus' appearances to the disciples.

Don't overly emotionalize the dialogue. Jesus is direct; it is Peter who must deal with the repeated questions that sting, probe, and totally disarm.

First, Jesus asks if Peter's love exceeds that of the other disciples; then he questions the sincerity and depth of that love.

Finally, Peter lets down his defenses.
A proverb about the loss of independence in old age is used to speak of Peter's future death.

Note that his anticipated martyrdom will "glorify God."

Jesus' final words speak to us as well as Peter.

---

deceased; the beloved disciple entered, saw, and believed.

This tale of the all-night fishers is as much a story of our own lives, as it is a tale of a crew on the Sea of Tiberius long ago. We are at times daunted by what seems to be a gloomy and difficult fishing expedition. We may feel overwhelmed by a catchless cast. There is a part of us that is slow and thick, reticent to greet the stranger on the shore, yet another part of our interior lives is on the lookout to recognize the stranger and greet him for who he really is. Then there is that part of us that, once informed of his identity, responds unhesitatingly, with all the vigor that characterized Peter's response when he dove into the sea.

We ask ourselves, who is this apostle Peter, once informed of the Gospel presence, who rushes to approach the mystery? It is that part of me that, at the urging of another, will rise to greet the Lord, as he did also at the beginning of the Gospel when his brother Andrew had informed him of Jesus' presence. Peter is that part of you or me that would readily shake off the business of this world, but momentarily he is so involved in the task at hand that his vision is clouded. At times, the clamminess of the labor and the stodginess of our fishing companions dulls our ability to recognize or respond to our Lord. Then we ask, who is this beloved disciple, whose keen vision is ever ready to perceive and announce the Lord? It is my intuition and better instinct. Even after the routine of my Christian life may have numbed me, the beloved disciple is sensitive and alert to the Gospel, and is not timid to confess an eternal longing to meet the Master. K.S.

FOURTH SUNDAY OF EASTER

LECTIONARY #51

READING I   Acts 13:14, 43–52

A reading from the Acts of the Apostles

Paul and **Barnabas** continued on from **Perga**
   and reached **Antioch** in **Pisidia.**
On the **sabbath** they **entered** the **synagogue** and **took** their **seats.**
Many Jews and worshipers who were **converts** to **Judaism**
   followed Paul and **Barnabas,** who **spoke** to them
   and **urged** them to **remain faithful** to the **grace** of **God.**

On the **following sabbath** almost the **whole city** gathered
   to **hear** the **word** of the **Lord.**
When the **Jews** saw the **crowds,** they were **filled** with **jealousy**
   and with **violent abuse contradicted** what **Paul said.**
Both **Paul** and **Barnabas** spoke out **boldly** and **said,**
   "It was **necessary** that the **word** of **God** be **spoken** to **you first,**
   but since **you reject** it
   and **condemn** yourselves as **unworthy** of **eternal life,**
   we **now turn** to the **Gentiles.**
For **so** the **Lord** has **commanded** us,
   *I have made you a **light** to the **Gentiles,***
   *that you may be an **instrument** of **salvation***
   *to the **ends** of the **earth.**"

The **Gentiles** were **delighted** when they **heard** this
   and **glorified** the **word** of the **Lord.**

This is the fourth of eight consecutive weeks we read from Acts.

Perga = PER-guh
Antioch = AN-tee-ahk
Pisidia = pih-SID-ee-uh

Begin with energy to suggest the fiery preaching of the previous week that has brought a huge crowd to hear them again.

Apparently, Jews and non-Jews have gathered to hear them.

Now as then, jealousy can make us oppose even the Gospel. Speak more with sadness than indictment.

Paul is strong in his conviction that the Word must now be proclaimed to those willing to hear it, no matter their ethnicity.

Paul quotes Isaiah 49:6. Shift your tone for the quotation.

Share this news with joy.

READING I The visit of Paul and Barnabas to Antioch in Pisidia occurs early in Paul's first missionary journey through the Diaspora, the regions where Jews were dispersed beyond Israel. The activity described in today's reading will establish a pattern for Paul's ministry that continues into his second and third journeys. He begins by preaching on the Sabbath in the synagogue, where he speaks to this fellow Jews, centering his preaching on the good news of Jesus' Resurrection from the dead. When great crowds come to hear the word of the Lord

the following Sabbath, local Jewish leaders are filled with jealousy and express opposition to Jesus' teaching. Just as hostility did not stop Jesus from proclaiming the Kingdom of God, neither did it stop Paul and Barnabas from preaching. They continue to speak with prophetic boldness, telling their audiences that it was necessary that they, as Jews, should be the first to receive the good news.

The Jews' rejection of Paul's preaching, equivalent to rejecting God's word, is the catalyst for Paul to take the message to the Gentiles, who respond with delight, glo-

rifying the word of the Lord. This causes further jealousy and persecution by the Jewish leaders, who expel the two preachers from their territory. Rather than inhibiting Paul's mission, this results in his taking it to other cities, where he will again preach in the synagogues. He never rejects the Jewish people. Not inhibited by opposition, Paul and those who have come to believe are filled with joy and the Holy Spirit.

READING II Revelation, the last book in the New Testament, brings to fulfillment promises from the first book

Quicken your tempo to suggest the surging flood of opposition that begins to well up against Paul. Speak in the tone of the opponents.

Iconium = ī-KOH-nee-uhm

Don't rush the last line. Despite opposition from their own people, they are filled with joy in the Spirit.

For meditation and context:

All who were **destined** for **eternal life** came to **believe,**
    and the **word** of the **Lord continued** to **spread**
    through the **whole region.**
The **Jews,** however, incited the **women** of **prominence**
        who were **worshipers**
    and the **leading men** of the **city,**
    stirred up a **persecution** against **Paul** and **Barnabas,**
    and **expelled** them from their **territory.**
So they shook the **dust** from their **feet** in **protest against** them,
    and went to **Iconium.**
The **disciples** were **filled** with **joy** and the **Holy Spirit.**

RESPONSORIAL PSALM   Psalm 100:1–2, 3, 5 (3c)

**R. We are his people, the sheep of his flock.
or R. Alleluia.**

Sing joyfully to the LORD, all you lands;
    serve the LORD with gladness;
    come before him with joyful song.

Know that the LORD is God;
    he made us, his we are;
    his people, the flock he tends.

The LORD is good:
    his kindness endures forever,
    and his faithfulness, to all generations.

This is the third of six consecutive weeks we read from Revelation.

Remember you are proclaiming a vision that's meant to bring comfort. Read slowly and with reverence.

All of humanity is represented in God's throne room.

The "elder" asked John about those dressed in white and now provides his own answer.

READING II   Revelation 7:9, 14b–17

A reading from the Book of Revelation

I, John, had a **vision** of a **great multitude,**
    which **no one** could **count,**
    from **every nation, race, people** and **tongue.**
They stood before the **throne** and before the **Lamb,**
    wearing **white robes** and holding **palm branches**
        in their **hands.**

Then **one** of the **elders said** to me,
    "**These** are the **ones** who have **survived** the time
        of **great distress;** »

of the Old Testament, Genesis. The great multitude described by John brings to mind the multitude of descendants promised to Abraham (Genesis 17:4; 22:17), now comprising both Jews and Gentiles from every nation, who stand before God's throne and before the Lamb. They have survived "the time of great distress" (*thlipsis*), referring to the end-time persecution of the faithful. Their white robes and palm branches signify purity and the saving victory that belongs to and comes from God.

John does not use the name of Jesus or Christ in this vision, but repeatedly refers

to him as the Lamb. By using the image of the Lamb here and elsewhere in Revelation (twenty-nine times), John evokes both the sacrificial Passover lamb (Exodus 12), and the lamb led to the slaughter (Isaiah 53:7), with both images alluding to the death of Jesus. The multitudes whose robes have been washed in the blood of the Lamb have been faithful in persecution, some probably to the point of death. Now as they worship at the throne of God, they no longer experience any kind of suffering, but are sheltered and shepherded by the Lamb. They will know all the tender care prophesied by

Isaiah: no hunger or thirst, no scorching wind or sun (49:10). In a striking poetic reversal, the Lamb becomes the shepherd, leading the multitude to springs of life-giving water. The actions of God and the Lamb are comparable; in every way, God and the Lamb care for the faithful multitude.

GOSPEL   This Gospel passage is the finale and high point of the discourse in which Jesus identifies himself as the good shepherd. Active verbs convey the dynamic relationship between Jesus and his sheep: the sheep *hear* and *follow*;

they have **washed** their **robes**
and made them **white** in the **blood** of the **Lamb**.

> "For **this reason** they **stand** before **God's throne**
>   and **worship** him **day** and **night** in his **temple**.
> The one who **sits** on the **throne** will **shelter** them.
> They will **not hunger** or **thirst** anymore,
>   nor will the **sun** or **any heat strike** them.
> For the **Lamb** who is in the **center** of the **throne**
>   will **shepherd** them
>   and **lead** them to **springs** of **life-giving water**,
>   and **God** will **wipe away every tear** from their **eyes**."

GOSPEL   John 10:27–30

A reading from the holy Gospel according to John

Jesus said:
"My **sheep hear** my **voice;**
   I **know** them, and they **follow me.**
I give them **eternal life,** and they shall **never perish.**
No one can take them out of **my hand**.
My **Father,** who has given them **to me,** is **greater** than **all,**
   and **no** one can take them out of the **Father's hand.**
The **Father** and **I** are **one**."

Their reward is eternal joy in the shelter of the Lord.

This is Good News for all who sit before you. Let them know these assurances are also for them.

Anyone in your assembly longing for God's comfort should hear the hope embedded in this final line. Use eye contact with the assembly to be sure they hear it.

In a short reading, every word matters. This text is spoken entirely in the voice of Jesus.

Though originally spoken in response to opponents, in our liturgy the tone of the words might be softened and spoken with compassion and assurance.
"No one . . . " requires strength and conviction.

Jesus' words are reassuring. Pause before the final line that asserts that he and the one who is "greater than all" are one!

Jesus *knows* and *gives*. Hearing is an essential component of faith and discipleship, a foundational imperative prayed every day in Judaism: "Hear, O Israel." Such hearing indicates attentiveness and obedience. Having heard the voice of the shepherd, the flock then follows him, a verb used throughout the Gospels to signify becoming a disciple.

For his part, Jesus knows his sheep. Far more than an intellectual comprehension, knowing includes understanding and profound intimacy. The gift that he gives to his sheep is eternal life; the life (*zoe*) that Jesus bestows is not held off until a distant future, but is already given even now as a down payment for future fullness. As his sheep hear his voice, Jesus reveals to them the oneness he has with his Father. No one can snatch the sheep out of Jesus' hand, nor out of his Father's. Jesus uses a very strong verb here, *harpazo*, denoting seizing by force or snatching, which was used earlier in the discourse to describe the action of a wolf against the flock (10:12). Jesus and his Father protect their flock, sharing a common concern for their safety. Jesus concludes his discourse by announcing his oneness with the Father. Later in John's Gospel, Jesus gives to those who hear his voice an ever-deepening revelation about the oneness he has with the Father (e.g., 10:30) and the oneness he desires for his sheep (17:22). E.P.

FIFTH SUNDAY OF EASTER

LECTIONARY #54

READING I   Acts 14:21–27

A reading from the Acts of the Apostles

After **Paul** and **Barnabas** had proclaimed the **good news**
    to that **city**
    and made a **considerable number** of **disciples,**
    they returned to **Lystra** and to **Iconium** and to **Antioch.**
They **strengthened** the **spirits** of the **disciples**
    and **exhorted** them to **persevere** in the **faith,** saying,
    "It is **necessary** for us to undergo **many hardships**
    to **enter** the **Kingdom** of **God."**
They appointed **elders** for them in **each church** and,
    with **prayer** and **fasting, commended** them to the **Lord**
    in whom they had **put** their **faith.**
Then they traveled through **Pisidia** and reached **Pamphylia.**
After proclaiming the word at **Perga** they went down to **Attalia.**
From there they sailed to **Antioch,**
    where they had been **commended** to the **grace** of **God**
    for the **work** they had now **accomplished.**
And when they **arrived,** they called the **church together**
    and **reported** what **God** had **done** with them
    and how he had **opened** the **door** of **faith** to the **Gentiles.**

This is the fifth of eight consecutive weeks we read from Acts.

"That city" is Derbe. Each city is a place where sisters and brothers grasped the faith you still profess.

Lystra = LIS-truh
Iconium = ī-KOH-nee-uhm
Antioch = AN-tee-ahk

Speak with calm confidence and strength.

Note the complex sequence: (a) they appointed elders, (b) they prayed and fasted, (c) they entrusted them to God. Help us hear all three stages of the process.
Pisidia = pih-SID-ee-uh
Pamphylia = pam-FIL-ee-uh
Perga = PER-guh
Attalia = uh-TAHL-ee-uh
They were "commended" means that through prayer they were entrusted to God.

Like a family, the "church" awaits the news and gathers to hear of their success.

 READING I The travels of Paul and Barnabas recounted in Acts bring their first missionary journey to completion. As they preach first to Jews and then turn to Gentiles, the missionaries make numerous disciples, a term used in Acts to refer to those who believe in Jesus and are baptized. While making disciples is one part of their mission, they also work to encourage those who are already disciples. Many of those who converted to the faith suffered ridicule, hostility, and even rejection by their own families, as Jesus had predicted (e.g., Luke 21:16). Paul's exhortation

to persevere in the faith is a recognition that the young Church faced persecution.

After establishing Churches, Paul and Barnabas appoint leaders to care for the communities. The act of designating leaders was likely performed with a ritual of laying on of hands, seen elsewhere in Acts as a sign of conferring power, grace, or the Holy Spirit (6:6; 8:17; 9:17; 13:3). The appointed leaders, called elders, are comparable to Jewish officials who administered, advised, and set synagogue policies. Before continuing to the next town, Paul and Barnabas entrust them to the Lord's care.

As Paul and Barnabas complete their journey and return to Antioch, where they began, they report to the community God's actions through them. Of particular importance is the news of God's grace opening "the door of faith to the Gentiles." Admittance of Gentiles into the community of believers without undergoing circumcision was the first major controversy in the Church, addressed by the Council of Jerusalem, described in the chapter immediately following this reading.

For meditation and context:

RESPONSORIAL PSALM   Psalm 145:8–9, 10–11, 12–13 (see 1)

R. I will praise your name for ever, my king and my God.
or R. Alleluia.

The LORD is gracious and merciful,
    slow to anger and of great kindness.
The LORD is good to all
    and compassionate toward all his works.

Let all your works give you thanks, O LORD,
    and let your faithful ones bless you.
Let them discourse of the glory of your
        Kingdom
    and speak of your might.

Let them make known your might to the
        children of Adam,
    and the glorious splendor of your
        Kingdom.
Your Kingdom is a Kingdom for all ages,
    and your dominion endures through all
        generations.

This is the fourth of six consecutive weeks we read from Revelation.

Remember this is a vision. Give it a sense of wonder and persuade us that what you describe is indeed possible.

"Sea" represents all that is chaotic and deadly in life.

Speak this vision with the joy you'd have if looking at a daughter adorned to meet her bridegroom.

Intensify the majesty of the moment. The "voice" speaks slowly, with great authority but also compassion.

Speak these as promises and sustain eye contact with the assembly.

READING II   Revelation 21:1–5a

A reading from the Book of Revelation

Then **I, John,** saw a **new heaven** and a **new earth.**
The **former** heaven and the **former** earth had **passed away,**
    and the **sea** was **no more.**
I also saw the **holy city,** a **new Jerusalem,**
    coming down out of **heaven** from **God,**
    prepared as a **bride adorned** for her **husband.**
I heard a **loud voice** from the **throne** saying,
    "**Behold, God's dwelling** is **with** the **human race.**
He will **dwell** with them and they will be **his people**
    and **God himself** will **always** be with them as **their God.**
He will **wipe every tear** from their **eyes,**
    and there shall be **no more death** or **mourning, wailing** or **pain,**
    for the **old order** has **passed away.**"

The **One** who sat on the **throne** said,
    "**Behold,** I make **all things new.**"

READING II   "I saw a new heaven and a new earth." Thus begins the final vision in the Revelation of John. Writing for a persecuted Church, John uses symbols and images intended to give the faithful people hope and confidence in God's ultimate victory. What the visionary calls "the former heaven and the former earth" is the world in which John's audience is living. The old will give way to utter newness in which all the uncertainty and suffering of the present are no more. Everything that causes them suffering will be destroyed. The sea, the symbolic place of chaos and danger in the Hebrew tradition, is no more; death, mourning, and pain will also pass away. The entire old order is gone, transformed.

A new Jerusalem, coming down from heaven, will replace the former earthly city. The historical city of Jerusalem, symbolic place of God's dwelling, had been destroyed by the Romans in the year AD 70, long before Revelation was written. What the vision promises is not a restoration of stones and structures but of the people themselves. Jerusalem as a symbol stands for the people as a whole. The people themselves are to be adorned as a bride, beautiful and pure, welcoming God in their midst.

At the center of the vision is the most important assurance to the beleaguered people: God's abiding presence with them as their own God. The promise is personal and comforting. The final verse begins, "behold," calling people to listen carefully, for God promises to make all things new.

GOSPEL   As soon as Judas leaves the supper with Jesus and his friends, the long awaited hour of Jesus'

Now that the betrayer is gone, Jesus can speak about the saving events his treachery will set in motion. Speak not with disappointment but with joy and hope.

There is a sense of urgency and immediacy in these lines.

Note the tender salutation.

Jesus asks no more than what he has been willing to give.

Obedience to his will configures us to his image and allows the world to see him in us.

TO KEEP IN MIND

What does the reading ask your assembly to do or to be after hearing your proclamation? Focus on an intention every time you proclaim.

GOSPEL   John 13:31–33a, 34–35

A reading from the holy Gospel according to John

When **Judas** had **left** them, **Jesus** said,
    "**Now** is the **Son of Man glorified,** and **God** is **glorified in him.**
If **God** is **glorified** in him,
    God will **also glorify** him in **himself,**
    and **God** will **glorify** him **at once.**
My **children,** I will be with you only a **little while longer.**
I give you a **new commandment**: **love one another.**
As **I** have loved **you,** so **you also** should **love one another.**
This is how **all** will **know** that **you** are **my disciples,**
    if **you** have **love** for **one another.**"

---

passing from this world to the Father is set in motion. This hour is the appointed time of glorification of Jesus and his Father. Jesus had earlier declared, "the Father and I are one" (10:30); now we learn that such intimate union means that the glorification of Jesus is also the glorification of his Father. Jesus uses the word glorification (*doxazo*) five times in two verses, emphatically pointing to the deepest meaning of the coming hour. To be glorified is to be greatly praised, and to be clothed in splendor; it is a revelation of the mystery of Jesus' identity and purpose. The hour of

glorification stretches from Jesus being lifted up on the cross, to his death, Resurrection, and exaltation. It is a manifestation of Jesus loving his own "to the end" (13:1), loving them to the fullest extent.

Having focused on his glorification and that of his Father, he turns his attention to his disciples. Addressing them as "my children," Jesus displays a tender bond of affection as he prepares them for the coming hour. After telling them that he will be with them only a little while longer, he gives them clear instructions on how they

are to live in his absence. Throughout his ministry, Jesus had shown love through his teaching and signs of compassionate healing; he will express his love even more completely from the cross. Such self-giving love is to be the pattern of their own love. The greatest, most tangible sign of discipleship is the love Jesus' disciples have for one another. Their love, like his, gives glory to God! E.P.

SIXTH SUNDAY
OF EASTER

LECTIONARY #57

READING I   Acts 15:1–2, 22–29

A reading from the Acts of the Apostles

Some who had come down from **Judea** were **instructing**
    the **brothers**,
 "**Unless** you are **circumcised** according to the **Mosaic practice**,
 you **cannot** be **saved**."
Because there arose **no little dissension** and **debate**
    by **Paul** and **Barnabas** with them,
    it was decided that **Paul, Barnabas,** and **some** of the **others**
    should go up to **Jerusalem** to the **apostles** and **elders**
    about this question.

The **apostles** and **elders,** in agreement with the **whole church**,
    decided to choose **representatives**
    and to send them to **Antioch with Paul** and **Barnabas.**
The ones **chosen** were **Judas,** who was called **Barsabbas,**
    and **Silas, leaders** among the brothers.
This is the **letter** delivered by them:

"The **apostles** and the **elders,** your **brothers**,
    to the brothers in **Antioch, Syria,** and **Cilicia**
    of **Gentile** origin: **greetings.**
Since we have **heard** that **some** of **our number**
    who went out without **any mandate** from **us**
    have **upset** you with their **teachings**
    and **disturbed** your **peace** of **mind,**

From the start, your tone should suggest that there is tension to resolve.

It was Pharisee converts who insisted on the need for circumcision.

You can be sure Paul argued vehemently, but without success. So, the decision is "kicked upstairs" to Jerusalem.

Left out here is the discussion in Jerusalem. It is the *Jerusalem* elders who send representatives back to Antioch.
Antioch = AN-tee-ahk
Barsabbas = bar-SAH-buhs
Silas = SĪ-luhs

The goal of the letter is to unburden the Gentile believers, so your tone is apologetic and pastoral.

READING I Paul's journey throughout the Mediterranean region was greatly successful in bringing Gentiles to the faith. Unlike the Church in Jerusalem, Paul did not require circumcision for Gentile converts. How Gentiles were to become a part of the community of believers was the first major controversy of the early Church, bringing leaders together in Jerusalem to decide the question. In his letter to the Galatians, Paul writes about this controversy in harsh terms, stating that Peter was clearly wrong, and many of the Jews were hypocrites (Galatians 2:11, 13). In Luke's account in Acts, the controversy is handled more peacefully, and agreement reached by all parties. The narrative shows both the debated question and the process the Church used to solve it.

It isn't surprising that at least some Jewish Christians expected Gentiles to be circumcised. The first disciples of Jesus were Jews, and they continued to observe the religious practices of the people of the covenant. Since Gentiles who joined the Jewish faith accepted its rituals and practices, the believers in Jerusalem presumed that converts to the Christian faith would do the same. But Paul's practice among the Gentiles outside of Palestine did not require the ritual of circumcision. When Luke says there was "no little dissension" he means that there was in fact a great uproar and division. Because the unity of the Church was at stake, the two sides had to come together.

Much of the process for reaching a decision is omitted from today's reading, but it is helpful in understanding how the believers addressed their differing practices. The process begins with bringing the representatives together and debating, not

They spend much time substantiating the level of discernment that took place.

beloved = bee-LUHV-uhd

Stress the role of the Spirit in the decision. You can list the directives rather quickly.

The role of the Law is not eliminated; "If you . . . you will be doing what is right."

For meditation and context:

we have with **one accord** decided to choose **representatives**
and to **send** them to you along with our **beloved Barnabas**
    and **Paul,**
who have dedicated their **lives** to the **name**
    of our **Lord Jesus Christ.**
So we are sending **Judas** and **Silas**
who will **also convey** this **same message** by **word** of **mouth:**
'It is the **decision** of the **Holy Spirit** and of **us**
not to **place** on you **any burden** beyond **these necessities,**
namely, to **abstain** from **meat sacrificed** to **idols,**
from **blood,** from **meats** of **strangled animals,**
and from **unlawful marriage.**
If you keep **free** of **these,**
    you will be doing what is **right. Farewell.'"**

RESPONSORIAL PSALM   Psalm 67:2–3, 5, 6, 8 (4)

R. O God, let all the nations praise you!
or R. Alleluia.

May God have pity on us and bless us;
    may he let his face shine upon us.
So may your way be known upon earth;
    among all nations, your salvation.

May the nations be glad and exult
    because you rule the peoples in equity;
    the nations on the earth you guide.

May the peoples praise you, O God;
    may all the peoples praise you!
May God bless us,
    and may all the ends of the earth fear him!

in the sense of one side winning and the other losing, but investigating and discussing. Part of the investigating involves remembering and relating their experiences, that of Paul as well as Peter. James, the leader of the Jerusalem Church, correlates these experiences with Scripture, and makes a judgment that is announced in the letter reported in today's reading. The letter is then promulgated by personal representatives, Paul and Barnabas, to the Gentile Christians. The decision, ultimately coming from the Holy Spirit, does not demand circumcision, but only abiding by

norms that allow the Gentile and Jewish Churches to live in peace.

READING II Revelation uses and reinterprets highly symbolic biblical images that would be well known to the original audience of persecuted Christians near the end of the first century. Today's reading begins with a high mountain, symbolic place of revelation and divine nearness. The most developed symbol in the vision is the holy city, Jerusalem. When Revelation was written, the real, historical city was in ruins, the temple destroyed, and

the people discouraged by their loss. But the Jerusalem of the vision gleams with God's own splendor and is radiant. The city's massive high wall has twelve gates, inscribed with the names of the twelve tribes of Israel. Added to the names of the ancient tribes are the names of the Twelve Apostles of the Lamb who are the foundations of the city. The number twelve, both for Israel's tribes and Jesus' Apostles, signifies fullness or completeness, and suggests that the city itself is symbolic of the people as a whole, all of them chosen by God. The verse just before today's reading prepares

This is the fifth of six consecutive weeks we read from Revelation.

This is not your typical opening line, even in Scripture. Read slowly and significantly.

Here, your *tone* will communicate more than the words will!

READING II   Revelation 21:10–14, 22–23

A reading from the Book of Revelation

The **angel** took me in **spirit** to a **great, high mountain**
    and **showed** me the **holy city Jerusalem**
    coming **down** out of **heaven** from **God.**
It **gleamed** with the **splendor** of **God.**
Its **radiance** was like that of a **precious stone**,
    like **jasper, clear** as **crystal.**
It had a **massive, high wall**,
    with **twelve gates** where **twelve angels** were stationed
    and on which **names** were **inscribed,**
    the **names** of the **twelve tribes** of the **Israelites.**
There were **three** gates facing **east,**
    three **north,** three **south,** and three **west.**
The **wall** of the city had **twelve courses** of **stones**
        as its **foundation**,
    on which were inscribed the twelve **names**
    of the twelve **apostles** of the **Lamb.**

I saw **no temple** in the **city**
    for its **temple** is the **Lord God almighty** and the **Lamb.**
The **city** had **no need** of **sun** or **moon** to **shine** on it,
    for the **glory** of **God** gave it **light,**
    and its **lamp** was the **Lamb.**

Stress this reference to the twelve tribes of Israel.

Don't shy from these repetitions; give them a grand and regal tone.

As Israel was built on the foundation of the twelve tribes, the New Covenant is built on the foundation of the Twelve Apostles.

Give the explanation that the city needed no Temple or illumination with mounting conviction and joy.

for this personalized meaning of the city, when the guiding angel says, "Come here. I will show you the bride, the wife of the Lamb."

The vision is reminiscent of that of Ezekiel, whose picture of Jerusalem was also on a high mountain (40:2). Much of Ezekiel's account is of the temple itself, with its walls, gates, and courts, its rituals and sacrifices. But the Jerusalem of Revelation has no temple. The Lord God almighty and the Lamb are the temple, the divine dwelling place. The people abiding with this temple need neither sun nor

moon to shine on them, for the Lamb, the risen Lord Jesus, gives the people all the light they need. The visions of Revelation, so often filled with fearful symbols of destruction, present a vision of hope for the whole people, in whose presence is the living temple of God.

GOSPEL   In Jesus' lengthy communication to his disciples at their last supper together, he gives them words of comfort even as he prepares them for his impending suffering and death. In this portion of his discourse, Jesus juxta-

poses the sad news that he will soon be leaving them with the assurance that he will still remain with them, a paradox they cannot yet understand. Further, not only will Jesus himself be with them, but also the Father and the Holy Spirit, sharing such an intimacy that Jesus and his Father will make their dwelling, their permanent home, with those who love him.

As he is about to leave them, Jesus announces his farewell gifts. First, his Father will send them the Advocate (*paracletos*), the Holy Spirit. Shortly before the words spoken here, Jesus had already

GOSPEL   John 14:23–29

A reading from the holy Gospel according to John

Jesus said to his **disciples:**
 "Whoever **loves** me will **keep** my **word,**
 and my **Father** will **love him,**
 and we will **come** to him and **make** our **dwelling with** him.
Whoever does **not** love me does **not** keep my words;
 yet the **word** you **hear** is **not mine**
 but **that** of the **Father** who **sent** me.

"I have **told** you this while I am **with** you.
The **Advocate,** the **Holy Spirit,**
 whom the **Father** will **send** in **my name,**
 will **teach** you **everything**
 and **remind** you of **all** that I **told** you.
Peace I **leave** with you; my **peace** I **give** to you.
Not as the **world** gives do **I give** it to **you.**
Do **not** let your **hearts** be **troubled** or **afraid.**
You heard me **tell** you,
 'I am **going away** and I will come **back** to you.'
If you **loved** me,
 you would **rejoice** that I am **going** to the **Father;**
 for the **Father** is **greater** than **I.**
And now I have **told** you this before it **happens,**
 so that **when** it **happens** you may **believe.**"

Recall that the setting is the Last Supper. Jesus is preparing his closest friends for his farewell. Create a mood of intimacy and warmth.

Let "Whoever does not . . . " contrast with what went before.

Sending another advocate brings reassurance to teacher as well as students.

Here begins a new beat in the text. This is not the ritual speech of liturgy, so give it a more conversational tone.

This is a command, but spoken with compassion.

Keep in mind, Jesus has yet to ascend Calvary; anticipating his return to the Father helps him sustain his resolve.

This whole discourse has been a way of caring for and preparing them for the difficult hours ahead.

---

promised this personal gift: the Father "will give you another *paracletos* to be with you forever" (14:16). In saying that his Father would send another Advocate, Jesus is pointing to his own role of being their advocate during his lifetime, the one who stood alongside them as their guide, counselor, and comforter. Though Jesus will be leaving them immediately after their meal, the other *paracletos* will remain with them always, ever reminding them of Jesus and his teaching. This Advocate will teach them everything, ultimately giving them a deeper understanding of what Jesus taught them throughout his ministry.

A second gift that Jesus bestows is peace, a treasure that his Jewish disciples would understand as the Hebrew notion of *shalom*: completeness and harmony in every dimension of life. But Jesus tells them that his gift of peace is different from that offered by the world. His peace will remain with them even in the face of intense conflict, persecution, rejection, and death. The inner harmony and communion with the Father, the Son, and the Holy Spirit create an abiding peace beyond any human effort or comprehension. It is based on mutual love. Jesus' promise of the Advocate is a future gift; peace is a gift he gives to his friends even before he leaves the upper room to complete his hour of passing from this world to the Father. E.P.

THE ASCENSION OF THE LORD

LECTIONARY #58

READING I   Acts 1:1–11

A reading from the beginning of the Acts of the Apostles

In the **first** book, **Theophilus,**
   I dealt with **all** that **Jesus did** and **taught**
   until the **day** he was **taken up,**
   after giving **instructions** through the **Holy Spirit**
   to the **apostles** whom he had **chosen.**
He presented himself **alive** to them
   by **many proofs** after he had **suffered,**
   appearing to them during **forty days**
   and **speaking** about the **Kingdom** of **God.**
While **meeting** with them,
   he **enjoined** them **not** to depart from **Jerusalem,**
   but to **wait** for "the **promise** of the **Father**
   about which you have heard me **speak;**
   for **John baptized** with **water,**
   but in a few days **you** will be **baptized** with the **Holy Spirit.**"

When they had **gathered together** they asked him,
   "**Lord,** are you at **this time** going to **restore**
   the **Kingdom** to **Israel?**"
He **answered** them, "It is **not** for you to **know** the **times**
      or **seasons**
   that the **Father** has **established** by his **own authority.**
But you will receive **power** when the **Holy Spirit** comes **upon** you,
   and you will be **my witnesses** in **Jerusalem,**

Luke is inspiriting faith, so this background information is important and should be shared with purpose.

Theophilus = thee-OF-uh-luhs

He reviews how he ended his Gospel with the narrative of the Ascension, then begins Acts with that same story.

These are assertions of facts, not of faith. Jesus was *seen* after his Resurrection!

"Forty" is symbolic of an indefinite, but sacred, span of time.

Luke is quoting Jesus. Note, it is "the Father" who has promised to send the Spirit.

Their hearts still yearn for earthly power. By now, they should know better.

Jesus redirects their energy to the real purposes of the Father. Don't be abrupt, but speak with compassion.

Though they have no idea where this prophecy will take them, it fills them with hope.

Today, options are given for reading II. Contact your parish staff to learn which reading will be used.

READING I   The account of the Ascension of Jesus is the hinge whereby Luke connects the story of Jesus in his Gospel to the story of the Church in Acts. The two volumes overlap, with a narrative of the Ascension concluding the Gospel, and told again at the beginning of Acts. In the version in Acts, which we read today, Jesus' disciples, confused and anxious, question him about the restoration of the Kingdom to Israel. Instead, he speaks of what they are to do through the power of the Holy Spirit. In one succinct sentence, he gives them their commission, phrased as both a command and promise. Jesus promises that the Holy Spirit, whose power had filled Jesus throughout his lifetime, will also empower and sustain their mission. The Spirit will impel the disciples beyond their fear and lack of understanding to become Jesus' own witnesses (*martyroi*). As witnesses, they will testify to Jesus by preaching and healing in his name, and even by emulating his faithfulness to God in the face of persecution. As Jews, Jesus' disciples would likely expect to carry out their mission in Jerusalem, among their own people. But Jesus sends them to witness also to Samaritans and even to Gentiles, those who dwell at the ends of the earth. The short sentence provides an outline for the deeds of the Apostles throughout Acts.

After giving them the final instructions, Jesus is lifted from their sight. The disciples, not yet filled with the promised Holy Spirit, seem dazed and immobile. The

Paint the scene by reading slowly and "seeing" what you describe.

"Suddenly" breaks the mood of awed silence.

The "two men" are not harsh; they nudge the disciples to look to the future.

"Will return" has implications for us today as much as for them: Be ready!

For meditation and context:

throughout **Judea** and **Samaria,**
and to the **ends** of the **earth.**"
When he had **said** this, as they were **looking on,**
he was **lifted up**, and a **cloud took** him from their **sight.**
While they were looking **intently** at the **sky** as he was **going,**
suddenly two men dressed in **white garments**
stood beside them.
They said, "**Men** of **Galilee,**
why are you **standing** there looking at the **sky?**
This **Jesus** who has been **taken up** from you into **heaven**
will **return** in the **same way** as you have **seen** him
going into **heaven.**"

RESPONSORIAL PSALM   Psalm 47:2–3, 6–7, 8–9 (6)

R. God mounts his throne to shouts of joy: a blare of trumpets for the Lord.
or R. Alleluia.

All you peoples, clap your hands,
    shout to God with cries of gladness,
for the LORD, the Most High, the awesome,
    is the great king over all the earth.

God mounts his throne amid shouts of joy;
    the LORD, amid trumpet blasts.
Sing praise to God, sing praise;
    sing praise to our king, sing praise.

For king of all the earth is God;
    sing hymns of praise.
God reigns over the nations,
    God sits upon his holy throne.

READING II   Ephesians 1:17–23

A reading from the Letter of Saint Paul to the Ephesians

Brothers and **sisters:**
May the **God** of our **Lord Jesus Christ,** the **Father** of **glory,**
    give you a **Spirit** of **wisdom** and **revelation**
    resulting in **knowledge** of him.
May the **eyes** of your **hearts** be **enlightened,**
    that you may know what is the **hope** that belongs to **his call,**
what are the **riches** of **glory** »

You greet "brothers and sisters" with a prayer.

Father, Son, and Spirit are all mentioned in this prayer.

Increase your energy as you move through this part of the prayer.

two men in white garments, evocative of the heavenly messengers at the empty tomb on Easter morning, announce that the place of Jesus' Ascension will also be the place of his return. Until that happens, his disciples have their mission to fulfill.

READING II   **Ephesians.** The letter to the Ephesians is unusual among Paul's letters in that it does not address specific concerns of the local Church in Ephesus, but describes the life and belief of the Church as a whole. It was perhaps written as a letter intended to be

circulated among the other Churches around the Mediterranean, beginning with Ephesus. Thus the prayer in today's reading is for believers in every time and place. Paul prays that the Father of glory will extend the riches of glory throughout both time and space. Among these riches for which he prays are a Spirit of wisdom and revelation, of knowledge and enlightened hearts. The scope of these gifts seems to leave Paul almost breathless as he writes about the surpassing greatness of God's power.

Paul continues in soaring language about the riches already accomplished in

Christ. The greatest evidence of God's surpassing greatness is his raising Christ from the dead and seating him at his right hand. Paul is emphatic in describing the extent of Christ's glory: he is above *every* principality and the other celestial beings; Christ is far above *every* name, now *and* in the age to come. *All* things are under Christ's feet. The universal Church for which Paul prays is embraced in Christ's eternal and vast dominion. This Church is Christ's own body, over which Christ is the head. Because the Church is Christ's body, the members of

God's mercy allows us to share in Christ's exaltation. These words give Christ praise.

"Principality," "authority," "power," and "dominion" are four different ranks of angelic spirits. Don't blur them into one.

"He" is the Father; "him" and "his" refer to Christ. God made Jesus head of the Church: announce that great truth with joy.

in **his inheritance** among the **holy ones**,
and what is the **surpassing greatness** of **his power**
for us who **believe**,
in accord with the **exercise** of his **great might**:
which he **worked** in **Christ**,
raising him from the **dead**
and **seating** him at his **right hand** in the **heavens**,
far above **every principality**, **authority**, **power**, and **dominion**,
and **every name** that is **named**
not only in **this age** but **also** in the one to **come**.
And he put **all things** beneath his **feet**
and gave him as **head** over **all things** to the **church**,
which is his **body**,
the **fullness** of the **one** who **fills all things** in **every way**.

Or:

READING II   Hebrews 9:24–28; 10:19–23

A reading from the Letter to the Hebrews

Be aware from the start that you are comparing Christ's sacrifice with those of the Old Law.

Christ, not a human priest, intercedes for us in the very presence of God.

Your tone suggests the futility of this endless repetition.

Christ's one perfect sacrifice of himself requires no repetition.

This is an analogy: just as this is true, so is what follows.

Christ did not enter into a **sanctuary** made by **hands**,
    a **copy** of the **true** one, but **heaven itself**,
    that he might now **appear** before **God** on **our behalf**.
Not that he might offer himself **repeatedly**,
    as the **high** priest enters **each year** into the **sanctuary**
    with **blood** that is **not** his **own**;
    if **that** were **so**, he would have had to **suffer repeatedly**
    from the **foundation** of the **world**.
But **now once for all he** has **appeared** at the **end** of the **ages**
    to take away **sin** by **his sacrifice**.
Just as it is **appointed** that **men** and **women die once**,
    and after **this** the **judgment**, so also **Christ**,
    offered once to take away the **sins** of **many**,

---

the body in all times and places live in Christ's fullness.

Hebrews. The reading from Hebrews, drawing on images and rituals from the Jewish feast of Atonement, develops the permanent meaning of Christ's enthronement in heaven. The actions described in Leviticus (16:2–34) explain the rituals for the feast that came to be performed annually in the Jerusalem Temple. The ceremony involved the high priest offering sacrifice for his own sins as well as those of the people and sprinkling the blood of a sacrificial animal as a sign of atonement. In this earthly temple, the high priest used "blood

that was not his own." With this background, the author of Hebrews portrays Christ in the heavenly sanctuary, present with God and acting on our behalf. There is no need for an annual sacrifice, for Christ's sacrifice was "once for all." Just as all men and women die only once, Christ died once, offering his own blood that takes away sin and brings about salvation.

The author of Hebrews develops the portrait of Christ as high priest in more detail in verses omitted from today's reading (10:1–18). Our reading picks up with an exhortation, reminding the community what it means to believe that Christ is our

great high priest. We have confidence that he has opened for us an entrance into the heavenly sanctuary. Christ's own flesh is the "veil," which must be passed through for admittance into the sanctuary. We live with sincere hearts and absolute trust that, having been sprinkled with the water of Baptism, we can approach God. The final verse exhorts an unwavering "confession" (*homologia*), implying belief as well as living in accordance with that belief by obedience, fidelity, and loving relationship. The once-for-all sacrifice of Christ as our eternal high priest gives us hope, grounded in God's own promise.

Christ will return, not to atone again for sin, but to give us the salvation he won for us.

Our "confidence" is our Baptism. He's using his previous points to call for faith and confident hope.

You are challenging us to live according to our faith. Don't be timid.

Speak boldly and out of your own experience of God's mercy and fidelity.

will appear a **second** time, **not** to take away **sin**
but to bring **salvation** to those who **eagerly await** him.

Therefore, **brothers** and **sisters**, since through the **blood** of **Jesus**
we have **confidence** of **entrance** into the **sanctuary**
by the **new** and **living way** he opened for us through the **veil**,
that is, **his flesh**,
and since we have "a **great priest** over the **house** of **God**,"
let us **approach** with a **sincere heart** and in **absolute trust**,
with our hearts **sprinkled clean** from an **evil conscience**
and our **bodies washed** in **pure water**.
Let us hold **unwaveringly** to our **confession** that gives us **hope**,
for he who made the **promise** is **trustworthy**.

GOSPEL   Luke 24:46–53

He reminds them that he had always preached about suffering and repentance. Among the "witnesses" of Jesus are those sitting in your assembly.

As In Acts, Jesus says that the "Spirit" is the *Father's* promised gift to them.

What follows is all narration, spoken slowly. The mood is not without hope and expectation.
Blessed = blesd

After they pay "homage" their hearts swell with joy!

A reading from the holy Gospel according to Luke

Jesus said to his **disciples**:
"**Thus** it is **written** that the **Christ** would **suffer**
and **rise** from the **dead** on the **third day**
and that **repentance**, for the **forgiveness** of **sins**,
would be **preached** in **his name**
to **all** the **nations**, **beginning** from **Jerusalem**.
You are **witnesses** of these things.
And **behold** I am sending the **promise** of my **Father** upon you;
but **stay** in the **city**
until you are **clothed** with **power** from on **high**."

Then he **led** them out as far as **Bethany**,
raised his **hands**, and **blessed** them.
As he **blessed** them he **parted** from them
and was **taken up** to **heaven**.
They did him **homage**
and then returned to **Jerusalem** with **great joy**,
and they were **continually** in the **temple praising God**.

GOSPEL   Today's Gospel is a drama with two scenes. In the first, Jesus speaks with his disciples in Jerusalem and gives them a final teaching. In his opening words, not included in today's reading, he tells them that everything written about him in the law and prophets and psalms had to be fulfilled. Then, having opened their minds to understand the Scriptures, he summarizes the core proclamation about him: his suffering, death, and Resurrection that had been foretold in their ancient writings. With these few words, he provides a new way of interpreting the Scriptures; they are now to

be reread in light of Jesus' passing from death to life. As his followers take this message to all the nations, they are also to call people to repentance (*metanoia*). They are to be Jesus' own witnesses, testifying about him in word and deed. Such worldwide witnessing would be impossible without the Holy Spirit, the one who will clothe the disciples with the power they need to fulfill the mission Jesus gives them.

In the second scene of the drama, Jesus leads his disciples from Jerusalem to Bethany where he is taken up to heaven. This account is much shorter than the complementary one in Acts. Most important in

this shortened version is Jesus' blessing of his disciples, reminiscent of Moses' blessing to Israel. The disciples respond by showing Jesus homage—the word suggests they prostrated themselves in an act of worship. They then return to Jerusalem, center of the Jewish world and the place where Luke began his Gospel. While we might expect fear or dejection at Jesus' departure, the disciples return to Jerusalem with great joy and constant praise of God in the temple. E.P.

SEVENTH SUNDAY
OF EASTER

LECTIONARY #61

READING I   Acts 7:55–60

Narrators often have a point of view. Here, yours is that of a believer who admires Stephen.

Don't gloss over the reference to the "Holy Spirit."

Convey the peaceful demeanor with which Stephen tells his vision and faces his death.

The prince of lies can't handle the truth and so erupts in violence.

Speak slowly and knowingly of "Saul."

Again, convey Stephen's serenity and peace in the face of death.

Note that his last prayer is more command than request. Speak with assurance that God will answer.

"Fell asleep" is a euphemism for death.

A reading from the Acts of the Apostles

Stephen, filled with the **Holy Spirit,**
   looked up **intently** to **heaven** and **saw** the **glory** of **God**
   and **Jesus** standing at the **right hand** of **God,**
   and **Stephen** said, "**Behold,** I see the **heavens opened**
   and the **Son** of **Man** standing at the **right hand** of **God.**"
But they **cried out** in a **loud voice,**
   covered their **ears,** and **rushed** upon him **together.**
They **threw** him **out** of the **city,** and began to **stone** him.
The **witnesses** laid down their **cloaks**
   at the **feet** of a **young man** named **Saul.**
As they were **stoning Stephen,** he **called out,**
   "**Lord Jesus, receive my spirit.**"
Then he **fell** to his **knees** and **cried out** in a **loud voice,**
   "**Lord,** do **not hold** this **sin against** them";
   and when he **said** this, he fell **asleep.**

READING I The account of the death of Stephen proclaimed today presents him as a true witness to Christ. As a witness, he not only testifies by his words, but also by repeating in his own person the life-pattern of Jesus, particularly in the manner he faces suffering and death. Like Jesus, Stephen is filled with the Holy Spirit. That same Spirit had already inspired him to review the history of his Jewish audience, recounting the actions that show how they, like their ancestors, always opposed the Holy Spirit. When the people heard his accusations, "they were infuri-ated and they ground their teeth at him" (7:54). Rather than focusing on their hostil-ity, Stephen raises his eyes to heaven, where he sees Jesus, risen and ascended, standing at the right hand of God. Even more enraged when Stephen cries out what he had seen, the people cover their ears, rush upon him, throw him out of the city, and begin to stone him. Those who were stoning Stephen removed their cloaks and placed them at the feet of a young man named Saul. This is the first mention of Saul; this former persecutor of Christians will become the major figure in the second half of Acts.

Stephen's final outcries twice echo those of Jesus. First, he asks the Lord Jesus to receive his Spirit, analogous to Jesus cry-ing out, "Father, into your hands I com-mend my spirit" (Luke 23:46). Then, like Jesus asking his Father to forgive those who had crucified him, Stephen cries out in a loud voice, "Lord , do not hold this sin against them." The account of the death of Stephen presents him as the first of wit-nesses (*martyroi*) who testify to Jesus even to the point of death.

For meditation and context:

RESPONSORIAL PSALM   Psalm 97:1–2, 6–7, 9 (1a, 9a)

R. The Lord is king, the most high over all the earth.
or R. Alleluia.

The LORD is king; let the earth rejoice;
   let the many islands be glad.
Justice and judgment are the foundation of
   his throne.

The heavens proclaim his justice,
   and all peoples see his glory.
All gods are prostrate before him.

You, O LORD, are the Most High over all
   the earth,
   exalted far above all gods.

READING II   Revelation 22:12–14, 16–17, 20

A reading from the Book of Revelation

I, John, heard a **voice** saying to me:
   "**Behold,** I am **coming soon.**
I bring **with** me the **recompense** I will give to **each**
   according to his **deeds.**
I am the **Alpha** and the **Omega,** the **first** and the **last,**
   the **beginning** and the **end.**"

Blessed are they who **wash** their **robes**
   so as to have the **right** to the **tree** of **life**
   and enter the **city** through its **gates.**
"**I, Jesus,** sent my **angel** to give you **this testimony**
      for the **churches.**
I am the **root** and **offspring** of **David,**
   the **bright morning star.**"

The **Spirit** and the **bride** say, "**Come.**"
Let the **hearer** say, "**Come.**"
Let the **one** who **thirsts** come **forward,**
   and the **one** who **wants it** receive the **gift** of **life-giving water.**

The **one** who gives this **testimony** says, "**Yes,** I am **coming soon.**"
Amen! Come, Lord Jesus!

Start slowly. You are narrating a grand vision and we need to know that "Behold" is spoken not by the visionary, but by one *within* the vision.

There is both comfort and discomfort in knowing we will receive what we deserve.

Read this as a declaration of all that Christ brings and offers us.

Blessed = BLES-uhd or blesd

Make eye contact as you speak this beatitude and blessing over your assembly.

Jesus is both immanent ("the root . . . of David") and transcendent ("the . . . morning star").

We return to the voice of John. The Church's desire to be reunited with her Lord must sound in your voice.
 Beckon the hearts of your hearers!
The Lord announces his imminent return, and the Church responds in fervent prayer: "Amen! Come."

READING II   "Behold"—this opening word urges us to give full attention to the proclamation that follows. While visions and revelations often come from heavenly messengers, this one is from the risen Jesus himself, who gives to his audience a self-identification that stretches across time and space. These last words of the Bible do not so much bring it to a conclusion as open up hope and eager anticipation for the future. In identifying himself as Alpha and Omega, the first and last letters of the Greek alphabet, Jesus affirms that his presence embraces everything, past, present, and future, heaven and earth. Further, Jesus uses an "I am" (*ego eimi*) statement, a favored way in John's Gospel of announcing his identity. "*I am the root and offspring of David,*" means that Jesus is both source and fulfillment of God's promise to King David. As the morning star, he is the herald of the new, messianic age.

When Jesus comes again, he will bring recompense, judging all persons according to their deeds. The liturgical reading omits a harsh and lengthy description of the evil deeds of those who will be judged along with the faithful. Their lives are a sharp contrast to those who are called "blessed" (*makarioi*), the seventh beatitude in Revelation. Those who "wash their robes" may be referring to martyrdom for the sake of Jesus, or to Baptism, "the gift of life-giving water." Or more broadly, all are blessed whose lives are cleansed of the evil deeds so they live in right relationship with God and one another.

We can hear the final words of the reading as the response of all those who have heard and believed in Jesus' message. Believers of every age pray in joy and hope, "Amen. Come Lord Jesus!"

GOSPEL   John 17:20–26

A reading from the holy Gospel according to John

Lifting up his **eyes** to **heaven**, Jesus **prayed** saying:
"**Holy Father,** I pray **not only** for **them,**
   but also for those who will **believe** in **me** through **their word,**
   so that they may **all** be **one,**
   as **you, Father,** are in **me** and **I** in **you,**
   that **they also** may be in **us,**
   that the **world** may **believe** that **you** sent me.
And **I** have given **them** the **glory you** gave **me,**
   so that **they** may be **one,** as **we** are **one,**
   I in **them** and **you** in **me,**
   that they may be brought to **perfection** as **one,**
   that the **world** may **know** that **you** sent **me,**
   and that **you loved them** even as **you loved me.**
Father, they are **your gift** to me.
I wish that where **I** am **they also** may be **with me,**
   that they may **see my glory** that **you gave** me,
   because **you loved me** before the **foundation** of the **world.**
Righteous Father, the **world also** does **not know you,**
   but **I know you,** and **they know** that **you** sent **me.**
I made **known** to them **your name** and **I will** make it **known,**
   that the **love** with which **you loved me**
   may be in **them** and **I** in **them.**"

Pause after the opening narration to shift into a tone of prayer.

The ideas flow one from another. Don't speak like a lawyer making an argument, but let the poetry and sincerity of the prayer be manifest.

Christian unity testifies to Christ.

"Perfection" is only realized in "unity" that testifies to Jesus' divine origin.

Make eye contact as you speak this tender line.

Jesus longs for his followers to experience the fullness of his glory.

Jesus displays an intimate connection with the Father.

Take a significant pause, letting your listeners dwell in the prayer before initiating the closing dialogue.

TO KEEP IN MIND
Read all three commentaries. Suggestions in each can give you insight into your own passage.

GOSPEL Jesus' prayer at the Last Supper is both a personal address to his Father and a summary of his teaching for his disciples. Throughout his prayer, often referred to as "the high priestly prayer," Jesus speaks directly to his Father, giving it a striking intimacy that his disciples overhear. Jesus speaks in it as a priest who intercedes with God for the people. In the part of the prayer in today's reading, Jesus pleads for his disciples, along with those who will believe through their word. At the core of Jesus' petitions is his desire "that they may all be one." As Jesus is eternally one with the Father, he asks that their unity be extended, that the world come to believe.

Jesus prays that those the Father gave him may be brought to perfection. He is not praying for the moral perfection of his disciples, but that they may be "perfectly one," radiating a complete unity visible to the world. The process toward perfect unity has already begun, since Jesus has already given them the glory that his Father gave to him. Jesus is speaking here of a dynamic relationship of shared glory that is the foundation for the perfect unity of the community. Jesus prays also that the love he shares with his Father may be in his disciples as well. *Glory* and *love* are two ways of sharing in the divine presence that God continues to pour forth. Having heard Jesus' prayer, we join in praying for unity. E.P.

PENTECOST SUNDAY: VIGIL

LECTIONARY #62

READING I   Genesis 11:1–9

A reading from the Book of Genesis

The whole **world** spoke the same **language**, using the same **words**.
While the people were **migrating** in the east,
    they came upon a valley in the land of **Shinar** and **settled** there.
They **said** to one another,
    "**Come**, let us mold **bricks** and **harden** them with **fire**."
They used bricks for **stone**, and bitumen for **mortar**.
Then they said, "**Come**, let us build ourselves a **city**
    and a **tower** with its top in the **sky**,
    and so make a **name** for ourselves;
    otherwise we shall be **scattered** all over the earth."

The LORD came down to see the city and the **tower**
    that the people had built.
Then the LORD said: "If **now**, while they are **one** people,
    all speaking the **same** language,
    they have started to do **this**,
    nothing will **later** stop them from doing whatever they
        presume to do.
Let us then go down there and **confuse** their language,
    so that one will not **understand** what another says."
Thus the LORD **scattered** them from there all over the **earth**,
    and they **stopped** building the city.
That is why it was called **Babel**,
    because there the LORD **confused** the speech of all the world.
It was from that **place** that he **scattered** them all over the earth.

As narrator, you know this innocent age is lost.

Speak with the arrogance that motivates their defiance.

Shinar = SHI-nahr.

bitumen = bih-TYOO-m*n.

Their plan is in direct defiance of God's order to "fill the earth" (1:28). They plan to enhance their own reputation without any help from God.

This is a new scene. Suggest the disapproval with which God views the city and tower.

God is not being vindictive, but protecting humanity from itself.

If an ancient child asked "Why do people speak different languages?", here is the reply.

Speak with conviction that what God has accomplished is just.

There are many options for the readings today. Consult your parish staff to learn which readings will be used.

READING I   **Genesis 11:1–9.** After creation and the first sin, the next chapters in Genesis recite an escalation of evil throughout the world, culminating in a plan to build a tower with its top in the sky. Such a tower would, in the minds of the builders, give them power and prestige. They fear that without such renown, they would be scattered far and wide.

The historical context behind the story provides insight into its importance for the ancient audience. The Babylonians were powerful enemies feared by Israel, and this account is an ironic mockery of them. It explains how Babylon got its name and reflects the attitude of the biblical writers to the Babylonians' hubris. According to Isaiah, the king of Babylon boasted, "Above the stars of God I will set up my throne. . . . I will ascend above the tops of the clouds; I will be like the Most High" (Isaiah 14:13–14). As a sign that the king's words were no empty boast, the people erected towers called ziggurats, sometimes rising over two hundred feet. These primitive sky-scrapers often included a shrine at the top to honor one of their gods.

In the Genesis account, the grand scheme of an imposing tower is completely turned around. Instead of giving the nation and its king the desired "name," their enterprise earns the name of "babel," meaning "confusion" or even "stuttering." The tower that was to give them power brings about the confusion of tongues instead. What was to be an extraordinary achievement appears so small that the Lord God has to

RESPONSORIAL PSALM   Psalm 33:10–11, 12–13, 14–15

R. Blessed the people the Lord has chosen to be his own.

The LORD brings to nought the plans
  of nations;
  he foils the designs of peoples.
But the plan of the LORD stands forever;
  the design of his heart, through all
  generations.

Blessed the nation whose God is the LORD,
  the people he has chosen for his own
  inheritance.
From heaven the LORD looks down;
  he sees all mankind.

From his fixed throne he beholds
  all who dwell on the earth,
He who fashioned the heart of each,
  he who knows all their works.

Or:

READING I   Exodus 19:3–8a, 16–20b

A reading from the Book of Exodus

Moses went up the **mountain** to **God**.
Then the LORD **called** to him and said,
  "**Thus** shall you say to the house of **Jacob**;
  tell the Israelites:
  You have seen for **yourselves** how I treated the **Egyptians**
  and how I **bore** you up on **eagle** wings
  and brought you here to **myself**.
Therefore, if you **hearken** to my voice and keep my **covenant**,
  you shall be my **special possession**,
  dearer to me than all **other** people,
  though **all** the earth is **mine**.
You shall be to me a **Kingdom** of **priests**, a **holy** nation.
That is what you must tell the **Israelites**."
So Moses went and **summoned** the elders of the people.
When he set before them
  all that the LORD had **ordered** him to tell them,
  the people all answered **together**,
  "**Everything** the LORD has said, we will **do**."

Exodus = EK-suh-duhs

With the opening narration you must intimate that Moses' ascent up the mountain is no ordinary climb; he is about to meet his God.

God recounts Israel's deliverance from slavery with incredible intimacy: God brings Israel not to the mountain, but "to *myself*"; the covenant is "*my* covenant,"' Israel is God's "special possession," the nation that is "holy."

Stress the conditions God sets.

"Kingdom of priests" refers to the nation as a whole. Among the nations, Israel is as special as are the priests among the people.

This is a solemn yet joyful statement of assent to God's conditions.

---

come down from the heavens to observe their little tower. As the account concludes, it is clear that the world is in need of the intervention of the Lord God once again. The One who confuses and scatters is the only One who can restore and create anew.

Exodus 19:3–8a, 16–20b. When Moses had his encounter at the burning bush, the Lord told him, "I have witnessed the affliction of my people" (Exodus 3:7). As the story continues, the Lord often speaks of the enslaved Israelites as "my people"; the significance of that designation is beautifully described in today's reading.

Moses has gone up to the mountain of God while the once-enslaved people are encamped in front of the mountain. On Sinai, God reveals to Moses that the reason for freeing "my people" from slavery was to enter into a covenant with them. God describes these people as a "special possession," a term used to refer to one's personal and treasured property. As "a Kingdom of priests and a holy nation," the people are set apart to honor God with reverence, and are consecrated to God's service. Their holiness is founded on God's own holiness and his choice of them as his own:

"You shall be holy, for I, the Lord, am holy; I, who have set you apart from the other nations to be my own" (Leviticus 20:26).

A covenant is a two-way relationship. God has freed the people of Israel and chosen them as his own. For their part, the people answer that they will do everything that the Lord has said. Although the terms of the covenant have not yet been spelled out, the people's answer is immediate and unanimous. This resolve will be tested over and over, not only in the desert, but throughout their history.

Describe the great theophany (manifestation of God's powerful presence) with a sense of awe.

On the morning of the **third** day
> there were peals of **thunder** and **lightning**,
> and a heavy **cloud** over the mountain,
> and a very loud **trumpet** blast,
> so that all the people in the camp **trembled**.

But **Moses** led the people out of the camp to meet **God**,
> and they **stationed** themselves at the **foot** of the mountain.

Fire and smoke are common manifestations of God. Wind and fire imagery dominate Pentecost.

Mount **Sinai** was all wrapped in **smoke**,
> for the LORD came down upon it in **fire**.

The smoke **rose** from it as though from a **furnace**,
> and the whole mountain trembled **violently**.

"Trumpet" may be a metaphor for a strong, driving wind.

The **trumpet** blast grew **louder** and **louder**, while Moses
> was **speaking**,
> and God **answering** him with **thunder**.

Speak slowly here. There is great suspense in this line.

When the LORD came **down** to the top of Mount Sinai,
> he **summoned** Moses to the **top** of the mountain.

RESPONSORIAL PSALM   Daniel 3:52, 53, 54, 55, 56

R. Glory and praise for ever!

"Blessed are you, O Lord, the God of our
> fathers,
> praiseworthy and exalted above all
> forever;
And blessed is your holy and glorious name,
> praiseworthy and exalted above all for all
> ages."

"Blessed are you in the temple of your holy
> glory,
> praiseworthy and glorious above all
> forever."

"Blessed are you on the throne of your
> Kingdom,
> praiseworthy and exalted above all
> forever."

"Blessed are you who look into the depths
> from your throne upon the cherubim,
> praiseworthy and exalted above all
> forever."

"Blessed are you in the firmament of heaven,
> praiseworthy and glorious forever."

Or:

The final scene of the reading is a spectacular theophany. The priestly nation gathers in a kind of liturgy led by Moses to meet God. Thunder, lightning, smoke, and fire are images that both reveal and conceal the great majesty and holiness of God. The holy God is in their midst, having chosen them to live in holiness like God's own. The scene is a foreshadowing of another theophany, which we celebrate at Pentecost.

Ezekiel 37:1–14. The prophet Ezekiel, exiled in Babylon along with other Jews in the sixth century BC, experienced the devastating loss of homeland and Temple. The

land of promise and God's dwelling in the Temple were signs of life and blessing, while exile in a foreign land was a sign of death, pictured by Ezekiel's jarring image of dry bones strewn about the plain in every direction. The bones—"How dry they were!"—symbolize the lifelessness of the devastated people. The Lord makes Ezekiel walk all around the field as if to make sure that he understands the extent of the loss he shares with his fellow exiles. Only when the prophet sees how great is the death all around him does God begin to change the image to one of hope and restoration.

"Prophesy," God commands Ezekiel. Bring the word of the Lord to the dry bones. Tell them that God will put spirit and sinews and flesh on these bones, so they will come to life again. Sinews and flesh are not enough for the bones to live; the "rattling" sounds like a feeble attempt of the bones to rise from their dry and dusty state. Only the spirit will give them life. Since the bones are strewn in every direction, the spirit will come from the four winds to breathe into them. Throughout this Hebrew text, one word appears over and over: *ruah*, breath, wind, and spirit. We can

This is a solemn yet joyful statement of assent to God's conditions.

RESPONSORIAL PSALM   Psalm 19:8, 9, 10, 11

R. Lord, you have the words of everlasting life.

The law of the LORD is perfect,
    refreshing the soul;
The decree of the LORD is trustworthy,
    giving wisdom to the simple.

The precepts of the LORD are right,
    rejoicing the heart;
The command of the LORD is clear,
    enlightening the eye.

The fear of the LORD is pure,
    enduring forever;
The ordinances of the LORD are true,
    all of them just.

They are more precious than gold,
    than a heap of purest gold;
Sweeter also than syrup
    or honey from the comb.

Or:

Ezekiel = ee-ZEE-kee-uhl

To enhance rather than slight the unique features of this text (the refrain-like repetitions, and the extraordinary visions), you will need extra preparation time. The style and content of this writing is quite different from contemporary prose, so prepare until you are comfortable with and enjoying the rich imagery and poetic flow of the language.

Ezekiel finds himself transported into the midst of this scene of devastation.

God orders Ezekiel to prophesy. Speak these words with authority.

Don't over-dramatize these events; they should have an air of reality.

READING I   Ezekiel 37:1–14

A reading from the Book of the Prophet Ezekiel

The hand of the LORD came upon me,
    and he **led** me out in the **spirit** of the LORD
    and set me in the center of the **plain**,
    which was now **filled** with **bones**.
He made me **walk** among the bones in every direction
    so that I saw how **many** they were on the surface of the plain.
How **dry** they were!
He **asked** me:
    Son of **man**, can these bones come to **life**?
I answered, "Lord GOD, you **alone** know that."
Then he said to me:
    Prophesy over these bones, and **say** to them:
    Dry **bones**, hear the word of the LORD!
Thus says the Lord GOD to these **bones**:
    See! I will bring **spirit** into you, that you may come to **life**.
I will put **sinews** upon you, make **flesh** grow over you,
    cover you with **skin**, and put **spirit** in you
    so that you may come to **life** and know that **I** am the LORD.
I, **Ezekiel**, **prophesied** as I had been **told**,
    and even as I was **prophesying** I heard a **noise**;
    it was a **rattling** as the bones came together, **bone** joining **bone**.
I saw the **sinews** and the **flesh** come upon them,
    and the **skin** cover them, but there was no **spirit** in them.

---

almost feel the powerful force of the *ruah*: the wind brings breath into the dry bones; when the spirit sent by God comes into them, they will live.

God's word to the Jews in exile symbolized for them a promise of restored life in Israel; return to their own land will be a kind of Resurrection from the dry bones of their exile. Later interpretations of both Jews and Christians see in Ezekiel's vision a hope for Resurrection from the dead. Such hope is well founded, based on Lord's final words of today's prophetic text: "I have promised and I will do it."

Joel 3:1–5. Prophets in the Bible are men and women filled with the spirit to communicate God's message, sometimes with words of comfort and other times with criticism and call to conversion. Whatever the message, it was inspired by God's spirit. Moses, the model prophet, expressed this understanding of spirit-filled prophets when some people complained about seemingly unauthorized people prophesying. Moses replied, "Would that all the people of the Lord were prophets! Would that the Lord might bestow his spirit on them all!" (Numbers 11:29). The prophecy that we hear from Joel goes fur-

ther than the hope that Moses expressed. "I will pour out my spirit on all flesh." Sons and daughters, young and old, even those enslaved, will be filled with God's spirit. Like the wind (*ruah*), God's spirit (*ruah*) cannot be contained or limited, and may rest upon anyone.

When will this extensive outpouring of the spirit occur? Joel calls it simply and vaguely "the day of the Lord." His prophecies were likely written late among the Old Testament books, at a time when there was a rise of apocalyptic thinking. One of the characteristics of this view was an expectation of God's ultimate triumph over

These repetitions, like the repeated phrases of a song, add beauty to the text and etch its message in our memories. Don't treat them like redundancies to be gotten around as quickly as possible.

Only when they receive God's spirit do the bones come alive.

This promise should arouse hope in the listener.

The fulfillment of the promise will prove God's sovereignty.

Make sure you have given proper attention to words like: "spirit," "life," "winds," and "breathe." The last line contains two ideas: "I promised," and "I will do it." Don't run them together.

Then the LORD said to me:
  Prophesy to the **spirit**, **prophesy**, son of man,
  and **say** to the spirit: Thus says the Lord **GOD**:
  From the four winds **come**, O spirit,
  and **breathe** into these **slain** that they may come to **life**.
I prophesied as he **told** me, and the spirit **came** into them;
  they came **alive** and stood **upright**, a vast **army**.
Then he said to me:
  Son of **man**, these bones are the whole **house** of **Israel**.
They have been saying,
  "Our bones are **dried up**,
  our hope is **lost**, and we are cut **off**."
Therefore, **prophesy** and **say** to them: **Thus** says the Lord **GOD**:
  O my **people**, I will open your **graves**
  and have you **rise** from them,
  and bring you **back** to the land of Israel.
Then you shall **know** that I am the LORD,
  when I **open** your graves and have you **rise** from them,
  O my **people**!
I will put my **spirit** in you that you may **live**,
  and I will **settle** you upon your **land**;
  thus you shall **know** that I am the LORD.
I have **promised**, and I will **do** it, says the LORD.

RESPONSORIAL PSALM   Psalm 107:2–3, 4–5, 6–7, 8–9

R. Give thanks to the Lord; his love is everlasting.
or R. Alleluia.

Let the redeemed of the LORD say,
  those whom he has redeemed from the
    hand of the foe
And gathered from the lands,
  from the east and the west, from the
    north and the south.

They went astray in the desert wilderness;
  the way to an inhabited city they did
    not find.
Hungry and thirsty,
  their life was wasting away within them.

They cried to the LORD in their distress;
  from their straits he rescued them.
And he led them by a direct way
  to reach an inhabited city.

Let them give thanks to the LORD for
    his mercy
  and his wondrous deeds to the children
    of men,
Because he satisfied the longing soul
  and filled the hungry soul with
    good things.

Or:

evil, encompassing not only this world but the cosmos as well. Joel's "day of the Lord" refers to this powerful display of God's power. Like other apocalyptic writings, Joel uses startling images to convey God's triumph: fire and smoke, a darkened sun and a moon turned to blood. For some people, this will be a day of terror, a day of judgment; for those who call on the name of the Lord, it will be a time of rescue and fulfillment of God's promises. At Pentecost, Peter used this text from Joel to explain how it was fulfilled in the outpouring of the Holy Spirit. All of those who received God's

Spirit on that day became prophets, empowered to proclaim the mighty works of God.

READING II Saint Paul was well aware of the reality of suffering. He experienced it in his own life, meditated deeply on the sufferings of Christ, and observed suffering around him. Today's reading is part of a longer reflection on suffering, in which he tells the Roman community that we are "joint heirs with Christ, if only we suffer with him so that we may also be glorified with him" (8:17). In this

part of his teaching, Paul looks at the distress of this present suffering as comparable to labor pains, intense suffering that is prelude to new life. Three times in this passage, he uses the motif of the groaning associated with giving birth to develop the relationship between present suffering and hope for salvation.

First, Paul says that creation is groaning. His view that creation suffers and flourishes along with the suffering and flourishing of humanity is part of the biblical story, particularly in apocalyptic writings. They share with Paul an expectation

READING I   Joel 3:1–5

A reading from the Book of the Prophet Joel

> **Thus** says the LORD:
> I will pour out my **spirit** upon all **flesh**.
> Your **sons** and **daughters** shall **prophesy**,
>   your **old** men shall dream **dreams**,
>   your **young** men shall see **visions**;
> even upon the **servants** and the **handmaids**,
>   in those days, I will pour out my **spirit**.
> And I will work **wonders** in the **heavens** and on the **earth**,
>   **blood**, **fire**, and columns of **smoke**;
> the **sun** will be turned to **darkness**,
>   and the **moon** to **blood**,
> at the coming of the **day** of the LORD,
>   the **great** and **terrible** day.
> Then everyone shall be **rescued**
>   who calls on the **name** of the LORD;
> for on Mount **Zion** there shall be a **remnant**,
>   as the LORD has said,
> and in **Jerusalem survivors**
>   whom the LORD shall **call**.

This text forms the basis of much of Peter's Pentecost sermon (Acts 2:17–21). Prophesy = PROF-uh-sī.

Stress the variety of those who will receive the Spirit.

This is unexpected: "Even upon the servants." Stress these words appropriately. There is a more sober mood here. Images are not terrifying, but awe-inspiring.

Those who call on God need not fear the "terrible day" of the Lord.

"Zion" and "Jerusalem" combine with "remnant" and "survivors" to create a sense of joyful hope.

For meditation and context:

RESPONSORIAL PSALM   Psalm 104:1–2, 24 and 35c, 27–28, 29bc–30 (see 30)

R. Lord, send out your Spirit, and renew the face of the earth.
or R. Alleluia.

Bless the LORD, O my soul!
   O LORD, my God, you are great indeed!
You are clothed with majesty and glory,
   robed in light as with a cloak.

How manifold are your works, O LORD!
   In wisdom you have wrought them all—
the earth is full of your creatures;
   bless the LORD, O my soul! Alleluia.

Creatures all look to you
   to give them food in due time.
When you give it to them, they gather it;
   when you open your hand, they are filled
      with good things.

If you take away their breath, they perish
   and return to their dust.
When you send forth your spirit,
   they are created,
   and you renew the face of the earth.

---

that the imminent end-time distress of creation itself will precede God's dramatic, final intervention.

Second, our own groaning, according to Paul, is part of our hopeful waiting. We share with creation the expectation that the present suffering will be transformed very soon. The end is near, when adoption as God's own children and the redemption of our bodies will be realized.

The third reference to groaning is that of the Holy Spirit, a phrase that is not easily understood. The mysterious groaning of the Spirit is "inexpressible." As God's own

breath, the Spirit's groaning may refer to the Spirit's breathing within us through the birth pangs, giving voice when we have none, and interceding for us in our weakness.

GOSPEL The Jewish Feast of Tabernacles, also called the Feast of Booths, ingathering, or Sukkoth, is a fall pilgrimage feast that lasts a full week. It is an occasion for remembering and celebrating many experiences and events in Israel's history. As a celebration of the end of the harvest, people set up booths or tents, symbolic of the temporary huts in

which harvesters would live. The huts also have a religious symbolism, recalling the quickly made desert dwellings of the people in their forty-year sojourn. Another symbol used throughout the feast as celebrated in Jerusalem at the time of Jesus was the pouring of water on the altar in the Temple. A priest would draw the water from the Pool of Siloam as Isaiah 12:3 was sung: "With joy you will draw water at the fountain of salvation." As water was drawn and poured, the people would remember with great joy the saving waters of their history: water from the rock in the desert,

READING II   Romans 8:22–27

A reading from the Letter of Saint Paul to the Romans

The phrase "labor pains" is unexpected. Don't rush past the image.

While we have already tasted life in the Spirit, we long for the fullness only the Kingdom can offer.

Brothers and sisters:
We know that all creation is groaning in labor pains even
    until now;
    and not only that, but we ourselves,
    who have the firstfruits of the Spirit,
    we also groan within ourselves
    as we wait for adoption, the redemption of our bodies.
For in hope we were saved.
Now hope that sees is not hope.
For who hopes for what one sees?
But if we hope for what we do not see, we wait with endurance.

There is a lively, colloquial feel to Paul's logic here.

The Spirit even prays within us when we don't know how to pray.

Don't rush past this beautiful image: "The one who searches hearts."

In the same way, the Spirit too comes to the aid of our weakness;
    for we do not know how to pray as we ought,
    but the Spirit himself intercedes with inexpressible groanings.
And the one who searches hearts
    knows what is the intention of the Spirit,
    because he intercedes for the holy ones
    according to God's will.

GOSPEL   John 7:37–39

A reading from the holy Gospel according to John

Suggest that he rose and spoke with great vigor at the words "Let anyone . . . ." Make eye contact with the assembly.

On the **last** and **greatest** day of the **feast**,
    Jesus stood up and **exclaimed**,
    "Let anyone who **thirsts** come to **me** and **drink**.
As Scripture says:
    *Rivers of living **water** will flow from **within** him* who
        believes in me."

"From within him . . . " is one of those rare instances when you should stress the preposition.

Although this sounds parenthetical, sustain the energy. It's important.

Jesus' glorification was his Death and Resurrection.

He said this in reference to the **Spirit**
    that those who came to **believe** in him were to **receive**.
There **was**, of course, no Spirit **yet**,
    because **Jesus** had not yet been **glorified**.

Zechariah's prophecy of water flowing from Jerusalem (14:7, 8), and Ezekiel's vision of life-giving water streaming from the Temple (Ezekiel 47:1–12).

Jesus had come to Jerusalem for the feast in secret, and then began teaching openly in the Temple. When the festival had reached the peak of joyful celebration on the last and greatest day, Jesus announces a new meaning for the symbol of water so much a part of the people's memories. Bringing together several biblical texts, Jesus promises living water to those who thirst and believe in him. His words also suggest that living water, the Spirit, will flow out of believers as well. Those who first heard Jesus' promise at the Feast of Tabernacles had to await the outpouring of the Spirit, since Jesus had not yet been glorified and had not yet risen and poured out his Spirit. E.P.

PENTECOST SUNDAY: DAY

LECTIONARY #63

READING I Acts 2:1–11

A reading from the Acts of the Apostles

When the **time** for **Pentecost** was **fulfilled,**
    they were **all in one place together.**
And **suddenly** there came from the sky
    a **noise** like a **strong driving wind,**
    and it **filled** the **entire house** in which they **were.**
Then there appeared to them **tongues** as of **fire,**
    which **parted** and came to **rest** on **each one of them**.
And they were **all filled** with the **Holy Spirit**
    and began to **speak** in **different tongues,**
    as the **Spirit enabled** them to **proclaim.**

Now there were **devout Jews** from **every nation** under **heaven**
    staying in **Jerusalem**.
At this **sound**, they **gathered** in a **large crowd**,
    but they were **confused**
    because **each one** heard them speaking in his **own language**.
They were **astounded**, and in **amazement** they asked,
    "Are not **all these people** who are **speaking Galileans**?
Then how does **each** of **us hear** them in his **native language**?
We are **Parthians**, **Medes**, and **Elamites**,
    inhabitants of **Mesopotamia**, **Judea** and **Cappadocia**,

---

"Pentecost" doesn't refer to the Christian solemnity we celebrate today, but to the Jewish festival of the Feast of Weeks. Start slowly and then surprise us with the spectacular events that suddenly unfold.
See Exodus 19:1–15 that recounts the giving of the Law and note the similarities with this event.
The "tongues" signify that each of these disciples is set apart for this new moment in God's plan of salvation.

The crowds were required to make a pilgrimage to Jerusalem for this major holiday that required abstaining from work.

You can speak with subdued amazement and astonishment as you ask the questions of the pilgrims.
Galileans = gal-ih-LEE-uhnz
Parthians = PAHR-thee-uhnz
Medes = meedz
Elamites = EE-luh-mīts
Mesopotamia = mes-uh-poh-TAY-mee-uh
Judea = joo-DEE-uh
Cappadocia = cap-uh-DOH-she-uh

There are options for the readings today. Consult your parish staff to learn which readings will be used.

READING I Many of the events of Jesus' life occur at major Jewish feasts, giving the feasts new unexpected meaning. The first reading from Acts occurs on one of the great pilgrimage feasts, Pentecost, fifty days after Passover. Described in Leviticus as a harvest festival, it later became a commemoration of Moses' reception of the Torah on Mount Sinai. On that holy mountain, peals of thunder, lightning, a heavy cloud, and the sound of trumpet blast were tangible signals of divine presence. At the festival celebrated by Jesus' disciples in Jerusalem, fire and the sound of rushing wind coming from the heavens are reminiscent of the signs on Sinai. According to the Jewish writer Philo, when the fire streamed forth from heaven to Sinai, "the flame became articulate speech in the language familiar to the audience." He explained further, "The voice of men is audible, but the voice of God truly visible" (*Decalogue 46*). The Sinai event is a foreshowing of the Pentecost event.

Like the Sinai fire described by Philo, the tongues at Pentecost are both visible and audible: the word "tongue" (*glossa*) refers first to the visible fiery tongue resting on each person, and then to the speech that is heard by the crowd. Like the theophany on Sinai, the one in Jerusalem manifests God's power and presence in dramatic fashion. The newness of the feast arises from the outpouring of the Spirit filling the whole house and each person, renewing and expanding the covenant of

Pontus = PON-thus

Phrygia = FRIJ-ee-uh

Libya = LIB-ee-uh

Cyrene = sī-REE-nee

Cretans = KREE-tuhns

The listing of nations has led to this closing statement: our differences don't impede us from hearing about God's mighty deeds!

For meditation and context:

Pontus and **Asia**, **Phrygia** and **Pamphylia**,
Egypt and the districts of **Libya** near **Cyrene**,
as well as **travelers** from **Rome**,
both **Jews** and **converts** to **Judaism**, **Cretans** and **Arabs**,
yet we hear them **speaking** in our **own tongues**
of the **mighty acts** of **God**."

RESPONSORIAL PSALM   Psalm 104:1, 24, 29–30, 31, 34 (30)

R. Lord, send out your Spirit, and renew the face of the earth.
or R. Alleluia.

Bless the LORD, O my soul!
  O LORD, my God, you are great indeed!
How manifold are your works, O LORD!
  The earth is full of your creatures.

If you take away their breath, they perish
  and return to their dust.
When you send forth your spirit,
    they are created,
  and you renew the face of the earth.

May the glory of the LORD endure forever;
  may the LORD be glad in his works!
Pleasing to him be my theme;
  I will be glad in the LORD.

> **TO KEEP IN MIND**
> Pray the text, using your favorite method of praying with Scripture.

Corinthians = kohr-IN-thee-uhnz

READING II   1 Corinthians 12:3b–7, 12–13

A reading from the first Letter of Saint Paul to the Corinthians

Brothers and **sisters:**
No one can say, "**Jesus** is **Lord**," except by the **Holy Spirit**.

There are **different kinds** of **spiritual gifts** but the **same Spirit;**
  there are **different forms** of **service** but the **same Lord;**
  there are **different workings** but the **same God**
  who produces **all** of them in **everyone**.
To **each individual** the **manifestation** of the **Spirit**
  is given for some **benefit**.

As a **body** is **one** though it has **many parts**,
  and **all** the **parts** of the **body**, though **many**, are **one body**,
  so also Christ. »

More instruction follows here: speak it slowly but with a sense of the joyful hope embedded in the lines.

Sinai. The fire and trumpet blast on Sinai were momentary signs of God's presence, while the Spirit is an abiding divine presence given "to you and to your children and to all those far off" (Acts 2:39).

READING II **Romans 8:8–17.** Paul contrasts living in the flesh and living in the spirit, not as two components of the human person, but as two ways that a person relates to God and to the world. Living in the flesh, according to Paul, means to be earthbound, mired in the things of this world. Such people are centered on

self, not on God, pleasing themselves rather than God. They do not belong to Christ. To emphasize the consequences of living according to the flesh, Paul writes "the body is dead because of sin." Since "body" refers to the whole human person, the impression is of a person who is dead even before physical death.

In contrast, being in the spirit is life immersed in Christ. Paul uses the word "spirit" (*pneuma*) to speak of the Holy Spirit, sometimes referred to as "the Spirit of Christ"; *pneuma* also refers to the human spirit that orients a person to be guided by

and in communion with the Spirit of God. Paul's repeated use of the small but significant preposition *in* throughout the description creates a sketch of the intimacy between the Holy Spirit and the human spirit: the Spirit of God dwells in you; Christ is in you; the Spirit who raised Jesus from the dead dwells in you.

Those led by the indwelling Spirit are sons and daughters of God. Just as Jesus, speaking in Aramaic, addressed God as "Abba," so too can those who have been adopted into his family. Those who are coheirs with Christ, with his own Spirit

The Spirit is the glue that binds us. Speak the differences—"Jews . . . free" in a positive tone, but speak of the oneness in the Spirit with even deeper joy.

For in **one Spirit** we were **all baptized** into **one body,**
    whether **Jews** or **Greeks, slaves** or **free persons,**
    and we were **all** given to drink of **one Spirit.**

Or:

READING II   Romans 8:8–17

A reading from the Letter of Saint Paul to the Romans

Make this a bold declaration.

Brothers and **sisters:**
Those who are in the **flesh cannot please God.**
But **you** are **not** in the **flesh;**

After a pause, announce this good news to your listeners.

    on the **contrary, you** are in the **spirit,**
    if only the **Spirit** of **God dwells** in you.

Contrast this statement with the one that follows.

Whoever does **not** have the **Spirit** of **Christ** does **not belong**
      to him.

Stress "is" not "in." The repeated "if" statements suggest we have an important role in our salvation.

But if Christ **is in** you,
    although the **body** is **dead** because of **sin,**
    the **spirit** is **alive** because of **righteousness.**
If the **Spirit** of the **one** who **raised Jesus** from the **dead dwells**
      in **you,**
    the **one** who **raised Christ** from the **dead**
    will give **life** to **your mortal bodies also,**
    through his **Spirit** that **dwells** in **you.**
Consequently, brothers and **sisters,**
    we are **not debtors** to the flesh,
    to live **according** to the flesh.

Speak these lines with authority. Paul is teaching about what leads to life and death; convey the importance of this instruction.

For if you live according to the **flesh,** you will **die,**
    but if by the **Spirit** you put to **death** the **deeds** of the **body,**
    you will **live.**

For those who are **led** by the **Spirit** of **God** are **sons** of **God.**
For you did not receive a **spirit** of **slavery** to fall back into **fear,**
    but you received a **spirit** of **adoption,**
    through whom we cry, "**Abba, Father!**"

---

dwelling in them, can expect to share both in his suffering and in his glory. Paul's theological exposition has an ethical purpose: to encourage believers to exhibit the behaviors, attitudes, and relationships that reflect their communion with the Holy Spirit.

1 Corinthians 12:3b–7, 12–13. The Corinthian community to whom Paul wrote was beset with serious divisions. Early in the letter, he urged them to "agree in what you say, and that there be no divisions among you" (1:10). Among the causes of their disagreements were jealousy and rivalry (3:3), divisive attitudes that Paul

addressed throughout the letter. In today's reading, we can well imagine Paul's consternation at people's envy when one person's spiritual gift appears more important than another's. He begins by skillfully admitting that, as they know, there are different gifts, different forms of service, and different workings. What they haven't realized is that the same Spirit is the source of all of these gifts. And every one of such manifestations of the Spirit is given for some benefit, or for "the common good." In verses omitted from our reading, Paul lists a wide variety of gifts, concluding the list

by saying, "the same Spirit produces all of these, distributing them individually to each person as he wishes."

In the next step of his argument, Paul uses the image of the body to show that the diversity of the gifts of the Spirit is just as necessary for the community as the different parts of the body are for an individual. In verses following today's reading Paul develops a conversation between various parts of the body. If one part says to another "I don't need you," the body wouldn't be complete or function well. In the same way, each gift of the Spirit is

The **Spirit himself** bears **witness** with **our spirit**
    that we are **children** of **God**,
    and if **children**, then **heirs**,
    heirs of **God** and **joint heirs** with **Christ**,
    if only we **suffer** with him
    so that we may **also** be **glorified** with him.

For meditation and context:

The Pentecost Sequence is an ancient liturgical hymn praising the Holy Spirit. It is also called the Golden Sequence, and is the source of the hymn, "Come, Holy Ghost."

SEQUENCE *Veni, Sancte Spiritus*

Come, Holy Spirit, come!
And from your celestial home
  Shed a ray of light divine!
Come, Father of the poor!
Come, source of all our store!
  Come, within our bosoms shine.
You, of comforters the best;
You, the soul's most welcome guest;
  Sweet refreshment here below;
In our labor, rest most sweet;
Grateful coolness in the heat;
  Solace in the midst of woe.
O most blessed Light divine,
Shine within these hearts of yours,
  And our inmost being fill!

Where you are not, we have naught,
Nothing good in deed or thought,
  Nothing free from taint of ill.
Heal our wounds, our strength renew;
On our dryness pour your dew;
  Wash the stains of guilt away:
Bend the stubborn heart and will;
Melt the frozen, warm the chill;
  Guide the steps that go astray.
On the faithful, who adore
And confess you, evermore
  In your sevenfold gift descend;
Give them virtue's sure reward;
Give them your salvation, Lord;
  Give them joys that never end. Amen.
  Alleluia.

In this very dense excerpt, Jesus' Resurrection, Ascension, and imparting of the Spirit occur on the same day. For more background, see the Gospel commentary of the Second Sunday of Easter.
The first sentence contains much information. Don't rush through it.

The mention of Jesus shifts the gloomy mood.

Here he shows his pierced side; in Luke he shows his "hands and feet."

Jesus must console a second time.

GOSPEL John 20:19–23

A reading from the holy Gospel according to John

On the evening of that **first day** of the **week**,
    when the **doors** were **locked**, where the **disciples** were,
    for **fear** of the Jews,
    Jesus came and **stood** in their **midst**
    and said to them, "**Peace** be **with you**."
When he had said this, he **showed** them his **hands** and his **side**.
The disciples **rejoiced** when they **saw** the **Lord**.
Jesus said to them **again**, "**Peace** be **with you**.
As the **Father** has **sent me**, so **I send you**." »

equally necessary for the life, the well-being, and the common good of the body of Christ. Through Baptism, they are formed into one body and drink of the one Spirit. There should therefore be no divisions among them.

GOSPEL | **John 14:15–16, 23b–26.** When Jesus gives his farewell discourse to his disciples, he teaches them one last time about his identity and how they are to live faithful to him. He also promises that they will not be left alone. Like his Jewish ancestors Jacob and Moses,

Jesus uses this occasion to give those closest to him his final instructions. Echoing Moses' words addressed to Israel in the desert (e.g., Deuteronomy 5:10, 7:9, and 11:1), Jesus tells his followers, "If you love me, you will keep my commandments," and "whoever loves me will keep my word." To "keep" (*tereo*) Jesus' words and commandments does not denote servile obedience; the word means more fully "to give careful attention to; to keep and preserve."

Jesus' commandments and words are life giving, and are themselves an expression of his love for his disciples. Their

response is to love him in return and to keep all that he has communicated to them. Later in his farewell discourse, Jesus expands his teaching that links loving and keeping: "If you keep my commandments, you will remain in my love, just as I have kept my Father's commandments and remain in his love" (15:10).

As he is about to leave them, Jesus assures his friends that the Father will send them another Advocate (*paracletos*), one who will stand beside them as their counselor and support, especially in times of trial. Jesus has already been their Advocate;

Don't rush the word "breathed." That "breathing" is the reason this text is proclaimed today.

And when he had said this, he **breathed** on them
    and said to them,
  "**Receive** the **Holy Spirit**.
Whose **sins** you **forgive** are **forgiven** them,
    and whose **sins** you **retain** are **retained**."

Or:

GOSPEL   John 14:15–16, 23b–26

A reading from the holy Gospel according to John

Imagine Jesus speaking these words directly to your assembly.

Jesus said to his disciples:
  "If you **love** me, you will **keep** my **commandments**.
and I will ask the **Father**,
    and he will give you another **Advocate** to be **with** you **always**.

Give "Advocate" a tone that suggests one who cares and comforts.

Don't let these short sentences elicit a choppy, rote delivery. Making a "dwelling with him" is a tender image.

Disregard for his Word is of no small consequence because his Word comes from the Father.

"Whoever **loves me** will **keep** my **word**,
    and my **Father** will **love** him,
    and we will **come** to him and **make** our **dwelling with** him.
Those who do **not** love me do **not** keep my words;
    yet the word you **hear** is **not mine**
    but that of the **Father** who **sent** me.

Jesus' tone is reassuring and encouraging.

"I have **told** you this while I am **with** you.
The **Advocate**, the **Holy Spirit** whom the **Father**
    will **send** in **my name**,
    will teach you **everything**
    and **remind** you of **all** that I **told** you."

Remember that throughout Jesus is comforting friends who are about to endure the trauma of his Death.

now they will have another one sent by the Father. The Advocate, the Holy Spirit, will remind the disciples of all that Jesus has told them, including his commandments and words. Then Father, Son, and Holy Spirit will make their dwelling place within each of his disciples.

John 20:19–23. The words, actions, and symbols in this scene from John's Gospel have a liturgical resonance; many of the things that happen when the community gathers for liturgy occur also in this appearance of the risen Jesus. The event is on the first day of the week, the day when believers commemorate the Resurrection of Jesus. The whole group of disciples, still fearful, see the crucified one standing in their midst alive, and speaking to them. He offers them peace, a greeting, a gift, and a revelation of him as their risen Messiah. When Jesus gives his gift of peace, whether to the first disciples or to those who even today gather in his name, their fears and anxieties are transformed to joy. The peace that Jesus gives creates wholeness and harmony, and is a source of transformation of individuals and the entire community.

Jesus lets his followers know immediately that the gifts that he gives them are to be shared. He sends them, just as his Father has sent him, bestowing on them another gift: the very breath of God, the Holy Spirit as the source of their power. When the community, filled with the Holy Spirit, leaves the assembly, they are to offer the gift that Jesus has given them: forgiveness in his name. E.P.

THE MOST HOLY TRINITY

LECTIONARY #166

READING I   Proverbs 8:22–31

A reading from the Book of Proverbs

Poetry communicates with sound and rhythm as well as meaning. Think of this text as a melody of praise and rejoicing.

An even, consistent reading throughout will kill the life of this text. Sense the up and down movement of rhythm and energy. Some lines require a burst of energy to convey the joy they contain.

Wisdom lauds her own majesty and ancient origins. "I was here before *everything* else," she asserts proudly!

Thus says the **wisdom** of **God:**
"The LORD **possessed** me, the **beginning** of his **ways,**
    the **forerunner** of his **prodigies** of long **ago**;
from of **old I** was **poured forth,**
    at the **first, before** the **earth.**
When there were no **depths I** was brought **forth,**
    when there were no **fountains** or **springs** of **water;**
before the **mountains** were **settled** into place,
    before the **hills,** I was **brought forth;**
while as yet the **earth** and **fields** were not **made,**
    nor the first **clods** of the **world.**

Here begins the second description of the creation of the universe.

Don't drone through this "when he" litany; let your energy rise like a fountain spraying with increasing force.

"Craftsman" can be interpreted as "confidant" and suggests great intimacy between the Creator God and Lady Wisdom. Note how Wisdom "delights" and "plays" before the Lord and then "plays" on earth and "delights" in human beings.

The revelation that Wisdom delights in humanity is the intriguing finale to this reading.

"When the **Lord** established the **heavens I** was **there,**
    when he marked out the **vault** over the **face** of the **deep;**
when he made **firm** the skies **above,**
    when he fixed **fast** the **foundations** of the **earth;**
when he set for the **sea** its **limit,**
    so that the **waters** should not **transgress** his **command;**
then was **I beside** him as his **craftsman,**
    and **I** was his **delight** day by day,
playing before him all the while,
    playing on the surface of his **earth;**
    and **I** found **delight** in the human **race."**

READING I   The voice we hear in this lovely poem is Wisdom, personified as a woman, sometimes referred to as "Lady Wisdom." She is a mysterious figure, so sublime that she seems almost divine, possessing attributes of God himself. In her self-portrait, she says that she was the "forerunner . . . was poured forth . . . and brought forth," poetic ways of presenting herself as the first of God's creations. Once she came into being, she worked alongside God as a coworker at creation. Her assertion that she was there before fountains and mountains, before the hills and fields is so beautifully described that it is easy to envision Lady Wisdom accompanying God at each stage of creation. Wisdom's presence in the beginning reveals that creation itself is a reflection of God's wisdom, designed in harmony, beauty, and goodness.

Just as God delights in Wisdom, she delights in the human race. Both the poem and creation itself culminate with humankind. After the verses in today's reading, Lady Wisdom will speak to those who have heard her poem, advising them to "listen to me" and assuring them that the one who finds her finds life, a teaching that is often associated with the Torah. In fact, an ancient Jewish interpretation sees Wisdom identified with the Torah that was present with God even before the creation of the earth. In the New Testament, Paul sees Jesus as the very presence of God's wisdom: "Christ is the power of God and the wisdom of God" (1 Corinthians 1:24). We fittingly apply Wisdom's words to Jesus: "Happy those who keep my ways. . . . The one who finds me finds life" (Proverbs 8:33, 35).

For meditation and context:

RESPONSORIAL PSALM   Psalm 8:4 5, 6–7, 8–9 (2a)

R. O Lord, our God, how wonderful your name in all the earth!

When I behold your heavens, the work of
    your fingers,
  the moon and the stars which you set
    in place—
What is man that you should be mindful
  of him,
  or the son of man that you should care
    for him?

You have made him little less than
    the angels,
  and crowned him with glory and honor.
You have given him rule over the works of
  your hands,
  putting all things under his feet.

All sheep and oxen,
  yes, and the beasts of the field,
the birds of the air, the fishes of the sea,
  and whatever swims the paths of the seas.

READING II   Romans 5:1–5

A reading from the Letter of Saint Paul to the Romans

Brothers and sisters:
Therefore, **since** we have been **justified** by **faith**,
  we have **peace** with **God** through our **Lord Jesus Christ**,
  through whom we have gained **access** by **faith**
  to this **grace** in which we **stand**,
  and we **boast** in **hope** of the **glory** of **God**.
Not **only** that, but we even **boast** of our **afflictions**,
  knowing that **affliction** produces **endurance**,
  and **endurance**, proven **character**,
  and proven **character, hope**,
  and **hope** does **not disappoint**,
  because the **love** of **God** has been poured **out** into our **hearts**
  through the **Holy Spirit** that has been **given** to **us**.

You are presenting a logical argument that requires each step to reach its conclusion, so be sure each step is clearly presented.

Despite his use of logic, Paul's argument is infused with joy; don't leave out that aspect.

Pause before introducing this startling assertion. A trace of a smile would not be inappropriate.
Remain upbeat as you increase energy on the new word of each line.
"And hope . . ." is a statement of faith, not a legal argument. Speak from your own conviction.
The Trinitarian formula is completed with the naming of the Holy Spirit. The Spirit sustains our joy.

 "We have been justified by faith." Paul's opening words affirm that we have already been justified, already brought into right relationship with God. Justification and the other effects of Christ's death and Resurrection are both a present and future reality, sometimes described as the "already and not yet" of salvation. In the present time, we believe and act and strive in hope of the future fullness of God's saving acts in Christ.

As Paul describes the accompanying fruits of justification, he brings together the present graces and the future expectation.

In the present, we have peace with God through Christ, through whom we have access to the grace in which we stand. At the same time, we boast in hope of the glory of God, focusing on the future. While boasting ordinarily stems from one's own actions, the boasting here is based on God's saving actions through Christ and in the power of the Spirit. Even suffering is reason for boasting, since the suffering that Paul refers to is the end-time affliction and distress before God's final intervention. The sequence progresses from suffering to endurance to character, and ultimately to

hope, bringing Paul back to his theological emphasis: our present experience of being already justified is grounds for the hope of future completeness and glory.

The most palpable gift and reason for hope is that the love of God has already been poured into our hearts through the Holy Spirit. The Spirit is God's abiding presence, constantly breathing within us, generously bestowing God's love and empowering us to love in return.

GOSPEL   In his farewell address, Jesus speaks to his friends,

GOSPEL   John 16:12–15

A reading from the holy Gospel according to John

Jesus said to his **disciples**:
"I have **much more** to tell you, but you **cannot bear** it **now.**
But when he **comes**, the **Spirit** of **truth,**
 he will **guide** you to **all truth.**
He will **not** speak on his **own,**
 but he **will speak** what he **hears,**
  and will **declare** to you the things that are **coming.**
He will **glorify** me,
 because he will **take** from what is **mine** and **declare** it to you.
Everything that the **Father** has is **mine;**
 for this **reason** I told you that he will **take** from what is **mine**
  and **declare** it to **you.**"

Pause after the opening narration, and be sure your tone conveys compassion.

"But when he comes . . . " suggests a time when they *can* bear to hear the other "things."

What is "coming" is greater understanding of Jesus' teaching.

The Trinity works in one accord sharing the one truth that comes from the Father.

Use eye contact to ensure your assembly understands these words are also intended for them.

thoroughly aware of their troubled hearts. Though he still had more to say to them, he knew well how much they could bear. To reveal too much too soon would be a burden too weighty for them to carry, leading to confusion and doubt. Thus, instead of burdening them beyond their capacity, Jesus reassures them, "The Advocate, the holy Spirit that the Father will send in my name—he will teach you everything and remind you of all that I told you" (14:26). Jesus tells them further that the Spirit will guide them to all truth and declare the things that are to come. Jesus' own teach-ing, like that of the Spirit, is not his own words in isolation; as Jesus had declared earlier in the Gospel, "My teaching is not my own but is from the one who sent me" (7:16; see 8:28; 12:49). As Advocate and guide, the Spirit, also sent by the Father, will continue to teach what Jesus himself had taught. After Jesus' departure, the Spirit will instruct the disciples, unfolding mysteries that they were not yet able to understand or bear.

Jesus also tells his friends that every-thing the Spirit teaches will be taken "from what is mine," adding, "all that belongs to the Father is mine." The teaching of the Spirit, comparable to Jesus' teaching, flows from what they have received from the Father. There is a mutual ownership of everything that is taught. Having spoken earlier about the intimacy he shares with the Father and Spirit, Jesus here provides an early glimpse into the mystery of the Trinity, the feast that we celebrate today. E.P.

THE MOST HOLY BODY AND BLOOD OF CHRIST

LECTIONARY #169

READING I   Genesis 14:18–20

Your task is to ensure all the details are heard: "Melchizedek," "bread and wine," "priest," "God Most High," "blessed," and so forth

Melchizedek = mel-KIZ-ih-dek
Salem = SAY-luhm
Deliver the "blessing" as if you were praying it yourself.
Blessed / blessed = BLES-uhd

Pause before announcing Abram's generous response and speak of it with admiration.

A reading from the Book of Genesis

In those days, **Melchizedek,** king of **Salem,**
　　brought out **bread** and **wine,**
　　and being a **priest** of **God Most High,**
　　he **blessed Abram** with these **words:**
　　"**Blessed** be **Abram** by **God Most High,**
　　　　the **creator** of **heaven** and **earth;**
　　and blessed be **God Most High,**
　　　　who **delivered** your **foes** into your **hand.**"
Then **Abram** gave him a **tenth** of **everything.**

For meditation and context:

RESPONSORIAL PSALM   Psalm 110:1, 2, 3, 4 (4b)

R. You are a priest for ever, in the line of Melchizedek.

The LORD said to my Lord: "Sit at my
　　right hand
　　till I make your enemies your footstool."

The scepter of your power the LORD will
　　stretch forth from Zion:
　　"Rule in the midst of your enemies."

"Yours is princely power in the day of your
　　birth, in holy splendor;
　　before the daystar, like the dew, I have
　　begotten you."

The LORD has sworn, and he will not repent:
　　"You are a priest forever, according to the
　　order of Melchizedek."

READING I The encounter of Abram and the priest-king Melchizedek is brief and mysterious, an abrupt interruption in the long Abraham saga. Melchizedek's name, based on two Hebrew words, indicates the character of his kingship: *melek* means *king*, and *sedek* denotes *just* or *righteous*. His actions in this scene are expressions of his righteousness. Melchizedek engages in a religious ritual that includes offering of bread and wine and a twofold blessing. The god he serves is *El Elyon*, "God Most High." This is the chief god of the Canaanites, as well as one of the many titles given to the God of the Hebrews (e.g., Psalm 47:3). As the highest of gods, El Elyon is the creator of heaven and earth. Melchizedek's bringing out bread and wine is likely an offering of thanksgiving for Abram's recent victory over the other kings, accomplished by El Elyon, "who delivered your foes into your hand."

Melchizedek first blesses Abram in the name of God Most High. This blessing is an imparting of the god's kindness, brought down to earth on those who are blessed. In the first episode in Abram's story, the Lord blessed him so abundantly that "all the communities of the earth shall find blessing in you" (Genesis 12:3). Even Melchizedek would be blessed by Abram's presence. Melchizedek's second blessing, that of God Most High, is an exclamation of praise, a frequent opening to prayers in the biblical tradition.

Abram's role in this short narrative is minor compared to Melchizedek's. His one action is to give him a tenth of everything, a tithe-offering that is also an act of praise or blessing of God.

Corinthians = kohr-IN-thee-uhnz

Paul is writing to correct abuses that infected the Corinthians' celebration of the Eucharistic meal.

Paul stresses his teaching is "from the Lord." "Handed over" immediately recalls Jesus' Death and the sacrificial nature of Eucharist. Jesus takes, blesses, breaks, and gives. He does the same in today's Gospel narrative.

To "do this in remembrance" is to makes him present among us.

This line is as poignant the second time as the first.
This sentence is spoken in Paul's voice; he points past the present to our eternal destiny with Christ.

READING II   1 Corinthians 11:23–26

A reading from the first Letter of Saint Paul to the Corinthians

Brothers and **sisters**:
I **received** from the **Lord** what I **also handed on** to **you**,
　　that the **Lord Jesus**, on the night he was **handed over**,
　　took bread, and, after he had given **thanks**,
　　broke it and **said**, "**This** is my **body** that is for **you**.
Do this in **remembrance** of **me**."
In the **same** way also the **cup**, after **supper**, saying,
　　"This **cup** is the **new covenant** in my **blood**.
Do this, as **often** as you **drink** it, in **remembrance** of me."
For as **often** as you **eat** this **bread** and **drink** the **cup**,
　　you **proclaim** the **death** of the **Lord** until he **comes**.

The healings are another sign of the Kingdom's abundance; they're an important prelude to this story.
Don't take Luke's details for granted for they add great texture and humanity to the story.

The "deserted place" may symbolize the wilderness of our hearts.

Jesus places the responsibility on them, knowing full well they can't respond.

Now that the impossibility of the situation is well established, Jesus helps them see with Kingdom eyes.

Again, Luke's details root the story in concrete reality.

GOSPEL   Luke 9:11b–17

A reading from the holy Gospel according to Luke

Jesus spoke to the crowds about the **Kingdom of God**,
　　and he **healed** those who **needed** to be **cured**.
As the day was drawing to a **close**,
　　the **Twelve** approached him and **said**,
　　"**Dismiss** the **crowd**
　　so that they can go to the surrounding **villages** and **farms**
　　and find **lodging** and **provisions**;
　　for we are in a **deserted** place here."
He said to them, "**Give** them some **food yourselves**."
They replied, "Five **loaves** and two **fish** are **all** we **have**,
　　unless we **ourselves** go and **buy** food for **all** these people."
Now the men there numbered about **five thousand**.
Then he said to his disciples,
　　"Have them **sit down** in groups of about **fifty**." ❯❯

READING II   Paul is handing on a tradition that began the night that Jesus was handed over. This was a tradition already known by the Christian community in Corinth. They were already celebrating the Eucharistic liturgy, although in a manner that showed all too clearly their factions and lack of care for one another. To counteract their divisive behavior, Paul retells the account of the origin of the Lord's Supper, which was always to be both a source and sign of unity. Each time they "do this" in remembrance of the Lord, he is again present with them in the sign of bread and wine. Through their sharing in Jesus' body and blood, they are brought into communion with him and with one another.

Paul is convinced that the Corinthians should already know this. He had asked them earlier in the letter, "The cup of blessing that we bless, is it not a participation (*koinonia*) in the blood of Christ? The bread that we break, is it not a participation in the body of Christ?" (10:16). The communion of which Paul writes is an unbreakable covenant bond with Christ and one another. Paul explains further that because of their communion in the "one loaf"—the bread that is Christ himself—they are formed into one body. Having reflected on Paul's understanding of the double meaning of "body of Christ," St. Augustine urged believers, "You are the body of Christ, and its members. . . . When you hear 'The body of Christ,' you answer 'Amen.' Be a member of the body of Christ, so that your 'Amen' may be true" (*Sermon 272*). Our celebration of Corpus Christi rejoices in Christ's presence in the sacramental signs of bread and wine, and his presence in ourselves, the body of Christ gathered in his name.

Slow your pace and assume a more solemn tone as you narrate, with eucharistic language, Jesus' compassionate response.

They **did** so and made them **all sit** down.
Then taking the five **loaves** and the two **fish**,
    and looking up to **heaven**,
    he said the **blessing** over them, **broke** them,
    and **gave** them to the **disciples** to set before the **crowd**.
They all **ate** and were **satisfied**.
And when the leftover **fragments** were picked up,
    they filled **twelve** wicker **baskets**.

These details underscore the theme of abundance and the concrete reality of the miracle.

THE 4 STEPS OF *LECTIO DIVINA* OR PRAYERFUL READING

1. *Lectio:* Read a Scripture passage aloud slowly. Notice what phrase captures your attention and be attentive to its meaning. Silent pause.

2. *Meditatio:* Read the passage aloud slowly again, reflecting on the passage, allowing God to speak to you through it. Silent pause.

3. *Oratio:* Read it aloud slowly a third time, allowing it to be your prayer or response to God's gift of insight to you. Silent pause.

4. *Contemplatio:* Read it aloud slowly a fourth time, now resting in God's word.

GOSPEL Luke's account of the multiplication of the loaves and fish is the first of three narratives in his Gospel that have a Eucharistic connotation. The Last Supper itself and the story of two disciples on the road to Emmaus share similar features that offer insights into the meaning of the shared meal. The evening setting, "when the day was drawing to a close," besides being the ordinary time for the main meal, connects the three accounts, creating a solemn atmosphere as they long for Jesus to remain with them. In all three episodes, Jesus teaches those who are with him before sharing in the meal; in this account, he spoke to the crowds about the Kingdom of God. Jesus' actions over the bread, identical in the three scenes, add to the solemnity and Eucharistic overtones: he took the bread, said the blessing, broke the loaves, and gave it to them.

Besides the similarities, the distinctiveness of today's account suggests additional meaning. It foreshadows the Last Supper even as it hints about the lasting significance for the Church. Coupled with his teaching, Jesus heals those in need, pointing to the healing effects of the Eucharistic bread. Because Jesus provides for the multitudes in abundance, even when the provisions are meager, we understand that the Church will not be left without the bread that sustains it. When Jesus' disciples and those who come after them are obedient to his instructions, they will feed the crowds with food that truly satisfies. E.P.

THIRTEENTH SUNDAY IN ORDINARY TIME

LECTIONARY #99

READING I   1 Kings 19:16b, 19–21

A reading from the first Book of Kings

The LORD said to **Elijah**:
 "You shall anoint **Elisha**, son of **Shaphat** of **Abel-meholah**,
 as **prophet** to **succeed** you."

Elijah set out and came upon **Elisha**, son of **Shaphat**,
 as he was **plowing** with **twelve yoke** of **oxen**;
 he was **following** the **twelfth**.
Elijah went **over** to him and **threw** his **cloak** over him.
Elisha left the oxen, **ran** after **Elijah**, and **said**,
 "**Please**, let me **kiss** my **father** and **mother goodbye**,
 and I will **follow** you."
Elijah answered, "**Go back!**
Have I done **anything** to you?"
Elisha left him, and taking the yoke of **oxen**, **slaughtered** them;
 he used the **plowing** equipment for **fuel** to **boil** their **flesh**,
 and gave it to his **people** to **eat**.
Then **Elisha left** and **followed Elijah** as his **attendant**.

God is *not* displeased. The great prophet Elijah, who fought mightily against idolatry, will eventually need a successor; Elisha will become his apprentice until that time. Practice distinguishing "Elijah" (ee-LĪ-juh) from "Elisha" (ee-LĪ-shuh).

Shaphat = SHAY-fat
Abel-meholah = AY-b*l-muh-HOH-lah
Emphasize the number of oxen.

A "cloak" represented the personality and authority of its owner.

Elisha is not denied this courtesy.

The import of this line is: "I'm not stopping you."

Elisha is leaving behind all claims to his family wealth.

And, eventually, Elisha became Elijah's successor.

READING I   The prophet Elijah is often remembered for his miraculous deeds, his bold confrontation with the prophets of Baal, and his departure in a fiery chariot. Some remarkably ordinary deeds, however, also proved to be important, including his call of Elisha recounted in today's reading. After the Lord commands Elijah to anoint Elisha as prophet to succeed him, Elijah comes upon the young man while he is out plowing with twelve yoke of oxen. Such an ordinary setting for God's call of Israel's leaders is frequent in the Bible. Moses was tending sheep, the judge Gideon was threshing wheat, and Samuel was sleeping when God called. In the midst of such mundane activities, God's intervention was often dramatic, but in today's scene we see no appearance of an angel, no burning bush, no mysterious voice in the night. Elijah himself says nothing, but simply throws his cloak over Elisha, perhaps as a symbol of clothing Elisha with the same authority and power of Elijah himself; it may also symbolize that Elijah is taking the young man under his protection.

Whatever the meaning, Elisha clearly understood that Elijah was calling him. He asks only that he be able to bid his father and mother farewell. His farewell involves much more than saying his goodbyes to his parents. He slaughters all his oxen, uses his plowing equipment for fuel, and feeds his people. He leaves behind all his family, his work, and his wealth. Having left all things, Elisha proceeds to follow Elijah as his attendant.

READING II   The freedom that Christians experience, according to Paul, is rooted in Christ's action. It does not come about because of human energy, but

For meditation and context:

RESPONSORIAL PSALM   Psalm 16:1–2, 5, 7–8, 9–10, 11 (see 5a)

R. You are my inheritance, O Lord.

Keep me, O God, for in you I take refuge;
   I say to the LORD, "My Lord are you."
O LORD, my allotted portion and my cup,
   you it is who hold fast my lot.

I bless the LORD who counsels me;
   even in the night my heart exhorts me.
I set the LORD ever before me;
   with him at my right hand I shall not be
      disturbed.

Therefore my heart is glad and my
      soul rejoices,
   my body, too, abides in confidence,
because you will not abandon my soul to
      the netherworld,
   nor will you suffer your faithful one to
      undergo corruption.

You will show me the path to life,
   fullness of joys in your presence,
   the delights at your right hand forever.

Galatians = guh-LAY-shuhnz

Christian "freedom" means we don't have to save ourselves by observing the Law; we keep the Law in order to love fully. Stress only "freedom" in the second line.

The "yoke of slavery": Paul is saying, don't trade one form of slavery for another.

Speak as if to a group you taught and loved that is now backsliding. Persuade them they must hold on to the truth they learned.

God's Law requires "love," not circumcision.

Apparently, Paul is concerned about destructive behaviors among the Galatians.

Make use of the clear balances in these lines to underscore Paul's message of the opposition of "flesh" and "Spirit."

End on a note of Good News: freedom is yours in the Spirit!

READING II   Galatians 5:1, 13–18

A reading from the Letter of Saint Paul to the Galatians

Brothers and **sisters**:
For **freedom Christ** set us free;
   so stand **firm** and do not submit **again** to the yoke of **slavery**.

For **you** were called for **freedom**, brothers and sisters.
But do **not** use this **freedom**
   as an opportunity for the **flesh**;
   rather, **serve** one another through **love**.
For the **whole law** is fulfilled in **one statement**,
   namely, *You shall **love** your **neighbor** as **yourself**.*
But if you go on **biting** and **devouring** one another,
   beware that you are not **consumed** by one another.

I say, then: **live** by the **Spirit**
   and you will certainly not **gratify** the **desire** of the **flesh**.
For the **flesh** has **desires against** the **Spirit**,
   and the **Spirit** against the **flesh**;
   these are **opposed** to each other,
   so that you may **not do** what you **want**.
But if **you** are **guided** by the **Spirit**, you are **not** under the **law**.

---

because Christ himself has set us free through his saving death and Resurrection. In today's passage, Paul develops how believers are to live with this God-given freedom.

In order to understand freedom, it is necessary also to understand its opposite: enslavement. The "yoke of slavery" to which Paul refers is strict Torah observance, specifically circumcision. Other preachers had insisted on the necessity of circumcision for Gentile believers, but Paul counters that salvation does not come from circumcision or adherence to the

Torah, but through Christ. Paul tells his Gentile converts not to submit "again" to the yoke of slavery, since formerly they had been enslaved to idols. Now they should stand firm in resisting a new form of slavery preached by those Paul calls "false brethren."

Paul also makes it clear that freedom is not the same as license. Living in freedom means living by the Spirit, and not in the flesh. By "flesh," Paul means being mired down in things of this world, and enslaved to selfish desires. In the verse following today's reading, he lists a wide vari-

ety of works of the flesh, ranging from sexual immorality to jealousy and even outbursts of fury. But living in the Spirit is totally different. Echoing Jesus' own teaching, Paul sums up the whole law as well as living in the Spirit: "You shall love your neighbor as yourself."

GOSPEL   The first verse in today's Gospel marks the beginning of Jesus' journey to Jerusalem. Having called disciples, preached the good news, healed people and exorcised demons in Galilee, Jesus determines (literally, in Greek,

GOSPEL Luke 9:51–62

A reading from the holy Gospel according to Luke

When the days for **Jesus'** being **taken up** were **fulfilled**,
  he **resolutely** determined to **journey** to **Jerusalem**,
  and he sent **messengers** ahead of him.
On the **way** they entered a **Samaritan** village
  to **prepare** for his **reception** there,
  but they would **not welcome** him
  because the **destination** of his **journey** was **Jerusalem**.
When the disciples **James** and **John** saw this they **asked**,
  "**Lord**, do you want us to call down **fire** from **heaven**
  to **consume** them?"
Jesus **turned** and **rebuked** them, and they journeyed
    to **another** village.

As they were **proceeding** on their journey someone **said** to him,
  "I will **follow** you **wherever** you go."
Jesus **answered** him,
  "**Foxes** have **dens** and birds of the **sky** have **nests**,
  but the **Son** of **Man** has **nowhere** to rest his head."

And to **another** he said, "**Follow** me."
But **he** replied, "**Lord**, let me go **first** and bury my **father**."
But he **answered** him, "Let the **dead** bury their **dead**.
But **you**, **go** and **proclaim** the **Kingdom** of **God**."
And **another** said, "I will **follow** you, Lord,
  but **first** let **me** say **farewell** to my family at **home**."
To **him** Jesus said, "**No one** who sets a **hand** to the **plow**
  and **looks** to what was left **behind** is **fit** for the **Kingdom**
    of **God**."

The text begins on a sober note alluding to Jesus' upcoming Passion. Stress Jesus' resolute determination and his plans for the journey.

Begin upbeat, so the rejection in Samaria surprises us. Their hostility toward "Jerusalem" leads to Jesus' rejection.

The disciples' righteous anger blinds them to the ways of the Kingdom.

This potential disciple is all eagerness!

Jesus does not sugar-coat the demands of discipleship, which he himself has embraced first.

If the youth followed Jesus and then the need arose to bury his father, surely Jesus would give him leave. The point is the primacy of the call.

This disciple seems already half-turned away to go say "farewell."

Sometimes filial piety takes precedence (as with Elisha) but other times nothing can be permitted to distract us from our calling. Don't let this be a harsh injunction, but a call to heroic fidelity.

"sets his face") to go to Jerusalem. Now the time is fulfilled for his being "taken up" (*analempsis*), a term that can refer simultaneously to Jesus' death and to his Ascension, two moments in the one mystery of Christ's journey through death to resurrected life. In his journey to Jerusalem, Jesus deliberately chose to go to dangerous and controversial places, instructing his own disciples as well as people he met on the way.

Jesus could have bypassed Samaria on his way to Jerusalem. Since Jews and Samaritans had an antagonistic relationship dating back centuries, it is not surprising that Samaritans did not welcome Jesus. Even the suggestion by James and John to call down fire from heaven would not be surprising to Jews of Jesus' day, for the great prophet Elijah had also called down fire on Israel's enemies (2 Kings 1:10). But Jesus rebukes the two sons of thunder. Refusing to allow a violent response to the Samaritans, Jesus simply continues on his way to Jerusalem.

Next Jesus encounters three potential followers. As Jesus speaks to each individually, his disciples are present to overhear what he says about discipleship. He is teaching each of them, as well as everyone who hears this Gospel, about the demands of discipleship: those who follow Jesus must be ready to be without home and security; discipleship takes precedence over family ties and obligations; and the relationship of Jesus and his disciples is permanent and unconditional. E.P.

FOURTEENTH SUNDAY
IN ORDINARY TIME

LECTIONARY #102

READING I   Isaiah 66:10–14c

A reading from the Book of the Prophet Isaiah

> **Thus** says the LORD:
> **Rejoice** with **Jerusalem** and be **glad** because of her,
>   all **you** who **love** her;
> **exult**, **exult** with her,
>   all **you** who were **mourning** over her!
> Oh, that you may suck **fully**
>   of the **milk** of her **comfort**,
> that you may **nurse** with **delight**
>   at her **abundant** breasts!
> For **thus** says the LORD:
> **Lo**, I will spread **prosperity** over **Jerusalem** like a **river**,
>   and the **wealth** of the **nations** like an **overflowing torrent**.
> As **nurslings**, you shall be **carried** in her **arms**,
>   and **fondled** in her **lap**;
> as a **mother comforts** her **child**,
>   so will **I comfort you**;
>   in **Jerusalem** you shall **find** your **comfort**.
>
> When you **see** this, your heart shall **rejoice**
>   and your bodies **flourish** like the **grass**;
> the LORD's **power** shall be **known** to his **servants**.

Isaiah = ĭ-ZAY-uh

Don't weaken the power of Isaiah's words by holding back on these striking images.

The text consists of couplets that repeat in the second line what was said in the first. To avoid sounding redundant, increase energy from the first to the second line. Remember, you are speaking these words as if to survivors of a great ordeal. Let them soothe and comfort.

God is promising to do the impossible, so speak with authority, but also with persuasive love.

Jerusalem is depicted as a nursing mother; in short order, God appropriates that same image.

The final lines speak of the future. Speak slowly and with great conviction that "heart" and "bodies" will be transformed by the Lord's "power."

READING I In the prophecy from Isaiah, the Lord speaks to people newly returned, or perhaps still on the way home, from exile in Babylon. Upon their return, they found their beloved Jerusalem, including the Temple, in ruins. While they are mourning this bleak reality, God urges them to rejoice in the midst of their present sorrow because of what God will do for Jerusalem in the future. God offers them one of the most comforting and reassuring of images: a mother nursing her child. The verses just before those we read today describe Jerusalem giving birth,

and now she will care for her offspring. The returned exiles are about to begin their life as those newly born.

The image of Mother Jerusalem is replete with words and phrases that emphasize the extent of God's generosity; you will "suck fully" on "abundant breasts"; God will "spread prosperity" like a river, and wealth of nations like an "overflowing torrent." In the Hebrew text, the word we hear as "prosperity" is *shalom*, a rich concept that means wholeness, harmony, and completeness. Jerusalem, a name associated

with *shalom*, will manifest the harmony that its name signifies.

The abundance that God promises is accompanied by Mother Jerusalem's tenderness: "you will be carried in her arms and fondled in her lap." The image expresses the constant care and delight that the mother takes in her children, surrounding her child with affection. In every way, the Jerusalem of the future is cause for rejoicing in the present. All of Jerusalem's children will respond with exultation and delight.

For meditation and context:

RESPONSORIAL PSALM   Psalm 66:1–3, 4–5, 6–7, 16, 20 (1)

R. Let all the earth cry out to God with joy.

Shout joyfully to God, all the earth;
  sing praise to the glory of his name;
  proclaim his glorious praise.
Say to God, "How tremendous are
  your deeds!"

"Let all on earth worship and sing praise
  to you,
  sing praise to your name!"
Come and see the works of God,
  his tremendous deeds among the children
  of Adam.

He changed the sea into dry land;
  through the river they passed on foot;
therefore let us rejoice in him.
  He rules by his might forever.

Hear now, all you who fear God,
  while I declare what he has done for me.
Blessed be God who refused me not
  my prayer or his kindness!

READING II   Galatians 6:14–18

A reading from the Letter of Saint Paul to the Galatians

Brothers and **sisters**:
May I **never boast** except in the **cross** of our **Lord Jesus Christ**,
  through which the **world** has been **crucified** to me,
  and **I** to the **world**.
For **neither** does **circumcision** mean **anything**,
  nor does **uncircumcision**,
  but only a **new creation**.
Peace and **mercy** be to all who **follow** this **rule**
  and to the **Israel** of **God**.

From now **on**, let **no one** make **troubles** for me;
  for I **bear** the **marks** of **Jesus** on my **body**.

The **grace** of our **Lord Jesus Christ** be with your **spirit**,
  brothers and sisters. Amen.

Galations = guh-LAY-shuhnz

This is the fifth consecutive week we read from Galatians. Here, Paul is both teacher and a healer, so his tone cannot be abrasive.

Pause after "boast" and then forcefully state of what one *can* boast—the Cross of Christ!

Don't stress what doesn't matter, but what does—"a new creation." Your listeners are that new creation!
This is a *prayer* for peace for all who follow Christ.

Don't let these words sound whining or bragging; Paul considers his suffering a prIvIlege.
End with a prayer that sounds like a prayer.

After such a fulsome portrait of Mother Jerusalem, the prophet adds to the motherhood image. Now God is presented as a mother comforting her children. The abundance of Mother Jerusalem is possible only because God also acts as a mother, comforting her children. Now the people will rejoice in the motherly comfort offered by the holy city and by their loving God. Then the people's bodies will "flourish like the grass," giving us a concluding image of continued abundance.

| READING II | In the final verses of his letter to the Galatians, Paul writes to the community in his "own hand" (6:11), giving his concluding remarks a deeply personal tone. Having argued throughout the letter against those who demanded circumcision, Paul summarizes the heart of his Gospel here: the cross of our Lord Jesus Christ. Paul is so immersed in Christ that he can say he is co-crucified with him (2:19), and has died to the world. Although the "world" (*kosmos*) is sometimes a neutral term referring to the earth and its inhabitants, Paul uses the word here to refer to those in opposition to God, those who reject the cross of Christ. The "world" signifies the old order in contrast to the new creation inaugurated by the cross of Christ. Paul writes further about the new creation in his Second Letter to the Corinthians: "If anyone is in Christ, there is a new creation: everything old has passed away; see, everything has become new" (2 Corinthians 5:17).

Those who live in the new creation follow the rule (*kanon*) of the cross of Christ; a *kanon* is a measuring rod, an apt metaphor for measuring how well believers are living

GOSPEL Luke 10:1–12, 17–20

A reading from the holy Gospel according to Luke

As the Twelve were sent to the tribes of Israel, the seventy-two are sent to the nations, believed to be seventy-two in number.

In all he says, the solicitousness of Jesus for his disciples is strongly apparent. "So ask . . ." is more prayer than admonition.

He warns them of the dangers ahead.

Don't overdramatize the instructions; Jesus is preparing them for their labors, not telling a story.

Jesus anticipates the frustrations they may encounter and the remedies they may be tempted to utilize.

Speak this declaration with authority.

[At **that** time the **Lord** appointed seventy-two **others**
    whom he sent **ahead** of him in **pairs**
    to every **town** and **place** he intended to **visit**.
He **said** to them,
    "The **harvest** is **abundant** but the **laborers** are **few**;
    so ask the **master** of the **harvest**
    to send out **laborers** for his **harvest**.
Go **on** your way;
    behold, I am sending you like **lambs** among **wolves**.
Carry no **money bag**, no **sack**, no **sandals**;
    and greet **no one** along the **way**.
Into whatever **house** you enter, **first** say,
    '**Peace** to this **household**.'
If a peaceful person **lives** there,
    your **peace** will **rest** on him;
    but if **not**, it will **return** to you.
Stay in the **same house** and **eat** and **drink** what is **offered** to you,
    for the **laborer deserves** his **payment**.
Do **not** move **about** from **one** house to **another**.

in light of the cross of Christ. They are to live neither according to the standards of the world nor according to the standard imposed by the Law. Paul wishes them peace and mercy, a twofold blessing asking for God's abiding gifts to them as individuals and as a community.

Circumcision left its mark on the flesh of those who submitted to the Law's requirement, but Paul bears the marks of Jesus in his flesh. Because Paul has been co-crucified, the scars of persecution reflect his union with Christ and his cross. When he says that he boasts in the cross of

Christ, Paul can point to the marks of the cross on his own body as a sign of his co-crucifixion.

After the harsh language of much of Galatians, the concluding benediction asks for God's grace on the community. In spite of their sharp disagreements, they remain a family of brothers and sisters united in our Lord Jesus Christ. To everything he has written, Paul says "Amen." Though there is no punctuation in the Greek text, we can almost hear an exclamation point!

| GOSPEL | In sending out seventy-two disciples, Jesus inaugurates the mission of spreading the Gospel to the whole world. In Genesis 10, seventy-two symbolizes the number of inhabitants of the whole world. If the disciples are to go out to such a massive and diverse population, they must be well prepared. Thus Jesus alerts them to the realities they will encounter, and explains how they are to proceed on their mission.

Jesus frequently uses images that would be easily understood by his followers. The harvest metaphor would be familiar in

Whatever **town** you **enter** and they **welcome** you,
    eat what is set **before** you,
    cure the **sick** in it and **say** to them,
    'The **Kingdom** of **God** is **at hand** for **you**.']
Whatever town you **enter** and they do **not** receive you,
    go out into the **streets** and **say**,
    'The **dust** of your **town** that **clings** to our **feet**,
    even that we **shake off against** you.'
Yet know **this**: the **Kingdom** of **God** is at **hand**.
I **tell** you,
    it will be **more** tolerable for **Sodom** on that day
        than for **that** town."

Speak without malice, but with stern warning.

Jesus' prophecy is not without compassion.

Pause briefly, then begin with renewed energy.

The seventy-two returned **rejoicing**, and said,
    "**Lord**, even the **demons** are **subject** to us because
        of your **name**."
Jesus said, "I have observed **Satan** fall like **lightning**
    from the **sky**.
Behold, I have given you the **power** to '**tread** upon **serpents**'
    and **scorpions**
    and upon the **full force** of the **enemy**
    and **nothing** will **harm** you.
Nevertheless, do **not rejoice** because the **spirits** are **subject** to you,
    but **rejoice** because your **names** are **written** in **heaven**."

Jesus is downplaying their enthusiasm.

To paraphrase: "Yes," he says calmly, "you have received power . . . "

"But here is the true cause for rejoicing!"

[Shorter: Luke 10:1–9 (see brackets)]

the agrarian environment of first-century Palestine (even among his fishermen followers), as well as from its usage in the Bible. God, the Lord of the harvest, is the one who provides the needed rain and watches over the harvest (Jeremiah 5:24). Though the workers must apply themselves, the bounty ultimately depends on the harvest master.

The second image is lambs among wolves. This frightful image is founded on the reality of daily life for shepherds as well as their flocks. Jesus' missionaries might also remember Isaiah's hopeful prophecy of the wolf lying down with the lamb, but Jesus warns them that he is sending them on a dangerous journey. Their success even among wolves will depend on the one who sent them.

After presenting symbolic pictures of the disciples' mission, Jesus moves to practical directives. They are not to be weighed down by anything that would prevent them from continuing on their missionary journey. Instructions in greetings, lodging, even eating and drinking, emphasize the urgency of their task: waste no time on nonessentials and focus instead on proclaiming the Kingdom of God.

Just as a successful harvest leads to rejoicing, so too do disciples rejoice in the success of their mission, including their being able to cast down Satan by Jesus' name. Even more than joy for their present success, they should rejoice in their names being written in heaven. Success in the present is only the beginning of eternal rejoicing. E.P.

FIFTEENTH SUNDAY IN ORDINARY TIME

LECTIONARY #105

READING I Deuteronomy 30:10–14

A reading from the Book of Deuteronomy

Moses said to the **people**:
"If **only** you would **heed** the **voice** of the LORD, your **God**,
and keep his **commandments** and **statutes**
that are **written** in this **book** of the **law**,
when you **return** to the LORD, your **God**,
with **all** your **heart** and **all** your **soul**.

"For this **command** that I **enjoin** on you **today**
is **not** too **mysterious** and **remote** for you.
It is **not** up in the **sky**, that you should say,
'**Who** will **go up** in the **sky** to **get** it for us
and **tell** us of it, that we may **carry** it **out**?'
Nor is it across the **sea**, that you should say,
'**Who** will **cross** the **sea** to **get** it for us
and **tell** us of it, that we may **carry** it **out**?'
No, it is something **very near** to **you**,
already in your **mouths** and in your **hearts**;
you have **only** to **carry** it **out**."

Deuteronomy = d<u>oo</u>-ter-AH-nuh-mee or dy<u>oo</u>-ter-AH-nuh-mee

Be sure your assembly hears who the speaker is.
Let Moses speak the first sentence with solemn authority.

The balance of the text is a cold dose of reality splashed upon the people.

Don't make these analogies overly serious. Moses is clearly exaggerating to make his point: You don't have to fly to the heavens or cross the sea to get this!

Pause before the final sentence. This is the climax of the text and the heart of his message.

READING I Attentive listening is a fundamental response to the Word of God. "Hear (*Shema*), O Israel" is the beginning of the daily prayer called the Shema that takes its name from the opening call to listen. After listening and acknowledging the one God, the people are to love the Lord their God with their whole being. In today's reading from Deuteronomy, Moses uses a similar pattern as he urges the people to heed the voice of God and to keep God's commandments with all their heart and soul. Moses tells the people they must return (*sub*) to the Lord, reminding them that they have often turned away. Shortly before today's verses, Moses had already begun his emphasis on returning or repenting. The people's action of repentance is closely aligned with God's action of restoring them, with the same verb (*sub*) used both for divine and human action.

In this part of his admonitions, Moses teaches that returning to the Lord is not slavishly keeping the commandments. Rather, the people are to return to the Lord with a wholehearted, loving relationship

For meditation and context:

RESPONSORIAL PSALM   Psalm 69:14, 17, 30–31, 33–34, 36, 37 (see 33)

R. Turn to the Lord in your need, and you will live.

I pray to you, O LORD,
    for the time of your favor, O God!
In your great kindness answer me
    with your constant help.
Answer me, O LORD, for bounteous is
      your kindness;
    in your great mercy turn toward me.

I am afflicted and in pain;
    let your saving help, O God, protect me.
I will praise the name of God in song,
    and I will glorify him with thanksgiving.

"See, you lowly ones, and be glad;
    you who seek God, may your
      hearts revive!
For the LORD hears the poor,
    and his own who are in bonds he
      spurns not."

For God will save Zion
    and rebuild the cities of Judah.
The descendants of his servants shall
      inherit it,
    and those who love his name shall
      inhabit it.

or:

For meditation and context:

RESPONSORIAL PSALM   Psalm 19:8, 9, 10, 11 (9a)

R. Your words, Lord, are Spirit and life.

The law of the LORD is perfect,
    refreshing the soul.
The decree of the LORD is trustworthy,
    giving wisdom to the simple.

The precepts of the LORD are right,
    rejoicing the heart.
The command of the LORD is clear,
    enlightening the eye.

The fear of the LORD is pure,
    enduring forever.
The ordinances of the LORD are true,
    all of them just.

They are more precious than gold,
    than a heap of purest gold;
sweeter also than syrup
    or honey from the comb.

READING II   Colossians 1:15–20

Colossians = kuh-LOSH-uhnz

Start with strength making the first statement a declaration of your own faith.

He is leading to the assertion that even the angelic beings were created by Christ, so none can be superior to him.

A reading from the Letter of Saint Paul to the Colossians

Christ Jesus is the **image** of the **invisible God**,
    the **firstborn** of **all creation**.
For in **him** were **created** all things in **heaven** and on **earth**,
    the **visible** and the **invisible**,
    whether **thrones** or **dominions** or **principalities** or **powers**;
    all things were **created through him** and **for him**. **»**

and do what God commands. There are no excuses. With a series of negatives, Moses dismisses the idea that the Law is impossible for the people to understand; it is not too mysterious, not remote, not up in the sky, not across the sea. God's law is so near that it is in the people's speech and in their hearts. If they listen attentively to God's voice today and follow God's commandments, they will thrive in the land of the promise.

READING II The canticle from Colossians is a majestic poem, perhaps used originally in a baptismal liturgy, extolling Christ in sweeping, cosmic language. Just before the canticle itself, Paul introduced it by praying that the community would give thanks to God, who has given them the inheritance of the saints, rescued them, and brought them into the Kingdom of Christ in whom the believers have been redeemed and forgiven.

The God who has acted so graciously cannot be seen, yet Christ the beloved Son is the very image of God, the *icon* who makes the invisible God visible. Throughout the canticle, the dominion of Christ has no limits. The words "all things" and "everything" repeatedly emphasize Christ's reign over the entirety of creation, embracing the visible and invisible, heaven and earth, angelic beings above and the Church below, time and eternity.

He is **before** all things,
   and in **him** all things **hold together**.
He is the **head** of the **body**, the **church**.
He is the **beginning**, the **firstborn** from the **dead**,
   that in **all** things he himself might be **preeminent**.
For in **him all** the **fullness** was pleased to **dwell**,
   and **through** him to **reconcile** all things for **him**,
   making **peace** by the **blood** of his **cross**
   through him, whether those on **earth** or those in **heaven**.

GOSPEL   Luke 10:25–37

A reading from the holy Gospel according to Luke

There was a scholar of the **law** who stood up to **test** him and said,
   "**Teacher**, what must I **do** to inherit **eternal life**?"
Jesus **said** to him, "What is **written** in the **law**?
How do **you** read it?"
He said in reply,
   "You shall love the Lord, your God,
   with all your heart,
   with all your being,
   with all your strength,
   and with all your mind,
   and your neighbor as yourself."
He **replied** to him, "You have answered **correctly**;
   do this and you will **live**."

But because he wished to **justify** himself, he said to **Jesus**,
   "And **who** is my **neighbor**?"
Jesus replied,
   "A **man** fell **victim** to **robbers**
   as he went down from **Jerusalem** to **Jericho**.
They **stripped** and **beat** him and went **off leaving** him **half-dead**.

Rejoice in this assertion; rather than arguing the point, celebrate Christ's dominion over all things.
His "body, the church" is sitting right in front of you. Speak to them.

Slow down for the final line that introduces the sobering reminder that what Christ did he did at great cost.

Let your tone signal that the man's motivation is insincere.

Jesus is aware of the lawyer's insincerity.

The man is learned and gives the "right" answer.

Jesus seems content to leave it at that and move on.

But the lawyer is determined to hear more from Jesus.

Now we see that Jesus had more to say all along. He dives into the story with energy.

Twice Christ is described as "first-born." As the firstborn of all creation, Christ holds a unique and preeminent place, not as a created being, but as the one in whom all else was created. Christ is also the first-born from the dead, the one who leads the way in re-creation by rising from the dead. As the first to rise, he is the source of Resurrection for his brothers and sisters. His death and Resurrection are the means of establishing reconciliation and peace, bringing together those once estranged.

The Canticle expresses the fundamental faith not only of the early Church but also the faith of believers in every age. In Christ we are born; in him we are sustained; in him we are reborn to eternal life.

GOSPEL   The lawyer in today's Gospel asks Jesus two questions, each with a different motivation. The first, regarding how to inherit eternal life, is meant to test Jesus. Rather than answering, Jesus turns the question back to the lawyer. Since he is a scholar of the law, he should know what is written there. When he brings together passages from the Torah, he makes the two mandates to love into a single commandment. Though the lawyer has exhibited correct knowl-

Jesus' narration should not betray a negative attitude toward "priest" or "Levite."

Note the extensive detail Jesus provides. The Samaritan is going to extraordinary lengths.

"The next day" starts a new beat. Begin with renewed energy.

Jesus' question requires insight and conversion.

The lawyer doesn't hesitate to name the virtue that distinguished the Samaritan as "neighbor." Pause briefly after "The one . . . ." Then, with sincerity, share the rest of his response.

Picture Jesus looking directly into the eyes of the lawyer. Jesus' words are a call to deep conversion.

A **priest** happened to be going down that road,
    but when he **saw** him, he **passed by** on the **opposite** side.
Likewise a **Levite** came to the place,
    and when **he saw** him, **he passed by** on the **opposite** side.
But a **Samaritan** traveler who came upon him
    was moved with **compassion** at the sight.
He **approached** the victim,
    poured oil and **wine** over his **wounds** and **bandaged** them.
Then he **lifted** him up on his own **animal**,
    took him to an **inn**, and **cared** for him.
The **next** day he took out **two** silver **coins**
    and **gave** them to the **innkeeper** with the instruction,
    'Take **care** of him.
If you **spend more** than what I have **given** you,
    I shall **repay** you on my way **back**.'
Which of these three, in **your** opinion,
    was **neighbor** to the robbers' victim?"
He answered, "The **one** who **treated** him with **mercy**."
Jesus said to him, "**Go** and **do likewise**."

edge, Jesus adds "do this and you will live." Knowledge is not enough; love of God and neighbor must be carried out in action.

The lawyer's second question stems from his wish to justify himself, likely combined with a desire to test Jesus further. Can Jesus correctly identify the meaning of neighbor? Jesus responds with a parable. Three people making the journey to Jericho see someone lying half-dead. The first two travelers, a priest and a Levite, see the man and pass by on the opposite side. The picture is clear: they choose to ignore him, and distance themselves. The parable says nothing about their motive, only about their actions. The motive of the third passerby, however, is clearly stated: he is moved by compassion. His actions are described in detail: he approached the man, poured oil, bandaged him, lifted him up, took him to an inn, cared for him, and even gave the innkeeper coins for his continued care.

The lawyer began with a question, and Jesus again turns the lawyer's question around: "Which one was neighbor to the robbers' victim?" The lawyer is almost forced to answer, "The one who treated him with mercy." The lawyer's correct answer must again be played out in action: "Go and do likewise." E.P.

SIXTEENTH SUNDAY IN ORDINARY TIME

LECTIONARY #108

READING I   Genesis 18:1–10a

A reading from the Book of Genesis

The LORD appeared to **Abraham** by the **terebinth** of **Mamre**,
  as he sat in the **entrance** of his **tent**,
  while the day was growing **hot**.
Looking **up**, Abraham saw **three men standing** nearby.
When he **saw** them, he **ran** from the entrance of the tent
    to **greet** them;
  and **bowing** to the ground, he said:
  "**Sir**, if I may ask you this **favor**,
  please do not go on **past** your servant.
Let some **water** be brought, that you may **bathe** your **feet**,
  and then **rest** yourselves under the **tree**.
Now that you have come this **close** to your **servant**,
  let me **bring** you a little **food**, that you may **refresh** yourselves;
  and **afterward** you may go on your **way**."
The **men** replied, "**Very well**, **do** as you have **said**."

Abraham **hastened** into the tent and told **Sarah**,
  "**Quick**, three measures of fine **flour**! **Knead** it
    and **make rolls**."
He **ran** to the **herd**, picked out a **tender**, **choice steer**,
  and gave it to a **servant**, who quickly **prepared** it.
Then Abraham got some curds and **milk**,
  as well as the **steer** that had been prepared,

Wait till all are settled, then announce that the "*Lord*" appeared to Abraham.
Terebinth = TAYR-uh-binth
Mamre = MAHM-ray

Narrate from Abraham's point of view: At first, he has no idea who the three are, but then senses the presence of divinity.

Note that he addresses the visitors in the singular.

He indicates that he will make little fuss, but then goes overboard.

"Do as you have said," should convey pleasure and gratitude.

His instructions to Sarah should convey a desire to serve rather than to impress his guests.

Slow the pace here to indicate his ability to focus on and be present to the guests.

READING I The opening sentence in the first reading tells us that the Lord appeared to Abraham, although Abraham himself does not know the identity of his three visitors. Our knowing that the Lord is present in disguise creates a sense of mystery and raises questions as the story unfolds. Is only one of the visitors the Lord in human guise, with two attendants? Or are the three so closely united that in addressing one of them, Abraham is addressing all three? Such questions have intrigued both Jewish and Christian interpreters through the centuries, leading to a variety of explanations. One Christian understanding sees the three visitors as representative of the Holy Trinity, expressed beautifully in the well-known icon by Andrei Rublev.

The story itself leaves such questions unanswered and in the realm of mystery. The narrative focuses instead on the beginning of the fulfillment of God's promise that Abraham would be the father of a multitude. In this scene, Abraham asks his visitors to favor him by not passing by, by resting and sharing in a "little food." What Abraham, Sarah, and their servant provide is far more than a "little food," but is an extravagant feast. The abundance offered by Abraham and Sarah is more than matched by the wondrous favor that the Lord in disguise offers them. One of the visitors tells Abraham that by the same time the next year, Sarah, well past child-bearing age, will have a son. The divine promise will be fulfilled.

READING II Our second reading, from Colossians, begins with a profound paradox: Paul rejoices in his sufferings. As he writes this letter, Paul is in

and **set** these before the three men;
and he **waited** on them under the **tree** while they **ate.**

They **asked** Abraham, "**Where** is your wife **Sarah**?"
He replied, "**There** in the **tent.**"
One of them said, "I will **surely return** to you
    about **this** time next **year,**
    and **Sarah** will then have a **son.**"

Don't rush this question.

This is the great promise that will be fulfilled in Isaac.

For meditation and context:

RESPONSORIAL PSALM   Psalm 15:2–3, 3–4, 5 (1a)

R. He who does justice will live in the presence of the Lord.

One who walks blamelessly and does justice;
    who thinks the truth in his heart
    and slanders not with his tongue.

Who harms not his fellow man,
    nor takes up a reproach against his
        neighbor;
by whom the reprobate is despised,
    while he honors those who fear the LORD.

Who lends not his money at usury
    and accepts no bribe against the innocent.
One who does these things
    shall never be disturbed.

READING II   Colossians 1:24–28

A reading from the Letter of Saint Paul to the Colossians

Brothers and **sisters:**
Now I **rejoice** in my sufferings for **your** sake,
    and in my **flesh** I am filling **up**
    what is **lacking** in the **afflictions** of **Christ**
    on behalf of his **body,** which is the **church,**
    of which **I** am a **minister**
    in accordance with God's **stewardship given** to me
    to bring to **completion** for you the **word** of **God,**
    the **mystery** hidden from **ages** and from generations **past.** »

Colossians = kuh-LOSH-uhnz

Read slowly because you are saying something surprising—that he "rejoices" in "suffering."
It will take a homilist's insight to clarify the meaning of this assertion, but if you don't ensure that they hear it, there won't be anything for him to clarify.
Paul is asserting his rightful role as apostle and servant of the Gospel.
Speak with joy of this mystery that has now been made known.

prison, and he asks the community "Remember my chains" (4:18). Whether imprisonment or other myriad hardships that Paul endured (e.g., 2 Corinthians 11:23ff.), he tells the community at Colossae that it is "for your sake," and "on behalf of his body, which is the Church." Paul is participating in Christ's own suffering as a minister (*diakonos*) of the Gospel, putting his entire life at the service of his brothers and sisters in the faith. Such participation in Christ's own suffering is cause for Paul's joy.

As Paul suffers for the sake of his fellow believers, he fills up what is lacking in Christ's afflictions. Since Christ has died once for all (see Romans 6:10), how can Christ's sufferings be incomplete? Paul explains that Christ's suffering continues in his body, the Church. Paul is both a member of that body and a minister to it, exercising stewardship over the household of the faith.

In his ministry of stewardship, Paul brings the word of God to the community, announces the hidden mystery to them, makes the Gospel known, admonishes, and

teaches everyone. Paul proclaims "Christ in you," the abiding presence of the risen one, giving each member of the body hope for glory. Even if Paul's present reality, as well as that of the community, entails suffering, Christ's dwelling in them is a gift now as well as a pledge for future glory, as they are being perfected, or brought to completion, in Christ.

GOSPEL   The story of the two sisters Martha and Mary is often understood as contrasting the contemplative and active lifestyles. Origen (185–254)

What has been "made known" to the Gentiles is the reality of Christ's oneness with his body, the Church.

But **now** it has been **manifested** to his **holy ones**,
> to whom **God** chose to make **known** the **riches** of the **glory**
> of this **mystery** among the **Gentiles**;
> it is **Christ** in **you**, the **hope** for **glory**.
It is **he** whom we **proclaim**,
> **admonishing everyone** and **teaching everyone**
>> with **all wisdom**,
> that we may **present everyone perfect** in **Christ**.

Through you, Paul is proclaiming Christ anew! Stress the verbs "admonishing" and "teaching" and save the stress on "everyone" until the end.

GOSPEL   Luke 10:38–42

A reading from the holy Gospel according to Luke

Jesus entered a **village**
> where a **woman** whose name was **Martha welcomed** him.
She had a **sister** named **Mary**
> who sat **beside** the **Lord** at his feet **listening** to him speak.
Martha, **burdened** with much **serving**, came to him and **said**,
> "**Lord**, do you not **care**
> that my **sister** has left me by **myself** to do the serving?
Tell her to **help** me."
The Lord said to her in **reply**,
> "**Martha**, **Martha**, you are **anxious** and **worried**
>> about **many** things.
There is need of **only one** thing.
Mary has chosen the **better** part
> and it will **not** be **taken** from her."

You're telling a story, and the setting and character names are important. Don't rush.

Let your tone convey the unusual nature of Mary's choice and stress her *listening*.

Martha is "burdened." Your tone should convey the negative judgment Jesus will make about her state of mind and heart.

She speaks to him familiarly, like a member of the family.

Remarkably, she tells Jesus what to do. Jesus seems mildly amused by her consternation.

Though he loves her, Jesus is clear with Martha about what is the *better* part.

---

was widely influential in promoting this view by writing, "One may confidently affirm that Martha symbolizes action, Mary contemplation." In spite of Origen's confident interpretation, Luke may have had something else in mind.

Both Martha and Mary can be counted among Jesus' disciples. In this scene, Jesus gives advice to Martha, as he had done to other disciples, lest she center her attention on the wrong things. His admonition to her is important for all disciples. She is anxious about many things, while her sister is attentive to only one: Jesus himself. Jesus is not denigrating active service (*diakonia*), but cautions about anxiety and worry. Martha's fretfulness brings to mind Jesus' parable about a seed falling among thorns, symbolic of people choked by the anxieties of life (8:14). The seed, according to the parable, is the Word of God that disciples should embrace with generous and good hearts, a stance seen in Mary listening at Jesus' feet. Later in the Gospel, Jesus tells his followers that they shouldn't worry about what to say in their defense, for the Holy Spirit will teach them (12:11–12). Like Mary, they need to listen to hear God's Spirit.

Because Jesus is well aware of the demands of service for the sake of the Gospel and the anxieties that often accompany it, he tells his disciples, including Martha, to keep their attention on Jesus even in the midst of their activity. The one thing necessary is to embrace the word of God, Jesus himself, with a generous and good heart. E.P.

SEVENTEENTH SUNDAY IN ORDINARY TIME

LECTIONARY #111

READING I Genesis 18:20–32

A reading from the Book of Genesis

In **those** days, the LORD said:
"The **outcry** against **Sodom** and **Gomorrah** is so **great**,
    and their **sin** so **grave**,
   that I must go **down** and **see** whether or not their **actions**
      fully **correspond** to the **cry** against them that **comes** to me.
I mean to find **out**."

While **Abraham's visitors** walked on **farther** toward **Sodom**,
    the LORD remained **standing** before **Abraham**.
Then **Abraham** drew **nearer** and said:
   "Will you sweep away the **innocent** with the **guilty**?
Suppose there were fifty **innocent** people in the **city**;
   would you **wipe out** the place, **rather** than **spare** it
   for the **sake** of the **fifty innocent people** within it?
Far be it from **you** to do such a thing,
   to make the **innocent** die with the **guilty**
   so that the **innocent** and the **guilty** would be treated **alike**!
Should not the **judge** of all the **world** act with **justice**?"
The LORD **replied**,
   "If I find **fifty** innocent people in the city of Sodom,
   I will **spare** the **whole place** for **their** sake."
Abraham spoke up **again**:
   "**See** how I am **presuming** to speak to my Lord,
   though I am but **dust** and **ashes**! »

The outcry comes from the victims of injustice. As defender of the weak and the poor, God must respond. Speak with strength, not vindictiveness.

God will "go down" to verify if the "outcry" is justified.

"Abraham's visitors" are the three (divine) visitors Abraham hosted in his tent who announced he'd have a son within the year.

Abraham is alarmed at what might happen and immediately intervenes!
His tone is bold at the start.

Abraham speaks to God as if God were an earthly king worried about his reputation. He also appeals to God's sense of Justice.

Abraham becomes more apologetic and deferential as he pushes for greater indulgence.

Abraham is clever, but not insincere.

READING I Among God's first promises to Abraham was that "all the communities of the earth shall find blessing you" (Genesis 12:3). In the scene in today's reading, Abraham asks God for blessing even on the sinful city, Sodom. In his pleading, Abraham becomes a model of intercession for sinners. Later in the desert, Moses will similarly ask the Lord, "If you would only forgive their sin!" (Exodus 32:32). The prophets will also intercede for the people: "Forgive, O Lord God! How can Jacob stand? He is so small!" (Amos 7:2).

While Abraham became a model for intercession as well as a standard of righteousness, Sodom became a symbol of widespread sinfulness. The prophet Jeremiah, preaching against the sinfulness of Jerusalem's prophets, used Sodom as a well-known example: "Adultery, living in lies, siding with the wicked, so that no one turns from evil; To me they are all like Sodom" (Jeremiah 23:14). All of Sodom's sins, whether against their fellow citizens or against the visitors to their city, were ultimately abuses "committed against the Lord" (Genesis 13:13).

Abraham mediates for such a sinful city for the sake of the righteous people living within it, using language that is both boldly insistent and deferential. He seems shocked at the notion that God would act unjustly: "Far be it from you to do such a thing, to make the innocent die with the guilty." Should the fifty innocent people be unfairly punished? Or forty? Thirty? Abraham stops his questions when he gets to ten innocent people, leaving the Lord who is just to make the decision.

The Talmud will later see Abraham as a model for how all of Israel is to relate to

Quicken your pace in order to sneak in one more request.

Imagine a conversation with your employer asking for a larger and larger raise and the finessing you would need to do to keep pushing for more.
God's tone can remain consistent throughout—even and without overt emotion.
Read at a brisk pace without belaboring the exchange between Abraham and God.

Carefully set up the final request, then spring the surprisingly small number of ten.

Pause after he replied and solemnly announce the Lord's final response.

For meditation and context:

What if there are five **less** than **fifty** innocent people?
Will you destroy the **whole city** because of those **five**?"
He answered, "I will **not** destroy it, if I find **forty-five** there."
But Abraham **persisted**, saying "What if only **forty** are
    found there?"
He replied, "I will **forbear** doing it for the **sake** of the **forty**."
Then Abraham said, "Let **not** my Lord grow **impatient** if I go on.
What if only **thirty** are found there?"
He replied, "I will **forbear doing** it if I can find but **thirty** there."
Still Abraham went **on**,
    "Since I have thus **dared** to speak to my **Lord**,
      what if there are no more than **twenty**?"
The LORD answered, "I will **not destroy** it, for the **sake**
    of the **twenty**."
But he **still** persisted:
    "**Please**, let **not** my Lord grow **angry** if I **speak** up this
      last time.
What if there are at **least ten** there?"
He replied, "For the **sake** of those **ten**, I will **not destroy** it."

RESPONSORIAL PSALM Psalm 138:1–2, 2–3, 6–7, 7–8 (3a)

R. Lord, on the day I called for help, you answered me.

I will give thanks to you, O LORD, with all
    my heart,
    for you have heard the words of
      my mouth;
    in the presence of the angels I will sing
      your praise;
I will worship at your holy temple
    and give thanks to your name.

Because of your kindness and your truth;
    for you have made great above all things
      your name and your promise.
When I called you answered me;
    you built up strength within me.

The LORD is exalted, yet the lowly he sees,
    and the proud he knows from afar.
Though I walk amid distress, you
      preserve me;
    against the anger of my enemies you raise
      your hand.

Your right hand saves me.
    The LORD will complete what he has done
      for me;
your kindness, O LORD, endures forever;
    forsake not the work of your hands.

God: "I deeply love you, for even when I gave you abundant greatness, you make yourselves small before Me. I gave greatness to Abraham, and he said *I who am but dust and ashes*." Abraham's fatherly role has implications for future generations, as the Lord declared, "I have singled him out that he may direct his sons and his posterity to keep the way of the Lord by doing what is right and just" (Genesis 18:19). Both Abraham and the Lord God show future generations what justice entails.

READING II In the short reading from Colossians, Paul provides a succinct explanation of the meaning of Baptism. The terminology he uses, similar to that of another baptismal passage at Romans 6, is distinctively Pauline. Paul created new vocabulary to describe a new reality, using a series of compound verbs with the prefix *syn*, meaning *with*; his new vocabulary can be translated as *co-buried, co-raised*, and *co-living*. The experience of being immersed into Christ at Baptism means that the baptized participate in the Paschal Mystery of Christ's death and Resurrection.

Those who are baptized into Christ have no need of the ritual of circumcision. Just before today's baptismal instruction, Paul tells the Colossians that they were "circumcised with a circumcision not administered by hand," but rather "with the circumcision of Christ." In Paul's understanding, Baptism can be regarded as a spiritual circumcision that accomplishes what the physical ritual could not. Those that Paul describes as "dead in transgressions and the uncircumcision of the flesh"

READING II Colossians 2:12–14

A reading from the Letter of Saint Paul to the Colossians

Brothers and **sisters**:
You were **buried** with him in **baptism**,
in which you were also **raised** with him
through **faith** in the **power** of **God**,
who **raised** him from the **dead**.
And even when you were **dead**
in **transgressions** and the **uncircumcision** of your **flesh**,
he **brought** you to **life** along **with** him,
having **forgiven** us all our **transgressions**;
obliterating the bond **against** us, with its **legal** claims,
which was **opposed** to us,
he also **removed** it from our midst, **nailing** it to the **cross**.

Colossians = kuh-LOSH-uhnz

Begin slowly and continue slowly or this text will become a blur. Remember, you are announcing Good News.
Your faith in the power of God who raised Christ brought about your own Resurrection.

Despite our sinfulness, God reached out to save us.

God raised us to life together with Christ.

Don't rush the powerful image of our debt being nailed to the cross.

GOSPEL Luke 11:1–13

A reading from the holy Gospel according to Luke

Jesus was **praying** in a **certain** **place**, and when he had **finished**,
one of his **disciples** said to him,
"**Lord**, **teach** us to **pray** just as **John** taught **his** disciples."
He said to them, "When you **pray**, say:
Father, **hallowed** be your **name**,
your Kingdom come.
Give us each day our **daily bread**
and **forgive** us **our sins**
for **we ourselves** forgive **everyone** in **debt** to **us**,
and do **not subject** us to the **final test**."

And he said to them, "Suppose one of you has a **friend**
to whom he goes at **midnight** and says, ❯❯

Be sure to highlight that Jesus is in prayer.

Moved by Jesus' ability to pray, they ask for instruction.

Keep the prayer upbeat. Each intercession stands alone, so end one before beginning the next.

Pause briefly before beginning the following narration.

---

are probably the Gentile members of the community. Though some of the Christian preachers had demanded circumcision for Gentile converts, Paul vehemently rejected the practice, particularly in his letter to the Galatians. God brought the uncircumcised Gentiles to life and forgave all their transgressions through their Baptism into Christ.

Paul develops his baptismal teaching with another comparison: a bond of debt. He presents the image of a legal document that lists an account of debt to be paid because of transgressions. Unpaid debts can result in punishment or condemnation.

But Christ's death has cancelled that debt! Paul envisions the document listing the debt owed as nailed to the cross. Unlike the mocking inscription the Romans nailed on Christ's cross, God has nailed onto the cross the notice that debt due to sin has been erased.

GOSPEL As Jesus and his disciples make their way to Jerusalem, he has been teaching them by word and example how to follow him on the way. At one point on the journey, they see Jesus praying, prompting one of his dis-

ciples to ask that Jesus teach them to pray as John the Baptist had taught his disciples. Jesus gives them a threefold teaching. He begins by telling them simply, "When you pray, say," followed by a brief prayer addressed to the Father. Next he presents a parable illustrating the need for persistence. Then he concludes with sayings that further develop how a loving father responds to a child who asks.

The prayer that Jesus teaches is communal in nature, with believers together addressing God as Father. In teaching this prayer, Jesus is also outlining how his

His request is made with clear expectation of a positive response.

He is tired and annoyed. His attitude says, "How could you even *think* I would get out of bed at this hour?"

Like a teacher asserting a point of which you are certain.

Don't rush this classic saying of Jesus. Address each phrase to a different section of the assembly.

Experience may seem to contradict this strong declaration. Speak with conviction.

Speak the examples at a good pace; the point is the father's willingness to satisfy his child, not the specific details.

Consistent with his emphasis on the Spirit, Luke substitutes "Holy Spirit" for Matthew's "good gifts."

'**Friend**, **lend** me three loaves of **bread**,
for a **friend** of mine has **arrived** at my **house** from a **journey**
and I have **nothing** to **offer** him,'
and he says in reply from **within**,
'Do **not bother** me; the door has **already** been **locked**
and my **children** and **I** are already in **bed**.
I **cannot** get **up** to give you **anything**.'
I **tell** you,
    if he does **not** get up to give the visitor the loaves
    because of their **friendship**,
    he **will** get up to give him **whatever** he needs
    because of his **persistence**.

"And I **tell** you, **ask** and you will **receive**;
    seek and you will **find**;
    knock and the door will be **opened** to you.
For **everyone** who **asks**, **receives**;
    and the one who **seeks**, **finds**;
    and to the one who **knocks**, the **door** will be **opened**.
What **father among** you would hand his **son** a **snake**
    when he **asks** for a **fish**?
Or **hand** him a **scorpion** when he **asks** for an **egg**?
If **you** then, who are **wicked**,
    know **how** to give **good** gifts to your **children**,
    how much more will the **Father** in **heaven**
    give the **Holy Spirit** to those who **ask** him?"

disciples are to live as children of one Father. They begin by honoring the holiness of God, a common feature in Jewish prayer: "Sanctified be his great name." Praying that God's Kingdom will come also has background in Judaism: "His Kingdom rules over all" (Psalm 103:19). Jesus' prayer asks that God's rule may be made effective here and now, and would likely remind his disciples how Jesus had proclaimed the Kingdom of God, making it present through his words and actions. The petitions that follow are, in fact, features of the Kingdom of God: bread each day and forgiveness both given

and received. The final petition, similar to Jesus' prayer in the garden (22:40), asks that the disciples be spared from the final, apocalyptic testing.

Like Jesus' prayer, the parable is quite short, depicting a scenario that the disciples could well imagine. Since *we* have heard the persistent and bold prayer of Abraham in the first reading today, we have a double illustration of the necessity of perseverance in prayer. The boldness of Abraham is well matched by the friend's persistence, *anaideia* in Greek, a term that means "shameless resolve."

The final segment of teaching reinforces the necessity of repeatedly asking God for what we need. Ask, seek, knock. The verb forms imply continued action and can be understood as "keep on asking, seeking, knocking." The Father will not be turned away by such persistence but will give good things to the children who ask, even giving them the Holy Spirit. E.P.

EIGHTEENTH SUNDAY IN ORDINARY TIME

LECTIONARY #114

READING I   Ecclesiastes 1:2; 2:21–23

A reading from the Book of Ecclesiastes

> **Vanity** of **vanities**, says **Qoheleth**,
>   **vanity** of **vanities**! **All** things are **vanity**!
>
> Here is one who has **labored** with **wisdom** and **knowledge**
>   and **skill**,
>   and **yet** to **another** who has **not labored** over it,
> he must **leave property**.
> This **also** is vanity and a **great misfortune**.
> For **what profit comes** to **man** from all the **toil** and **anxiety**
>   of **heart**
>   with which he has **labored** under the **sun**?
> **All** his days **sorrow** and **grief** are his **occupation**;
>   even at **night** his mind is **not** at rest.
> This **also** is **vanity**.

Ecclesiastes = ih-klee-zee-AS-teez

Qoheleth = koh-HEL-uhth
This classic refrain will also end the book. Speak the second iteration slower than the first. And increase your intensity further on "*All* is vanity."
The attitude underlying these lines is cynical and pessimistic. Don't hide that fact.

Avoid anger, but make this blunt statement without equivocation.

You or someone you know has made similar assertions. Convey the frustration that leads to such declarations.

It's all so futile!

Don't overstate the final line. But, after a slight pause, speak it with conviction.

READING I   The unknown author of the Book of Ecclesiastes probably composed his book around the year 300 BC. He writes in the name of King Solomon, thereby giving authority to his teaching. He identifies himself also as Qoheleth (*Ecclesiastes* in Greek), not a name, but a designation of his occupation as a preacher or teacher.

The opening words of today's reading, "Vanity of vanities," is at the heart of his preaching. He uses *vanity* (*hebel*) almost forty times in this short book, with a repeated refrain, "All is vanity." The Hebrew word *hebel* has a basic meaning of vapor or puff of wind, signifying something transitory, fleeting, and insubstantial. Even if a person labors with wisdom, knowledge, and skill, his days will end with his death, the only certainty. Qoheleth asks a rhetorical question, "What profit comes to man from all the toil and anxiety of heart with which he has labored?" His question nudges those who hear to ask the question of themselves.

Qoheleth suggests several answers as he continues the theme of "all is vanity." Since death is our ultimate destiny, make the best of the present day. Though "all is vanity" suggests a profound pessimism, the preacher admits that joy in the fruit of one's labor is a gift from God (2:24; 3:13). Further, in order to live as happily as possible in the present, each person should fear the Lord. Far from being a cowering terror, fear of the Lord is a sense of awe and reverence before God and the divine plan: "I know that it shall be well with those who fear God, for their reverence toward him" (8:12).

For meditation and context:

RESPONSORIAL PSALM   Psalm 90:3–4, 5–6, 12–13, 14, 17 (95:8)

R. If today you hear his voice, harden not your hearts.

You turn man back to dust,
    saying, "Return, O children of men."
For a thousand years in your sight
    are as yesterday, now that it is past,
    or as a watch of the night.

You make an end of them in their sleep;
    the next morning they are like the
        changing grass,
which at dawn springs up anew,
    but by evening wilts and fades.

Teach us to number our days aright,
    that we may gain wisdom of heart.
Return, O LORD! How long?
    Have pity on your servants!

Fill us at daybreak with your kindness,
    that we may shout for joy and gladness all
        our days.
And may the gracious care of the LORD our
        God be ours;
    prosper the work of our hands for us!
    Prosper the work of our hands!

READING II   Colossians 3:1–5, 9–11

Colossians = kuh-LOSH-uhnz

"If" sets up an "if/then" clause: "if" you were raised, "then" seek . . . .

Contrast "above" and "on earth."
Having "died" in Christ is a positive thing spoken with gratitude!

Speak with authority and urgency. "Earthly" things are like a cancer sure to kill the life of our spirit.

Make eye contact on this very direct injunction.
Don't ignore the clothing imagery used here.

A reading from the Letter of Saint Paul to the Colossians

Brothers and **sisters**:
If you were **raised** with **Christ**, **seek** what is **above**,
    where **Christ** is **seated** at the **right hand** of **God**.
Think of what is **above**, **not** of what is on **earth**.
For **you** have **died**,
    and your **life** is **hidden** with **Christ** in **God**.
When **Christ** your **life appears**,
    then **you too** will **appear** with him in **glory**.

Put to **death**, then, the **parts** of you that are **earthly**:
    immorality, **impurity**, **passion**, **evil desire**,
    and the **greed** that is **idolatry**.
Stop **lying** to one another,
    since you have taken off the **old** self with its **practices**
    and have put on the **new** self,
    which is being **renewed**, for **knowledge**,
    in the **image** of its **creator**.

READING II As Paul continues his baptismal instruction in the Letter to the Colossians, he develops his teaching with a familiar pattern: a statement of the Church's faith, followed by how people are to live in light of that faith. In both parts of his teaching, Paul develops a series of sharp contrasts: things above and things of the earth; death and life; present hidden life and future life appearing in glory; old and new, symbolized by the taking off and putting on of clothing.

Through Baptism, believers are co-raised with Christ, who is seated above at the right hand of God. Since the realm of Christ is above, those who are baptized should focus both their seeking and their thinking on what is above. Having died with Christ in Baptism, their present life is not outwardly visible, but hidden with Christ; when Christ himself appears in glory, the once-hidden life will also appear in glory. Just as Christians share in Christ's death and Resurrection, so too will they share in his glory at his *parousia*, his glorious coming again at the end of time.

Having proclaimed believers' participation in Christ's death, Resurrection, and glory, Paul instructs his audience how they are to live. Earthly things include a list of behaviors, not an entire catalog, but a representation of the earthly things that contrast with things that are above. Since Baptism entails taking off the old garments of sinful behavior and putting on the new ones, the discarded clothing must not be put on again. Rather, the new self with new garments is in a continuous process of being renewed in the very image of the creator God.

As good as this diversity is, it no longer matters in light of our oneness.

Oneness trumps diversity because our oneness is Christ!

Here there is not **Greek** and **Jew**,
   circumcision and **uncircumcision**,
   barbarian, **Scythian**, **slave**, **free**;
   but **Christ** is **all** and **in all**.

GOSPEL   Luke 12:13–21

A reading from the holy Gospel according to Luke

Someone in the **crowd** said to **Jesus**,
   "**Teacher**, tell my **brother** to **share** the **inheritance** with me."
He **replied** to him,
   "**Friend, who** appointed **me** as your **judge** and **arbitrator**?"
Then he said to the **crowd**,
   "Take **care** to **guard against all greed**,
   for though **one** may be **rich**,
   one's **life** does not consist of **possessions**."

The petitioner is speaking over the crowd seeking to get Jesus' attention.

Jesus' salutation, "Friend," should soften the impact of his refusal to be drawn in.

Lift your voice for Jesus' address to the crowd.

Then he told them a **parable**.
"There was a **rich** man whose **land** produced a **bountiful harvest**.
He **asked** himself, '**What** shall I **do**,
   for I do **not** have **space** to **store** my **harvest**?'
And he said, '**This is** what I shall do:
   I shall **tear down** my **barns** and build **larger** ones.
There I shall **store all** my grain and **other goods**
   and I shall **say** to myself, "**Now** as for **you**,
   you have so **many** good things stored up for **many years**,
   rest, eat, drink, be merry!" '
But **God** said to him,
   'You **fool**, **this night** your **life** will be **demanded** of you;
   and the things you have **prepared**, to **whom** will they **belong**?'
Thus will it be for **all** who store up treasure for **themselves**
   but are **not rich** in **what matters** to **God**."

Though he's still addressing the crowd, Jesus can assume a quieter storytelling tone. Subtly differentiate between the "rich man," God, and Jesus' narrator voice.

He's pleased with his solution!

His pride is the result of hard and honest work. Nonetheless, he's deluding himself.

God's voice shatters his smug complacency

With good eye contact, direct these blunt words to your assembly.

GOSPEL   A variety of people approach Jesus as he makes his way to Jerusalem, often asking him challenging questions. The man in today's scene doesn't ask a question, but makes a demand of Jesus. The issue has to do with an inheritance that could include money, land, and livestock. In Luke's Gospel, wealth and poverty, rich people and poor people, are an important theme, suggesting that there were both poor and wealthy people in Luke's community. The concerns of the man making the demand on Jesus, as well as the man in the parable, are likely concerns of Luke's audience listening to the account in the Gospel.

Before presenting a parable to the man, Jesus gives a succinct warning: "Take care to guard against all greed (*pleonexia*)"; the word implies insatiableness, avarice, and a restlessness to acquire more. At times *pleonexia* also involves defrauding and cheating. The rich man in the parable is a perfect example of *pleonexia*. Whereas those who are concerned with the things of God bring their questions to God, or search the tradition for insight, the man in the parable asks only himself. Seemingly without need of time for deliberation, he decides to tear down the inadequate barns and build larger ones. Thinking that this will give him many years of security, he is instead shown to be a fool. The treasure he builds for himself leaves him impoverished in what matters to God. E.P.

NINETEENTH SUNDAY IN ORDINARY TIME

LECTIONARY #117

READING I   Wisdom 18:6–9

A reading from the Book of Wisdom

Begin with a tone of gratitude and prayer.

The people, despite their slavery, could rejoice in their knowledge that God would save them.

The single act of passing through the sea saved the Israelites and destroyed their enemies. Speak with a sense of awe and gratitude.

They prepared for their time of deliverance "in secret" by offering sacrifice and waiting in faith.

> The **night** of the **passover** was known **beforehand** to our **fathers**,
>   that, with **sure knowledge** of the **oaths** in which they
>   put their **faith**,
> they might have **courage**.
> Your people **awaited** the **salvation** of the **just**
>   and the **destruction** of their **foes**.
> For when you **punished** our **adversaries**,
>   in this you **glorified** us whom you had **summoned**.
> For in **secret** the **holy children** of the **good**
>   were offering **sacrifice**
> and putting into **effect** with one **accord** the
>   **divine institution**.

For meditation and context:

RESPONSORIAL PSALM   Psalm 33:1, 12, 18–19, 20–22 (12b)

R. Blessed the people the Lord has chosen to be his own.

Exult, you just, in the LORD;
   praise from the upright is fitting.
Blessed the nation whose God is the LORD,
   the people he has chosen for his
      own inheritance.

See, the eyes of the LORD are upon those
      who fear him,
   upon those who hope for his kindness,
to deliver them from death
   and preserve them in spite of famine.

Our soul waits for the LORD,
   who is our help and our shield.
May your kindness, O LORD, be upon us
   who have put our hope in you.

READING I The night of Passover, replete with startling wonders and divine power, is so central to the identity of Israel that it is remembered and reinterpreted throughout Israel's history. In today's reading from Wisdom, a later generation speaks to God about the original Passover event. According to Wisdom, the ancestors were well prepared for Passover since they had known about it ahead of time. They put their faith in God's oaths and God's fidelity to promises as they awaited salvation from their enslavement in Egypt. Wisdom depicts their rescue in sharp contrast to the fate of their Egyptian oppressors, who meet destruction and punishment even as Israel is glorified.

As Israel keeps courageous vigilance for God to act in their favor, they offer sacrifice, a reference to their killing of unblemished lambs, and use the lambs' blood as a sign of protection. The keeping of Passover, including sharing in a meal laden with symbols, praying, and keeping vigil, was a divine institution to be celebrated in obedience to God's command: "all the Israelites must keep a vigil for the Lord throughout their generations" (Exodus 12:42).

Like other Passover reinterpretations, the Wisdom tradition regards people of later generations, including its own audience, to be beneficiaries: "you glorified us whom you had summoned." The descendants, like their forebears, are not only recipients of God's saving acts, but they must also live in faith, act with courage,

READING II   Hebrews 11:1–2, 8–19

A reading from the Letter to the Hebrews

[**Brothers** and **sisters**:
Faith is the **realization** of what is **hoped** for
    and **evidence** of things **not seen**.
Because of it the **ancients** were well **attested**.

By **faith** Abraham **obeyed** when he was **called** to go **out** to a place
    that he was to **receive** as an **inheritance**;
    he **went out**, **not knowing where** he was to go.
By **faith** he sojourned in the **promised** land as
      in a foreign **country**,
    dwelling in **tents** with **Isaac** and **Jacob**,
      heirs of the **same promise**;
    for he was looking **forward** to the city with **foundations**,
    whose **architect** and **maker** is **God**.
By **faith** he received **power** to **generate**,
    even though he was **past** the **normal** age
    —and Sarah **herself** was **sterile**—
    for he thought that the one who had **made** the promise
      was **trustworthy**.
So it was that there came **forth** from **one** man,
    himself as **good** as **dead**,
    descendants as **numerous** as the **stars** in the **sky**
    and as **countless** as the **sands** on the **seashore**.]

All these **died** in **faith**.
They did **not receive** what had been **promised**
    but **saw** it and **greeted** it from **afar**
    and **acknowledged** themselves to be **strangers** and **aliens**
      on **earth**,
    for those who **speak thus show** that they are **seeking**
      a **homeland**. »

Use the greeting to secure everyone's attention, then declare confidently this classic explanation of what faith is.

"Attested" means "commended" or "given approval." Read this line slowly and deliberately.

Stress "by faith" each time it recurs.

Abraham left his home and willingly lived simply to achieve God's will.

"As good as dead" is a colorful exaggeration. Speak it with some playfulness.

They died still holding on to faith despite not having seen its complete fulfillment. Speak with admiration.

TO KEEP IN MIND
Pay attention to the pace of your reading. Varying the pace gives listeners clues to the meaning of the text. The most common problem for proclaimers new to the ministry is going too fast to be understood.

---

keep vigil, and celebrate the divine institution of Passover.

READING II The reading from Hebrews begins with a statement about faith, not as a definition, but as a motivating foundation for people who live by faith. Throughout the reading, including the foundational statement, the word "faith" (*pistis*) has several meanings, as it does throughout the Bible. At times faith means trust, or assurance, signifying a rela-tionship between God and people who put their confidence in God. In both the Hebrew and Greek, "faith" also signifies faithful-ness, an attribute seen both in God's abid-ing faithfulness to the covenant and the expected response of God's people.

These first two meanings center on the relationship between God and individu-als, or between God and the whole people. A third meaning of *pistis* is the content of what is believed; creeds and dogmas are expressions of this kind of faith. Although faith in this sense does not have the same relational emphasis as the first two mean-ings, professions of faith, such as in a creed, arise from the trust people have in the God of revelation, and in God's own fidelity. In the examples of persons of faith in the Hebrew Scriptures, each of these meanings has a place.

The primary example of an Old Testament person of faith in today's read-ing is Abraham, although other examples precede him in Hebrews: Abel, Enoch, and

If they had been **thinking** of the land from which they had **come**,
    they would have had **opportunity** to **return**.
But **now** they desire a **better** homeland, a **heavenly** one.
Therefore, God is **not ashamed** to be called their **God**,
    for he has **prepared** a **city** for them.

By **faith** Abraham, when put to the **test**, offered up **Isaac**,
    and he who had **received** the **promises** was ready
        to **offer** his **only son**,
of whom it was said,
    "Through **Isaac** descendants shall **bear** your **name**."
He reasoned that **God** was able to **raise** even from the **dead**,
    and he received **Isaac back** as a **symbol**.

[Shorter: Hebrews 11:1–2, 8–12 (see brackets)]

GOSPEL   Luke 12:32–48

A reading from the holy Gospel according to Luke

[Jesus said to his **disciples**:]
    "Do not be **afraid** any **longer**, little **flock**,
    for your **Father** is **pleased** to give you the **Kingdom**.
Sell your belongings and give **alms**.
Provide **money** bags for yourselves that do **not** wear **out**,
    an **inexhaustible treasure** in **heaven**
        that no **thief** can reach nor **moth destroy**.
For where your **treasure** is, **there also** will your **heart** be.

["**Gird** your **loins** and **light** your **lamps**
    and be like **servants** who await their master's return
        from a **wedding**,
    ready to open **immediately** when he **comes** and **knocks**.
Blessed are those **servants**
    whom the master finds **vigilant** on his arrival.
Amen, I say to you, he will **gird** himself,
    have them **recline** at **table**, and **proceed** to **wait** on **them**.

Let your voice suggest that you, too, desire that "better homeland."

This is the climactic example of Abraham's exemplary faith. Speak with awareness of how remarkable a demonstration of faith this was.

Abraham's faith was so strong that he trusted God would find a way to undo what he was asked to do. Use ritardando on the final phrase.

The challenging directives that follow are shared in the context of God's unfailing love and the dismissal of fear.

While these are imperatives, the tone should be one of gentle persuasion.

Take a substantial pause after sharing this profound truth.
Renew your energy and deliver these instructions with upbeat vitality.

Blessed = BLES-uhd or blesd

Jesus offers one of his stunning reversals in the image of the master waiting on his own servants.

Noah. The faith of these individuals was a shadowy preview of the fuller faith exhibited by Abraham. The first instance of Abraham's faith is his obedience when God called him out of his own land to go where God led him, though he did not know where he was going. Here, Abraham's faith is an act of trust, for he had to leave all that was known and secure. Only a profound trust could move anyone to take such a leap into the unknown. Abraham also believed the content of God's promise, which became a sort of creed not only for Abraham, but also for later generations. They believed in the promise of land, numerous descendants, and blessing on all families of the earth.

Having left his own country, Abraham continued his journey to the still distant and unknown land, trusting that God would fulfill his promise of land, descendants, and blessing. In the next example of Abraham's faith, he "received the power to generate." At this point, we hear that he thought the one who made the promise was "trustworthy," emphasizing the confident trust dimension of his faith. His confidence was not misplaced, for God began to fulfill the promise, ultimately fulfilled in descendants as numerous as stars of the sky.

The final example of Abraham's faith is one that tested his earlier trust and belief in God's promises. Could Abraham, in faith, offer to God the child of the promise, Isaac? The interpretation of the author of Hebrews is that Abraham reasoned that "God was able to raise even from the dead, and he received Isaac back as a symbol." This enigmatic statement suggests that for Abraham, his son became a sign of hope for future Resurrection. Such a belief is a profound act of trust in God's power.

And should he **come** in the **second** or **third** watch
and find them **prepared** in this way,
blessed are those servants.
Be **sure** of **this**:
if the **master** of the house had **known** the hour
when the **thief** was coming,
he would **not** have let his house be broken **into**.
You also must be prepared, for at an **hour** you do **not expect**,
the **Son** of **Man** will **come**."]

Then **Peter** said,
"**Lord**, is this parable meant for **us** or for **everyone**?"
And the Lord **replied**,
"**Who**, **then**, is the **faithful** and **prudent steward**
whom the **master** will put in **charge** of his **servants**
to distribute the **food allowance** at the **proper time**?
Blessed is that servant whom his **master** on **arrival** finds **doing** so.
Truly, I **say** to you, the **master** will put the servant
in charge of **all** his property.
But if **that servant** says to himself,
'My master is **delayed** in coming,'
and begins to **beat** the menservants and the maidservants,
to **eat** and **drink** and get **drunk**,
then that servant's **master** will **come**
on an **unexpected day** and at an **unknown hour**
and will **punish** the servant **severely**
and assign him a **place** with the **unfaithful**.
That servant who **knew** his master's will
but did **not** make **preparations nor act** in **accord** with his **will**
shall be beaten **severely**;
and the **servant** who was **ignorant** of his master's will
but **acted** in a way **deserving** of a **severe** beating
shall be beaten **only lightly**.
Much will be **required** of the **person entrusted** with much,
and still **more** will be demanded of the person **entrusted**
with **more**."

[Shorter: Luke 12:35–40 (see brackets)]

At every step of Abraham's life, he was faithful to the God who had called him from his own land. Jews and Christians alike see in him a worthy example of faith manifest in trust, faithfulness, and belief in all that God reveals.

GOSPEL In Jesus' teaching to his disciples from the Gospel of Luke, we see how those who follow Jesus are to exhibit some of the same characteristics we saw in the first two readings. The courageous vigilance of the ancestors at the first Passover, and the multifaceted faith of Abraham are expected of Jesus' disciples as well. Similar to Abraham who left home and security to go where God directed him, Jesus' disciples, the "little flock," are to find their treasure not in the security of possessions, but in the Kingdom of God. Along with letting go of unnecessary belongings, they are to share what they have with those in need through the giving of alms.

According to Wisdom, the Israelites at Passover were vigilant as they waited for God to rescue them. Now Jesus' disciples are to be equally ready for the coming of their master. Whether that refers symbolically to the final return of the Lord in glory, perhaps delayed or coming at an unknown hour, or to his presence in their midst any day and every day, those who are well prepared for the master's coming are described as "faithful and prudent." Their faithfulness, like Abraham's, means continuing to follow Jesus' pattern of loving service, no matter the trials and challenges that face them. With prudence, they act as responsible stewards, carefully using their gifts for the needs of all in the household. E.P.

THE ASSUMPTION OF THE BLESSED VIRGIN MARY: VIGIL

LECTIONARY #621

READING I   1 Chronicles 15:3–4, 15–16; 16:1–2

A reading from the first Book of Chronicles

David assembled all **Israel** in **Jerusalem** to bring the **ark** of
     the LORD
  to the place that he had **prepared** for it.
David also called together the sons of **Aaron** and the **Levites**.

The **Levites** bore the ark of God on their **shoulders** with **poles**,
  as **Moses** had **ordained** according to the word of the LORD.

David commanded the **chiefs** of the **Levites**
  to appoint their **kinsmen** as **chanters**,
  to play on musical **instruments**, **harps**, **lyres**, and **cymbals**,
  to make a loud **sound** of **rejoicing**.

They **brought** in the ark of God and set it within the **tent**
  which David had **pitched** for it.
Then they offered up burnt **offerings** and **peace** offerings to God.
When David had **finished** offering up the burnt offerings and
     peace offerings,
  he **blessed** the people in the **name** of the LORD.

Chronicles = KRAH-nih-k*ls

Since the "ark" can be seen as a metaphor for Mary, speak of it with great care and reverence.

David has amassed a large and solemn assembly. The details of the careful handling of the ark are important; don't rush past them.

The joy of the festival is amplified by the presence of singers and musicians. Your tone should suggest the joyful, epic nature of this celebration.

A hushed tone will help you convey the solemn and dramatic nature of this special moment.

"Burnt offerings" required the offering of an entire animal. "peace offerings" required that only the fat be offered on the altar.

Establish eye contact and speak with great dignity of David blessing the people in God's name.

READING I The reading from 1 Chronicles is a narrative description of King David bringing the Ark of the Covenant, also called the Ark of the Lord, to Jerusalem, to "the place that he had prepared for it." Following the reading, the responsorial from Psalm 132 is a complementary poetic version of the procession of the Ark to its dwelling place in the Temple. Both narrative and poetry depict liturgies with priests and Levites attending the sacred object to Jerusalem. The joyful procession involves carrying the Ark on the shoulders of the Levites in obedience to the

instructions in the Torah (Numbers 7:9). As the people accompany the Ark, recaptured from the Philistines, they celebrate with music and sounds of rejoicing. Not only do the people accompany the Ark, but God himself, present in the Ark, is also accompanying the people.

The liturgical celebration highlights the people's belief in the Ark as the place of God's presence among them, the place where God meets his people, and where people seek God's will for them. It is a tangible reminder of God's abiding covenant promise: "I will dwell in the midst of the

Israelites and will be their God" (Exodus 29:44). Because of God's presence, ritual purity was demanded of anyone handling the Ark, thereby requiring both priests and Levites to sanctify themselves.

The ancient liturgies honoring the Ark of the Lord have an echo in the liturgy we celebrate for the solemnity of the Virgin Mary's Assumption. Mary, another dwelling place for God, has long been regarded as an image of the Ark. The feast celebrates her being taken up to the new and heavenly Jerusalem. This understanding was beautifully expressed in the eighth-century com-

For meditation and context:

TO KEEP IN MIND

Pace: The rate at which you read is influenced by the size of your church, the size of the congregation, and the complexity of the text. As each increases, rate decreases.

Corinthians = kohr-IN-thee-uhnz

This text is pure celebration disguised as progressive reasoning. Paul uses logic to celebrate the great truth of Christianity: death, our most fearsome foe, will one day meet its death!
Read carefully, for what we anticipate is not yet here.

Take joy in announcing the ultimate victory of life over death! Increase your intensity from the first to the second question.

First you share the logic: "sting . . . sin"; "power . . . law."
Then, the gratitude that in Christ that formula has been shattered.

RESPONSORIAL PSALM   Psalm 132:6–7, 9–10, 13–14 (8)

R. Lord, go up to the place of your rest, you and the ark of your holiness.

Behold, we heard of it in Ephrathah;
    we found it in the fields of Jaar.
Let us enter into his dwelling,
    let us worship at his footstool.

May your priests be clothed with justice;
    let your faithful ones shout merrily for joy.
For the sake of David your servant,
    reject not the plea of your anointed.

For the LORD has chosen Zion;
    he prefers her for his dwelling.
"Zion is my resting place forever;
    in her will I dwell, for I prefer her."

READING II   1 Corinthians 15:54b–57

A reading from the first Letter of Saint Paul to the Corinthians

Brothers and sisters:
When that which is **mortal** clothes itself with **immortality**,
    then the **word** that is **written** shall come **about**:

> **Death** is swallowed up in **victory**.
> **Where**, O death, is your **victory**?
> **Where**, O death, is your **sting**?

The **sting** of **death** is sin,
    and the **power** of sin is the **law**.
But thanks be to **God** who gives **us** the victory
    through our **Lord** Jesus **Christ**.

ment of Saint John Damascene: "Today, the living and holy ark of the living God, the one whose womb carried her own Creator, rests in the Temple of the Lord."

READING II In chapter 15 of the First Letter to the Corinthians, Paul presents his most extensive theological explanation of the Resurrection. He developed his teaching so fully because some Christians in Corinth were questioning the Resurrection; others in Corinth asked about how people were to be raised, with what kind of body. Following his detailed theological explanation, Paul presents his conclusion in today's reading. He creatively combines biblical references from the prophets Isaiah (25:8) and Hosea (13:14), with the words "death" and "victory" being the catchwords that allow him to combine the two texts. Paul envisions death personified, as did Hosea. Further, he uses the word *victory* in his Hosea reference, although the prophet Hosea himself did not use that word. Like other Jewish interpreters of his era, Paul is thus taking a broad license both in his citation and in his interpretation as he develops a new meaning for the Hebrew Scriptures to fit a new context.

In his lengthy explanations about the fact and meaning of Resurrection in this chapter of 1 Corinthians, Paul is presenting the very core of Christian belief. Paul is strongly affirming that in Christ's Resurrection, Christ's glorious victory is so complete that he conquers sin along with death itself. Paul's final word moves from theology to thanksgiving. The whole community should give thanks to God, because our Lord Jesus Christ gives us the victory over sin and death.

GOSPEL   Luke 11:27–28

A reading from the holy Gospel according to Luke

While **Jesus** was **speaking**,
a **woman** from the **crowd called** out and said to him,
"Blessed is the **womb** that **carried** you
and the **breasts** at which you **nursed**."
He replied,
"**Rather**, **blessed** are those
who **hear** the word of God and **observe** it."

Proclaim the introductory lines as if addressing the large crowd that surrounds Jesus.

Do as the woman did and raise *your* voice.
Blessed / blessed = BLES-uhd or blesd
The woman's voice is full of admiration!

Drop your voice to announce Jesus' response, then speak it with appreciation for the people who submit their wills to God's, among whom, Mary is our best model.

THE 4 STEPS OF *LECTIO DIVINA* OR PRAYERFUL READING

1. *Lectio:* Read a Scripture passage aloud slowly. Notice what phrase captures your attention and be attentive to its meaning. Silent pause.

2. *Meditatio:* Read the passage aloud slowly again, reflecting on the passage, allowing God to speak to you through it. Silent pause.

3. *Oratio:* Read it aloud slowly a third time, allowing it to be your prayer or response to God's gift of insight to you. Silent pause.

4. *Contemplatio:* Read it aloud slowly a fourth time, now resting in God's word.

GOSPEL   As Jesus was making his way to Jerusalem, he cast out a mute demon, an action that led some in the crowd to be amazed, while others accused Jesus of casting out demons by the power of Beelzebul, prince of demons. In a lengthy, well-crafted response, including the image of a Kingdom divided against itself, Jesus silences his critics. Whether impressed by Jesus' casting out of a demon or by his ability to put an end to the controversy, one woman in the crowd shouts out that Jesus' mother is blessed, implying that his mother is to be honored for bearing such a son. The woman is speaking from the wellspring of Jewish tradition in which blessings proclaim God's freely given kindness both to individuals and groups. Jesus himself used such blessings or beatitudes in his teaching, most notably in the Sermon on the Mount.

Responding to the woman's calling out his mother's blessedness, Jesus adds another beatitude: "Blessed are those who hear the word of God and observe it." Not denying that his mother is blessed, Jesus explains the deeper reason that she is a recipient of God's graciousness. His mother has heard the word of God and has kept it. She is, in fact, not only his mother, but also a model for disciples. Like her, all disciples are to listen attentively to God's word and live in obedience to it. The beatitude is meant both for Jesus' mother and for all his disciples. E.P.

THE ASSUMPTION OF THE BLESSED VIRGIN MARY: DAY

LECTIONARY #622

READING I   Revelation 11:19a; 12:1–6a, 10ab

A reading from the Book of Revelation

God's **temple** in heaven was **opened**,
  and the **ark** of his **covenant** could be seen in the temple.

A great **sign** appeared in the sky, a **woman** clothed with the **sun**,
  with the **moon** under her **feet**,
  and on her **head** a **crown** of twelve **stars**.
She was with **child** and **wailed** aloud in **pain** as she labored to
    give **birth**.
Then **another** sign appeared in the sky;
  it was a huge red **dragon**, with seven **heads** and ten **horns**,
  and on its heads were seven **diadems**.
Its **tail** swept away a third of the **stars** in the sky
  and **hurled** them down to the **earth**.
Then the dragon **stood** before the woman about to give birth,
  to **devour** her child when she gave birth.
She gave birth to a **son**, a **male** child,
  destined to **rule** all the nations with an iron **rod**.
Her child was caught up to **God** and his **throne**.
The woman herself **fled** into the **desert**
  where she had a place prepared by **God**. »

You are narrating a vision filled with powerful imagery that requires a grand and solemn tone worthy of the cosmic events described here.

Speak in a positive tone of the "sign," for it refers to the woman chosen by God.
All the symbols are significant, so be sure to stress each one.
That she is pregnant and in childbirth is surprising information; be sure you don't make it sound ordinary or insignificant.
Announce "another sign" with a negative tone, for now you are introducing the archenemy who seeks the lives of the woman and her child.
This is indeed a powerful adversary!

Avoid cheap dramatics, but be sure to convey the destructive horror that threatens mother and child.
Despite the circumstances, convey a sense of peace as you announce the child's birth.

The peace is short-lived; with energy and quickened tempo speak of these efforts to secure safety.

READING I   A woman clothed with the sun, accompanied with moon and stars: the image is stunning and dramatic. But who is this woman? She is given no name, simply referred to as "a woman," who gives birth to a child. Revelation and other apocalyptic writings are filled with multifaceted symbolism open to a variety of interpretations. An important clue as to the woman's identity is the connection that Revelation has with the Gospel of John. The language of this mysterious passage echoes some of the language of John. In John's Gospel, the mother of Jesus is never identified as "Mary," but is twice referred to simply as "woman," both times by Jesus, first at the wedding at Cana and then from the cross. The designation as "woman" in Revelation and her giving birth to a male child who is destined to rule all the nations readily identifies this unnamed woman as the mother of Jesus. Given the multiple symbols possible, the woman has sometimes been understood as an image for Israel or the Church. Mary brings these symbols together; she is the mother of Jesus who, born from Israel, fulfilled Israel's hopes and promises, and she is the mother of the Church, the first disciple, and a symbol of the Church itself.

Whether understood as Israel, the mother of Jesus, or the Church, the woman faces a cosmic conflict. The seven-headed dragon, a fierce and violent beast, is determined to devour the newborn child. The dragon, strong as it is, does not win, for the child is rescued, even caught up to the throne of God, signifying a divine saving action for the child. The woman's fleeing into the desert to the place prepared by

Then I heard a loud **voice** in heaven say:
   "Now have **salvation** and **power** come,
      and the **Kingdom** of our **God**
      and the **authority** of his **Anointed** One."

For meditation and context:

RESPONSORIAL PSALM   Psalm 45:10, 11, 12, 16 (10bc)

R. The queen stands at your right hand, arrayed in gold.

The queen takes her place at your right hand
   in gold of Ophir.

So shall the king desire your beauty;
   for he is your lord.

Hear, O daughter, and see; turn your ear,
   forget your people and your father's house.

They are borne in with gladness and joy;
   they enter the palace of the king.

READING II   1 Corinthians 15:20–27

A reading from the first Letter of Saint Paul to the Corinthians

Corinthians = kohr-IN-thee-uhnz

First, Paul establishes the premise: Christ rose from the dead, the first of many to follow.

Paul utilizes progressive reasoning to make his point. Like a teacher, lead your listeners from one point to the next.

What follows the colon is an explanation of how things must progress in "proper order."

Paul shares a profound, mystical truth. Speak slowly of this weighty subject.

All pretenders to Christ's throne will be "destroyed." Don't shy from making full use of this strong language.

Speak the final line as if you were warning death to be on alert!

Brothers and sisters:
Christ has been **raised** from the **dead**,
   the **firstfruits** of those who have fallen **asleep**.
For since **death** came through **man**,
   the **Resurrection** of the dead came **also** through man.
For just as in **Adam** all **die**,
   so too in **Christ** shall all be brought to **life**,
   but **each** one in proper **order**:
Christ the **firstfruits**;
   then, at his **coming**, those who **belong** to Christ;
   then comes the **end**,
   when he hands over the Kingdom to his God and **Father**,
   when he has **destroyed** every **sovereignty**
   and every **authority** and **power**.
For he must reign until he has put all his **enemies** under his **feet**.
The **last** enemy to be destroyed is **death**,
   for "he subjected **everything** under his feet."

God appears to be a time and place of safety and anticipation.

   Revelation was written in a specific historical context, most probably in the last decade of the first century AD. The Christians were facing persecution under Roman emperors, the dragons of Revelation. Beyond the historical context, the language and symbolism throughout Revelation has a timeless quality about it as it depicts a too-often repeated conflict between good and evil, between God's people and those opposed. Israel, Jesus, and the Church have experienced the sym-

bolic dragons. God's action for the woman and her son reveals that God is more powerful than the dragons that face God's people. The woman, mother of Jesus and mother of the Church, remains as a great sign of God's saving fidelity.

READING II   Paul's exposition to the Corinthians about the Resurrection in today's reading follows his handing on to them the tradition "of first importance" that he had also received. Referred to as the *kerygma*, indicating the earliest proclamation of the good news,

Jesus' death and Resurrection stands as the most fundamental belief of the early Church. Given its central significance, Paul is dismayed that some among the Corinthian community are saying that there is no Resurrection of the dead. When they deny that those who die will not be raised, they are, according to Paul, also denying the Resurrection of Jesus, making Jesus' preaching (*kerygma*) and their faith empty and futile.

   Paul's response to them is twofold: he first reaffirms Christ's own Resurrection, and then explains how his Resurrection is a

GOSPEL   Luke 1:39–56

A reading from the holy Gospel according to Luke

Mary set out
  and traveled to the **hill** country in **haste**
  to a town of **Judah**,
  where she entered the house of **Zechariah**
  and greeted **Elizabeth**.
When Elizabeth **heard** Mary's greeting,
  the infant **leaped** in her **womb**,
  and **Elizabeth**, **filled** with the Holy **Spirit**,
  cried out in a loud voice and said,
  "**Blessed** are you among **women**,
  and blessed is the **fruit** of your **womb**.
And how does this **happen** to me,
  that the mother of my **Lord** should come to me?
For at the moment the **sound** of your greeting reached my **ears**,
  the **infant** in my womb leaped for **joy**.
Blessed are you who **believed**
  that what was **spoken** to you by the Lord
  would be **fulfilled**." »

(margin notes)

You want to create a sense of "haste" without blurring the words or meaning.

Zechariah = zek-uh-RĪ-uh

The role of the Spirit, as in all of Luke's Gospel account, is important here.

Express these familiar lines with joy! Elizabeth speaks with prescience of Mary as "mother of [her] Lord."

Blessed / blessed = BLES-uhd
Elizabeth lauds Mary for her trust in God.

Mary's great *Magnificat* comprises the balance of the text.

---

sign of his solidarity with humanity. When Paul writes of the Resurrection "from the dead," he is referring to more than Christ's Resurrection from death; he is also saying that Christ has risen from among those who have died. In his death, Christ shared the fate of all human beings, for "in Adam all die." Paul goes on to explain that as all die, so too, "in Christ shall all be brought to life." Paul's logic runs: as Christ and the descendants of Adam are together in death, they will also be together in Resurrection. Christ's Passover from death to life is thus not only about his own rescue

from death, but is also the source and pattern for our own.

Christ's Resurrection is the beginning, the "firstfruits" to be followed by the rest of the harvest. As the Risen One, he will put all enemies under his feet, subjecting the last and greatest enemy, death itself. Paul's explanation of the *kerygma* not only corrects the misunderstandings of the Corinthians, but gives them the good news of hope in their own Resurrection. The hope-filled teaching of Resurrection has already found fulfillment in the Blessed Mother, whose Assumption we celebrate today.

GOSPEL   In the opening chapters of his Gospel, Luke the evangelist simultaneously develops portraits of Jesus and of his mother. Today's Gospel is the second scene in which Luke continues his beautiful sketch of Mary. She has traveled "in haste" to a town in Judah because her cousin Elizabeth, long past childbearing age, is in the sixth month of her pregnancy. Mary herself has newly conceived her son by the power of the Holy Spirit. When the two women meet, Elizabeth's greeting adds important elements to Mary's portrait. Mary and her son, "the fruit of her

And Mary said:

> "My **soul** proclaims the **greatness** of the Lord;
>   my spirit **rejoices** in God my **Savior**
>   for he has with **favor** on his lowly servant.
> From this day all generations will call me **blessed**:
>   the Almighty has done **great** things for me
>   and **holy** is his **Name**.
>   He has **mercy** on those who **fear** him
>   in **every** generation.
> He has shown the **strength** of his arm,
>   and has **scattered** the proud in their **conceit**.
> He has cast down the **mighty** from their **thrones**,
>   and has **lifted** up the **lowly**.
> He has filled the **hungry** with **good** things,
>   and the **rich** he has sent away **empty**.
> He has come to the **help** of his servant **Israel**
>   for he has **remembered** his promise of **mercy**,
>   the promise he made to our **fathers**,
>   to **Abraham** and his children for **ever**."

Mary **remained** with her about three **months**
  and then **returned** to her **home**.

These are words of praise and gratitude, so speak them with joy!

Remember, this is a poetic text meant to be sung. Share the images one at a time.

blessed: blesd

Lift out the significant contrasts of "mighty" and "lowly" and "hungry" and "rich."

If you "see" the images and the characters she names you won't rush this beautiful text.

Conclude the Canticle and then pause. The closing narration tells us Mary remained with Elizabeth until the birth of John.

womb," are both called blessed. The blessings are declarations of praise and thanksgiving; mother and son alike are to be praised because of God's presence and kindness within them. Elizabeth's asking how it is that "the mother of my Lord" should come to her is likely an allusion to David's wonder at God's presence in the Ark of the Covenant (2 Samuel 6:9). Mary, like the ark, is the container of God's very presence. Elizabeth proclaims another blessing, this time with another word underlying our English word *blessed*. This is the declaration of beatitude, of God's freely given kindness to Mary. Elizabeth says specifically that her cousin is blessed because she has believed that God's word to her would be fulfilled.

The scene then shifts to Mary's own words. Mary had already identified herself as the Lord's lowly servant (literally a "slave woman") when she gave her absolute yes to the angel's message at the Annunciation. She again speaks of herself as the Lord's lowly servant on whom God has shown great favor. Everything that she proclaims in her joyful poetic prayer is about what God has done in the past, is doing in the present, and will do in the future. Although Luke has been sketching Mary's own portrait, she looks entirely on God, developing one of the richest and loveliest portraits of the God of blessing, kindness, and mercy.
E.P.

TWENTIETH SUNDAY IN ORDINARY TIME

LECTIONARY #120

READING I   Jeremiah 38:4–6, 8–10

A reading from the book of the prophet Jeremiah

In those days, the **princes** said to the **king**:
"**Jeremiah** ought to be put to **death**;
  he is **demoralizing** the **soldiers** who are **left** in this **city**,
  and all the **people**, by **speaking** such things to them;
  he is **not interested** in the **welfare** of our **people**,
  but in their **ruin**."
King **Zedekiah** answered: "**He** is in **your** power";
  for the **king** could do **nothing** with them.
And so they **took Jeremiah**
  and **threw** him into the **cistern** of Prince **Malchiah**,
  which was in the **quarters** of the **guard**,
  letting him down with ropes.
There was **no water** in the **cistern**, only **mud**,
  and **Jeremiah sank** into the **mud**.

Ebed-melech, a court official,
  went there from the **palace** and said to him:
  "**My lord king**,
  these **men** have been at **fault**
  in all they have **done** to the **prophet Jeremiah**,
  casting him into the cistern.
He will **die** of **famine** on the **spot**,
  for there is **no more food** in the **city**." »

Their anger and hostility should be immediately apparent.

Their self-interest persuades them they are doing the right thing.

Zedekiah sounds like Pilate in abdicating responsibility.

Use the details to suggest the horror of being lowered into this sure death trap.

Pause before starting this new beat that brings hope back into the story.

His tone is confident; these are the words of a truly righteous man.

READING I   Jeremiah prophesied in the seventh century BC, when the Babylonian empire was on the rise. At the time of today's prophecy, King Zedekiah reigned in Jerusalem, placed on the throne by Babylon. Zedekiah, however, defied Babylon, leading to a year-and-a-half siege of the holy city. During this time, Jeremiah prophesied, proclaiming a message that enraged the princes who claimed that Jeremiah was demoralizing the soldiers still left in the city. Jeremiah had announced, "This city shall certainly be handed over to the army of the king of Babylon; he shall

capture it." His prophecy conflicted with the military strategies of the princes, who brought their accusations against him to Zedekiah. Fearful and weak, at one moment listening to Jeremiah and at another to the princes, Zedekiah gives in to the princes' demands. He gave them free rein, saying of Jeremiah, "He is in your power." Though the princes had claimed that Jeremiah should be put to death, suggesting an immediate execution, they chose instead to throw him into a muddy cistern, intending to make him a humiliating

spectacle whose prophetic word would be ridiculed.

A foreign court official named Ebed-melech warns Zedekiah that Jeremiah will die of famine if he isn't rescued from the cistern. The king who had approved the violent action against Jeremiah orders Ebed-melech to rescue the prophet before he dies. Zedekiah's instability and weakness reflects the instability and weakness of the nation itself. Standing against the faithlessness of the king, the princes, and the people, Jeremiah, released from the cistern, continues to fulfill the role that

Now, Zedekiah speaks with greater confidence and authority for he knows he's doing the right thing.

Then the **king** ordered **Ebed-melech** the **Cushite**
to take three men along with him,
and **draw** the **prophet Jeremiah** out of the **cistern**
before he should **die**.

For meditation and context:

RESPONSORIAL PSALM   Psalm 40:2, 3, 4, 18 (14b)

R. Lord, come to my aid!

I have waited, waited for the LORD,
  and he stooped toward me.

The LORD heard my cry.
He drew me out of the pit of destruction,
  out of the mud of the swamp;
he set my feet upon a crag;
  he made firm my steps.

And he put a new song into my mouth,
  a hymn to our God.
Many shall look on in awe
  and trust in the LORD.

Though I am afflicted and poor,
  yet the LORD thinks of me.
You are my help and my deliverer;
  O my God, hold not back!

READING II   Hebrews 12:1–4

A reading from the letter to the Hebrews

Pause briefly after the salutation.

If you have statues or stained glass depicting the communion of saints, you might want to throw a glance in that direction as you speak this line.

The key words in these lines are "persevere" and "Jesus."

Stress Jesus' willingness to suffer for us.

"So that you may not grow weary . . ." should be spoken with great sincerity.

A fast delivery will obscure the meaning of the final sentence. Read slowly, with awareness of the great cost of discipleship.

Brothers and **sisters**:
Since we are **surrounded** by so great a **cloud** of **witnesses**,
  let us **rid** ourselves of **every burden** and **sin** that **clings** to us
  and **persevere** in running the **race** that lies **before** us
  while keeping our **eyes fixed** on Jesus,
  the **leader** and **perfecter** of **faith**.
For the **sake** of the **joy** that lay **before** him
  he **endured** the **cross**, **despising** its **shame**,
  and has taken his **seat** at the **right** of the **throne** of **God**.
Consider how he **endured** such **opposition** from **sinners**,
  in order that you may not **grow weary** and **lose heart**.
In **your struggle** against **sin**
  you have not yet **resisted** to the **point** of **shedding blood**.

God had given him: "To root up and to tear down, to destroy and to demolish, to build and to plant."

READING II After the review of people of faith from the Jewish tradition, the author of Hebrews moves from the past to the present. "A great cloud of witnesses" including both the ancestors and more recent people of faith surround us today. We can envision a crowd watching and encouraging us, pictured as athletes running a race. The witnesses are able to give sound advice because they have com-

pleted the race themselves. They know it is necessary for runners to rid themselves of any burden that would encumber their movement forward. The greatest burden that weighs on us is sin, making running arduous and painful. We must rid ourselves of the weight of sin, casting it off like clothing that clings to us and prevents us from running. The surest way to reach what lies before us is to keep our eyes on the ultimate goal, Jesus himself.

Having completed the race, Jesus is the perfect model of faith and endurance. Though he was not burdened by sin, he

took upon himself the burden of the cross. He knew the joy that awaited him at the completion of the race. Sinless himself, he endured the opposition of those who were sinners. In his faithful perseverance, Jesus was leader and model for all of us who run the race, so that we may not grow weary or lose heart. Many of those witnesses, as well as Jesus himself, persevered to the point of shedding blood. Though we have not witnessed so completely, the fidelity of those who have gone before us reminds us to keep our eyes fixed on Jesus, no matter the cost.

GOSPEL   Luke 12:49–53

A reading from the holy Gospel according to Luke

Jesus said to his **disciples**:
  "I have **come** to set the **earth** on **fire**,
    and how I **wish** it were **already blazing**!
There is a **baptism** with which I **must** be **baptized**,
    and how **great** is my **anguish** until it is **accomplished**!
Do you **think** that I have **come** to establish **peace** on the **earth**?
No, I tell you, but rather **division**.
From now **on** a **household** of **five** will be **divided**,
    three against **two** and **two** against **three**;
    a **father** will be **divided** against his **son**
    and a **son** against his **father**,
    a **mother** against her **daughter**
    and a **daughter** against her **mother**,
    a **mother-in-law** against her **daughter-in-law**
    and a **daughter-in-law** against her **mother-in-law**."

Pause after the introduction and speak with authority.

He longs for the fire to blaze because it is a purifying fire.
He is referring to his own death.

It would be naive to think so!

Speak with regret as you list the relationships that will be marred by dissension and division. The list is intentionally somewhat exhaustive to convince us no relationships are exempt from the possibility of division.

GOSPEL   Fire is a multifaceted symbol in both the Jewish and Christian traditions, an apt image for the wide range of fiery experiences, sometimes warm and comforting and other times frightening and destructive. A pillar of fire symbolized the divine presence that accompanied Israel through the desert, but another kind of fire was envisioned when Israel worshiped the golden calf, and the Lord warned that "my wrath may burn hot against them and I may consume them." Fire is a biblical image for purification and judgment, as well as of the Holy Spirit who descended in the form of fiery tongues. When Jesus says that he came to cast fire upon the earth, more than one symbolic meaning may be inferred. He may be longing for the fire of the Holy Spirit to be ignited in his disciples and also be longing for the fires that refine and purify the people.

Along with wishing that the fire he came to bring were already blazing, Jesus is also in anguish that his baptism be accomplished. While we most often think of water baptism, the basic meaning of baptism is to be immersed, or to be plunged deeply into something. The baptism that Jesus anticipates is the immersion into his passion and death. His passing from death to life will set the fire blazing, the fire that purifies and separates and destroys. Jesus is speaking here to his disciples, warning them of the consequences of following him, and challenging them to choose what kind of fire they will experience. E.P.

TWENTY-FIRST SUNDAY IN ORDINARY TIME

LECTIONARY #123

READING I   Isaiah 66:18–21

Isaiah = Ī-ZAY-uh

Immediately, the tone is lofty and authoritative but with underlying tenderness and comfort.

Speak of the "sign" as something truly rare and unexpected!

Tarshish = TAHR-shish
Put = POOT
Lud = LUHD
Tubal = TOO-buhl
Javan = JAY-vuhn

You are not describing an ordinary event, but something marvelous and undreamed of: foreigners going to extraordinary lengths to return Jewish refugees to their homeland.

The return of scattered Israelites will be an offering of worship to God.

This news is remarkable. Announce it with joy and wonder.

A reading from the Book of the Prophet Isaiah

Thus says the LORD:
I know their **works** and their **thoughts**,
and I **come** to gather **nations** of **every language**;
   they shall **come** and **see** my **glory**.
I will set a **sign** among them;
   from **them** I will send **fugitives** to the **nations**:
   to **Tarshish**, **Put** and **Lud**, **Mosoch**, **Tubal** and **Javan**,
   to the **distant coastlands**
   that have never **heard** of my **fame**, or **seen** my **glory**;
   and they shall **proclaim** my **glory** among the **nations**.
They shall bring **all** your **brothers** and **sisters** from all the **nations**
   as an **offering** to the LORD,
   on **horses** and in **chariots**, in **carts**, upon **mules**
      and **dromedaries**,
   to **Jerusalem**, my **holy mountain**, says the **Lord**,
   just as the **Israelites** bring **their offering**
   to the **house** of the LORD in **clean vessels**.
Some of these I will take as **priests** and **Levites**, says the LORD.

READING I   The first reading, from the last chapter of Isaiah, presents a final prophecy depicting a grand transformation extended to all the nations. One startling revelation about the coming newness is the role given to all the nations. The nations (*goyim*) are peoples, Gentiles, who are not of the tribes and family of Israel. The Lord will gather Gentiles of every language, and "they will see my glory," the divine, weighty splendor and majesty made manifest. As the prophecy continues, the Lord affirms that up until now the nations have "not seen my glory." In the future,

however, God's glory will be proclaimed among them, reaching distant peoples who have never heard of God's fame, nor had any experience of God's glory.

God gives the nations the role of bringing back to Jerusalem "all your brothers and sisters" from the lands where they have been scattered. The vision is of a vast array of God's people, coming on every form of transport, suggesting a scene of women and men, and of the wealthy and the poor. Not only will the Gentiles bring back the dispersed people of Israel, but they will also present them as an offering

to the Lord. The Israelites themselves will bring the usual offering of grains, perhaps in the form of bread and cakes, while the foreign nations will bring the people of Israel themselves as an offering to God. An essential purpose of the gathering of Israel and the nations is thus for worship. The final verse, though ambiguous, seems to describe an extraordinary transformation. From the Gentile nations, God will make priests and Levites, giving them a cultic role ordinarily reserved for families of Israel.

For meditation and context:

RESPONSORIAL PSALM   Psalm 117:1, 2 (Mark 16:15)

R. Go out to all the world and tell the Good News.
or R. Alleluia.

Praise the LORD, all you nations;
    glorify him, all you peoples!

For steadfast is his kindness toward us,
    and the fidelity of the LORD endures
        forever.

READING II   Hebrews 12:5–7, 11–13

A reading from the Letter to the Hebrews

This text is meant to rouse and encourage. Be sure your tone communicates that.

Brothers and **sisters**,
You have **forgotten** the **exhortation** addressed to you as **children**:
"My **son**, do not **disdain** the **discipline** of the **Lord**
    or lose **heart** when **reproved** by him;
    for whom the **Lord loves**, he **disciplines**;
        he **scourges** every **son** he **acknowledges**."
Endure your **trials** as "**discipline**";
    God treats you as **sons**.
For what "**son**" is there whom his **father** does **not discipline**?
At the time,
    all discipline seems a **cause** not for **joy** but for **pain**,
    yet **later** it brings the **peaceful fruit** of **righteousness**
    to those who are **trained** by it.

So **strengthen** your **drooping hands** and your **weak knees**.
Make **straight paths** for your **feet**,
    that what is **lame** may **not** be **disjointed** but **healed**.

Imagine a grandparent speaking to a teenager who thinks his or her parents are too strict. Helps the teen see things from the other side.

This is an appeal to common sense. Speak with conviction.

Adopt a slower pace here to explain that time lends perspective.

Make eye contact and encourage, like a coach at halftime.

He's saying: "Walk the straight and narrow so that the joints already bruised will heal rather than break!" Again, you're trying to encourage.

 The reading from Hebrews begins with a sharp reprimand to the sons (today we would include daughters as well), saying that they have forgotten the exhortation addressed to them as children. The exhortation combines a wisdom teaching from the Book of Proverbs (3:11) with Moses' instruction found in Deuteronomy (8:5), followed by the advice that believers should endure their trials as discipline. The word that connects the three segments of the exhortation is "discipline." The underlying Greek word is *paideia*, a term that refers to the rearing and education of a child that includes instruction in every sphere: intellectual, religious, social, and physical. The *paideia* that aims to bring the child to maturity must include chastening and correcting, and sometimes punishment for misdeeds, as a parent would do to a beloved child.

The audience members of Hebrews are supposed to consider themselves as the adult children of the Lord. In the midst of whatever suffering or trials they are undergoing, they are to look to the Lord as the parent who is disciplining them. The training that God employs is a strong verb, *gymnazo*, suggesting the vigorous exercise that people perform in the gymnasium. Those being trained must strengthen their hands, knees, and feet, bringing the person to healing and wholeness. The Lord's discipline and training, though it may be painful in the present, is so that the mature person will exhibit the peaceful fruit of righteousness.

GOSPEL While Jesus is making his way to Jerusalem, an unnamed person asks if only a few people can be saved. Though the question is framed broadly, seeming to ask about other

GOSPEL   Luke 13:22–30

A reading from the holy Gospel according to Luke

Jesus passed through **towns** and **villages**,
　　teaching as he went and **making** his **way** to **Jerusalem**.
Someone **asked** him,
　　"**Lord**, will **only** a **few people** be **saved**?"
He **answered** them,
"**Strive** to **enter** through the **narrow** gate,
　　for **many**, I tell you, will **attempt** to **enter**
　　but will not be **strong** enough.
After the **master** of the **house** has **arisen** and **locked** the door,
　　then will you stand **outside knocking** and **saying**,
　　'**Lord**, **open** the **door** for us.'
He will **say** to you in **reply**,
　　'I do **not know where** you are **from**.'
And **you** will **say**,
　　'We **ate** and **drank** in your **company** and you **taught**
　　　in our **streets**.'
Then **he** will **say** to you,
　　'I do **not know where** you are **from**.
Depart from me, **all** you **evildoers**!'
And there will be **wailing** and **grinding** of **teeth**
　　when you see **Abraham**, **Isaac**, **and Jacob**
　　and **all** the **prophets** in the **Kingdom of God**
　　and **you yourselves** cast **out**.
And people will come from the **east** and the **west**
　　and from the **north** and the **south**
　　and will **recline** at **table** in the **Kingdom** of **God**.
For **behold**, some are **last** who will be **first**,
　　and some are **first** who will be **last**."

The opening narration should convey Jesus' great concern for the people.

This question is not dispassionate.
Rather than responding with bad news, Jesus' reply offers the way that leads to salvation.

This is one of Jesus' "hard sayings." There is no way to lessen the difficult teaching conveyed here. To do so would be a disservice to your assembly.

This reply will be repeated; keep it grave each time. It has the weight of saying, "I don't know who you are."

Though the parable suggests the choice is God's, we know it is we who say no, not God.

This is a dire image of exclusion from the banquet. Its stark imagery is intentional!

Those coming from the four winds are the Gentiles who precede those first invited.

---

people, Jesus' answer is personal: "you" must strive to enter through the narrow gate. The verb could be translated "keep on striving," because entering through the narrow gate will entail a lifelong effort, like that of an athlete who must keep up the effort to win the prize. The narrow gate, like the eye of the needle too small for the camel to pass through, highlights the difficulty of responding wholeheartedly to Christ and the demands of discipleship.

The master of the house, understood to be Jesus himself, has arisen (the verb *arisen*, *egeiro*, is used for Resurrection) and

locked the door, suggesting the final judgment. At that time, there will be no further opportunity to ask for entrance. Nearness to Jesus, being close enough to eat and drink in his company and to hear his teaching, does not ensure admittance through the narrow gate. Proximity, whether based on physical accompaniment, or the nearness of blood ties or religious affiliation, is not necessarily a sign of a faithful relationship. Indeed, though some people seem to be close to Jesus, he will say to them, "I do not know where you are from." In contrast, many who are far off have in fact responded

more fully than those who seem to be near to Jesus.

The final saying reverses the expected status of the first and the last, of those who are close by tradition and practice and those who are far. The ones from afar have become first, and will recline at table in the heavenly feast. E.P.

TWENTY-SECOND SUNDAY IN ORDINARY TIME

READING I   Sirach 3:17–18, 20, 28–29

A reading from the Book of Sirach

My **child**, conduct your affairs with **humility**,
   and you will be **loved more** than a **giver** of **gifts**.
Humble yourself the **more**, the **greater** you **are**,
   and you will find **favor** with **God**.
What is **too sublime** for you, **seek not**,
   into **things** beyond your **strength search not**.
The **mind** of a **sage** appreciates **proverbs**,
   and an **attentive ear** is the **joy** of the **wise**.
Water quenches a **flaming fire**,
   and **alms atone** for **sins**.

RESPONSORIAL PSALM   Psalm 68:4–5, 6–7, 10–11 (see 11b)

R. God, in your goodness, you have made a home for the poor.

The just rejoice and exult before God;
   they are glad and rejoice.
Sing to God, chant praise to his name;
   whose name is the LORD.

The father of orphans and the defender
      of widows
   is God in his holy dwelling.
God gives a home to the forsaken;
   he leads forth prisoners to prosperity.

A bountiful rain you showered down, O God,
      upon your inheritance;
   you restored the land when it languished;
your flock settled in it;
   in your goodness, O God, you provided it
      for the needy.

Sirach = SEER-ak

The salutation should set your tone!

These first two sentences give commands: "conduct . . . humble yourself"! The goal is to persuade.

Maintain a slow pace and serene tone throughout. After each pair of lines, pause and breathe to renew your energy and then share the new idea.

Pause and sustain eye contact before announcing, "The word of the Lord."

For meditation and context:

TO KEEP IN MIND

A *didactic* text makes a point or teaches something. Help your assembly to follow the argument and understand what's being taught.

READING I   The Book of Sirach opens with a statement that underlies all of the instruction, advice, and proverbs in the book: "All wisdom comes from the Lord." Whether it is a contrast between wise and foolish behavior or practical suggestions such as how to choose friends, all wisdom comes from the Lord. Today's reading is presented as counsel given by a teacher to an adult student, addressed as "my child." The teacher is Jesus Ben Sira, who lived in the late third and early second century BC. Ben Sira himself sought wisdom through prayer and study, and imparted it to his students both verbally and in writing.

Throughout his instruction, Ben Sira advises his students to cultivate virtues, developing life-long habits essential to living wisely. The virtue promoted in today's reading is humility. Sirach encourages humility first because a humble person will be loved more than a giver of gifts, a motive that appears more self-centered than virtuous. More important than the love given by human persons is the favor found with God.

Rather than seeking things too sublime or beyond one's strength, the humble person listens to the wisdom transmitted through proverbs, and finds joy in wise teaching. (Perhaps Sirach is encouraging his students to be attentive to his own instruction!) Wisdom is more than intellectual pursuit, but must be manifest in one's way of life. The final verse today states that giving of alms will serve as atonement for sin. Both humility and almsgiving draw the wise person into right relationship with the Lord.

READING II   Hebrews 12:18–19, 22–24a

A reading from the Letter to the Hebrews

Brothers and **sisters:**
You have **not** approached that which could be **touched**
    and a **blazing fire** and **gloomy darkness**
    and **storm** and a **trumpet** blast
    and a **voice speaking words** such that **those** who **heard**
    begged that **no message** be further **addressed** to them.
No, you have **approached Mount Zion**
    and the **city** of the **living God**, the **heavenly Jerusalem**,
    and countless **angels** in festal **gathering**,
    and the **assembly** of the **firstborn enrolled** in **heaven**,
    and **God** the **judge** of **all**,
    and the **spirits** of the **just** made **perfect**,
    and **Jesus**, the **mediator** of a new **covenant**,
    and the **sprinkled blood** that speaks more **eloquently**
        than that of **Abel**.

Pause after the salutation, then, as if with a shake of the head, speak of those things that are not *part of our experience in Christ. Your tone says, "Yes these were fearful things, but they don't exist any longer!"*

God's voice was so terrifying that the people wanted to shut it out!

Your tone should communicate the very different climate of the new covenant.

Name each segment of the citizenry of the new Jerusalem with pride and delight. Each is more assurance of the safety and goodness of this Holy City.

GOSPEL   Luke 14:1, 7–14

A reading from the holy Gospel according to Luke

On a **sabbath Jesus** went to **dine**
    at the home of one of the leading **Pharisees**,
    and the **people** there were **observing** him **carefully**.

He told a **parable** to those who had been **invited**,
    noticing how they were choosing the **places** of **honor**
        at the **table**.
"When you are **invited** by someone to a **wedding banquet**,
    do not **recline** at table in the **place** of **honor**.

Slow your pace at the end of the first sentence to draw attention to the watching eyes of the Pharisees.

Don't assume a judgmental tone here.

To hold their attention, Jesus' tone would need to avoid harshness and remain upbeat. The lesson will be clearer if the tone is not judgmental.

READING II The reading from Hebrews depicts two vivid and varied scenes embracing the past and present, earth and heaven, human and divine, with dramatic sights and sounds, and emotions ranging from dread to festivity. The first part of the reading reminds the audience of an event long past that took place on Mount Sinai, the place where God made covenant with Israel. There God's presence was experienced in the vision of fire, in darkness and storm, and in the sound of a trumpet blast and a voice so fearful that the audience begged not to hear any fur-

ther message. The people did not approach the awesome God of Mount Sinai, and they pleaded with Moses, "Let not God speak to us, or we shall die" (Exodus 20:19).

But now, says the author of Hebrews, you have approached another mountain, Mount Zion, which is both an earthly and a heavenly dwelling of the living God. The fear and inability to approach the awesome God of Sinai is transformed into a festal gathering and approachability of Mount Zion. Moses was the mediator at Sinai, and now Jesus is the mediator of the new covenant. Some of the faithful, "the firstborn

enrolled in heaven," along with "the spirits of the just" have already transcended the earthly Zion in Jerusalem to the heavenly, eternal Zion. Accompanying these faithful people are countless angels, heavenly beings who were thought to be hovering over Mount Zion.

One of the ways that the Letter to the Hebrews portrays Jesus is as the great high priest. Jesus has offered his own blood in an offering much more eloquent and effective than the offering of Abel. The people are all able to draw near in joy and confi-

The host would find this awkward, to say the least.

Jesus' tone says, "Here is a better way!"

Take time with this important saying.

Now Jesus is in full teacher mode. His concern is for the neglected poor, but also for the rich who need to learn this lesson in order to rise with the "righteous."

blessed = blesd

Offer this assurance with great conviction.

A more **distinguished** guest than you may have been
    invited by him,
and the **host** who invited **both** of you may **approach you**
    and **say**,
'**Give** your **place** to **this man**,'
and then you would **proceed** with **embarrassment**
to take the **lowest** place.
Rather, when you are **invited**,
    go and **take** the **lowest place**
so that when the **host comes** to **you** he may say,
'My **friend**, **move up** to a **higher** position.'
Then you will **enjoy** the **esteem** of your **companions** at the **table**.
For **every one** who **exalts** himself will be **humbled**,
    but the one who **humbles** himself will be **exalted**."
Then he **said** to the **host** who **invited** him,
    "When you hold a **lunch** or a **dinner**,
do **not** invite your **friends** or your **brothers**
or your **relatives** or your **wealthy neighbors**,
in case they may **invite** you **back** and you have **repayment**.
Rather, when you hold a **banquet**,
    invite the **poor**, the **crippled**, the **lame**, the **blind**;
    blessed indeed will you be because of **their inability**
        to **repay you**.
For **you** will be repaid at the **Resurrection** of the **righteous**."

dence to the dwelling place of such a mediator and high priest.

GOSPEL In the Gospel according to Luke, events that take place in the context of a meal are opportunities for Jesus to teach all gathered at table. The meal in today's Gospel is a Sabbath dinner at the home of a prominent Pharisee. While the guests are carefully watching Jesus, he is also observing them, noticing how they are choosing for themselves the places of honor. Jesus has seen similar status seeking before: "You love the

best seat in the synagogues and salutations in the market place" (11:43).

In the first century, the concept of honor was highly valued. Taking a place of honor showed everyone how important, how highly respected, a person was. Honor and pride were high values, while shame and humility were to be avoided. Jesus turns the common perception around. By exercising humility, a person will ultimately be honored by being offered a higher place. Jesus' saying, "The one who humbles himself will be exalted," is about much more than places at table, but describes a whole

way of life: humility before God and one another.

Having addressed the assembled guests, Jesus then gives advice to the host. Rather than inviting wealthy friends and people who can give in return, the host should invite the poor and those who have no ability to pay him back. Jesus again turns around the values of the culture. Make those who have no honor according to accepted standards become the honored guests. Such action will earn more than dinner invitations, for the repayment will be at the final Resurrection. E.P.

TWENTY-THIRD SUNDAY IN ORDINARY TIME

LECTIONARY #129

READING I   Wisdom 9:13–18b

A reading from the Book of Wisdom

Who can **know** God's **counsel**,
  or who can **conceive** what the LORD **intends**?
For the **deliberations** of **mortals** are **timid**,
  and **unsure** are our **plans**.
For the **corruptible body burdens** the **soul**
  and the **earthen shelter** weighs down the **mind**
    that has **many concerns**.
And **scarce** do we **guess** the things on **earth**,
  and what is within our **grasp** we find with **difficulty**;
  but when **things** are in **heaven**, **who** can **search** them out?
Or **who** ever **knew** your **counsel**, except **you** had given **wisdom**
  and **sent** your **holy spirit** from on **high**?
And **thus** were the **paths** of those on **earth** made **straight**.

Since these questions will be out of context and unexpected, pause between them to let your listeners ponder.

Don't sound harsh; this is a reflection on the human condition, not a condemnation.

The text is saying that our humanity is limited in its ability to grasp the greater truths.

Express both joy and gratitude that God has given us at least a degree of understanding.

End on a note of humble gratitude.

READING I   The Book of Wisdom, though written by an unknown author, presents its teachings as if the wise king Solomon is speaking. Today's reading is from the prayer of Solomon in which he asks God, "Give me wisdom." He requests further that wisdom "may be with me and work with me, that I may know what is your pleasure." According to Solomon, wisdom knows and understands all things and will guide him and make his deeds acceptable. Having extolled wisdom, Solomon questions in the opening verse today, "Who can know God's coun-

sel?" While wisdom knows all things, human deliberations, including Solomon's own, are timid, resulting in unsure plans. Our bodies burden our souls, and weigh down our minds. Because of such burden and weight, we must guess about things on earth, and can grasp them only with difficulty. Since even things of earth cannot be comprehended by human effort alone, things of heaven are clearly beyond our grasp.

After Solomon's probing questions and musing, in which he seems downcast by the limitations of mere mortals, he again addresses God directly. The question in

which he asks who could know divine counsel contains an implicit answer: only those to whom God has given wisdom through the holy spirit sent from on high will know God's counsel. The holy spirit, though not yet understood as the Holy Spirit of Christian tradition, is at least a foreshadowing. The spirit is a source of wisdom, and guides the wise on their life's paths. The final sentence in today's reading is followed by an even greater affirmation of wisdom's power: "Men learned what was your pleasure and were saved by Wisdom."

For meditation and context:

RESPONSORIAL PSALM   Psalm 90:3–4, 5–6, 12–13, 14, 17 (1)

R. In every age, O Lord, you have been our refuge.

You turn man back to dust,
   saying, "Return, O children of men."
For a thousand years in your sight
   are as yesterday, now that it is past,
   or as a watch of the night.

You make an end of them in their sleep;
   the next morning they are like the
     changing grass,
which at dawn springs up anew,
   but by evening wilts and fades.

Teach us to number our days aright,
   that we may gain wisdom of heart.
Return, O Lord! How long?
   Have pity on your servants!

Fill us at daybreak with your kindness,
   that we may shout for joy and gladness all
    our days.
And may the gracious care of the Lord our
   God be ours;
   prosper the work of our hands for us!
   Prosper the work of our hands!

READING II   Philemon 9–10, 12–17

A reading from the Letter of Saint Paul to Philemon

I, **Paul**, an **old** man,
   and now also a **prisoner** for **Christ Jesus**,
   urge you on behalf of my **child Onesimus**,
   whose **father** I have **become** in my **imprisonment**;
   I am **sending him**, that is, my own **heart**, **back** to you.
I should have **liked** to **retain** him for **myself**,
   so that he might **serve** me on your **behalf**
   in my **imprisonment** for the **gospel**,
   but I did not want to do **anything** without your **consent**,
   so that the **good** you **do** might not be **forced** but **voluntary**.
Perhaps **this** is why he was **away** from you for a while,
   that you might have him **back forever**,
   no longer as a **slave**
   but **more** than a **slave**, **a brother**,
   beloved especially to **me**, but even **more** so to **you**,
   as a **man** and in the **Lord**.
So **if you** regard **me** as a **partner**, **welcome him** as you would **me**.

Philemon = fi-LEE-muhn

Paul does not refrain from using every persuasive angle: I am *old* and a *prisoner*.
Onesimus = oh-NES-uh-muhs

Stress Paul's designation of Onesimus as his "child."

Paul continues to pour it on: Onesimus is his very "*heart*"!

He's saying, I overcame my own desires in order to do the right thing (suggesting, perhaps, that Philemon now also do the right thing).

Paul grows more serious and philosophical here. Slow your pace.

Onesimus' conversion should impact Philemon even more than Paul.

beloved = bee-LUHVD

Paul clinches his argument with an appeal to Philemon's esteem for their relationship.

READING II   While Paul was in prison, a runaway slave named Onesimus came to Paul in his imprisonment. Since running away from his master makes Onesimus subject to severe punishment, Paul writes to his master, Philemon, on Onesimus' behalf. Even though the letter is brief, the shortest of biblical books, it is filled with emotion and clever strategies to convince Philemon to do as Paul asks.

To begin with, Paul stresses his relationship with Onesimus, writing of him as "my child" and "my own heart." Paul may have baptized Onesimus, or at least have been closely involved in his conversion to Christ. With such a close relationship founded on their shared faith, Paul is subtly urging Philemon to see Onesimus as Paul sees him: as a beloved brother. In addition, by telling Philemon that he wants him to act voluntarily, Paul is reminding Philemon of the respect and authority that Paul wields. Both as an old man and as a prisoner suffering for the sake of the Gospel, Paul's word should carry weight.

Paul does not specify exactly what it means to take Onesimus back as a brother. When he writes "no longer as a slave," Paul may not be advocating the legal release of Onesimus, but he certainly is pointing to the new relationship he will have with Philemon and the church that meets in his house. Philemon should welcome Onesimus just as he would have welcomed Paul. Writing of the kind of welcome that Paul would expect, he tells Philemon at the conclusion of the letter to prepare a guest room for him. If Paul actually visits Philemon's house, he will see for himself how Onesimus has been welcomed.

GOSPEL   Luke 14:25–33

A reading from the holy Gospel according to Luke

Great **crowds** were traveling with **Jesus**,
    and he **turned** and **addressed** them,
        "If **anyone** comes to me without **hating** his **father** and **mother**,
        wife and **children**, **brothers** and **sisters**,
        and even his **own life**,
        he **cannot** be my **disciple**.
Whoever does **not** carry his **own cross** and **come after me**
        cannot be my **disciple**.
Which of you **wishing** to construct a **tower**
    does not **first** sit down and **calculate** the **cost**
    to see if there is **enough** for its **completion**?
Otherwise, after laying the **foundation**
    and finding himself **unable** to **finish** the **work**
    the onlookers should **laugh** at him and **say**,
        '**This** one **began** to **build** but did not have the **resources**
            to **finish**.'
Or what **king marching** into **battle** would not **first sit down**
    and **decide** whether with **ten** thousand troops
    he can **successfully** oppose **another king**
    advancing upon him with **twenty** thousand troops?
But if **not**, while he is **still** far **away**,
    he will **send** a **delegation** to ask for **peace** terms.
In the **same way**,
    anyone of you who **does not renounce all** his **possessions**
    cannot be my **disciple**."

Lift your voice to suggest his address to the large crowd.

Notice, it's not only family, but even ourselves we must be willing to renounce.

The urgent energy lessens for this section.

Offer the second example, "Or what king . . ." immediately, without taking a pause.

Contrast "*ten*" and "*twenty*" thousand.

Pause here before declaring, with sustained eye contact, the final admonition.

GOSPEL   As Jesus makes his way to Jerusalem, great crowds are traveling with him. In addition to Jesus' disciples, the multitude most likely included those who were simply curious, the sick who were eager for healing, and opponents listening in the hope of accusing him. Whatever their motives, Jesus explains clearly the cost of following him as a disciple. The first requirement, to hate one's family members, seems extreme and contrary to Jesus' teaching about love. However, Jesus is using a Semitic idiom, meaning that disciples should show an absolute, unwavering preference for Jesus above all others. The parallel passage in Matthew's Gospel expresses it, "Whoever loves father or mother more than me is not worthy of me" (11:37).

The second requirement of discipleship is to carry one's cross and come after Jesus. No one will be able to take up a cross without being prepared to do so. The parables of a person constructing a tower and a king marching into battle stresses the necessity of being equipped to bring the project to completion. Only those who prefer Jesus above all others will be prepared to endure the suffering that discipleship demands.

The third condition of discipleship, renunciation of possessions, completes the requirement of devoted preference a disciple must have for Jesus. A disciple chooses Jesus over human relationships, the possessions of material goods, or positions of honor and power. E.P.

TWENTY-FOURTH SUNDAY IN ORDINARY TIME

LECTIONARY #132

READING I   Exodus 32:7–11, 13–14

A reading from the Book of Exodus

The LORD said to Moses,
"Go down at **once** to your **people**,
    whom you brought **out** of the land of **Egypt**,
    for they have become **depraved**.
They have soon turned **aside** from the way I pointed **out**
        to them,
    making for themselves a **molten calf** and **worshiping** it,
    sacrificing to it and crying out,
    '**This** is your God, O **Israel**,
    who brought you **out** of the land of **Egypt**!'
I see how **stiff-necked** this people is," continued the Lord
        to Moses
"Let me **alone**, then,
    that my **wrath** may blaze up **against** them to **consume** them.
Then I will make of you a **great nation**."

But Moses **implored** the LORD, his God, saying,
"**Why**, O LORD, should your **wrath** blaze up
        against your **own people**,
    whom **you** brought out of the land of Egypt
    with such **great power** and with so **strong** a **hand**?
Remember your **servants Abraham**, **Isaac**, and **Israel**,
    and how you **swore** to them by your **own self**, saying, **»**

Note that God and Moses will take turns, like exasperated parents, labeling the Israelites "*your* people."
Stress that it is the Lord who speaks.

Don't hold back expressing God's anger and frustration.

God's disappointment is over their repeated infidelity and for mistaking a human object for the eternal God.

Rather than rage, these words can sound like an angry person hoping to be "held back" from taking retribution.

Moses' voice should be a blend of humility and confidence in God's merciful love.

Recall the patriarchs with tenderness and repeat God's promise with the assurance with which God first pronounced it.

READING I The episode of the Israelites making a molten calf that they worship in the desert is the context for one of the most engaging dialogues in the Bible. It begins with the Lord telling Moses, "Go down to your people whom you brought out of Egypt." Yet earlier, when speaking to Moses at Mount Horeb, the Lord had looked with compassion on the enslaved Israelites, repeatedly referring to them as "my" people: "I will send you to Pharaoh to lead my people out of Egypt" (Exodus 3:10). But now, because of Israel's idolatry, the Lord no longer identifies them as "my people"; they now belong to Moses. The Lord's plan is for the divine wrath to blaze up against Israel to consume them. Then the Lord will make of Moses a great nation, seeming to reverse God's ancient promise to Abraham, now transferred to Moses.

After such a rejection of the people by the Lord, it is Moses' turn to speak. At Mount Horeb, in their first meeting, Moses had not hesitated to argue, trying to make the Lord choose someone else to lead the people. Now he shows the same determination and boldness in speaking to God, asking why the Lord should show wrath against "your own people, whom you brought out of the land of Egypt." Moses is saying that the people still belong to the Lord. They are your people, not mine! Moses also reminds the Lord of the promise to Abraham, that he would have numerous descendants. Moses is arguing that the original promise to Abraham should not now be given to Moses, but that the Lord should remain faithful to the divine word.

Moses' plea to the Lord is both audacious and unselfish. The Lord listened to such an impassioned speech and turned

'I will make your **descendants** as **numerous** as the **stars**
  in the **sky**;
and **all** this **land** that I **promised**,
  I will **give** your **descendants** as their **perpetual heritage**.'"
So the LORD **relented** in the **punishment**
  he had **threatened** to **inflict** on his **people**.

Take a substantial pause before announcing God's change of heart.

For meditation and context:

RESPONSORIAL PSALM   Psalm 51:3–4, 12–13, 17, 19 (Luke 15:18)

R. I will rise and go to my father.

Have mercy on me, O God, in your goodness;
  in the greatness of your compassion wipe
    out my offense.
Thoroughly wash me from my guilt
  and of my sin cleanse me.

A clean heart create for me, O God,
  and a steadfast spirit renew within me.
Cast me not out from your presence,
  and your Holy Spirit take not from me.

O Lord, open my lips,
  and my mouth shall proclaim your praise.
My sacrifice, O God, is a contrite spirit;
  a heart contrite and humbled, O God, you
    will not spurn.

READING II   1 Timothy 1:12–17

A reading from the first Letter of Saint Paul to Timothy

Beloved:
I am **grateful** to him who has **strengthened** me, **Christ Jesus**
    our **Lord**,
  because he **considered** me **trustworthy**
  in **appointing** me to the **ministry**.
I was once a **blasphemer** and a **persecutor** and **arrogant**,
  but I have been **mercifully treated**
  because I **acted** out of **ignorance** in my **unbelief**.
Indeed, the **grace** of our **Lord** has been **abundant**,
  along with the **faith** and **love** that are in **Christ Jesus**.
This saying is **trustworthy** and deserves **full acceptance**:
  Christ Jesus came into the **world** to **save sinners**.
Of these **I** am the **foremost**.

Beloved = bee-LUHV-uhd

Be aware of where you are headed; Paul is not expressing generic gratitude but thanks for God's inexplicable mercy!

He's not bragging, but confessing his earlier ignorance and arrogance.

Don't speak of his "ignorance" as an excuse; Paul is nothing but grateful here.

This is a grand and solemn truth best spoken with heartfelt simplicity.

---

away from the threatened punishment. In spite of Israel's infidelity, the people remain the Lord's own.

READING II Near the middle of the reading from 1 Timothy, Paul writes, "the grace of our Lord has been abundant." Both before and after this statement of faith, Paul gives evidence from his own life of the abundance of grace, bestowed freely and generously. As a Jew well versed in his tradition, Paul would know that the Lord God of Israel is the one who bestows grace. Like the God

of Israel, Christ Jesus did not deal with Paul as his own sins merited.

Having formerly been a blasphemer, persecutor, and arrogant man who acted in ignorance, Paul experienced the greatest of graces in being treated mercifully by Christ. Paul saw his indebtedness due to sin vast indeed. But now Christ Jesus, who came into the world to save sinners, uses Paul to display divine patience and mercy. Paul's life, transformed by grace, is to be an example of the mercy that God offers to all sinners. The foremost of sinners becomes the foremost example of the

mercy of Christ Jesus. Having begun his narration in gratitude, Paul concludes with a prayer of praise.

GOSPEL "This man welcomes sinners and eats with them." Complaining with what they considered a harsh insult, the Pharisees and scribes make a profoundly ironic statement, unrecognized by themselves, but surely comprehended by anyone who hears the Gospel. Jesus' welcoming sinners and eating with them is a joyful proclamation of the good news, but the Pharisees regard such

Connect his thoughts: (a) I was chosen (b) because as a great sinner (c) I'm an example of God's mercy!

Paul ends with a moment of deep prayer. Don't list God's attributes like grocery items. Each reveals a profound dimension of the mystery of God.

The makeup of the crowd attracted to Jesus disturbs the Pharisees, who find reason to grumble.

They don't bother whispering; they want him to hear their displeasure.

Imagine Jesus moving among the crowd, catching one person's eye and then another. These stories should be animated and upbeat.

The tone throughout says, "This is obvious; everyone (even you!) would behave this way!"

Here Jesus speaks for God and the ways of God's Kingdom—sure to anger his critics.

Note Luke's use of a female image to present God's love for sinners.

As above, emphasize the *public* rejoicing.

But for **that reason** I was **mercifully treated**,
   so that in **me**, as the **foremost**,
      Christ Jesus might **display** all his **patience** as an **example**
      for those who would come to **believe** in him for **everlasting life**.
To the **king** of **ages**, **incorruptible**, **invisible**, the **only God**,
   honor and **glory forever** and **ever**. **Amen**.

GOSPEL   Luke 15:1–32

A reading from the holy Gospel according to Luke

[**Tax collectors** and **sinners** were all drawing **near** to **listen**
      to **Jesus**,
   but the **Pharisees** and **scribes** began to **complain**, saying,
   "**This** man **welcomes sinners** and **eats** with them."
So to **them** he addressed this **parable**.
"**What man** among you having a **hundred** sheep
      and losing **one** of them
   would not **leave** the **ninety-nine** in the desert
   and go after the **lost one** until he **finds** it?
And when he **does** find it,
   he **sets** it on his **shoulders** with **great joy**
   and, upon his arrival **home**,
   he **calls** together his **friends** and **neighbors and says** to them,
   '**Rejoice** with me because I have **found** my **lost sheep**.'
I tell you, in **just** the **same way**
   there will be **more joy** in **heaven** over **one sinner** who **repents**
   than over **ninety-nine righteous people**
   who have **no need** of **repentance**.

"Or **what woman** having **ten coins** and **losing one**
   would not **light** a **lamp** and **sweep** the **house**,
   searching carefully until she **finds** it?
And when she **does** find it,
   she **calls** together her **friends** and **neighbors**
   and **says** to them,
   '**Rejoice** with me because I have **found** the **coin** that I **lost**.' »

actions as shockingly scandalous. The Pharisees and scribes are so dismissive of Jesus that they do not even refer to him by name. Although they talk about "this man," rather than to him, Jesus addresses them directly.

Jesus begins with a parable asking "What man among you?" The Pharisees are to imagine themselves as participants in the parable. The first two parables that Jesus tells them are notably brief, and follow the same structure. One lost sheep and one lost coin motivate a shepherd and a woman to search out what is lost. For one

sheep and one coin, seemingly so insignificant, the searchers are surprisingly diligent. The shepherd leaves the other ninety-nine sheep in the desert, going on the quest over a vast area, needing to look behind, around, and under the various hiding places in the desert environment. The woman, though conducting her search over a much smaller area, is similarly thorough; she lights a lamp, sweeps, and searches carefully. Through their determination, the two searchers find what is lost and rejoice in the finding. Their joy must be shared, so they invite friends and neighbors to cele-

brate the finding of what was lost. The pattern of the two parables is thus loss, searching, finding, rejoicing, and sharing of the joy. Finally, each episode is compared to the joy over one repentant sinner. The saying about a repentant sinner indicates that both the shepherd and the woman are images for the God who rejoices at the finding of each sinner restored to sheepfold and household.

The third parable is much longer, with well-drawn characters: the father, the elder son, and the younger son. Like the sheep and the coin, the younger son becomes

In **just** the **same way**, **I tell you**,
    there will be **rejoicing** among the **angels** of **God**
    over **one sinner** who **repents**."]

Then he said,
    "A man had **two sons**, and the **younger** son said to his **father**,
    '**Father give** me the **share** of your **estate** that should **come**
        to me.'
So the **father divided** the **property between** them.
After a few **days**, the younger son **collected** all his **belongings**
    and **set** off to a **distant country**
    where he **squandered** his inheritance on a **life** of **dissipation**.
When he had **freely** spent **everything**,
    a **severe famine** struck that **country**,
    and he **found** himself in dire **need**.
So he **hired** himself **out** to one of the local **citizens**
    who sent him to his **farm** to tend the **swine**.
And he **longed** to **eat** his **fill** of the **pods** on which the **swine** fed,
    but **nobody gave** him any.
Coming to his **senses** he **thought**,
    'How **many** of my father's hired **workers**
    have **more** than **enough** food to eat,
    but here am **I**, **dying** from **hunger**.
I shall **get up** and **go** to my **father** and I shall **say** to him,
    "**Father**, I have **sinned** against **heaven** and **against you**.
I no longer **deserve** to be **called your son**;
    treat me as you would **treat one** of your **hired workers**."'
So he **got up** and **went back** to his **father**.
While he was **still a long way off**,
    his **father** caught **sight** of him,
    and was **filled** with **compassion**.
He **ran** to his son, **embraced** him and **kissed** him.
His son **said** to him,
    '**Father**, I have **sinned** against **heaven** and **against you**;
    I no longer **deserve** to be called **your son**.'
But his **father** ordered his **servants**,

Pause before launching into the story of the prodigal as if deciding that more needs to be said about forgiveness and repentance.

Suggest the father's dismay as he accedes to his son's demands.

Don't rush this mention of his dissolution. Take note of the strong words "squandered" and "life of dissipation."

Your tone should reveal how great an indignity it was for a Jew to feed a Gentile's pigs.

This seems less a conversion than a move for self-preservation. But still it requires humility and trust.

This time he is just rehearsing. The sincerity will come later.

The character of the father is revealed in this initiative toward the son.

Now, give the son's confession the sound of sincerity.

lost. While a lost sheep and lost coin have no blame attached to their being lost, the son appears to be guilty in two distinct ways. First, asking for his inheritance while his father is still living is a flagrant violation of the respect due his father. Such a request is tantamount to wishing his father dead. The son leaves almost immediately with his inheritance, which he squanders on a life of dissipation, the second way in which he is guilty of wrongdoing. Selfish, arrogant, and irresponsible, the young man throws away all he had been given, and finds himself in dire need.

When he comes to his senses, he thinks immediately of his father. Having been brought low, the young man is ready to admit his sin to his father and take on the role of a mere hired hand. While the parable does not say that the father searched for his son, he does seem to be on watch for him, catching sight of him when the young man is still a long way off. Ignoring the usual demeanor and behavior expected of the patriarch of a household, the father, filled with compassion, runs to his son, embraces him, and kisses him. The son cannot even complete his planned

speech before the father orders the best attire and a great feast. With words and actions that echo the first two parables, the loving father is ready to celebrate the finding of his lost son.

Were the parable to end with the celebration, the third parable would fit, at least broadly, the pattern of the first two: finding the lost, joy, and celebration. However, the next scene goes beyond the pattern and is directed specifically to Jesus' audience of grumbling Pharisees and scribes. Like the elder son, they are unhappy about meals shared with sinners.

The father's voice is filled with excitement and breathless joy.

'**Quickly** bring the **finest robe** and put it **on** him;
put a **ring** on his **finger** and **sandals** on his **feet**.
Take the **fattened calf** and **slaughter** it.
Then let us **celebrate** with a **feast**,
  because this **son** of **mine** was **dead**, and has **come** to **life** again;
  he was **lost**, and has been **found**.'
Then the **celebration began**.

"Now the older son" introduces a dark cloud that temporarily blocks the sun of the joyful celebration.

Now the **older** son had been **out** in the **field**
  and, on his way **back**, as he **neared** the **house**,
  he heard the **sound** of **music** and **dancing**.
He **called** one of the **servants** and **asked** what this might **mean**.
The servant said to him,

The "servant" shares the father's joy over the younger son's return.

  'Your **brother** has **returned**
  and your **father** has **slaughtered** the **fattened calf**
  because he has him **back safe** and **sound**.'

Pause briefly before reintroducing the father.

He became **angry**,
  and when he **refused** to enter the house,
  his **father came out** and **pleaded** with him.
He said to his father in reply,
  '**Look**, **all** these **years I served you**
  and not **once** did I disobey **your orders**;
  yet you **never** gave me **even a young goat** to **feast** on
    with **my friends**.

The son feels wronged and entitled to his anger.

But when **your son returns**,
  who **swallowed** up **your property** with **prostitutes**,
  for **him** you **slaughter** the fattened **calf**.'
He **said** to him,

The father's tone needs to convey sincere compassion.

  '**My son**, **you** are here with me **always**;
  everything I have is **yours**.
But **now** we **must celebrate** and **rejoice**,
  because your **brother** was **dead** and has **come** to **life** again;
  he was **lost** and has been **found**.'"

Use ritardando (slowing gradually toward the end) on this final line.

[Shorter: Luke 15:1–10 (see brackets)]

Both the elder son and Jesus' opponents distance themselves from those they should recognize as brothers. Rather than brother, the young man is "your son," and rather than fellow Jews, Jesus' table-partners are lumped together as "sinners." Elder son and Pharisees alike judge others to be unworthy and seem to resent what appears to be undeserved mercy.

How might the father response to such resentment? It would not be surprising if he were to reprimand his first-born,

telling him to stop being so petty, judgmental, and self-centered. Instead, he speaks with such tenderness. He calls him "my son," and assures him that he is always with him, and even that "everything I have is yours." Now is the time to celebrate the restoration to life, the finding of the lost. This is Jesus' response to the Pharisees and scribes as well. He neither rejects them nor scolds them, but through the parable, invites them to join in the celebration.

The loving father in the parable is a third image for God in these three parables. His eager welcome and celebration at the return of his son illustrates God's overwhelming mercy that extends even to the sinners so disdained by the Pharisees. E.P.

TWENTY-FIFTH SUNDAY IN ORDINARY TIME

LECTIONARY #135

READING I Amos 8:4–7

A reading from the Book of the Prophet Amos

> **Hear this**, you who **trample** upon the **needy**
>   and **destroy** the **poor** of the **land**!
> "**When** will the **new moon** be **over**," you ask,
>   "that we may **sell** our **grain**,
>   and the **sabbath**, that we may **display** the **wheat**?
> We will **diminish** the **ephah**,
>   **add** to the **shekel**,
>   and **fix** our **scales** for **cheating**!
> We will **buy** the **lowly** for **silver**,
>   and the **poor** for a **pair** of **sandals**;
>   even the **refuse** of the **wheat** we will **sell**!"
> The Lᴏʀᴅ has **sworn** by the **pride** of **Jacob**:
>   **Never** will I **forget** a **thing** they have **done**!

Make eye contact. The prophet's goal is to get people to hear God's warning!

Convey the impatience of the greedy who want to get back to making money.

Ephah = EE-fah (a unit of dry measure)

Shekel = SHEK-*l (a unit of weight)

Their plots become increasingly sinister and heartless.

Pause, then announce God's solemn promise. The threat here is greater than in the opening line.

TO KEEP IN MIND

Exhortatory texts make an urgent appeal to listeners. They may encourage, warn, or challenge, and often include a call to action. You must convey the urgency and passion behind the words.

READING I Amos is often referred to as "the prophet of justice." In the face of the blatant injustice of the wealthy and powerful in Israel, Amos urged, "let justice surge like water, and goodness like an unfailing stream" (5:24). Prophesying for only one year, around 760 ʙᴄ, Amos saw harsh treatment of the poor of the land, while the wealthy—including king, priests, and other supposedly religious people—appeared self-satisfied and complacent. Today's reading is a clear example of the attitudes and actions that Amos so abhorred.

The prophet presents a vivid picture. The unjust actions of his audience involve more than simply ignoring those who are poor and needy. Their injustice is equivalent to trampling the poor into the earth so completely that it destroys them. In his first indictment against Israel, Amos had already set the scene with the same image: "They trample the heads of the weak into the dust of the earth, and force the lowly out of the way" (2:7). What makes their actions even more egregious is the pseudo-religious lifestyle of the wealthy. They seem to regard their participation in feasts and prayers as an indication that they are in right relationship with God. But Amos announces the word of the Lord against them: "I hate, I spurn your feasts, I take no pleasure in your solemnities" (5:21).

The prophecy we hear today illustrates well why the Lord would take no pleasure in the religious observances of those who exploited the poor. The celebration of the new moon at the beginning of each month included feasting and sacrifices. Since no work was permitted on the new moon or Sabbath, the wealthy merchants were eager for the days to be over

254

For meditation and context:

RESPONSORIAL PSALM   Psalm 113:1–2, 4–6, 7–8 (see 1a, 7b)

**R. Praise the Lord who lifts up the poor.
or Alleluia.**

Praise, you servants of the LORD,
　　praise the name of the LORD.
Blessed be the name of the LORD
　　both now and forever.

High above all nations is the LORD;
　　above the heavens is his glory.
Who is like the LORD, our God, who is
　　enthroned on high
　　and looks upon the heavens
　　　and the earth below?

He raises up the lowly from the dust;
　　from the dunghill he lifts up the poor
to seat them with princes,
　　with the princes of his own people.

READING II   1 Timothy 2:1–8

Beloved = bee-LUHV-uhd

With urgency, you are giving instructions.
Speak with authority.

Don't rush the benefits of praying for our
leaders.

God expects us to pray. Speak in a
gentler tone.

This is the instruction of a loving teacher.

God gave him this responsibility that all might
be saved.

End softly and humbly, calling for prayer that
is characterized by the peace you pray for.

A reading from the first Letter of Saint Paul to Timothy

Beloved:
First of all, I **ask** that **supplications**, **prayers**,
　　petitions, and **thanksgivings** be offered for **everyone**,
　　for **kings** and for **all** in **authority**,
　　that we may lead a **quiet** and **tranquil** life
　　in all **devotion** and **dignity**.
This is **good** and **pleasing** to **God** our **savior**,
　　who wills **everyone** to be **saved**
　　and to come to **knowledge** of the **truth**.
　　　For there is **one God**.
　　　There is also **one mediator** between **God** and **men**,
　　　the **man Christ Jesus**,
　　　who **gave** himself as **ransom** for **all**.
This was the **testimony** at the **proper time**.
For **this** I was **appointed preacher** and **apostle**
　　—I am **speaking** the **truth**, I am **not lying**—,
　　teacher of the **Gentiles** in **faith** and **truth**.

It is my **wish**, then, that in **every place** the men should **pray**,
　　lifting up holy hands, without **anger** or **argument**.

---

so they could begin their cheating again. They used their scales both to falsify the weight of produce and to determine the price. Then, having further impoverished the needy, they plan to sell them into servitude, in violation of the Torah itself (Leviticus 25:36ff.).

　　The final verse is a sharp and frightening warning: the Lord will not forget what these people have done.

READING II   The second reading opens and closes with Paul urging that prayer be offered for everyone and in

every place. Just as Jesus had instructed his disciples how to pray, Paul instructs Timothy how the community under his leadership should pray when they are gathered for worship. In the first-century context of the Roman Empire, praying for kings and all in authority means praying for those who have power over the Christian community, who can threaten and persecute them. Praying for such powerful political figures has a twofold purpose. First, it contributes to a quiet and tranquil life by publicly attesting that, far from opposing the

emperor and others in government, Christians respect and even pray for them.

　　Second, praying for those with political power springs from Jesus' own prayer and mission. He taught his disciples, "Pray for those who persecute you" (Matthew 5:44). His very reason for coming into the world is "that the world might be saved through him" (John 3:17). Jesus' prayer and mission put kings and emperors (as well as political leaders today) in their proper place. Like all the rest of humanity, they are under God's rule and God's will to save.

GOSPEL   Luke 16:1–13

A reading from the holy Gospel according to Luke

Jesus is in full teacher mode; start briskly.

[**Jesus** said to his **disciples**,]
    "A **rich** man had a **steward**
    who was **reported** to him for **squandering** his **property**.
He **summoned** him and said,
    'What is this I **hear** about you?

The rich man's inquiry is stern.

Prepare a full **account** of your **stewardship**,
    because you can **no longer** be my **steward**.'

The manager remains calm, resorting to logic rather than panic.

The **steward** said to himself, '**What** shall I **do**,
    now that my **master** is taking the **position** of **steward**
        away from me?
I am **not strong** enough to **dig** and I am **ashamed** to **beg**.
I **know** what I shall **do so** that,
    when I am **removed** from the **stewardship**,
    they may **welcome** me into their **homes**.'

Your tone implies he has taken full charge of the situation.

He called in his master's **debtors one** by **one**.
To the **first** he said,
    '**How much** do you **owe** my master?'
He replied, '**One hundred measures** of **olive** oil.'
He said to him, '**Here** is your **promissory** note.

He makes every effort to sound magnanimous.

Sit down and quickly **write** one for **fifty**.'
Then to **another** the steward said, 'And **you**,
        how much do **you owe**?'

Pause before citing the master's commendation.

He replied, '**One hundred kors** of **wheat**.'
The steward **said** to him, '**Here** is **your** promissory note;
    write one for **eighty**.'

Closely connected to praying for everyone is the proclamation of the one God and one mediator, Jesus Christ. This short poetic verse was probably an early liturgical profession of faith. Through both prayer and creed, the first-century believers affirmed the universality of Jesus' mediation: he gave himself as a ransom for all. Himself a human, Jesus is the living link between God and humanity; Paul uses the same word, *anthropos*, both for the man Jesus and for humanity.

Paul, preacher and apostle, concludes with his desire that everyone should pray.

Lifting up holy hands, an ancient prayer gesture found at Psalm 28:2 and depicted in the catacombs, expresses reverence, supplication, and humility.

GOSPEL   The parable about a household steward in today's Gospel follows the parable about the prodigal son. Though the original audiences of the two parables are different, anyone who hears these Gospels proclaimed is its true audience. Those who listen attentively to the two parables will hear echoes of the son's actions in those of the steward. Both

son and steward act wrongly to the one in authority over them. When the son receives his inheritance from his father, he squanders it; the steward is accused of wasting his master's property. When their actions lead them to a dire situation, each thinks about how to survive.

Following the similarities in the depictions of son and steward, we can well expect them to face similar consequences. The father's surprising welcome of his son with no berating or punishment creates an expectation in Jesus' listeners that the actions of the master will also be surpris-

And the master **commended** that dishonest steward
  for acting **prudently**.

Your tone comments on the master's attitude, helping us understand that prudence is being praised, not dishonesty.

Jesus draws a lesson from his story.

"For the **children** of **this world**
  are more **prudent** in **dealing** with their **own generation**
  than are the **children** of **light**.
I **tell** you, make **friends** for **yourselves** with **dishonest wealth**,
  so that when it **fails**, you will be **welcomed**
    into **eternal dwellings**.

Make eye contact. This teaching counters the notion that we can cheat "just a little bit."

[The **person** who is **trustworthy** in **very small** matters
  is also **trustworthy** in **great ones**;
  and the **person** who is **dishonest** in **very small** matters
  is also **dishonest** in **great ones**.
If, therefore, you are **not trustworthy** with **dishonest wealth**,
  who will **trust** you with **true** wealth?

Slow the pace here. For some, this will be a "hard saying," difficult to accept.

If you are **not trustworthy** with what **belongs** to **another**,
  who will **give** you what is **yours**?
No servant can serve **two** masters.
He will **either hate** one and **love** the **other**,
  or be **devoted** to one and **despise** the other.
You cannot serve both God and mammon."]

The last sentence is a solemn pronouncement spoken with authority.

[Shorter: Luke 16:10–13 (see brackets)]

ing. While society would expect the steward to be punished, the master, like the father, neither berates nor punishes him. Instead he praises him for acting prudently (*phronesis*). The basis of the commendation is his clever way of thinking, his insight and resourcefulness, his wisdom and prudence.

Not only does the master of the household withhold a negative assessment of the steward's actions, so too does Jesus. Evidently including the steward among "the children of this world," Jesus says that they are more resourceful in gaining earthly wealth for themselves than the children of

light are in gaining eternal wealth. Jesus is not judging the steward's honesty or dishonesty, but is comparing his resourcefulness to the lack of such daring on the part of his own disciples.

The collection of sayings following the parable—which are only loosely connected to the parable—gather together various teachings about the proper use of wealth. Jesus' disciples are stewards of the household of God and must act with trustworthiness in all their actions, from the very small to the great. Throughout Luke's Gospel, Jesus repeatedly instructs his followers

about the proper use of money. Their master must be God, not mammon. The final word of the reading, *mammon*, seems almost personified as the wealth and power that can exercise lordship over a person. The only lordship that leads to life is that of the Lord Jesus. E.P.

TWENTY-SIXTH SUNDAY IN ORDINARY TIME

LECTIONARY #138

READING I   Amos 6:1a, 4–7

A reading from the Book of the Prophet Amos

Thus says the LORD, the **God** of **hosts**:
Woe to the **complacent** in **Zion**!
Lying upon **beds** of **ivory**,
   stretched **comfortably** on their **couches**,
they eat **lambs** taken from the **flock**,
   and **calves** from the **stall**!
Improvising to the **music** of the **harp**,
   like **David**, they **devise** their own **accompaniment**.
They **drink wine** from **bowls**
   and **anoint** themselves with the **best oils**;
   yet they are **not** made **ill** by the **collapse** of **Joseph**!
Therefore, **now** they shall be the **first** to go into **exile**,
   and their **wanton revelry** shall be **done away** with.

Even this opening narration should signal the harsh judgment to follow.

Your tone must tell us that this "complacency" is ill-gotten and ungodly.

Your energy and disapproval grow with each item added to this list.

They drink wine by the bowlful!

This is where their focus should be. Pause before the final sentence.

Speak slowly. This is not God's vengeance, but the sad consequence of their choices!

For meditation and context:

RESPONSORIAL PSALM   Psalm 146:7, 8–9, 9–10 (1b)

R. Praise the Lord, my soul!
or R. Alleluia.

Blessed is he who keeps faith forever,
   secures justice for the oppressed,
   gives food to the hungry.
The LORD sets captives free.

The LORD gives sight to the blind;
   the LORD raises up those who were
     bowed down.
The LORD loves the just;
   the LORD protects strangers.

The fatherless and the widow he sustains,
   but the way of the wicked he thwarts.
The LORD shall reign forever;
   your God, O Zion, through all
     generations. Alleluia.

READING I   When Amos was prophesying, Israel was enjoying political, economic, and military strength. More accurately, the wealthy were enjoying such abundance, while the poor suffered at their hands. Those who controlled all the prosperity were so far from living according to the covenant that Amos developed a lamentation over them in terminology that sounds like a funeral dirge. Although the nation appears to be alive and well, Amos laments over them, as if they had already died.

One of the words of Amos' lamentation, "woe" (*hoy*, 5:18), is the opening word in today's reading: "Woe to the complacent in Zion." Those whom Amos describes as complacent, lying on beds of ivory, are the objects of his funeral lament. Their food of lambs and calves, the music of the harp, drinking of wine, and anointing with oil belong to the celebration of a religious feast. Yet their actions are no more than a parody of worship; they are using the trappings of the sacred to indulge in self-serving excesses.

While there is no mention of the poor and needy, their very absence highlights the exclusivity of the gathering. The poor would rarely be able to afford meat of any kind, but the wealthy are eating the meat used for sacrifice. They also drink an excess of wine from bowls, and anoint themselves with the best oils.

The single word "therefore" in the final verse introduces the consequences of their lifestyle. The collapse of their nation, when they will be the first sent into exile, will come because of their own sinful disdain

READING II   1 Timothy 6:11–16

A reading from the first Letter of Saint Paul to Timothy

But **you**, **man** of **God**, pursue **righteousness**,
  devotion, **faith**, **love**, **patience** and **gentleness**.
Compete **well** for the **faith**.
Lay hold of **eternal life**, to which you were **called**
  when you made the **noble confession** in the presence
    of **many witnesses**.
I charge you before **God**, who gives **life** to **all** things,
  and before **Christ Jesus**,
  who gave **testimony** under **Pontius Pilate**
    for the **noble confession**,
  to **keep** the **commandment** without **stain** or **reproach**
  until the **appearance** of our **Lord Jesus Christ**
  that the **blessed** and **only** ruler
  will make **manifest** at the **proper** time,
  the **King** of **kings** and **Lord** of **lords**,
  who **alone** has **immortality**, who dwells
    in **unapproachable light**,
  and whom **no** human being has **seen** or **can see**.
To **him** be **honor** and **eternal power**. **Amen**.

Catch your listeners' attention immediately with the unexpected salutation, then slowly list the virtues we are to pursue.

What's at stake is our "eternal life." Be sure to make this sound important.

"I charge you" is fraternal encouragement, not scolding.

"The commandment" refers to all commandments.

The two titles are similar, but increase your energy from the first to the second.
Beloved = bee-LUHV-uhd

Speak the last line from memory.

GOSPEL   Luke 16:19–31

A reading from the holy Gospel according to Luke

Jesus said to the **Pharisees**:
"There was a **rich man** who dressed in **purple garments**
    and **fine linen**
    and dined **sumptuously** each day. »

Unique to Luke, this parable, addressed to the Pharisees, calls us all to repentance in due season.

---

for the poor, while they make a mockery of authentic worship.

READING II Paul begins his exhortation to Timothy by addressing him as "man of God." The designation, used of Hebrew prophets, indicates that Paul sees Timothy as one chosen by God who will carry on Paul's prophetic role as a leader in the faith. In today's reading, Paul gives Timothy a final instruction; he doesn't delineate specific tasks for Timothy to perform, but presents to him a way of life that flows from his Baptism. Paul begins with a list of virtues that Timothy should pursue, implying energetic dedication to living as Jesus did: in righteousness, devotion, and the other virtues manifest in Jesus.

The energy of pursuing virtue is also needed for Timothy to compete well for the faith. Like an athlete striving to win the prize, Timothy is to strain forward toward the finish line. Because eternal life is a gift already possessed as a down payment, Timothy can lay hold of it even now as he runs toward the completion of the race and the fullness of eternal life.

At Baptism, Timothy had made a noble confession, or profession of faith. The faith that Timothy professes, like that of everyone in the Church, includes adherence to the teaching handed down, the pursuit of virtue, and keeping the commandments. Having exhorted Timothy to virtue and faith, Paul turns his focus to Christ in a poetic text that may have been part of a baptismal profession of faith. This rich proclamation about Christ, King of Kings and Lord of Lords, moves naturally to prayer, concluding with a faith-filled "Amen!"

Luke's concern for the contrast between rich and poor is manifested in his language. Contrast "purple garments and fine linen" with the more pungent language that refers to Lazarus ("sores," "scraps," "dogs," and "licked").
Contrast the serene fate of Lazarus with the rich man's torment.

He has no compunction about asking to be waited upon.

Keep Abraham's response temperate, without a trace of vindictiveness. He calls him "child," a kindness that makes the irreversible fate all the more chilling.
This "chasm" is of our making, not God's.

His concern for his brothers seems genuine, but he wants them "warned" rather than relying on their consciences to lead them to just and merciful living.

He grows more urgent in his naiveté. He sets up the irony of Abraham's final comment.

Here is the heart of the message; this hard truth can't be diluted.

And lying at his door was a **poor man** named **Lazarus**,
　　covered with **sores**,
　who would **gladly** have eaten his fill of the **scraps**
　that **fell** from the rich man's **table**.
Dogs even used to **come** and **lick** his **sores**.
When the **poor man died**,
　he was carried away by **angels** to the **bosom** of **Abraham**.
The **rich man also died** and was **buried**,
　and from the **netherworld**, where he was in **torment**,
　he **raised** his **eyes** and saw **Abraham** far **off**
　and **Lazarus** at his **side**.
And he **cried** out, '**Father Abraham**, have **pity** on me.
Send Lazarus to **dip** the tip of his **finger** in **water** and **cool**
　　my **tongue**,
　for I am **suffering torment** in these **flames**.'
Abraham replied,
　'**My child**, **remember** that you received
　what was **good** during your **lifetime**
　while **Lazarus** likewise **received** what was **bad**;
　but **now he** is **comforted** here, whereas **you** are **tormented**.
Moreover, between **us** and **you** a **great chasm** is established
　to **prevent anyone** from **crossing** who might **wish** to go
　from **our side** to **yours** or from **your side** to **ours**.'
He said, 'Then I **beg** you, **father**,
　send him to my **father's house**, for I have **five brothers**,
　so that he may **warn** them,
　lest they **too come** to this **place** of **torment**.'
But **Abraham replied**, 'They have **Moses** and the **prophets**.
Let them **listen** to **them**.'
He said, 'Oh **no**, father **Abraham**,
　but if **someone** from the **dead** goes to them, they will **repent**.'
Then **Abraham** said, 'If they will **not** listen to **Moses**
　　and the **prophets**,
　neither will they be **persuaded** if someone should **rise**
　　from the **dead**.'"

GOSPEL　Jesus tells the Pharisees a parable that illustrates in picturesque detail God's action proclaimed in the Magnificat: reversing the situations of the arrogant, the mighty, and the rich, and of the lowly and hungry (Luke 1:51–53). The rich man of the parable, dressed in purple and eating sumptuously every day, is the epitome of those whom God casts down, while the poor and hungry Lazarus is exalted to the side of Abraham.

The depiction of Lazarus during his lifetime is painfully graphic. Covered with sores that dogs used to come and lick, he would have been glad for even a scrap of food from the rich man's table. His poverty and sores seemed a sign of God's rejection. Having lived in such destitution, the image of Lazarus being carried by angels to Abraham's bosom is beautiful and comforting. God has indeed lifted up the lowly.

The portrayal of the rich man is a sharp contrast. Blind to the poor man at his door during his lifetime, the rich man suffers the torments of the nether world at his death. Though cast down from his exalted state, even in death the rich man has not changed his selfishness. He asks Abraham in effect to treat Lazarus as his servant: send Lazarus to cool his tongue with water, and then send Lazarus to warn his brothers. Abraham responds that since his brothers did not listen to Moses and the prophets, they will not listen even if someone were to rise from the dead. The final words of the parable create a broader perspective: those who are blind to the poor and deaf to the prophets will also be blind and deaf to the Resurrection of Jesus. E.P.

TWENTY-SEVENTH SUNDAY IN ORDINARY TIME

LECTIONARY #141

READING I Habakkuk 1:2–3; 2:2–4

Habakkuk = huh-BAK-kuhk or HAB-uh-kuhk

Are these the words of a single intercessor or of several praying about different sets of circumstances?

Fix a concrete situation of desperate need in your mind to lend passion and energy to these concerns.

Pause to allow time to transition to the more solemn tone of this section where the prophet quotes God.

This is a promise that faith will not be disappointed.

See with the eyes of faith, not those of the body!

Faith is always the mark of those who find favor with God and who can endure without losing heart.

A reading from the Book of the Prophet Habakkuk

How long, O LORD? I cry for **help**
   but you do not **listen**!
I cry out to you, "**Violence!**"
   but you do **not intervene**.
Why do you let me see **ruin**;
   why must I look at **misery**?
Destruction and **violence** are before me;
   there is **strife**, and **clamorous discord**.
Then the LORD **answered** me and said:
   Write down the **vision clearly** upon the **tablets**,
   so that one can **read** it **readily**.
For the **vision** still has its **time**,
   presses **on** to **fulfillment**, and will **not disappoint**;
if it **delays**, **wait** for it,
   it will **surely come**, it will **not** be **late**.
The **rash one** has **no integrity**;
   but the **just one**, because of his **faith**, shall **live**.

READING I | The first two chapters of Habakkuk consist of a dialogue between Habakkuk and the Lord. In today's reading, Habakkuk accuses God of not listening to his cry for help and not intervening in the face of violence. The prophet sees ruin, misery, and destruction, realities repeated so often in Israel's history that they could refer to almost any period. Even readers today can identify with the situations that Habakkuk laments.

In verses omitted from the lectionary, God responds to Habakkuk's complaint. With words that would seem to increase the prophet's dismay, God describes the power and violence that Israel endures. After God's part of the dialogue, the prophet again speaks, not surprisingly, with another complaint. He says that God has made the people like fish of the sea, like creeping things without a ruler, suggesting that God has reversed the order of things established in creation. Habakkuk is keeping watch to see what answer God will give to his complaint.

We hear the divine response in the second part of today's reading. God offers a vision that the prophet is to write down, so that it can be read. The fulfillment of this vision is certain and will not disappoint, even though it will come in its own time. The final verse presents two kinds of people who await the vision's arrival. One is rash, proud, or "puffed up," having no integrity. In contrast, the just person has faith. That person, while waiting for God's promises to be fulfilled, remains faithful and steadfast, confident in God's promise, no matter the circumstances or delay.

READING I | Paul's two letters to Timothy are referred to as

For meditation and context:

Beloved = bee-LUHV-uhd

The salutation is tender but the message is strong and challenging.

Set afire what is already within you—that you received in Holy Orders! "Power," "love," and "self-control" are three *distinct* qualities. Differentiate them.

These words comprise a spiritual pep-talk from someone whose own life circumstances are dark and painful.

Recall the suffering you've endured in life that could embolden you to invite others to not fear suffering.

Even today, millions suffer daily for the faith. How might they encourage others to safeguard it?

RESPONSORIAL PSALM   Psalm 95:1–2, 6–7, 8–9 (8)

R. If today you hear his voice, harden not your hearts.

Come, let us sing joyfully to the LORD;
   let us acclaim the Rock of our salvation.
Let us come into his presence with
      thanksgiving;
   let us joyfully sing psalms to him.

Come, let us bow down in worship;
   let us kneel before the LORD who
      made us.
For he is our God,
   and we are the people he shepherds, the
      flock he guides.

Oh, that today you would hear his voice:
   "Harden not your hearts as at Meribah,
      as in the day of Massah in the desert,
where your fathers tempted me;
   they tested me though they had seen
      my works."

READING II   2 Timothy 1:6–8, 13–14

A reading from the second Letter of Saint Paul to Timothy

Beloved:
I **remind** you to **stir** into **flame**
   the **gift** of **God** that you have through the **imposition**
      of my **hands**.
For **God** did not give us a **spirit** of **cowardice**
   but rather of **power** and **love** and **self-control**.
So do **not** be **ashamed** of your **testimony** to our **Lord**,
   nor of me, a **prisoner** for **his sake**;
   but **bear your** share of **hardship** for the **gospel**
      with the **strength** that comes from **God**.

Take as your **norm** the **sound words** that you **heard** from **me**,
   in the **faith** and **love** that are in **Christ Jesus**.
Guard this **rich trust** with the **help** of the **Holy Spirit**
   that **dwells within** us.

"pastoral epistles" because they give guidance to Timothy as a pastor, or shepherd, of the church. Paul is Timothy's own pastor, giving him guidance, encouragement, warnings, and personal example, the same characteristics that Timothy himself is to offer to the Church. Writing from prison, Paul urges Timothy to exhibit courage and to accept hardship and the other challenges associated with being a pastor, always relying on the gift of God that Timothy received through the laying on of hands. This ancient custom is an initiation rite into office and is a sign of the transmis-

sion of authority, such as Moses conferring authority to Joshua (Numbers 27:18–23), and the Apostles to the seven reputable men (Acts 6:6). The laying on of hands gave Timothy a participation in the same mission Paul exercised, the mission of being a shepherd for the nascent Church.

Writing from prison, Paul reminds Timothy that God did not give them a spirit of cowardice, and warns him not to be ashamed of his testimony, and to bear his share of hardship. Having exhibited courage and endured suffering, Paul is a living example for Timothy of the steadfastness

needed to be a pastor. Although Paul presents himself as an example through both his words and actions, neither his fidelity nor Timothy's are accomplished by their own efforts. Paul repeatedly emphasizes the power and presence of God, both in himself and in Timothy. The gift of God includes the spirit of power and love and self-control. God provides strength; no matter the situation, both Paul and Timothy can rely on the help of the Holy Spirit who dwells within them.

TwenTy-Seventh Sunday in Ordinary Time ■ OcTOBER 6, 2019   263

GOSPEL   Luke 17:5–10

A reading from the holy Gospel according to Luke

Speak their request slowly, stressing both "increase" and "faith."

Don't scold; Jesus is giving a lesson on the power of faith.

Speak with the expectation that you will be believed!

The **apostles** said to the **Lord**, "Increase our **faith**."
The **Lord replied**,
  "If you have **faith** the size of a **mustard seed**,
  you would **say** to this **mulberry** tree,
  '**Be uprooted** and **planted** in the **sea**,' and it would **obey** you.

Your tone asks, "Who would make such a ridiculous offer?"

These are not harshly stated orders but expected interaction between master and servants.

Of course not!

"**Who** among you would **say** to your **servant**
  who has **just** come in from **plowing** or **tending sheep**
    in the field,
  '**Come here immediately** and **take** your **place** at **table**'?
Would he **not rather say** to him,
  '**Prepare** something for **me** to **eat**.
Put on your **apron** and **wait** on me while I **eat** and **drink**.
You may **eat** and **drink** when I am **finished**'?
Is he **grateful** to that **servant** because he **did** what
    was **commanded**?
So should it **be** with **you**.
When you have **done all** you have been **commanded**,
  say, 'We are **unprofitable servants**;
  we have **done** what we were **obliged** to **do**.'"

The Gospel is not endorsing self-abusive humility, but a healthy awareness that doing one's duty is not extraordinary.

GOSPEL   As the Apostles continue with Jesus on the journey to Jerusalem, they have witnessed his teaching and his expectations of discipleship: a radical following of him. He has just warned them about causing little ones to stumble, and that they must forgive without bounds. Apparently recognizing the littleness of their faith, they say to him, "Increase our faith." Jesus' response is reassuring, for even a tiny faith, no larger than a mustard seed, is powerful. The image of the seed suggests further that faith must be deeply planted and allowed to grow.

The next part of Jesus' teaching seems an abrupt change of subject, but in fact illustrates that those who have faith are to be servants. The household slaves are obliged to work for their master. They perform tasks as varied as plowing, tending sheep, and waiting at table without expecting a word of thanks. They are simply doing their duty. Being faithful to their obligations as slaves is its own reward. When this short parable is linked to the disciples' request for an increase of faith, we see that faith entails being a servant, doing as the master, the Lord Jesus, commands.

It is significant that Jesus' instructions about being a faithful servant are given to the Apostles. They will become leaders in the early Church, and in that capacity they will maintain their role as slaves, doing what the Lord asks of them without expectation of reward. The service itself is their reward. E.P.

TWENTY-EIGHTH SUNDAY IN ORDINARY TIME

LECTIONARY #144

READING I   2 Kings 5:14–17

A reading from the second Book of Kings

Naaman went down and **plunged** into the **Jordan seven times**
    at the **word** of **Elisha**, the **man** of **God**.
His **flesh** became **again** like the **flesh** of a little **child**,
    and he was **clean** of his **leprosy**.

Naaman returned with his whole **retinue** to the **man** of **God**.
On his **arrival** he **stood** before **Elisha** and **said**,
    "**Now** I **know** that there is **no God** in **all** the **earth**,
    except in **Israel**.
Please accept a **gift** from your **servant**."

Elisha replied, "**As** the L ORD **lives** whom I **serve**, I will **not**
    take it,"
    and **despite Naaman's urging**, he **still refused**.
Naaman said: "If you will **not accept**,
    please let me, your **servant**, have **two mule-loads** of **earth**,
    for I will **no longer** offer **holocaust** or **sacrifice**
    to **any other god** except to the L ORD."

READING I   Naaman was a commander of the army of the king of Aram, highly respected and valued by the king even though he was a leper. Having heard that there was a powerful prophet in Israel, the Aramean king sent a letter to the king of Israel requesting that he cure Naaman of his leprosy. Dismayed and fearful, Israel's king, knowing he had no power over life and death, saw the request as an excuse to quarrel. But Elisha the prophet, hearing of the king's distress, told him to send Naaman to him.

When Naaman met Elisha, the prophet gave him simple instructions: wash seven times in the Jordan River. Enraged at the request, stating that the waters of his own country were better than the waters of Israel, Naaman at first refused. When his servants convinced him to undergo the washing, Naaman relented, and plunged into the Jordan seven times.

The scene in today's reading reveals not only Naaman's cleansing from leprosy, but also his transformation from arrogant resistance to humble acceptance, and his new faith in the God of Israel. The sevenfold plunging is symbolic of total cleansing. So complete is his cleansing and his allegiance that he offers a gift to Elisha. Elisha's refusal of Naaman's gift is a sign that the Lord alone is worthy of such honors. In fact, Elisha was not even present at Naaman's healing, accomplished by God's own power. Naaman's final request is to take two mule-loads of earth from Israel. Cured in Israel's waters, Naaman will offer sacrifices only on Israel's "land," symbolized by the earth that he takes back with him. The God of Israel can then be worshiped in Naaman's distant country.

For meditation and context:

RESPONSORIAL PSALM   Psalm 98:1, 2–3, 3–4 (see 2b)

R. The Lord has revealed to the nations his saving power.

Sing to the LORD a new song,
　for he has done wondrous deeds;
his right hand has won victory for him,
　his holy arm.

The LORD has made his salvation known:
　in the sight of the nations he has revealed
　　his justice.
He has remembered his kindness and his
　faithfulness
　toward the house of Israel.

All the ends of the earth have seen
　the salvation by our God.
Sing joyfully to the LORD, all you lands:
　break into song; sing praise.

READING II   2 Timothy 2:8–13

Beloved = bee-LUHV-uhd

A slight pause after "remember" and moving slowly through the sentence will highlight this important opening.
Paul is imprisoned for his faith.

Contrast the freedom enjoyed by God's Word to go where it will.

This is a joyful declaration: he suffers willingly for the good of others!

Be sure to balance "died"/"live" and "persevere"/"reign."

A reading from the second Letter of Saint Paul to Timothy

Beloved:
Remember Jesus Christ, **raised** from the **dead**,
　a **descendant** of **David**:
　such is my **gospel**, for which I am **suffering**,
　　even to the point of **chains**, like a **criminal**.
But the **word** of **God** is **not chained**.
Therefore, I bear with **everything** for the **sake** of **those**
　　who are **chosen**,
　so that **they too** may **obtain** the **salvation** that is
　　in **Christ Jesus**,
　together with **eternal glory**.
This **saying** is **trustworthy**:
　If we have **died** with him
　　we shall also **live** with him;
　if we **persevere**
　　we shall also **reign** with him. »

READING II The second reading opens and closes with succinct affirmations of faith. The first one is a short presentation of Paul's own Gospel that expresses the core of Christian faith: Jesus Christ, raised from the dead. As a descendant of David, Jesus is the Christ, the anointed one who brings to fulfillment God's ancient promises. Paul's imprisonment is a participation in the death and Resurrection of Jesus, the anointed one; like Jesus, Paul bears his suffering so that others may also share in salvation. As believers await eternal glory, they already

have a share in salvation; even now they have a down payment of what they await.

Paul's second affirmation of faith, a trustworthy saying, is a poetic verse with the feel of a liturgical hymn, perhaps used at Baptism or as baptismal catechesis. As he does elsewhere in his letters, Paul inserts the hymn into his instructions, thereby drawing on what his audience already knows to reinforce his own teaching. The teaching addressed to Timothy is meant for the whole community.

Believers' immersion into Christ's death and Resurrection in Baptism means

that they have died with him and are risen to new life. This saying expresses both a present reality and promise of a future fulfillment. After announcing the fundamental belief of dying and rising with Christ, the remaining verses add how believers are to live: in perseverance and fidelity. The final verse contrasts human infidelity with God's absolute faithfulness. For God to be unfaithful would be a denial of God's very nature.

GOSPEL In the first reading, Naaman was a single foreign leper

But if **we deny him**
  he will deny us.
If we are **unfaithful**
  he remains **faithful**,
  for he **cannot deny himself.**

Note the suggestions for placing stress. Paul says that Christ remains faithful to himself and God; his righteousness requires that he judge our unfaithfulness.

GOSPEL   Luke 17:11–19

A reading from the holy Gospel according to Luke

As **Jesus** continued his **journey** to **Jerusalem**,
  he traveled through **Samaria** and **Galilee**.
As he was entering a **village**, **ten lepers** met him.
They **stood** at a **distance** from him and **raised** their **voices**, saying,
  "**Jesus**, **Master**! Have **pity** on us!"
And when he **saw** them, he said,
  "**Go show** yourselves to the **priests**."
As they were **going** they were **cleansed**.
And one of them, **realizing** he had been **healed**,
  returned, **glorifying God** in a loud **voice**;
  and he **fell** at the **feet** of **Jesus** and **thanked** him.
He was a **Samaritan**.
Jesus **said** in **reply**,
  "**Ten** were **cleansed**, were they **not**?
Where are the **other nine**?
Has **none** but this **foreigner** returned to give **thanks** to **God**?"
Then he **said** to him, "**Stand up** and **go**;
  your **faith** has **saved** you."

Let your tone suggest the serious nature of his journey.
Samaria = suh-MAYR-ee-uh

The Law required this distance. Raise your volume.

"When he saw them" should suggest his immediate compassion.

The priests had to authenticate cures of leprosy.
Is their reaction marked by joy, awe, gratitude?
We should hear the joy of the healed Samaritan in this narration.

Remember, Jesus admires the Samaritan. He regrets that the others did not come to claim a greater healing.
Make these words sincere and full of assurance.

---

who was cleansed. In the Gospel, the horror of the disease and the power of the cure are magnified: ten lepers are afflicted, and ten are healed. Having traveled through Samaria and Galilee, Jesus meets these lepers as he enters an unnamed village. While Jews and Samaritans ordinarily did not associate with one another, their ethnic and religious identity were obliterated by the disease of leprosy as they traveled together. They must stand at a distance even from Jesus as they cry out to him, addressing him as Master (*epistates*), a title

that Jesus' disciples used. They beg, not for alms, but for Jesus' pity or mercy (*eleeson*) on them.

    Jesus' response to them resonates with the account of Naaman and Elisha. Both Elisha and Jesus command the lepers to go away for their cleansing. Neither Elisha nor Jesus are actually present when the lepers are healed. And like Naaman, the Samaritan, a foreigner and an outcast, offers thanks. Both Naaman and the healed Samaritan recognize that God's hand is at work in the healings. The Samaritan offers

no gift as Naaman had done, but his expression of faith is expansive. He glorifies God, falls at Jesus' feet, and thanks him.

    This account, unique to Luke's Gospel, develops several important Lukan themes: the role of Jesus as a powerful prophet; the merciful action of God present in Jesus; the praise and thanks that is due to God; and the inclusion of foreigners in God's saving deeds. E.P.

TWENTY-NINTH SUNDAY IN ORDINARY TIME

LECTIONARY #147

READING I Exodus 17:8–13

A reading from the Book of Exodus

In those days, **Amalek** came and waged **war** against **Israel**.
Moses, therefore, said to **Joshua**,
  "Pick out certain **men**,
  and **tomorrow** go out and **engage Amalek** in **battle**.
I will be standing on top of the **hill**
  with the **staff** of **God** in my **hand**."
So **Joshua did** as **Moses told** him:
  he **engaged Amalek** in battle
  after **Moses** had **climbed** to the top of the hill
    with **Aaron** and **Hur**.
As long as **Moses** kept his **hands** raised **up**,
  Israel had the **better** of the fight,
  but when he let his **hands rest**,
  Amalek had the **better** of the fight.
Moses' hands, however, grew **tired**;
  so they put a **rock** in **place** for him to **sit** on.
Meanwhile Aaron and **Hur supported** his **hands**,
  one on **one** side and **one** on the **other**,
  so that his **hands** remained **steady** till **sunset**.
And **Joshua mowed** down **Amalek** and his **people**
  with the **edge** of the **sword**.

Amalek = AM-uh-lek

Moses takes decisive action to rebuff Amalek's attack. He is determined and strong.

His "staff" represents God's powerful presence.
Your sober tone announces the beginning of battle.

Aaron = AYR-uhn

Hur = her

A shift in tone can signal the differing impact that the upraised and resting hands had on the battle.

Speak with urgency: they aren't simply making him comfortable but ensuring Israel's victory!

Connect the "steady" hands with the consequence that follows. This is God's victory: speak with gratitude, not disdain.

READING I While the Israelites are journeying in the desert, the nomadic, marauding Amalekites wage war against them. According to Moses (Deuteronomy 25:18), Amalek had no fear of God as he harassed the weak and weary people, and cut off from the rear all those who lagged behind. The details in today's account focus neither on Amalek nor the weary Israelites, but on Moses, supported by Aaron and Hur, while Joshua engages Amalek in battle.

Moses' action of holding his staff in upraised hands as he stands on top of the hill has several possible meanings. The staff may be a sign of God's power as it was at the parting of the Red Sea; the raised staff may also be a means of directing the battle or a sign of victory. Whatever the symbolism, the Israelites have the better of the fight as long as Moses' hands are raised. With his tiring hands supported by his brother, Aaron, and Hur, the son of Caleb, Moses is able to keep his hands steady until sunset. The victory over Amalek is then complete.

Although there is no mention of the God of Israel in this account, the military success of Joshua, the power of Moses' upraised staff, and the support of Aaron and Hur are understood in the context of God's abiding presence and power. God is the one who is victorious over the Amalekites. In the verse immediately following today's reading, the Lord tells Moses, "I will completely blot out the memory of Amalek from under the heavens." As the Israelites continue on their way through the desert, the Lord God will make the journey with them, always protecting and guiding them.

For meditation and context:

RESPONSORIAL PSALM　Psalm 121:1–2, 3–4, 5–6, 7–8 (see 2)

R. Our help is from the Lord, who made heaven and earth.

I lift up my eyes toward the mountains;
　whence shall help come to me?
My help is from the LORD,
　who made heaven and earth.

May he not suffer your foot to slip;
　may he slumber not who guards you:
indeed he neither slumbers nor sleeps,
　the guardian of Israel.

The LORD is your guardian; the LORD is
　your shade;
he is beside you at your right hand.
The sun shall not harm you by day,
　nor the moon by night.

The LORD will guard you from all evil;
　he will guard your life.
The LORD will guard your coming and
　your going,
　both now and forever.

READING II　2 Timothy 3:14—4:2

A reading from the second Letter of Saint Paul to Timothy

Beloved = bee-LUHV-uhd

This is more an earnest plea than an instruction.

Speak confidently of the reliability of Scripture.

This is a classic and bold declaration!

Conjure different images as you speak the words "teaching . . . refutation" to help you distinguish one from another.

Take a breath before starting this section and speak with solemn authority.

Use the imperatives to boldly invite your assembly to take on these important tasks. Within it are hearts that need to be convinced, reprimanded, or encouraged. Your heartfelt proclamation can help open their hearts to instruction.

Beloved:
Remain **faithful** to what you have **learned** and **believed**,
　because you **know** from **whom** you **learned** it,
　and that from **infancy** you have known the **sacred Scriptures**,
　which are **capable** of giving you **wisdom** for **salvation**
　through **faith** in **Christ Jesus**.
All Scripture is **inspired** by **God**
　and is **useful** for **teaching**, for **refutation**, for **correction**,
　and for **training** in **righteousness**,
　so that **one** who **belongs** to **God** may be **competent**,
　equipped for **every good work**.

I **charge** you in the presence of **God** and of **Christ Jesus**,
　who will **judge** the **living** and the **dead**,
　and by his **appearing** and his kingly **power**:
　proclaim the **word**;
　be **persistent** whether it is **convenient** or **inconvenient**;
　convince, **reprimand**, **encourage** through **all patience**
　　and **teaching**.

READING II As Paul exhorts Timothy to remain faithful to what he has learned and believed, he writes of two sources of their common belief: Sacred Scripture and Christ Jesus. The Scriptures in which both Paul and Timothy believe conveyed the Jewish traditions through accounts of God's actions of creating and redeeming, of making covenant, and remaining a powerful though unseen presence. There are stories of the ancestors and of God's people throughout history, accounts of how people are to live in right relationship with the Lord, and writings as

diverse as genealogies, detailed regulations, and poetic prayers. Through all of these writings, inspired by God, the Jews learned and passed on their identity from generation to generation.

Faith in Christ Jesus opened a new way of interpreting these ancient texts. Paul was Timothy's teacher in expounding how Jesus brought to fulfillment the hopes and promises of their tradition. Rather than abandoning their tradition, Jews like Paul and Timothy found in them an essential means of handing on their faith in the Christ, the promised Anointed One.

Paul charges Timothy to carry on the ministry of proclaiming the Word. When Paul urges Timothy to be persistent, whether it is convenient or inconvenient, he could well be referring to his own ministry of the word. For Paul it was more than a simple inconvenience: his fidelity in proclaiming his faith in Jesus resulted in hardships of every kind, including imprisonment. The Lord who was ever present in the past will remain present as Timothy hands on his faith to a new generation.

GOSPEL   Luke 18:1–8

A reading from the holy Gospel according to Luke

Let the opening narration itself be a consoling teaching about God's mercy.

Jesus told his **disciples** a **parable**
  about the **necessity** for them to **pray always**
    without becoming **weary.**

Begin with the robust confidence of the selfish judge.

He **said,** "There was a **judge** in a certain **town**
  who **neither feared God** nor **respected** any **human being.**

Your tone is of an all-knowing narrator who anticipates where the story is going.

And a **widow** in that town used to **come** to him and **say,**
  '**Render** a **just decision** for me against my **adversary.'**
For a **long time** the judge was **unwilling,** but **eventually**
    he thought,

There is no fear in his tone, only the desire to be rid of this nagging widow.

  'While it is **true** that I neither **fear God** nor **respect**
    any **human being,**
  because this **widow** keeps **bothering** me
  I shall **deliver** a just **decision** for her
    lest she finally **come** and **strike** me.'"

The brief narration serves as a pointer to the lesson about to follow.

The **Lord** said, "**Pay attention** to what the **dishonest judge says.**
Will not **God** then secure the **rights** of his **chosen** ones
  who **call out** to him **day** and **night**?

Jesus' tone suggests that the right response is obvious!

Will he be **slow** to **answer** them?
I **tell** you, he will **see to it** that **justice** is **done** for them **speedily.**

His final question underscores the fact that persistent faith, not endless verbiage in prayer, is the point of Jesus' parable.

But when the **Son** of **Man comes,** will he **find faith** on **earth**?"

GOSPEL   Jesus often taught in parables. At times, the meaning or application of the parable is given at the end, or it is left to hearers to determine its significance. In today's parable, however, the evangelist tells us ahead of time that the parable teaches Jesus' disciples the necessity of praying always. Jesus has already shown the importance of prayer by his own praying, beginning with prayer at his baptism, praying in the wilderness and on the mountaintop, sometimes praying alone and at other times in the presence of his disciples.

The two characters in the parable portray two different attitudes, each symbolic of stances toward God and prayer. The judge who "neither feared God nor respected human beings" sounds much like Amalek in the first reading, who also had no fear of God. The judge is not motivated by justice, but finally renders a just decision because the widow keeps bothering him.

Little is said of the widow other than her persistence. She was so demanding in her quest for justice that the judge feared that she might "come and strike me." Whether he feared violence on the widow's part, or her spreading the tale of his injustice, her bold determination finally results in a just decision for her. God, likewise, will secure the rights of his chosen ones who call out to him day and night.

In conclusion, Jesus questions whether the Son of Man—Jesus himself—will find faith on earth when he comes. This question posed to the disciples would likely move them to see the woman as an image of fidelity in prayer, an example that they should imitate. E.P.

THIRTIETH SUNDAY IN ORDINARY TIME

LECTIONARY #150

READING I Sirach 35:12–14, 16–18

A reading from the Book of Sirach

The LORD is a **God** of **justice**,
   who knows **no favorites**.
Though not **unduly partial** toward the **weak**,
   yet he **hears** the **cry** of the **oppressed**.
The **Lord** is **not deaf** to the **wail** of the **orphan**,
   nor to the **widow** when she **pours** out her **complaint**.
The **one** who **serves God willingly** is **heard**;
   his **petition** reaches the **heavens**.
The **prayer** of the **lowly pierces** the clouds;
   it does **not rest** till it **reaches** its **goal**,
nor will it **withdraw** till the **Most High responds**,
   judges justly and **affirms** the **right**,
and the **Lord** will **not delay**.

Sirach = SI-ruhk; SEER-ak

Begin with authority and sweep the assembly as you declare this consoling truth.

Contrast what God does and does not do!

Fix concrete images of "orphan" and "widow" in your mind so you are not speaking of abstractions but of real people.

In the following lines you are stating and restating a single idea—that earnest prayers accomplish their goal. Speak with conviction and with enough energy to persuade

The final line offers assurance that whenever it comes, God's mercy is never too late.

TO KEEP IN MIND

Always pause at the end of the reading, before you proclaim the closing dialogue ("The Word of the Lord" or "The Gospel of the Lord").

READING I According to Sirach, the Lord shows no partiality. Having asserted that God knows no favorites, Sirach goes on to describe the Lord's particular care for the weak, oppressed, orphaned, and widowed. Rather than being a manifestation of divine partiality, God's concern for those who cry out in their need shows God listening and acting as a just judge. God's justice means the Lord always acts to establish, maintain, and restore right relationships. In the Hellenistic milieu in which Sirach was written, the poor were commonly dismissed as unworthy and often oppressed by the strong and wealthy. In fact, those described as oppressed or wronged are literally the recipients of injustice (*edikemenou*). As a just judge, the Lord will right the wrongs that are committed against them. The cries and wails of those in need reach to the heavens, and are not withdrawn until the Most High responds.

The Lord's counterpart in responding to the needs of the lowly and poor is the audience to whom Sirach writes, young students whom he instructs in wisdom. Rather than accepting a cultural prejudice against the poor, Sirach looks to the Jewish tradition as a reliable guide. "Because of the precept, help the needy, and in their want, do not send them away empty-handed" (29:9). The Torah itself demands such attentiveness to the poor (e.g., Leviticus 23:22; Deuteronomy 15:8). Just as the Lord listens to their outcries and acts in justice, so too ought those who are truly wise: "Give a hearing to the poor man . . . let not justice be repugnant to you" (4:8, 9).

READING II Throughout his letters, Paul describes himself in many

For meditation and context:

RESPONSORIAL PSALM   Psalm 34:2–3, 17–18, 19, 23 (7a)

R. The Lord hears the cry of the poor.

I will bless the LORD at all times;
   his praise shall be ever in my mouth.
Let my soul glory in the LORD;
   the lowly will hear me and be glad.

The LORD confronts the evildoers,
   to destroy remembrance of them from the
    earth.
When the just cry out, the LORD hears them,
   and from all their distress he rescues them.

The LORD is close to the brokenhearted;
   and those who are crushed in spirit he
    saves.
The LORD redeems the lives of his servants;
   no one incurs guilt who takes refuge in
    him.

Beloved = bee-LUHV-uhd

Paul is preparing for death. "Libation" is wine poured out as a sacrificial offering. "Departure" is a euphemism for his death. His tone is confident and resigned.

Paul is keenly aware that he did all this only with Christ's help, so he speaks with gratitude.

Because he understands God's merciful love, he knows God will bless all those who remain faithful. Again, the timbre of the lines is gratitude.

Paul was wounded by this disloyalty, but his prayer for them is sincere.

This is why he can be generous and forgiving: Christ did not abandon him!

To the very end, Paul's trust will be unwavering.

Pause before the final line, then speak it as a prayer.

READING II   2 Timothy 4:6–8, 16–18

A reading from the second Letter of Saint Paul to Timothy

Beloved:
I am **already** being **poured out** like a **libation**,
   and the time of my **departure** is at **hand**.
I have **competed well**; I have **finished** the **race**;
   I have **kept** the **faith**.
From now on the **crown** of **righteousness** awaits me,
   which the **Lord**, the **just judge**,
   will **award** to me on that day, and **not only** to **me**,
   but to all who have **longed** for his **appearance**.

At my **first** defense **no one appeared** on my **behalf**,
   but **everyone deserted** me.
May it **not** be held **against** them!
But the **Lord stood by** me and **gave** me **strength**,
   so that **through** me the **proclamation** might be **completed**
   and all the **Gentiles** might **hear** it.
And I was **rescued** from the **lion's mouth**.
The **Lord** will **rescue** me from **every evil threat**
   and will bring me **safe** to his **heavenly Kingdom**.
To him be **glory forever** and **ever**. **Amen**.

ways, frequently referring to himself as apostle, servant, and slave, and he uses numerous metaphors to describe his life and ministry. In today's reading, written from prison, he develops two fitting metaphors to describe his present experience: his life is poured out like a libation, and he is running a race like an athlete. These two images are particularly poignant at this point in Paul's life as he sees that the time of his departure (*analusis*) is at hand. Referring to his impending death, Paul uses a metaphor employed by Homer for loosing a ship from its moorings in preparation for

setting sail. Paul's imprisonment is the final preparation for his departure. He sees his life as a living sacrifice, poured out like the ritual sacrifices of blood. We can imagine the incarcerated Paul with time to reflect on his life, looking at it now as a race that is almost completed. He has been a committed athlete in this race, and will earn no temporary laurel crown, but an eternal crown of righteousness. He is not maudlin or self-pitying as he sees the end drawing near, but longs for the Lord's appearance.

In the second part of the reading, Paul looks back at his life from another perspec-

tive. Though Paul had hoped that many of his coworkers would defend him, no one appeared. Yet, even in their absence, Paul does not stand alone. The Lord stands by him, giving him strength for the sake of bringing the Gospel to the Gentiles. Alluding again to his imminent departure, Paul confidently relies on the Lord who will bring him safely to his heavenly Kingdom.

GOSPEL   In Jesus' parables, he creates characters familiar to his audience, but developed in stories that turn around commonly held beliefs or

GOSPEL   Luke 18:9–14

A reading from the holy Gospel according to Luke

Jesus addressed this **parable**
    to those who were **convinced** of their **own righteousness**
    and **despised everyone else**.
"Two **people** went up to the **temple** area to **pray**;
    one was a **Pharisee** and the **other** was a **tax collector**.
The **Pharisee** took up his position and spoke this prayer
    to himself,
    'O **God**, **I thank you** that I am **not** like the **rest** of **humanity**—
    greedy, **dishonest**, **adulterous**—or even like this **tax collector**.
I fast **twice** a week, and I pay **tithes** on my **whole income**.'
But the **tax collector** stood off at **a distance**
    and would not even **raise** his **eyes** to **heaven**
    but **beat** his **breast** and **prayed**,
    'O **God**, be **merciful** to me a **sinner**.'
I **tell** you, the **latter** went home **justified**, **not** the **former**;
    for whoever **exalts** himself will be **humbled**,
    and the one who **humbles** himself will be **exalted**."

The introductory sentence sets the necessary context for Jesus' teaching.

Show no bias toward either character.

Note that the Pharisee is speaking "to himself."

Don't give the Pharisee an overly obnoxious tone; he thinks he's just telling the truth.

Read slowly, one phrase at a time, to suggest the tax collector's tentative approach.

His words are few, but heartfelt.

Pause before relating Jesus' assessment of the situation. He's turning an outcast into a role model and a pillar of society into a failure. Stress the contrasts as if trying to convince a skeptical crowd.

TO KEEP IN MIND
What does the reading ask your assembly to do or to be after hearing your proclamation? Focus on an intention every time you proclaim.

expectations. The Pharisee in today's parable, for example, would be regarded as righteous, honest, and upright, carefully attentive to keeping all the prescriptions of the Law. In contrast, people looked on tax collectors as just the opposite. They cheated the people by demanding more than was due, and gave the collected taxes to the Roman occupiers. People have clear expectations of both characters.

The Pharisee himself articulates how righteous he is and contrasts himself with the rest of humanity. He could likely see the tax collector out of the corner of his eye, a

prime case in point. Saying the prayer "to himself" may mean simply that he is praying quietly, with no one to hear his words. The phrase may also mean that the Pharisee is in fact speaking to himself about himself, rather than actually praying to God. The tax collector, not daring to even raise his eyes to heaven, is nonetheless speaking directly to God. He recognizes himself as a sinner and asks only for God's mercy. He does not deny his sinful life, but begs God to grant forgiveness.

Jesus is directing his parable to those who were convinced of their own righ-

teousness while despising others, as the Pharisee did. They are exalting themselves rather than God, while the humble tax collector has exalted God by admitting his sin and asking for mercy. E.P.

ALL SAINTS

LECTIONARY #667

READING I   Revelation 7:2–4, 9–14

A reading from the Book of Revelation

I, **John**, saw another **angel** come up from the East,
    holding the **seal** of the living **God**.
He cried out in a loud **voice** to the four angels
    who were given power to **damage** the **land** and the **sea**,
    "Do **not** damage the land or the sea or the trees
    until we put the **seal** on the foreheads of the **servants**
        of our God."
I heard the **number** of those who had been marked with the seal,
    one **hundred** and forty-four **thousand** marked
    from every **tribe** of the children of **Israel**.

After this I had a vision of a great **multitude**,
    which no one could **count**,
    from every **nation**, **race**, **people**, and **tongue**.
They stood before the **throne** and before the **Lamb**,
    wearing white **robes** and holding **palm** branches in
        their hands.
They cried out in a loud **voice**:

    "**Salvation** comes from our **God**, who is seated on the **throne**,
    and from the **Lamb**."
All the **angels** stood around the throne
    and around the **elders** and the four living **creatures**.
They **prostrated** themselves before the throne,
    worshiped God, and exclaimed: »

From word one, let your tone signal that you are describing an extraordinary vision. These are cataclysmic events you are describing. In the midst of the terror, the voice of an angel calls for a halt, so God's people can be "marked" for protection.

The number is less important than your solemn tone. Those sealed are protected by the one whose mark they bear.

"After this . . . " signals the start of a new, more expansive vision. "Every nation, race . . . " means every sector of humanity is represented.
The white robes and palm branches signify the victory of God's elect.

Lift your voice to give this acclamation a joyful chant-like quality.

All of heaven joins the exuberant hymn of praise.

READING I The Book of Revelation opens with John stating that the revelation has been given to him "to show his servants what must happen soon." John uses symbolic language and visions for this task. Today's reading consists of two visions, the first taking place on earth and the second in heaven, each looking ahead to what must happen soon.

In the first vision, we see a single angel coming from the east, symbolic of salvation. The saving angel prevents four destroying angels from damaging the land and sea, thereby announcing a reprieve from the final judgment until God's servants have received the seal on their foreheads. Used to signify ownership and protection, the seal has long been used to refer to Baptism. Those sealed by the angel, God's baptized servants, belong to God and are protected from the coming cataclysm. They number one hundred forty-four thousand, from every tribe of Israel. This number represents fulfillment and abundance, rather than a literal number.

The second vision looks and sounds like a great heavenly liturgy. The vast multitude wearing white robes symbolic of Resurrection, joy, and purity, hold palm branches in their hands. Only at the end of the vision do we learn that they have survived the great distress; like the threatened destruction of land and sea in the first vision, the great distress refers to God's final judgment. They cry out in a poetic acclamation well suited to a liturgy celebrating God's victory and our salvation. Everyone in heaven, including the great multitude, all the angels, the elders, and four symbolic living creatures join in an acclamation of profound faith.

Give us a sense that the cry of praise filled the heavens.

"**Amen. Blessing** and **glory**, **wisdom** and **thanksgiving**,
　　honor, **power**, and **might**
　be to our God **forever** and **ever. Amen.**"

The "elder" knows the answer to his own question. His tone is gentle and wise.

Then one of the **elders** spoke up and said to me,
　"Who are these wearing white **robes**, and where did they
　　come from?"
I said to him, "My **lord**, **you** are the one who knows."
He said to me,

The elder speaks with pride and admiration of those who survived persecution and trial.

That these multitudes entered the heavenly sanctuary, not through their own merit, but because of the work of the Lamb, should fill us with expectant hope.

　"These are the ones who have **survived** the time
　　of great distress;
　they have **washed** their robes
　and made them **white** in the **Blood** of the **Lamb**."

For meditation and context:

RESPONSORIAL PSALM　Psalm 24:1bc–2, 3–4ab, 5–6 (6)

R. Lord, this is the people that longs to see your face.

The LORD's are the earth and its fullness;
　the world and those who dwell in it.
For he founded it upon the seas
　and established it upon the rivers.

Who can ascend the mountain of the LORD?
　or who may stand in his holy place?
One whose hands are sinless, whose heart
　is clean,
　who desires not what is vain.

He shall receive a blessing from the LORD,
　a reward from God his savior.
Such is the race that seeks him,
　that seeks the face of the God of Jacob.

The passage is full of wonder at the love of God who makes us his beloved children. Focus on that love before you begin.

Beloved = bee-LUHV-uhd

Look at the assembly as you make this solemn affirmation.

READING II　1 John 3:1–3

A reading from the first Letter of Saint John

Beloved:
See what **love** the Father has **bestowed** on us
　that we may be called the **children** of God.
Yet so we **are**.
The reason the **world** does not know us
　is that it did not know **him**.

Regret tinges this admission that the world rejected Christ.

Pause briefly after "beloved" before continuing.

Beloved, we **are** God's children **now**;
　what we **shall** be has not yet been **revealed**.

READING II　In the desert, God formed a people, making them children of the Lord their God. It was out of love that God acted as a divine parent to them and made them God's own treasured people (Deuteronomy 14:1–2). In their long desert journey and throughout their history, the people of Israel experienced God's love in every circumstance, even when they rejected God's loving kindness. The same love that God bestowed on the ancestors has now been bestowed on the audience to whom John writes. They have

also seen, have also experienced, how God has loved them.

Having become God's beloved children, John's community exists in the midst of a world that does not know them. In the theology of John, knowing entails much more than an intellectual comprehension. Genuine knowing implies a right and loving relationship, such as that between the Father and the Son, and between the Lord and the children of God. Because the world does not know either the children or their Father, they can expect hostility and persecution. Yet by identifying the community as

beloved children of God, John is assuring them of God's abiding presence with them, even as God remained with their ancestors.

John includes all of us in his instruction. Even though we are already God's children, the fullness of our identity has not yet been revealed. When the time of fulfillment comes, we children of God will be like our Lord, and we shall see him as he is. In the meantime, we are to strive to live in the very purity that God radiates, perfect integrity, goodness, and holiness.

While some things are *unknown*, John confidently asserts that "At least we know *this* much."

This hope we have requires action on our part—to purify ourselves of all that pollutes the mind and heart.

We **do** know that **when** it is revealed we shall be **like** him,
    for we shall see him as he **is**.
Everyone who has this hope based on **him** makes himself **pure**,
    as **he** is pure.

GOSPEL · Matthew 5:1–12a

A reading from the holy Gospel according to Matthew

When Jesus saw the **crowds**, he went up the **mountain**,
    and after he had **sat** down, his **disciples** came to him.
He began to **teach** them, saying:

There are many effective ways to proclaim this familiar Gospel text. You can pause after each "blessed"; or prior to each "for they . . . "; or you might forgo pauses and deliver each Beatitude like a dart flying toward the bull's-eye. What is critical is that you keep a clear image of what (or better, whom) each Beatitude names. Have someone in mind for each of the eight "blesseds" and let their unique goodness color the way you proclaim.

These statements are meant to comfort those who live the Beatitudes and those who think they can't.

The message of these provocative statements is counter-cultural. How would your delivery be affected if some in your assembly got up and left in the middle of your speaking?

Leave time for silence between the Beatitudes so each can sink in.
Don't shy from emphasizing the word "blessed" each time it recurs.

Speak the final beatitude with awareness that some in your pews have indeed been insulted and slandered for the sake of the Kingdom.

Although the passage ends with an imperative, let your tone make it an invitation to dream God's Kingdom dream.

    "**Blessed** are the **poor** in **spirit**,
        for theirs is the Kingdom of **heaven**.
    Blessed are they who **mourn**,
        for they will be **comforted**.
    Blessed are the **meek**,
        for they will inherit the **land**.
    Blessed are they who **hunger** and **thirst** for **righteousness**,
        for they will be **satisfied**.
    Blessed are the **merciful**,
        for they will be shown **mercy**.
    Blessed are the clean of **heart**,
        for they will see **God**.
    Blessed are the **peacemakers**,
        for they will be called **children** of God.
    Blessed are they who are **persecuted** for the sake
            of **righteousness**,
        for theirs is the Kingdom of **heaven**.
    Blessed are **you** when they **insult** you and **persecute** you
        and utter every kind of **evil** against you **falsely** because
            of **me**.
    Rejoice and be **glad**,
        for your **reward** will be **great** in **heaven**."

GOSPEL | The Sermon on the Mount is the first of Jesus' discourses in Matthew's Gospel. In his first major teaching to his disciples, he gives them an overview of how they are to live as his community. By beginning with the beatitudes, Jesus offers his followers a challenging portrait, not only for those first followers gathered around them on the mountain, but for all who desire to be his disciples.

Jesus' Jewish audience would be familiar with beatitudes, statements of blessedness found frequently in the psalms. In fact, the first word in the Book of Psalms is "blessed," echoed by the first word in Jesus' inaugural sermon. In both psalter and sermon, beatitudes announce God's gracious kindness, freely bestowed in the present, with expectations of future fullness. Such announcements of divine blessing give a sense of identity to those who live in their light. Taken as a whole, the beatitudes develop a portrait of a disciple. The dispositions, attitudes, and actions express the right relationship, with both God and other people.

The first beatitude is a foundation for the rest. Whether materially poor or living in grandeur and success, those who are poor in spirit rely on God as the ultimate source of life and every blessing. As they put their trust in God, the poor in spirit also share in God's care for all of creation. Thus, their mourning, meekness, hunger and thirst for justice, actions of mercy, and peace making are a participation on God's own providence. The Kingdom of heaven is theirs! E.P.

THE COMMEMORATION OF ALL THE FAITHFUL DEPARTED (ALL SOULS)

LECTIONARY #668

READING I   Wisdom 3:1–9

A reading from the Book of Wisdom

The **souls** of the **just** are in the **hand** of **God**,
  and **no torment** shall **touch** them.
They **seemed**, in the **view** of the **foolish**, to be **dead**;
  and their **passing away** was thought an **affliction**
  and their **going forth** from us, utter **destruction**.
But **they** are in **peace**.
For if before **men**, indeed, they be **punished**,
  yet is their **hope** full of **immortality**;
chastised a **little**, they shall be **greatly blessed**,
  because **God tried** them
  and found them **worthy** of himself.
As **gold** in the **furnace**, he **proved** them,
  and as **sacrificial offerings** he **took** them to **himself**.
In the **time** of their **visitation** they shall **shine**,
  and shall **dart** about as **sparks** through **stubble**;
they shall **judge nations** and **rule** over **peoples**,
  and the Lord shall be their **King forever**.
Those who **trust** in him shall **understand truth**,
  and the **faithful** shall **abide** with him in **love**:
because **grace** and **mercy** are with his **holy ones**,
  and his **care** is with his **elect**.

The melodic opening line is the foundation for all that follows. Speak with joyful confidence.

Let your tone convey that here appearances don't match the reality.

This is another line to be delivered with utter conviction.

The purification that may come after death is not to be feared but welcomed as God's gift that prepares one for final judgment. Speak with authority.
blessed = blesd

The energy builds and the tempo quickens a bit as you offer the lovely image of souls shining like sparks.

The final sentence can be delivered at a slower pace, emphasizing the words "grace" and "mercy" that await God's elect.

There are many options for the readings today. Contact your parish staff to learn which will be used.

READING I   God is the creator of life, the one who "fashioned all things that they might have being" (Wisdom 1:14). God's gift of life, according to the Book of Wisdom, does not cease when a person dies. According to the Old Testament, death consigned a person to a shadowy existence in Sheol. Relationships are brought to an end. Even in the Greek world of the Wisdom writer, just a few decades before the birth of Christ, foolish people saw death as an affliction and utter destruction. Those who are wise know differently; the Sage proclaims that those who have lived justly will know blessedness and peace after death. Their relationship with God will continue. After death, they are in the hand of God and freed from the torments of life. No shadowy existence is expected, for "the just will live forever, . . . they shall receive the splendid crown" (5:15, 16).

The hope of immortality provides a way of looking at the present life. By affirming that the souls of the just are in the hand of God, Wisdom is implicitly promoting a just way of life. Justice, or righteousness, is the primary virtue in Wisdom. To live justly is to be in right relationship with God and one another. Beginning with the opening admonition, "Love justice," the Sage develops a multifaceted description of justice in the next five chapters of the book.

Without providing a clear or full picture of immortality, Wisdom still presents a strong foundation. The final lines in today's

For meditation and context:

RESPONSORIAL PSALM   Psalm 27:1, 4, 7, 8b, 9a, 13–14 (1a) (13)

R. The Lord is my light and my salvation.
or R. I believe that I shall see the good things of the Lord in the land of the living.

The Lord is my light and my salvation;
  whom should I fear?
The Lord is my life's refuge;
  of whom should I afraid?

One thing I ask of the Lord;
  this I seek:
To dwell in the house of the Lord
  all the days of my life,
that I may gaze on the loveliness of the Lord
  and contemplate his temple.

Hear, O Lord, the sound of my call;
  have pity on me and answer me.
Your presence, O Lord, I seek.
  Hide not your face from me.

I believe that I shall see the bounty of
  the Lord
  in the land of the living.
Wait for the Lord with courage;
  be stouthearted and wait for the Lord!

READING II   Romans 5:5–11

A reading from the Letter of Saint Paul to the Romans

Brothers and **sisters**:
Hope does **not disappoint**,
  because the **love** of **God** has been **poured out** into our **hearts**
  through the **Holy Spirit** that has been **given** to us.
For **Christ**, while we were **still helpless**,
  died at the appointed time for the **ungodly**.
Indeed, only with **difficulty** does one **die** for a **just person**,
  though **perhaps** for a **good person**
  one might **even find courage** to **die**.
But **God proves** his **love** for us
  in that while we were **still sinners Christ died** for us.
How much more then, since we are **now justified** by his **Blood**,
  will we be **saved** through **him** from the **wrath**.
Indeed, if, while we were **enemies**,
  we were **reconciled** to God through the **death** of his **Son**,
  how much more, once **reconciled**,
  will we be **saved** by his **life**.
Not only **that**, »

This is a bold statement to share with people who have lost loved ones. Speak from the knowledge of God's love within your own heart.

This is a bedrock Christian conviction: Christ died for us not when we were deserving, but when we were steeped in sin.

Even if one might die for a "good" person, the fact is Christ died for the undeserving—us.

If God showered mercy on us during our time of alienation, how can he not shower even more on us now that Christ has "reconciled" us?

End as joyfully as you began. The purpose of the text is not to argue a point, but to comfort with the truth of God's merciful love.

reading offer a sure hope: the faithful will abide with him in love (*agape*); God's grace (*charis*) and mercy (*eleos*) will be with God's holy ones. As God's love, grace, and mercy have sustained the just throughout their lives, the same divine attributes will be with them after death.

READING II   **Romans 5:5–11.** The reading from Romans opens with Paul confidently saying that hope does not disappoint. Then he unfolds, step by step, the reasons for such confidence, looking at the actions of the Father, Son, and Holy Spirit in the past, present, and future. The first reason for hope is that God has already poured love into our hearts through the Holy Spirit, a love that can refer simultaneously to the love that God has for us and the love we have for God. From either perspective, the love of God is freely bestowed by the power of the Holy Spirit.

After writing about the present gift of the Holy Spirit, Paul looks at Christ's action in the past. As a proof of God's love for us, Christ died for those whom Paul describes as helpless, ungodly, and sinners. His death in the past has continuing saving effects.

We are now justified by his blood and reconciled through his death. Justification and reconciliation are two ways of referring to God's ongoing actions of being brought back into right relationship, of forgiveness, and transformation.

Paul considers these saving effects, already received, as pointers to how God will act for us in the future. God's past and present actions assure Paul that God will do even more in the future, twice using the phrase "how much more." Ultimately, we will be saved through Christ from the wrath, that is, God's final conquering of

but we **also boast** of **God** through our **Lord Jesus Christ**,
through **whom** we have now **received reconciliation**.

Or:

READING II   Romans 6:3–9

A reading from the Letter of Saint Paul to the Romans

Brothers and **sisters**:
Are you **unaware** that **we** who were **baptized** into **Christ Jesus**
    were **baptized** into his **death**?
We were indeed **buried** with him through **baptism** into **death**,
    so **that**, just as **Christ** was **raised** from the **dead**
    by the **glory** of the **Father**,
    we **too** might **live** in **newness of life**.

For if we have **grown** into **union** with him through a **death**
    like his,
    we shall also be **united** with him in the **Resurrection**.
We know that our **old** self was **crucified** with him,
    so that our **sinful body** might be **done away** with,
    that we might **no longer** be in **slavery** to **sin**.
For a **dead** person has been **absolved** from sin.
If, then, we have **died** with **Christ**,
    we **believe** that we shall also **live** with him.
We know that **Christ**, **raised** from the **dead**, **dies** no **more**;
    death no longer has **power** over **him**.

Paul jolts us to attention with a rhetorical question: Don't you know that by being baptized in Christ you were baptized (initiated) into this death?
The joyful consequence of that dying in Christ is heralded here: We were "buried" like Christ so we could rise like him to "newness of life"!

"A death like his" refers to our Baptism. Paul is repeating his point to ensure we get it. Be sure your tone is gentle and reassuring.

"If then we have" is a repetition. But let your energetic tone keep it from sounding redundant.
The last two lines make the same assertion twice, so give greater stress to the second iteration. "We know" means "We are convinced!"

evil. A few short verses before today's reading Paul summarized what he, and all who believe, await: "We rejoice in our hope of sharing the glory of God."

Romans 6:3–9. To be baptized is to be immersed into the very person of Christ Jesus. Far more than an external initiation ritual, Baptism transforms the person, bringing about a profound union with Christ. Paul begins his baptismal teaching by asking his Roman audience a question, querying if they are unaware that through Baptism into Christ they have been baptized into his death. He answers his own question: not only have believers been bap-

tized into Christ's death, but they have also been buried with him, and will be united with him in his Resurrection. Such a weighty statement of faith, easily misunderstood, demands further explanation.

To die with Christ means that the believer has also been crucified and buried with him. Through union with Christ's crucifixion and death, the old self, the sinful body enslaved to sin, has been done away with. Having been united with Christ through a co-crucifixion and co-death, the baptized person will also be united with him in the Resurrection. Even now, believers have been immersed into Christ's

Paschal Mystery. They now live in Christ, so that the new life begun in Baptism will continue to grow as believers become more and more conformed to Christ's image.

The reading today concludes with this theological explanation of Baptism. Immediately after these verses, Paul develops the implications about how the baptized community ought to live. Those who are plunged into Christ's Paschal Mystery, brought from death to life, live a new life to God, continuing to live a cruciform existence in the pattern of Christ.

GOSPEL   John 6:37–40

A reading from the holy Gospel according to John

Jesus said to the **crowds**:
"**Everything** that the **Father gives** me will **come** to me,
    and I will **not reject anyone** who **comes** to me,
    because I **came** down from **heaven** not to do my **own will**
    but the **will** of the one who **sent** me.
And **this** is the **will** of the **one** who **sent** me,
    that I should not **lose anything** of what he **gave** me,
    but that I should **raise** it on the **last day**.
For **this is** the **will** of my **Father**,
    that **everyone** who **sees** the **Son** and **believes** in him
    may have **eternal life**,
    and I shall **raise** him on the **last day**."

Pause after the introductory phrase to shift to the compassionate and reassuring tone of Jesus.

Jesus' assertion that none be "lost" means we must weigh the evidence of our own experience against the infinite mercy of God.

Stress "this" here as in the previous sentence. God wants what we want—for everyone who has known Christ to share God's eternal life.

Make eye contact and, from memory, share the hope-filled final line.

GOSPEL In today's Gospel, Jesus is speaking to crowds who have followed him after his feeding of the five thousand. He has just revealed his mysterious identity to them, "I am the bread of life." He told them further that those who come to him will not hunger, and those who believe will not thirst. "Coming to Jesus" and "believing in him" appear to be synonymous ways of describing those who become his disciples. As the bread of life, Jesus will be their source of life-giving nourishment.

Having spoken about people coming to him, Jesus continues in today's reading, "Everything that the Father gives me will come to me." Although "everything" may refer to all creation as in the Colossian hymn (Colossians 1:15–20), the context and logic of the saying suggests that it means "every person." Jesus will not reject any person who comes to him because that is the will of his Father.

The Father's will and the Father's action are integral to Jesus' mission. The Father is the one who sent Jesus into the world, who wills that Jesus should not lose anything (or anyone) that the Father gave him. The Father also wills that those who see and believe Jesus may have eternal life. This means that believers have a share in the very life of God in the present, with fullness of eternal life when Jesus raises them up on the last day.

Jesus' discourse that reveals the intimate relationship between Jesus and his Father and their union of will is at the same time an invitation to the audience to listen to his words and believe in him. Those who believe will share in the bread of life, nourished by Jesus' body given for them. E.P.

THIRTY-FIRST SUNDAY IN ORDINARY TIME

LECTIONARY #153

READING I Wisdom 11:22—12:2

A reading from the Book of Wisdom

> **Before** the Lord the whole **universe** is as a **grain**
>   from a **balance**
> or a **drop** of morning **dew** come down upon the **earth**.
> But **you** have **mercy** on **all**, because you can **do all things**;
>   and you **overlook** people's **sins** that they may **repent**.
> For you **love all** things that **are**
>   and **loathe nothing** that you have **made**;
>   for what you **hated**, you would not have **fashioned**.
> And how could a thing **remain**, unless **you willed** it;
>   or be **preserved**, had it not been **called forth** by **you**?
> But you **spare** all things, because they are **yours**,
>   **O Lord** and **lover** of **souls**,
>   for your **imperishable spirit** is in **all** things!
> Therefore you **rebuke offenders little** by **little**,
>   **warn** them and **remind** them of the **sins**
>   they are **committing**,
>   that they may **abandon** their **wickedness** and **believe**
>   in **you**, **O Lord**!

You are telling God about the wonder of all his creation!

"But you . . . " conveys human amazement that God, so powerful, is willing to be so merciful.
God "overlooks" for a purpose—that we might repent!
Some ancient cultures believed God created both good *and* evil.

These rhetorical questions are meant to convey awe that God made and sustains all things in creation.

God not only loves creation, but God's "imperishable spirit" is *in* all things.

God does not shy from pointing out our shortcomings, but God's "rebuke" is a gift that leads to salvation.

Sustain eye contact through this final sentence. It is more a prayer than a declaration.

READING I The Book of Wisdom was likely written in the first century before Christ to a Jewish audience living in Alexandria, Egypt. As the author, often referred to as Pseudo-Solomon, instructs them in their traditions and beliefs, he displays a profound knowledge of their Scriptures and skillfully presents them for his Hellenistic audience. Today's reading is taken from a lengthy section of the book in which Pseudo-Solomon speaks to God. As he addresses God, he is instructing his audience about the divine nature, the relationship of God with all of creation,

what his audience is to believe, and how they are to behave.

The reading begins by emphasizing God's grandeur; the universe itself is a mere grain in the balance or drop of the morning dew when compared to God. Immediately following this image of divine splendor and majesty is a tenderly personal view of God. The Lord shows mercy on all, loves everything that he has created, preserves and spares all things, simply because they belong to God. God's mercy on all creation, rather than being in opposition to divine grandeur, is actually a mani-

festation of it, as the author acclaims, "You have mercy on all, because you can do all things."

Woven into the beautiful portrait of God are signs of how God's people should live. They should repent of their sins, abandon wickedness and believe in the Lord God. They can expect God to rebuke them little by little. As God warns them and reminds them of their sins, they ought always to remember that God's mercy extends to all.

For meditation and context:

RESPONSORIAL PSALM Psalm 145:1–2, 8–9, 10–11, 13, 14 (see 1)

R. I will praise your name for ever, my king and my God.

I will extol you, O my God and King;
    and I will bless your name forever
        and ever.
Every day will I bless you;
    and I will praise your name forever
        and ever.

The LORD is gracious and merciful,
    slow to anger and of great kindness.
The LORD is good to all
    and compassionate toward all his works.

Let all your works give you thanks, O LORD,
    and let your faithful ones bless you.
Let them discourse of the glory of
        your Kingdom
    and speak of your might.

The LORD is faithful in all his words
    and holy in all his works.
The LORD lifts up all who are falling
    and raises up all who are bowed down.

READING II   2 Thessalonians 1:11—2:2

Thessalonians = thes-uh-LOH-nee-uhnz

Pause after the salutation.

Give this the quality of an earnest prayer for your own assembly.

Each phrase conveys a new idea; take your time so you don't blur one into another.

Pause and take a breath before starting the second sentence. This is the "business" at hand that must now be addressed!

He's urging them not to be easily thrown off by rumors and lies.

"The day of the Lord" is no small matter to get wrong; correcting this misinformation is essential.

**A reading from the second Letter of Saint Paul
    to the Thessalonians**

Brothers and **sisters**:
We **always pray** for you,
    that our **God** may make you **worthy** of his **calling**
    and powerfully bring to **fulfillment every** good **purpose**
    and **every effort** of faith,
    that the **name** of our **Lord** Jesus may be **glorified** in **you**,
    and **you** in **him**,
    in accord with the **grace** of our **God** and **Lord Jesus Christ**.

We **ask** you, **brothers** and **sisters**,
    with regard to the **coming** of our **Lord Jesus Christ**
    and our **assembling** with him,
    not to be **shaken** out of your **minds** suddenly, or to be **alarmed**
    either by a "**spirit**," or by an **oral statement**,
    or by a **letter allegedly** from **us**
    to the **effect** that the **day** of the **Lord** is at **hand**.

READING II At the beginning of his Second Letter to the Thessalonians, Paul offers a prayer of thanks to God for the community, grateful for the growth of their faith, and the increase of their love for one another. He adds another prayer in today's reading, telling the Thessalonians that he always prays for them, asking that God may make them worthy of their call. The God who called them to faith and communion in the beginning is the one who will bring their efforts to fulfillment. Paul reminds them that God's powerful action within them is not for their

sake alone, but so that the name of the Lord Jesus may be glorified in them.

In the second part of the reading, Paul writes to correct their misunderstanding and apprehension about Jesus' coming (*parousia*). The Thessalonian Christians are being persecuted and afflicted with many trials. Such affliction was often seen as a sign of the end-times, and of God's final conquering of evil, referred to as the "Day of the Lord." Paul had already written about the topic in his first letter to the community. In both letters, he writes to assuage their worry, alarm, and exaggerated focus

on Christ's future coming. Those who, unlike Paul, claim that the day of the Lord is at hand are creating fear, not hope. Paul's emphasis is on abiding faith, vibrant love, participation in Christ's death and Resurrection in the present, and being conformed to him. That is the best way to be prepared for Christ's future coming.

GOSPEL The story of Zacchaeus and Jesus is replete with picturesque details, beginning with the depiction of Zacchaeus himself. As the chief tax collector, he would be despised by the crowds

There is no indication of Jesus' intent to encounter Zacchaeus.

Here is a rich man not used to being deprived of what he wants.

His unorthodox solution becomes the doorway to his salvation.

Jesus brings urgency into the situation, perhaps sensing an opportunity that must not be squandered.

Zacchaeus immediately responds with joy to Jesus' self-invitation.

Does Zacchaeus fear that the crowd will dissuade Jesus from entering his home? He doesn't risk it and takes remarkable action right there and then.

The Old Testament prescribes this level of restitution (see 2 Samuel 12:6), so Zacchaeus seems aware of the Law.

All three final lines are classic. Don't rush them, and sustain eye contact on the last line assuring your assembly this applies to them.

GOSPEL   Luke 19:1–10

A reading from the holy Gospel according to Luke

At that **time**, **Jesus** came to **Jericho** and intended
　　to pass **through** the town.
Now a **man** there named **Zacchaeus**,
　　who was a chief **tax** collector and also a **wealthy** man,
　　was seeking to **see who Jesus was**;
　　but he could **not see** him because of the **crowd**,
　　for he was **short** in **stature**.
So he **ran** ahead and **climbed** a **sycamore** tree in order to **see Jesus**,
　　who was about to **pass** that **way**.
When he **reached** the place, **Jesus looked** up and said,
　　"**Zacchaeus**, come down **quickly**,
　　for **today** I **must stay** at your **house**."
And he **came** down **quickly** and received him with **joy**.
When they **all saw** this, they began to **grumble**, saying,
　　"He has **gone** to **stay** at the **house** of a **sinner**."
But **Zacchaeus stood** there and said to the **Lord**,
　　"**Behold**, **half** of my **possessions**, **Lord**, I shall **give** to the **poor**,
　　and if I have **extorted anything** from **anyone**
　　I shall **repay** it **four times over**."
And **Jesus** said to him,
　　"**Today salvation** has come to this **house**
　　because **this** man **too** is a **descendant** of **Abraham**.
For the **Son** of **Man** has come to **seek**
　　and to **save** what was **lost**."

who will later refer to him as a sinner. A wealthy man such as Zacchaeus would ordinarily guard his dignity. Yet in this scene he abandons his dignity first by running, considered demeaning for a mature man, and then acts even more outrageously by climbing up a tree to see Jesus. Zacchaeus simply wanted to see Jesus, but it is Jesus who sees Zacchaeus in his lofty perch.

　　Jesus' words and Zacchaeus' response move the story rapidly forward: "come down quickly"; then without any hesitation "he came down quickly." In this first

encounter with Zacchaeus, Jesus uses two words that highlight important themes in Luke's Gospel: "must" and "today". Early in his ministry, Jesus declared, "To the other towns also I must proclaim the good news of the Kingdom of God" (4:43). There is a divine necessity and purpose in Jesus' preaching far and wide, as there is in visiting the house of Zacchaeus: God's plan is to bring the good news to all people. Beginning with the announcement of the birth of the savior, the word *today* signals the inauguration of God's saving action in the present.

　　When Zacchaeus joyfully receives Jesus into his house, he announces that he will give half his possessions to the poor and will repay four times over anything he has extorted. Neither Jesus nor Zacchaeus deny that he is a sinner. The important thing is that today salvation has come to his house, fulfilling Jesus mission of seeking and saving the lost. E.P.

THIRTY-SECOND SUNDAY IN ORDINARY TIME

LECTIONARY #156

READING I   2 Maccabees 7:1–2, 9–14

A reading from the second Book of Maccabees

It **happened** that **seven brothers** with their **mother** were **arrested**
and **tortured** with **whips** and **scourges** by the **king**,
to **force** them to eat **pork** in **violation** of **God's law.**
One of the brothers, **speaking** for the **others**, said:
"**What** do you **expect** to **achieve** by **questioning** us?
We are **ready** to **die** rather than **transgress** the **laws**
of our **ancestors.**"

At the point of **death** he said:
"You **accursed fiend**, you are **depriving** us of this **present life**,
but the **King** of the **world** will **raise** us up to **live again forever**.
It is for **his** laws that we are **dying** "

After him the **third** suffered their cruel **sport.**
He put out his tongue **at once** when told to do so,
and **bravely** held out his **hands**, as he spoke these noble **words:**
"It was from **Heaven** that I received these;
for the **sake** of his **laws** I **disdain** them;
from **him** I **hope** to **receive** them **again.**"
Even the **king** and his **attendants marveled**
at the young man's **courage**,
because he regarded his **sufferings** as **nothing**. **»**

Maccabees = MAK-uh-beez

The opening words belie the gruesome nature of what follows, so begin with a weighty tone.
Don't rush past the violent language: "tortured"; "whips"; "scourges."
They have considered their decision and this brother speaks it for the rest.

The identification of this as the "second" brother is left out. "He" substitutes for "the second brother."
He mocks their ignorance.

The cruelty of the persecutors is reinforced by the use of the word "sport."

He makes three statements: Where he got them, his willingness to sacrifice them, and his conviction that they will be restored.

Convey the wonder of the king at the young man's courage.

READING I   Belief in the Resurrection of Jesus from the dead is at the very center of Christian faith. In the world of first-century Judaism, however, not all Jews believed even in the possibility of Resurrection. The Sadducees saw no evidence in the Torah for God raising the dead, while Pharisees had faith in the Resurrection of the just at the end of the ages. Much of the Old Testament reflects a belief that the reward of the just would be given to their descendants, with the afterlife consisting of a shadowy existence in Sheol. One of the clearest testaments of

pre-Christian Jewish belief in the Resurrection is found in today's reading from Maccabees about seven brothers who are put to death. Written in a Hellenistic milieu in the second century before Christ, Maccabees reflects a development in some Jewish belief in the afterlife.

The story of the martyred brothers is filled with graphic details of torture, some of which are omitted from the lectionary. The harshness of the brothers' persecution brings their steadfastness into sharp focus, for they remain faithful to their tradition no matter what suffering they endure. The

motivation underlying their courage is their belief in the Resurrection of the dead. The first one to speak gives a clear statement of his belief. Though their tormentors are depriving them of this present life, the King of the world will raise them up to live again forever. The king who is persecuting them is not the King of the world; the Lord God of Israel, in whom the brothers and all faithful Jews put their trust, is a more powerful king who will give them life forever.

As the third brother is being cruelly tormented, he adds another dimension to their belief. Holding out his hands, he

Remember, you are speaking of four murders. Don't lose the weighty tone needed to relate this remarkable story.

His courage is rooted in his faith that he will rise again. His final comment reflects the conviction that evildoers would *not* rise from the dead.

After he had **died**,
> they **tortured** and **maltreated** the **fourth** brother
>> in the **same** way.

When **he** was **near death**, he said,
> "It is my **choice** to **die** at the **hands** of **men**
>> with the **hope God** gives of being **raised up** by him;
>> but for **you**, there will be **no Resurrection** to **life**."

For meditation and context:

RESPONSORIAL PSALM   Psalm 17:1, 5–6, 8, 15 (15b)

R. Lord, when your glory appears, my joy will be full.

Hear, O Lord, a just suit;
   attend to my outcry;
   hearken to my prayer from lips
      without deceit.

My steps have been steadfast in your paths,
   my feet have not faltered.
I call upon you, for you will answer me,
      O God;
   incline your ear to me; hear my word.

Keep me as the apple of your eye,
   hide me in the shadow of your wings.
But I in justice shall behold your face;
   on waking I shall be content in
      your presence.

READING II   2 Thessalonians 2:16—3:5

Thessalonians = thes-uh-LOH-nee-uhnz

**A reading from the second Letter of Saint Paul to
   the Thessalonians**

You begin with a prayer comprised of several phrases that communicate separate thoughts. Don't run them together.

"Good hope" refers to Christ's return at the end of time.

Invite your assembly to join the prayer Paul requests for the spread of the Gospel.

Don't make light of this sobering truth that there are those who work against the Gospel.

Brothers and **sisters**:
May our **Lord Jesus Christ himself** and **God** our **Father**,
   who has **loved** us and **given** us **everlasting encouragement**
   and **good hope** through his **grace**,
      encourage your **hearts** and **strengthen** them
         in every **good deed** and **word**.
Finally, **brothers** and **sisters**, **pray** for us,
   so that the **word** of the **Lord** may speed **forward** and be **glorified**,
   as it did among **you**,
   and that we may be **delivered** from **perverse** and **wicked people**,
   for **not all** have **faith**.

speaks of his hope that the God who gave him his hands will give them back to him. He believes that his body will be fully restored at the Resurrection. As yet another brother is being tortured, he affirms what all the brothers believe: hope that God will raise them up. He then adds that for those who are so maltreating them, there will be no Resurrection to life. The Maccabean belief in Resurrection of the body is not for the wicked, but only for the just.

READING II
Early in Paul's Second Letter to the Thessalonians, he offers a prayer of thanksgiving to God, and he reiterates it midway through: "we ought to give thanks to God for you always, brothers and sisters loved by the Lord" (2:13). Today's reading adds other prayers: first Paul's prayer for the community, and then Paul asking that they pray for him. An atmosphere of prayer, rooted in God's steadfast and loving relationship with the community, permeates the entire letter.

There was good reason for Paul to emphasize prayer to the nascent Church. The Christians in Thessalonica were enduring persecution and needed hope as they awaited the Lord Jesus' coming again (*parousia*). Paul's emphasis on prayer is a means of reminding the community that God's loving presence sustains them in the here and now, in the midst of their affliction. Paul prays that God will provide encouragement and strengthen them in every one of their good deeds and words.

Having prayed for the community, Paul then asks that they pray for him and his coworkers, so that the word of the Lord will speed forward and be glorified. Paul's prayer is thus not so much for himself as for the effectiveness of the word that he

But the Lord **is faithful**;
  he will **strengthen** you and **guard** you from the **evil one**.
We are **confident** of **you** in the **Lord** that what **we instruct you**,
  you are **doing** and will **continue** to do.
May the **Lord direct your hearts** to the **love** of **God**
  and to the **endurance** of **Christ**.

GOSPEL   Luke 20:27–38

A reading from the holy Gospel according to Luke

[Some **Sadducees**, those who **deny** that there is a **Resurrection**,
  came **forward**] and put this **question** to Jesus, saying,
  "**Teacher**, **Moses** wrote for us,
  *If someone's **brother** dies leaving a **wife** but **no child**,*
  *his **brother** must **take** the wife*
  *and raise up **descendants** for his brother.*
Now there were **seven** brothers;
  the **first** married a **woman** but **died childless**.
Then the **second** and the **third** married her,
  and likewise all the **seven died childless**.
Finally the **woman** also died.
Now at the **Resurrection** whose **wife** will **that woman be**?
For **all seven** had been **married** to her."
[**Jesus** said to them,
  "The **children** of **this age marry** and **remarry**;
  but those who are **deemed worthy** to **attain** to the **coming age**
  and to the **Resurrection** of the **dead**
  neither marry nor are **given** in **marriage**.
They can no longer **die**,
  for they are **like angels**;
  and they are the **children** of **God**
  because **they** are the **ones** who will **rise**. »

God's faithfulness is a source of comfort!

These words are also true of your assembly. Speak them sincerely.

With strong eye contact, you end with another prayer directed at your listeners.

The parenthetical comment is the most important information in the opening sentence. There is no need to signal their ulterior motives.

Their first statement sets the parameters for the legal question.

"Now" signals the complications that make the situation seemingly difficult to resolve.

With self-satisfaction, the Pharisee suggests he's presented a nut too hard to crack!

Stress "seven" as if to remind Jesus not to ignore the details of the story.
Jesus is not argumentative, for his teaching is as much for the crowd as for the leaders. His words paint a heavenly realm of serenity and joy.

---

preaches. The word (the entirety of the good news lived and proclaimed) is energetic and dynamic, almost appearing to be a person, as seen in the Hebrew tradition.

Underlying the prayers of Paul and the community is God's fidelity and abiding love. Having prayed that God strengthen the community, Paul affirms confidently that the Lord will indeed strengthen them and guard them. Paul's confidence extends to the community itself: "in the Lord" they are presently following Paul's instructions and will continue to do so. Paul's final prayer is an appeal directly to the Lord to order the hearts of the community so that God's love and Christ's steadfastness may be manifest in the believers in Thessalonica.

GOSPEL   After his extensive journey with his disciples, Jesus entered Jerusalem, where he immediately faced opposition from the chief priests, scribes, and leaders of the people. The various groups attempted to trap Jesus, posing questions, challenging his authority, and seeking to put him to death. Today's Gospel tells of the Sadducees who came forward with a question designed to embarrass Jesus. Addressing Jesus as "teacher," perhaps sarcastically, they cite Moses, a logical place to begin since their belief was based on the Torah. According to Moses, if a married man died childless, his brother was required to marry the widow in order to raise up descendants for his brother. Having heirs was important for economic and societal stability. Even more, in the context of this episode, the "raising up" of descendants was the means of a person living on.

This final teaching requires a higher level of energy. Jesus is using the Law they espouse to prove their contention wrong, but again, avoid an argumentative tone and strive, instead, to communicate the love of God that keeps us eternally alive.

That the **dead will rise**
> even **Moses** made known in the **passage** about the **bush**,
> when he called out '**Lord**,'
> the **God** of **Abraham**, the **God** of **Isaac**, and the **God** of **Jacob**;
> and he is not **God** of the **dead**, but of the **living**,
> for to **him all** are **alive**."]

[Shorter: Luke 20:27, 34–38 (see brackets)]

Having cited Moses, the Sadducees set up the story of seven brothers who die childless, one after another. In their tale, not only would Resurrection create a seemingly impossible determination of whose wife the widow would be, but there wouldn't even be descendants raised up in this life to carry on the family name. Jesus uses the opportunity to set his opponents straight. Fundamental to his teaching is the distinction between "this age" and "the coming age." In the coming age, those deemed worthy to attain the Resurrection of the dead will no longer marry, nor be given in marriage. In the coming age, neither men nor women will marry or die. They are "like angels," heavenly beings in which the Sadducees did not believe. Jesus says further that those raised from the dead "are the children of God because they are the ones who will rise." He teaches that by their Resurrection, they will have the abiding identity of God's own children.

Jesus concludes his answer to the Sadducees by citing the Torah, as the Sadducees themselves had done in initiating their challenge. The God who spoke to Moses in the scene of the burning bush is God of Abraham, God of Isaac, and God of Jacob. If the Lord is their God, even though they have died, they must still be alive, for the Lord is the God of the living. E.P.

THIRTY-THIRD SUNDAY IN ORDINARY TIME

LECTIONARY #159

READING I   Malachi 3:19–20a

A reading from the Book of the Prophet Malachi

Lo, the day is **coming**, **blazing** like an **oven**,
   when all the **proud** and all **evildoers** will be **stubble**,
and the **day** that is **coming** will set them on **fire**,
   leaving them **neither root nor branch**,
     says the Lord of **hosts**.
But for **you** who **fear** my **name**, there will **arise**
   the **sun** of **justice** with its **healing rays**.

Malachi = MAL-uh-kī

Be sure all are attentive before you begin. Pause after speaking the exclamation "Lo," then continue with high energy.

These are hard truths spoken without malice, but with conviction.
Holding back on this stern message deprives listeners of an important truth.
"But . . ." is spoken with strength, but in a comforting tone. God's fire can both destroy and heal.

For meditation and context:

RESPONSORIAL PSALM   Psalm 98:5–6, 7–8, 9 (see 9)

R. The Lord comes to rule the earth with justice.

Sing praise to the Lord with the harp,
   with the harp and melodious song.
With trumpets and the sound of the horn
   sing joyfully before the King, the Lord.

Let the sea and what fills it resound,
   the world and those who dwell in it;
let the rivers clap their hands,
   the mountains shout with them for joy.

Before the Lord, for he comes,
   for he comes to rule the earth;
he will rule the world with justice
   and the peoples with equity.

READING I Malachi's prophecy opens with a terrifying image. On the coming day, "the day of the Lord, the great and terrible day" (3:23), the Lord of hosts will judge the proud and evildoers with a blazing fire. All that will be left of them will be mere stubble, with neither root nor branch for possible future growth. When the people of Israel envisioned this Day of the Lord, they most often looked at other nations as recipients of God's harsh judgment, while they themselves would be vindicated. However, Malachi's prophecies are a series of sharp indictments against Israel, the people of the covenant who have acted corruptly and have not kept the faith of their ancestors. They are the proud and evildoers.

According to Malachi, when the people returned from exile and rebuilt the temple, their temple sacrifices were a sham. The priests did not lead the people in proper worship, and even accepted animals for oblation that were stolen, lame, and sick. The Lord's indictment extends beyond the priests, for the people have abandoned the Torah requirements: they have defrauded widows and orphans, have turned aside the stranger, and do not fear the Lord of hosts.

The graphic metaphors of the Day of the Lord, along with the indictments against both priest and people, are intended to make them aware of their behavior and challenge them to turn from their sinful ways. There is hope for those who repent. The final verse in today's reading offers another vision, far different from the devastating judgment of the day of the Lord. For the ones who fear God's name, the sun of justice will arise with its healing rays. This will be the dawning of a new day

READING II   2 Thessalonians 3:7–12

Thessalonians = thes-uh-LOH-nee-uhnz

Paul is all teacher today correcting and laying down the law. His tone immediately calls his listeners to attention!

Paul is just stating facts, not self-aggrandizing.

At his own expense, Paul offered a "model for [them]."

Paul is concerned about the disruption caused by the slackers in the community.

Paul claims the authority of Christ to order everyone to do their fair share.

**A reading from the second Letter of Saint Paul
   to the Thessalonians**

Brothers and **sisters:**
You **know** how one must **imitate** us.
For we did **not act** in a **disorderly** way **among** you,
   nor did we eat **food** received **free** from **anyone.**
On the **contrary**, in **toil** and **drudgery**, **night** and **day**
   we **worked**, so as not to **burden any** of you.
Not that we do not **have** the **right.**
Rather, we wanted to **present** ourselves as a **model** for you,
   so that you might **imitate** us.
In **fact**, when we were **with** you,
   we **instructed** you that if **anyone** was **unwilling** to work,
   neither should that one **eat.**
We hear that some **are conducting** themselves among you
   in a **disorderly** way,
   by not keeping **busy** but **minding** the **business of others.**
Such people we **instruct** and **urge** in the **Lord Jesus Christ**
   to **work quietly**
   and to **eat** their **own food.**

GOSPEL   Luke 21:5–19

Let the grand description of the Temple contrast with the fate Jesus predicts in the following lines.

Jesus takes no joy in this prediction.

A reading from the holy Gospel according to Luke

While **some** people were speaking about
   how the **temple** was adorned with **costly stones**
     and **votive offerings,**
   Jesus said, "**All** that you **see** here—
   the days will **come** when there will **not** be **left**
   a **stone** upon **another stone** that will not be **thrown down.**"

for those who have listened to the prophetic word and have turned to the Lord.

READING II The Second Letter to the Thessalonians is from Paul, Silvanus, and Timothy. Thus, the advice to the community explaining "how one must imitate us" includes all three letter writers as models for the community to imitate. Paul himself used Christ as the model for how he should conduct himself, as he urged the Christians in Corinth, "Be imitators of me, as I am of Christ" (1 Corinthians 11:1). All who believe in Christ are to be co-

imitators of Christ, along with Paul and his fellow missionaries (Philippians 3:17).

As Jesus worked tirelessly in proclaiming the Kingdom of God, Paul and his coworkers also labored night and day for their communities. Presenting themselves as a model to imitate, they encouraged each member of the community to conduct themselves in a like manner. Such instruction was needed, since Paul had heard that some among them acted in a disorderly way. Making a clever play on words, Paul says that some people there were not keeping busy but instead were "busybod-

ies." Instructing further that they "work quietly," Paul implies that people should peacefully do their own work without meddling officiously in the affairs of others. In the verse immediately following today's reading, Paul summarizes his exhortation: "Brothers and sisters, do not be remiss in doing good." Such a way of life would imitate Paul, Silvanus, Timothy, and most importantly, Jesus himself.

GOSPEL With the magnificent temple in Jerusalem in the background, Jesus addresses the people

Then they **asked** him,
"**Teacher**, **when** will this **happen**?
And what **sign** will there be when **all** these things
    are **about** to **happen**?"
He **answered**,
"**See** that you not be **deceived**,
  for **many** will come in my **name**, saying,
  'I am **he**,' and 'The **time** has **come**.'
Do **not follow** them!
When you hear of **wars** and **insurrections**,
  do **not** be **terrified**; for such things **must** happen **first**,
  but it will not **immediately** be the **end**."
Then he said to them,
"**Nation** will **rise** against **nation**, and **Kingdom** against
    Kingdom.
There will be **powerful earthquakes**, **famines**, and **plagues**
  from **place** to **place**;
  and **awesome sights** and **mighty signs** will come from **the sky**.

"**Before** all this **happens**, **however**,
  they will **seize** and **persecute** you,
  they will **hand you over** to the **synagogues** and to **prisons**,
  and they will have you **led** before **kings** and **governors**
  because of **my name**.
It will **lead** to your giving **testimony**.
Remember, you are **not** to **prepare** your defense **beforehand**,
  for I **myself** shall **give** you a **wisdom** in **speaking**
  that **all** your **adversaries** will be **powerless** to **resist** or **refute**.
You will even be **handed over** by **parents**, **brothers**,
    relatives and **friends**,
  and they will put **some** of you to **death**.
You will be **hated** by **all** because of my **name**,
  but not a **hair** on your **head** will be **destroyed**.
By your **perseverance** you will **secure** your **lives**."

Their eager curiosity alerts Jesus to how easily they might be fooled, so he responds with urgency, counseling caution.

Let your tone encourage composure.

These apocalyptic signs, dire as they are, will be preceded by even more painful personal struggles with governments and families.

Even in times of such distress we can give witness to our faith.

Jesus' tone suggests the sorrow with which his listeners would receive such unsettling news.

Slow down on the last two lines. Jesus, Shepherd of the sheep, speaks authoritatively of his care for those who cling to the sheepfold.

---

for the final time before his passion. He begins by telling them that the Temple will be destroyed. Without specifying the time, he says "the days will come," when this will happen, reminiscent of Malachi's writing of the Day of the Lord, the great and terrible day. Like Malachi's prophecy, Jesus speaks of a coming time of great devastation and turmoil. His speech is often referred to as his eschatological discourse; eschatology treats of the events that are connected with the "end," sometimes dealing with the fate of individuals, but more broadly with

God's final, triumphant conquering of evil and the vindication of the just.

Although the time when the end will come is uncertain, it is nonetheless assured that it will come. With the vivid imagery common to other scenarios of the last days, Jesus speaks of widespread human conflict as well as the upheaval of nature itself. Jesus' followers will experience more immediate suffering: they will be persecuted and imprisoned because of their faith in Jesus. Some will be betrayed by families, and some put to death. Yet

death will not destroy them. By their steadfastness, they will be saved.

In the Gospel account, Jesus is speaking before the destruction of the temple occurred in the year 70, decades after Jesus' lifetime. Heard by the later Church, Jesus' words carry the same note of being faithful to the end, enduring the suffering that will surely come to Jesus' followers, and relying on his promise and presence. The message is relevant to the Church of any generation. E.P.

OUR LORD JESUS CHRIST, KING OF THE UNIVERSE

LECTIONARY #162

READING I   2 Samuel 5:1–3

Hebron = HEB-ruhn

With the first line, set a tone of regal solemnity.

Although Saul was king, it was David who led the armies and won many victories.

It was God's will that David be king. Speak "shepherd" and "commander" with great reverence.

They negotiate a covenant and then formally anoint him king.

A reading from the second Book of Samuel

In those days, **all** the **tribes** of Israel came to **David**
    in **Hebron** and said:
    "**Here** we **are**, **your bone** and **your flesh**.
In days **past**, when **Saul** was our **king**,
    it was **you** who led the **Israelites out** and brought them **back**.
And the Lord said to you,
    'You shall **shepherd** my **people Israel**
    · and shall be **commander** of Israel.'"
When all the **elders** of Israel **came** to **David** in **Hebron**,
    King David made an **agreement** with them there
        before the Lord,
    and they **anointed** him **king** of Israel.

For meditation and context:

RESPONSORIAL PSALM   Psalm 122:1–2, 3–4, 4–5 (see 1)

R. Let us go rejoicing to the house of the Lord.

I rejoiced because they said to me,
    "We will go up to the house of the Lord."
And now we have set foot
    within your gates, O Jerusalem.

Jerusalem, built as a city
    with compact unity.
To it the tribes go up,
    the tribes of the Lord.

According to the decree for Israel,
    to give thanks to the name of the Lord.
In it are set up judgment seats,
    seats for the house of David.

READING I   David, son of Jesse, was first anointed by the prophet Samuel at the Lord's command. Later, the people of Judah anointed David as king over the house of Judah. In today's reading, David is anointed a third time, this time as king over all the tribes of Israel. Besides the ordinary practice of anointing as a sign of respect, anointing was a rite of consecration for prophets, priests, and kings. David's anointing three times marked him as king by both the choice of God and of the people.

When all the tribes of Israel came to David in Hebron, they stated three reasons for him to be anointed. First, they are "your bone and your flesh," descended from the same ancestors. Second, even when Saul was king, David took on the role of military leader, proving himself to be strong and wise. The third reason comes from the Lord, who gave David two roles: shepherd and commander. Shepherds were responsible for watching over their flocks, protecting them from predators, and tending to their overall well-being; so should a shepherd king be for the people. Military com-

manders led their people in battle, fighting alongside them against their enemies. Both designations regard the king as closely linked with the people.

As a result of the people's entreaty, David made a covenant with them before the Lord. Like other covenants in the ancient world, this one entails obligations on both parties. David agrees to rule with justice, and the people promise loyalty. The covenant made before the Lord gave David's anointing as king of all Israel a religious solemnity and divine blessing.

READING II　Colossians 1:12–20

A reading from the Letter of Saint Paul to the Colossians

Brothers and **sisters:**
Let us give **thanks** to the **Father**,
　who has made you **fit** to **share**
　in the **inheritance** of the **holy ones** in **light**.
He **delivered us** from the **power** of **darkness**
　and **transferred us** to the **Kingdom** of his **beloved Son**,
　in whom we have **redemption**, the **forgiveness** of **sins**.

　　He is the **image** of the **invisible God**,
　　　the **firstborn** of **all creation**.
　　For in **him** were **created** all things in **heaven** and on **earth**,
　　　the **visible** and the **invisible**,
　　　whether **thrones** or **dominions** or **principalities** or **powers;**
　　　all things were **created through him** and **for him**.
　　He is **before all** things,
　　　and **in** him **all things** hold **together**.
　　He is the **head** of the **body**, the **church**.
　　He is the **beginning**, the **firstborn** from the **dead**,
　　　that in **all** things he **himself** might be **preeminent**.
　　For in **him all** the **fullness** was **pleased to dwell**,
　　　and **through** him to **reconcile** all **things** for him,
　　　making **peace** by the **blood** of his **cross**
　　　through him, whether those on **earth** or those
　　　　in **heaven**.

Call your assembly to prayerful thanks that, in Christ, God made us worthy of salvation.

Because he loves us, God always takes the initiative. Proclaim this joyfully.

beloved = bee-LUHV-uhd

The ancient Christological hymn begins here.

Here are four categories of angels; distinguish each from the others.

Take joy and pride in naming these attributes of Christ, your Savior.

Employ a slower and more considered delivery here.

"The blood of his cross" helps set the stage for today's ironic Gospel.

READING II　Today's reading from Colossians includes a short prayer of thanksgiving and a hymn exalting Christ. The thanksgiving amplifies Paul's opening prayer of thanks to the Father and his prayer for the community. Although he doesn't mention Baptism, the tone and content have the ring of a baptismal liturgy. Through Baptism into Christ, we already have a share in the inheritance of the saints, are already delivered from darkness, and are already transferred into the Kingdom of his Son.

After the thanksgiving, the soaring hymn proclaims Christ's sovereignty. Both in his identity and in his accomplishments, Christ is profoundly related to humanity and to creation. The Father to whom gratitude is due is invisible, the author of creation and redeemer of the people. Now Paul proclaims Christ as the very image of God; in Christ, works of creation and redemption are accomplished.

So extensive is his dominion that every dimension of time and space is under his rule. Repetition of the word *all* (eight times in six verses) emphatically attests to the totality of his rule. In addition to repetition of *all*, three prepositional phrases that focus on Christ's saving power for creation are woven throughout the hymn: in him (three times), through him (three times), and for him (two times). These repetitions occur throughout the entire hymn, which has two distinct divisions. In the first, Christ is firstborn of all creation, and in the second he is firstborn from the dead. As firstborn, he has priority and absolute primacy over everything.

GOSPEL   Luke 23:35–43

A reading from the holy Gospel according to Luke

The rulers **sneered** at Jesus and said,
    "He **saved others**, let him **save himself**
    if he is the **chosen** one, the **Christ** of **God**."
Even the **soldiers** jeered at him.
As they **approached** to offer him **wine** they called out,
    "If **you** are **King** of the **Jews**, **save** yourself."
Above him there was an **inscription** that read,
    "**This** is the **King** of the **Jews**."

Now **one** of the **criminals** hanging there **reviled** Jesus, saying,
    "Are **you** not the **Christ**?
Save yourself and **us**."
The **other**, however, **rebuking** him, said in **reply**,
    "Have **you** no **fear** of **God**,
    for you are **subject** to the **same condemnation**?
And **indeed**, **we** have been **condemned justly**,
    for the **sentence** we **received corresponds** to our **crimes**,
    but **this** man has done **nothing** criminal."
Then he said,
    "**Jesus**, **remember** me when you **come** into your **Kingdom**."
He **replied** to him,
    "**Amen**, I **say** to **you**,
    today you will be with **me** in **Paradise**."

Notice that only the leaders and soldiers mock Jesus, not the crowd.

They spit their words at him in mocking insult.

You might echo the voice of Pilate who required this sign.

Does he turn his anger and self-hatred on the helpless man beside him?

His life of crime has not withered all his faith. It would seem he's inviting his fellow thief to a like conversion.

In the original Greek, the verb for "remember" suggests the thief repeated the phrase multiple times.

Jesus demonstrates his sovereignty in determining the man's fate. Speak the line slowly and simply.

GOSPEL   Rulers, soldiers, and even a criminal treated the crucified Jesus with contempt. They taunted him, jeering that he should save himself as he had saved others, "if he is the chosen one, the Christ of God." As the Christ, or Messiah, he would be the descendant of David of whom God promised, "I will make his royal throne forever" (2 Samuel 7:13). He would be a king even greater than David. The Roman soldiers would read the title on the cross differently, regarding the inscription, "This is the king of the Jews," as a challenge to Caesar. They dare Jesus, if he is truly a king, to save himself! Everyone who joins in the mockery has unwittingly, ironically, correctly identified Jesus. He is the chosen one, the Messiah, the King of the Jews. He is the one who saves.

The only person who understands Jesus' identity is one of the criminals hanging on a cross beside him. While the other criminal reviles Jesus, this man admits his guilt and states that Jesus has done nothing wrong. His request of Jesus is a profound statement of faith. Asking that Jesus remember him is not a request for simple reminiscence. Jesus is to remember him as God remembers the covenant. In such remembering, God fulfills promises with saving acts of love and mercy. The condemned man wants Jesus to remember him similarly when he comes into his Kingdom, thereby implicitly recognizing that even on the cross Jesus is indeed a king. Jesus responds to the man's plea as a king would to a petitioner: he announces salvation to the man "today," signifying that God's salvation is mightily present (e.g., 2:22; 19:9). E.P.